CHRISTIANITY IN TROPICAL AFRICA

CHRISTIANITY IN TROPICAL AFRICA

STUDIES PRESENTED AND DISCUSSED
AT THE SEVENTH INTERNATIONAL AFRICAN SEMINAR,
UNIVERSITY OF GHANA, APRIL 1965

Edited with an Introduction by
C. G. BAËTA

Foreword by
DARYLL FORDE

Published for the
INTERNATIONAL AFRICAN INSTITUTE
by the
OXFORD UNIVERSITY PRESS
1968

Oxford University Press, Ely House, London W.1
GLASGOW NEW YORK TORONTO MELBOURNE WELLINGTON
CAPE TOWN SALISBURY IBADAN NAIROBI LUSAKA ADDIS ABABA
BOMBAY CALCUTTA MADRAS KARACHI LAHORE DACCA
KUALA LUMPUR HONG KONG TOKYO

Printed in Great Britain by Richard Clay (The Chaucer Press), Ltd., Bungay, Suffolk

CONTENTS

FOREWORD

Early in the consideration of the programme of the series of International African Seminars which the Institute has organized, it was felt that the influence of Christianity and of Islam in Tropical Africa should be included as major subjects for discussion. Our recently published book on the influence of Islam in Tropical Africa, edited by Dr. I. M. Lewis, has presented the work of the seminar held at Ahmadu Bello University, Northern Nigeria, in January 1964. In the present volume we have been able to make more widely available the contributions and the results of the discussions at the seventh seminar on the influence of Christianity in Tropical Africa, which was held at the University of Ghana from 6 to 16 April 1965, under the Chairmanship of the Rev. C. G. Baëta, Professor of Religious Studies at Ghana.

The eighteen studies presented in this volume, in English or French with a summary in the other language, have been arranged for publication in three parts, the first two being concerned with the historical and analytical perspectives of Christianity and the third dealing with more recent trends and prospects for the future. Each group of papers is preceded by an account of the discussions which arose out of them. The subjects presented and discussed in this way range from historical accounts of the planting of Christianity in Africa, to relations between African communities, missions, traders, and colonial administrations, and between Catholics and Protestants in the Congo. The process of conversion is considered in its many aspects, including responses to the Gospel, psychological problems of 'guilt' and 'shame', the attitudes of African churches towards polygamy; church growth and independency are analysed on a tribal basis and there is an historical review of 'Ethiopianism'. Ways of communicating the Gospel, with special reference to modern methods, are discussed and suggestions concerning African contributions to theology in relation to traditional religious beliefs. The discussion of modern trends and future prospects includes a consideration of the position of the church in Africa today.

The Institute is indebted to the participants in this seminar for the time and thought they gave to the preparation of their papers. We are especially grateful to Professor Baëta for serving as Chairman, for editing the papers and the accounts of the discussions, and also for contributing a general introduction. We should also like to thank the University of Ghana and Dr. Conor Cruise O'Brien, then Vice-Chancellor, for receiving the seminar and making it most welcome.

This seminar was made possible by the continued generosity of the Ford Foundation, to whom our grateful thanks are again due.

In addition to those contributing papers the following also came to the seminar and took part in the discussions: Rev. Fr. John A. Bell, W.F., Director, African Research and Information Centre, Washington, D.C., U.S.A.; Dr. G. S. P. Freeman-Grenville, Institute of African Studies, University of Ghana; Nana Kobina Nketsia IV, Director, Ghana Institute of Art and Culture, Accra; Professor Daryll Forde, Director, International African Institute, London.

The following attended as observers: Dr. Kenneth M. Glazier, Stanford University, U.S.A.; Dr. Robert D. Carey, Stanford University, U.S.A.; Dr. William J. Samarin, Hartford Seminary Foundation, U.S.A.; Dr. (Mlle.) Claude Perrot, C.N.R.S., Paris and Abidjan; Sister Labouré and Sister John of the Catholic Medical Mission, Berekum, Ghana; Professor Immanuel Wallerstein, Department of Sociology, Columbia University, U.S.A.

GENERAL INTRODUCTION

At a previous seminar in this series it was felt that its subject could be reasonably circumscribed and dealt with fairly comprehensively in the papers that were presented and discussed. This seminar on the influence of Christianity in Tropical Africa was faced with precisely the contrary situation. There is practically no end to the topics and questions which might appropriately be considered, and the number of those which are obviously important is considerable; even to separate them neatly from one another would be an impossible task. In these circumstances all that could be hoped for was some elucidation of outstanding issues within the theme, and even these could not be followed very far. While their presentation here will no doubt fail to satisfy, there can be no question about the need, particularly at the present time, for some attempt at a more or less comprehensive view, and within a reasonable compass, of this broad subject. The International African Institute must be commended for undertaking a very worthwhile risk.

The subjects taken up in the preparatory papers were freely chosen by the authors on the basis of a general scheme proposing issues and problems that appeared to be most directly relevant to the theme. At the seminar each participant introduced for discussion a topic other than his own. This was done to encourage the linking of related fields and the contribution at the seminar of statements on specific points that arose. It has been my concern to provide a record which will indicate the extent of orderly development and cohesion that could in the circumstances be achieved. An introduction to each Part attempts to gather up some of the more salient points of the relevant discussions, and thus to a certain extent complements the essays grouped in that Part. In the nature of the case, however, this has not been uniformly possible. As Chairman of the Seminar, I should like to express my warm thanks to the participants, who, at my request, most generously furnished me with notes and memoranda on the contributions which they themselves had made to the discussions. These have been utilized as far as seemed possible in a brief commentary. Any value which this volume may be considered to possess is due to the very considerable time and thought which the participants devoted both before and during the meetings to the questions we discussed.

Intangible in many of its aspects, the Christian presence has been and remains, in the African scene, a massive and unavoidable fact and factor. The All Africa Conference of Churches unites sixty-one already autonomous African churches within its fellowship: 39 of these are also members of the World Council of Churches; several more are on the threshold of autonomy or on the waiting-list for formal admission into the continental or world bodies. African-born members of the Roman Catholic Hierarchy in Tropical Africa include 1 Vicar Apostolic, 19 archbishops, 57 bishops and auxiliary bishops (3 of them being Cardinals), and 2 Apostolic administrators. In round figures there are 26 million Catholics and 5 million catechumens in tropical Africa.[1] The total Christian population is variously given as 41½ or 62 millions.[2] There is reason to suppose that these figures, derived from official Church sources, represent far less than the actual numbers of professing Christians. The 1960 census in Ghana, for example, in which religious affiliation was registered by simply taking the self-declaration of persons of fifteen years and over, revealed the numbers of those claiming to be Christians (amounting to 42·8 of the total population) to be far in excess of the highest figures recorded by the Churches themselves. At the same time, whether Christianity has been a success in Africa or not, an oft-debated question, must probably remain a matter of opinion.

In numberless institutions of many different kinds as well as in the equally numerous and diverse voluntary organizations and free associations of men, women, and children; in the pervasive

[1] This figure is taken from *Bilan du Monde*, 1964 edition. It will be noted that Father J. B. Schuyler in his paper gives an estimate of 27 millions.

[2] The former figure is obtained by adding the numbers given for Catholics in 'Bilan' and for Protestants in the 1962 edition (latest available at time of writing) of *World Christian Handbook*; for the latter figure see Vicedom, *Christus und die Welt*, Heft 22.

influence and challenge of its message to men and demand upon their individual lives and their relationships with one another; in countless personal and group decisions made, and lives actually lived very differently from what they would otherwise have been; in the new high hopes and aspirations for individual and social destiny which it has awakened; in the sheer excellence of human performance in devotion and courageous, self-sacrificing service to others, and in yet other ways, Christianity still plays a role and exerts a force in tropical Africa which is none the less real or significant because it eludes full and conclusive analysis.

As is well known, Christian missionary enterprise has for a considerable time now been under very heavy fire (and not least in Africa) from colonial administrators, nationalists, rationalists, anthropologists, political theorists, tourists, and indeed practically everyone outside the churches having to do with the people concerned, who has cared to write on the subject. Some of this criticism is of course reflected in the seminar's papers and discussions. That some of it can be easily justified has on occasion led to such wholesale and undiscerning acceptance of summary negative judgements that a balanced view and understanding of the historical background has been largely wanting. As a result there is widespread today a readiness to repudiate the missionary past that is not based even on such acquaintance with it as is in fact readily available. It is not an uncommon experience to meet would-be critics (including contemporary missionaries) who, after indulging in sweeping condemnation of everything that was done in the past, calmly proceed to set forth, as new ideas, lines of thought which were not only thoroughly familiar, but had even been tested, in more than one place, many years ago.

It was no task of the seminar to vindicate missionary policies and actions of the past or present. But if it has succeeded, to a reasonable extent, in affording an introduction to the tremendous range and the sometimes baffling complexity of this whole field, then its purpose has been fully accomplished.

C. G. Baëta

PART ONE

HISTORICAL PERSPECTIVE

INTRODUCTORY REVIEW: FACTS AND PROBLEMS

(a) *The Need for Continuing Research*

The seminar frequently recurred to the need for more and continuing research on its subject. Professor Low recalled that while some very good use had been made of the mostly excellent archives of missionary bodies, the yield so far had tended to present too much chronicle and not enough history. New efforts now being undertaken should also seek to explore fundamental questions concerning the spread of Christianity in Africa, as had been done for early Christianity, for example, in A. D. Nock's *Conversion.* It was noted that a good deal of re-thinking, in principle, concerning the mission and its implications was in progress within the circles of the World Council of Churches' Division of World Mission and Evangelism, and that insights obtained here would doubtless further illuminate particular facts of mission history coming under study. The most important need was for posing the right questions.

Considerable attention was given to the areas in which it was desirable that research work should immediately proceed. One of these appeared to be that of the assumptions and the aims of the home-bases of missionary societies. It was an interesting fact, for example, that Anglican and Roman Catholic missions, working in Buganda for the same length of time and with what would appear to have been the same instruments, had produced two quite different kinds of elite; the one with a heavy emphasis on careers like journalism, the law, school-mastering, and politics; the other stressing the priesthood and positions in the chiefly hierarchy. Similarly, the particular religious ethos of the pietistic groups in Germany and Switzerland which, responding to the founding of the Basel Mission in 1815, so rapidly organized themselves into *Hilfsvereine* (supporting associations) had left its clear imprint on the work of this society and of other Protestant missions based on Central Europe, just as the peculiar enthusiasm of the Evangelical

Revival in England had unmistakably marked Methodist African missions. Before the centralization of direction of Roman Catholic missions in Rome in the nineteenth century the different policies of different Orders and national missions at different times were likewise clearly reflected in their areas of activities. Thus in order to understand the distinctive impact of various missions it was necessary to see as fully as possible their separate backgrounds of conviction, prevailing religious temperament, type and style of piety, avowed objectives, and the ways and means of carrying these into effect. All these factors form part and parcel of an influence which could otherwise be completely misunderstood and misinterpreted.

An important element in this necessary background to mission history is the role played by the Bible Societies. As shown in some of the essays presented here, the Bible Societies' conception of their own specific calling and function, and their activities to implement it, had major results which continue to be effective even today.

The question of the best unit within which to pursue such studies is also important if the most helpful results are to be obtained. Whereas the tribe as a linguistic unit would often appear to afford a useful basis and two recent works, each dealing in depth with the reaction of one tribe to mission (the Kalabari and the Basuto), have proved very acceptable, in some cases it would be difficult to cover, in this way, all the problems which fall to be considered. Some 'tribes' (e.g. the Ibo) would need to be regarded as more than one unit; while regional and administrative relationships with surrounding areas and the political structure of the entire territory within the colonial context, must be taken into account. Possibly the best approach is to study a distinctive tribe within these wider contexts as, for example, the Baganda within Uganda.

The search for materials should go well beyond the immediately relevant frontiers. Many valuable documents have been taken overseas by retiring missionaries to remain in private hands; and letters and notes written by African evangelists working outside their own tribal home, and in some cases by West Indian and

American Negro catechists who had been brought in to help, can yield fascinating information.

But the most remarkable and painful gap in source materials at present is that occasioned by the absence of histories of nineteenth- and twentieth-century Roman Catholic African missions. Whereas *bona fide* scholars can obtain access to the archives of the religious Orders chiefly concerned, the central and presumably most comprehensive Vatican collections remain out-of-bounds. So long as this continues, it is not possible to obtain a reasonably complete picture of the missionary enterprise in Africa. In view of the seriousness of this handicap the seminar expressed the hope that this reference to the matter would be read as a respectful plea to the Roman Catholic authorities, and particularly to African bishops, that urgent representations be made in Rome for some relaxation of the hundred-year closure rule in respect of African history. In this connexion the information that the Church Missionary Society was intending to reduce its own fifty-year rule was welcomed. On the other hand some other missions, for example Jehovah's Witnesses in New York, have effectively closed their archives altogether.

The call for a major and widespread operation to salvage documentation on the participation by indigenous Africans in the christianization of the continent was warmly welcomed at the seminar. The fragile and perishable nature of these materials makes the matter extremely urgent, while their wide dispersal and the difficulties of collection demand careful planning and organization as well as adequate funds and personnel. This is surely an area in which joint action by all interested parties—missions, African churches, historians, and others, possibly on a regional basis—holds out the best promise of fruitful results. Such an undertaking is a crying need for, when all is said and done, the brunt of evangelization has in fact been borne by African Christians. To name just one example in which even the responsibility for directing the effort was carried by them, there is the very remarkable case of the missionary enterprise of Baganda Christians from the 1890s onwards, from which emerged one of the saints of Africa, Apolo Kivebulaya. Biographies of the earliest men and women to be converted in an area, local stories of the struggles of the pioneering days, of personal and group initiatives undertaken to advance Christianity; these and like materials are waiting to be assembled to enrich our knowledge and deepen our understanding.

The story of the Christian influence in Africa should consider not only the effects of evangelization on a people but also those of the people and their religion on the character and growth of the Christian communities which come into being among them. In India, China, and Japan early Catholic endeavours, characterized by a remarkably pacific approach, deliberately developed the policy of adapting Christianity to the indigenous religions. In parts of Latin America, more as a result of a natural development than of deliberate policy, blends of Christianity and African religious beliefs have emerged which, though presenting features somewhat startling to most other Christians, appear to satisfy deeply the religious need of those who practise them. In Africa, however, a distinguishing mark of missions has been their almost unanimous refusal to incorporate elements of the local traditional cults in any shape or form within the Christian system of religious thought and practice. The reasons for this general line must be sought in considering missionary attitudes and policies. Of interest in this context are the problems to which it has given rise, the measure of success which has attended it and the nature of the resulting coexistence of the two kinds of religion, particularly at the grass-roots. It should be illuminating to discover how prevalent is the practice that is sometimes called 'wearing both braces and belt' (so that if either should give way the other should hold the trousers), as illustrated for example by Martin Luther Nsibirwa, the Katikiro of Buganda, distinguished as a Christian gentleman who, when he was murdered on the steps of Namirembe Cathedral in 1944, was found to be wearing many pagan amulets. But, apart from the missions, to what extent has full syncretism occurred? In this connexion obviously the very remarkable development of independent churches is of immediate relevance; what is its true significance? Bearing in mind the eruption of forms of 'enthusiasm' in the most unlikely places (the incidence of *sufi* in Islam and of *Bhakti* in Hinduism, both movements being, like independence, populist, revivalist and devotional reactions against orthodoxy), one starting point from which the African scene may be considered is the extent to which the new phenomena represent the self-assertion, in African Christianity, of the emotional and ecstatic elements present in most religions, or are an expression of a desire, however unformulated and for whatever reason, to take up some vital features of the old local cults and way of life into the world religion now adopted.

(b) *The Relations between the African Communities, Missions, Traders and the Colonial Administrations*

With the abolition of the slave trade it was held as axiomatic by all interested in African affairs that 'legitimate' or normal trade and commerce should be greatly developed to replace the traffic in slaves. Particularly in the West, Europe had maintained commercial contacts with the African territories practically without interruption since the earliest seafaring ventures of the Portuguese in the late fifteenth century, and although this traffic had come to dominate the scene, its abolition could not simply bring to a stop a relationship already long established between the two continents. In our context it is important to bear in mind how widespread and strong was the conviction among missionary strategists that the spread of trade and the development of agriculture, with ancillary minor industries, were essential conditions for the success of evangelization. Professor Shepperson pointed out that behind such ideas, which flourished in the 1860s and 1870s under the predominating influence of David Livingstone, lay Adam Smith's view that the hidden hand of Providence directed economic effort, as well as Reid's philosophy of 'common sense'.

Such is the background of the close links between Christianity and trade which could be seen when, for example, directors and other well known home-based personalities of missionary societies were also directors of trading companies operating in the same area of Africa. Professor Low provided a clear example from East Africa. Mr. T. F. Buxton, a prominent member of the parent committee of the C.M.S., was also a director of the

Imperial East Africa Co. Later he was director of the first major company in Uganda, the Uganda Company, which took over the Church Missionary Society's Industrial Institution and developed the export of cotton. Dr. Grau also instanced a similar case in West Africa from the Bremen Mission. One of its first missionaries sent to the Coast was to investigate the opportunities for legitimate trade, and as a result a merchant member of the parent committee, Herr Vietor, opened up trade in the Gold Coast and Togoland, his company giving employment to the mission-educated Africans.

Occasionally missions went directly into trading. The Basel Mission of the Gold Coast set up a trading company which developed cotton production and sought to introduce Christian trading standards, which largely meant the refusal to deal in fire-arms and liquor. Professor Shepperson recalled that the Scottish Free Church missionaries of Malawi founded a trading corporation which is still in existence. Between 1878 and the 1890s such interpenetration of mission and trade, with a fusion of economic and spiritual aspirations, was quite common.

The ideal was that the missionaries should form nuclei of industrious and frugal communities of believers and converts, living godly lives and providing all their own material needs. Farmers and artisans, as well as graduate teachers and doctors, were regarded as being just as much missionaries as the ordained preachers, and most of the latter were at the same time competent craftsmen, well able to practise a trade if need should arise.

While still supported by the home base they had to give a strict account of their expenditure of funds. In this connexion it is interesting to note that ideas which have recently become modern again, such as forming interdenominational or nondenominational missions, or serving the Lord in secular occupations as Christian lay witnesses in potential missionary areas or situations were already current and even partly put into effect. Thus missionaries imperceptibly became settlers, and worldly business, originally taken up out of necessity or the desire to make missions self-supporting, frequently came to be pursued to the disadvantage of evangelism.

But some societies strictly forbade trading activities of any kind. In the Gold Coast, alongside the Basel Mission which, as has been seen, had its own trading company, was the Wesleyan Methodist Mission which rejected any involvement in trade. Dr. Freeman-Grenville pointed out that the Universities' Mission to Central Africa was also strictly forbidden to trade, but noted that its missionaries came mainly from the English aristocracy and that most of them possessed private incomes. Father Bell recalled that Canon Law prevented Roman Catholic missionaries from engaging in trade but allowed them to undertake agricultural production (e.g. cotton and coffee) and even some mining in Uganda. Dr. Reardon commented that Catholic industrial settlements and plantations in the Congo had incurred charges of slavery because African labour had been used without remuneration. Father Schuyler noted the Topo Island plantation experiment of the *Société des Missions Africaines* near Badagry in Nigeria, which, at first regarded as a commendable work of charity, later gave rise to complaints that missionaries were competing in the commercial field.

Mr. Tufuoh distinguished five categories of missions as regards their connexion with trade: those which set up industrial missions, training artisans; those engaged in agricultural production; those in which mission personnel was involved in separate trading ventures; those which traded directly, and those which shunned trade altogether. While the last-mentioned group tended to be too little involved, for its own good, in African affairs, only the first generally escaped bitter criticism for engaging in activities incompatible with their proper business. Even here occasionally there could be friction when, for example, artisans trained in such industrial institutions began to compete, say, in the production of furniture.

If trading could be used to eke out mission funds, it also readily suggested itself to African mission agents as a means of supplementing their usually quite inadequate salaries. However, this provided an easy ground of criticism against them, generally from those financially much better placed. The charge of trading against the Rev. Moses Ladejo Stone of the First Baptist Church in Lagos led to the first secession in that area under African leadership. It now appears that Philip Quaque of Cape Coast, who has been heavily criticized on the score of trading, actually received his emoluments for some time, at least partially, in trade goods.

Relations between European traders and missionaries, and between these and the African communities, tended to reflect the identity or divergence of their prevailing interests. In Lagos and the Niger Delta during the 1860s and seventies, when European traders were conducting their business in partnership with educated Africans (some of them prominent Church members or close kin of leading African Clergy), there was harmony between them and the European and African missionaries. When, however, in the eighties European traders, their hands strengthened by the increasing consolidation of imperial rule, began to establish a trade monopoly on the Niger and to drive African traders out of business, they were supported in this economic war by European missionaries, whereas the African clergy sided with the African traders.

Occasionally circumstances united missionaries and traders in a common front against the colonial government. Dr. Reardon pointed out how, for example, in the Congo they co-operated to break the state monopolies which, up to 1903, had kept the traders out of the interior, and to do away with the disabilities imposed on Protestant missions that had made it practically impossible for them to secure mission sites. M. Bureau said that in the Cameroons missionaries arrived after traders and the colonial government, and were greatly dependent on both. Traders and missionaries alike settled around government posts and their common interests, particularly their fears of African revolts, kept the three foreign groups closely linked together.

Whereas missionary voices expressing misgivings about some of the excesses of the pacification during the early days of colonial rule were never completely silent, and occasionally a missionary society would take a stand against imperialist moves detrimental to Africans, such protests were on the whole few and far between. As Dr. Grau's paper shows, in missionary circles at the time strong disapproval was being expressed of the harshness and injustice during pacification. But no effective public objection was raised, for example, against reprehensible Portuguese, French, and Belgian colonialist methods. Dr. Webster cited individual missionaries, like Tom Harding and S. G. Pinnock in Yoruba country, who registered unequivocal disagreement with some high-handed actions and openly espoused the African cause, but were sharply dealt with both by the governments concerned and by their own missionary societies.

Lord Lugard in Nigeria dismissed missionary criticism of the administration as arising from envy of the district officer who was superseding the missionary in influence and prestige. A similar view was taken in East Africa by Harry Johnston, a colonial administrator who considered that missionaries were piqued at being eclipsed and replaced as the political power and self-made authorities over tribal chiefs. Missionaries had indeed challenged him on certain matters such as his objectionable mode of collecting taxes and some of his 'punitive expeditions', but otherwise they fully co-operated with him, supplying African assistants, interpreting and recommending obedience to regulations and generally building up the prestige of the Queen's representative. They showed sympathetic understanding of his difficulties to the extent of incurring severe criticism by some of the non-political Anglicans in the Y.M.C.A. and by such detached enthusiasts as Joseph Booth. This radical fundamentalist missionary identified himself very closely with African interests and aspirations and for this reason between 1892 and 1918 suffered deportation from Tanganyika, South Africa, and East Africa.[1]

Dr. Reardon's paper shows how missions often sought benefits from colonial governments and in return worked to make converts docile and submissive to foreign rule. It did not seem to have been realized that reliance on governmental power risked turning the mission into a mere tool in government hands or that the mission stood only to gain in goodwill and respect if it spoke out against malpractices plainly contrary to its own viewpoint and teaching.

[1] Further details of his remarkable career are to be found in G. Shepperson and T. Price: *Independent African* (Edinburgh, 1958).

For Roman Catholic missions in the Congo the favour of the colonial government became an embarrassment as it inhibited criticism that would otherwise doubtless have been raised, of many obvious and intolerable malpractices. The Protestants also, already heavily discriminated against and always hopeful of improving their relations with government or fearful lest these should further deteriorate, waited longer than they should have done before venturing to expose the wrongs perpetrated by the authorities.

On the relations between missions and colonial administrations it was noted that interest was greater and support more generous for national missions operating in colonies of the countries concerned, than for other missions. However, missions were often helpless to effect the changes they wished for in the colonial policies of their own nations. Examples are the ban on evangelization in Northern Nigeria and the Belgian policy of permitting only Belgian nationals to conduct missions in the Congo. The general question was raised as to the extent to which it was possible for a mission to dissociate itself from the government of a colony when that government was its own. Some believed the very serious difficulties in such a situation to be insurmountable and therefore urged that no mission undertaking should work in a colony of its homeland. But in fact the question does not really rest there: given the European source of imperialism, how far could any European (or, for that matter, any white) missionary hold himself completely aloof from the European (white) colonial government of the territory in which he worked?

For Central and East Africa Mr. Price and Professor Shepperson emphasized the point that it was the absence of any law and order in the area of their service, rendering effective evangelization impossible, which led missionaries like Livingstone and Mackay to invite colonial rule. Elsewhere the same need led to the setting up, as at Blantyre, of forms of religio-secular government controlled by the missions. In considering what the best arrangement might have been in the circumstances it is pertinent to bear in mind also the areas in which missions and missionaries had to do not only with colonial governments but with European settlers as well.

The opinion was stated that an exhaustive study of the seminar's topic would need to include the earlier story of the spread of Christianity in Roman North Africa, among the Copts, in Nubia and in the Congo prior to the nineteenth century, which might afford a basis for comparison with the results of the later efforts and might reveal the extent to which colonial expansion affected the character of christianization of the continent today.

(c) *Missionary Motivations, Policies, and Methods*

In principle the object of mission is simply to make God known wherever He was previously unknown. The most perceptive prophets of Israel saw the meaning of their nation's election in God's intention to use it for conveying knowledge of Himself to all the other peoples of the earth. The source of the Christian mission is God's own act in sending Jesus Christ into the world. By this personal means of communication, the incarnated Word of God, all men may come to understand God's mind and heart in relation to themselves and His will concerning how they should conduct their lives. This initiative was prompted by God's concern that men should achieve the greatest realization of their own best welfare, culminating in their sharing in the life of His nearer presence.

But this primary purpose appears to have been purely and solely the moving force only in the missions of apostolic and sub-apostolic times. Since then, while never absent, it has been accompanied by secondary motivations of all kinds, often to the extent of being completely overlaid by them. This is not in itself a perversion. By the very presupposition of concern for the welfare of its recipients, mission almost necessarily implies (apart from verbal communication of knowledge about God) some form of helpful practical assistance rendered to those to whom it comes, some sharing of whatever good things or service the missioners may be able to offer. One of the major signs heralding the work of Christ in the world was his healing of diseases, and he told his disciples that the greatest of them would be the servant of all.

Thus 'secondary purposes' in mission such as education, medicine, agriculture, and general civilizing efforts are legitimately undertaken in addition to the primary evangelistic task. At the same time they open the door widely to human factors with their inherent limitations and failings: ignorance or misunderstanding of the general social situation; misjudgement of the value of objectives set and methods used; inability to see into the future or even to forecast rightly the effects of carefully thought-out policies; sheer chance and change; the unconscious or deliberate harnessing of 'secondary purposes' to ends somehow advantageous to the missioners themselves and detrimental to the recipients of mission. However, the general tendency, in criticizing whatever has here turned out wrong, to assume faults of character, leaving almost entirely out of account the obviously relevant consideration of simple human fallibility, is in all probability really a reaction against the excessive idealization, in missionary propaganda, of missions and missionaries. But some resentment of their business itself is also discernible.

In discussing the extent to which procedures in the spread of Christianity in Africa differed from those employed by the other great world religion of the continent, Islam, it was noted that no use was made by Christians of 'holy war' (*jihad*).[2] It was observed, however, that in effect there might be parallels between conversions as a result of 'holy war' and those coming in the aftermath of European imperialist conquest. The point here is not, of course, whether or not people are forced at the point of the sword to adopt the conquering faith. Defeat in war would have meant for many the defeat of their old gods whose impotence and faithlessness was now conclusively and dramatically demonstrated. The logical result of this would be a widespread readiness to concede superiority to the creed of the successful invader. It may therefore be that European conquests in Africa, though not initiated by missionaries, in fact benefited the spread of Christianity in much the same way as 'jihads' operated (though more directly, of course) to the benefit of Islam. Thus on this point

[2] This is in marked contrast to what happened in South America, for example, where both Spanish and Portuguese missions did pursue 'holy war' policies.

students of the spread of Christianity may have insights to offer to students of the spread of Islam and of other religions.

The peculiarly Christian instruments for the propagation of the Faith have been the full-time professional missionary and the mission station. The dedication of their entire lives in single-minded devotion to their task, usually in the face of heavy odds including even death, has earned for missionaries a high esteem, whether this is acknowledged or not; indeed the adjective 'missionary' has come generally to connote courageous, selfless, and sacrificial service for the good of others. This in itself is a great heritage. As Professor Low pointed out, until the emergence of nationalist leaders few equals of such moral excellence had been seen. But missionaries were by no means merely evangelists and preachers. They were also leaders to whom the African communities looked for introduction to the highly complex new ways of life bursting in upon them, as well through the missionary's own coming as through the other channels of government and trade. Likewise the mission station was not merely a base for teaching the Christian discipline and manner of living and for propagating the Faith: it was also a pocket of this new invading civilization, displaying and mediating a wide range of its techniques. In introducing scientific explanations of natural phenomena and rationalizations in the moral sphere, this process affected the African religious sense as a desacralizing and secularizing force. Dr. Grau's paper introduces a mission which from the beginning declared a sympathetic and enlightened interest and respect for African customary beliefs and practices; and Professor Shepperson argued that missionary understanding and appreciation of African traditional cultures had often been undervalued. He instanced such missionaries as Dutt MacDonald of the Blantyre (Malawi) Mission, whose book *Africana*, written in the 1880s, revealed a penetrating understanding of African culture in this region. An even more important example was the career of Edwin W. Smith, a pioneer missionary in Zambia, who was later a leading figure in the founding of the International African Institute. His book, *The Golden Stool*, although elementary by the standards of contemporary social anthropology, introduced many Europeans to a sympathetic appreciation of the values of traditional African society. And other missionaries have produced works of a similar nature. However, until quite recently, the prevailing attitude has implied complete rejection of African culture, and the effort to assimilate Africans to the assumptions, values and practices of the Christian West. To quote Mr. Price's succinct formulation: 'Physically they [i.e. the missionaries] went out to Africa, psychologically the Africans had to come to them.' Such ethnocentrism did not necessarily stem from the arrogance with which it has usually been charged. Ethnocentrism could just as well have arisen from a generous-spirited eagerness to help. In any case in the circumstances it would have required genius to detect its basic fallacy. West Indians giving service in Africa met the same criticism as Europeans for the same reason: they came from a more complex and therefore higher culture.

A recent work on Christian missions in Africa carries the subtitle: 'The Making of a New Elite.'[3] To what extent was there an intention of establishing the Gospel through the creation of a new prestige group? Considering the lofty tone evident in the writings of early converts, how far did the quite common practice of isolating them from their communities foster a chosen race mentality and vitiate missionary efforts in general and their relationships with the other indigenous peoples in particular? Can it be demonstrated that the mission station or 'gathered colony' approach was in fact the only one that could have succeeded to any extent in planting Christianity in those pioneer days or was this practice mainly motivated by the missionaries' desire to set up around themselves the manner of life to which they were accustomed? Would the 'people movement approach', advocated by strategists like Allen from the U.K. and McGavran from the U.S.A., have avoided the pitfalls and proved more generally satisfactory and more successful?

The mission-compound method of creating a new Christian community appears to have realized, in good part, its purposes as traditionally understood, and that at not too high cost. The necessarily temporary character of these settlements greatly

[3] *Christian Missions in Nigeria 1841–1891*, by J. F. Ade Ajayi (Longmans).

reduced the seriousness of any social disruption which they occasioned; relations with the 'pagan' neighbours generally continued to be spontaneous and happy; it was not long before mission station people were settling back into the wider community and the latter was reflecting (e.g. in the construction of dwellings and the planning and maintenance of the village) the healthy influence emanating from the 'station'. Besides, it is noteworthy that an attempt by Crawford, a missionary in Katanga, to depart from this pattern proved a failure.

Within the mission station education was the main instrument used for establishing and maintaining the new values. Literacy was actively pursued as a means of getting the converts to read the Bible for themselves. The Protestant missionaries emphasized the importance of responsible personal conviction and decision in religion as in other matters. This was by no means a new thing in Africa. However, distress and disharmony could arise when Africans exercised their private judgement in a manner contrary to missionary expectation, as for example by employing the education received for purely secular purposes or by displaying indifference towards religion. The missionaries' refusal to accept such results revealed their fundamentally paternalistic attitude and led to frictions which eventually erupted in secessions. In this connexion Dr. Webster suggested that around 1880 there was a dramatic change in missionary attitudes. Whereas previously the policies in African education, the promotion of indigenous leadership and even on such an issue as polygamy had been very liberal, from then onward some resentment of highly-educated Africans and of their leadership became plainly discernible, and a harder line was taken on the polygamy question as indicated by the events leading to the eclipse of Bishop Crowther in Nigeria, the reversal of Henry Venn's pro-African policies after his death, and the prohibition by the Lambeth Conference of the baptism of polygamists. The course was now set for the hegemony of Europeans and of the positions taken up by them. Would missions have made a greater Christian impact if they had fully accepted equality and been less eager and more flexible in their effort to transfer the entire apparatus of European civilization to Africa?

I. PROBLEMS OF HISTORICAL PERSPECTIVE: THE PLANTING OF CHRISTIANITY IN AFRICA IN THE NINETEENTH AND TWENTIETH CENTURIES

RICHARD GRAY

One of the most surprising facts to emerge from a survey of historical writing in this field is the almost complete absence of writers who have taken a stand outside the Christian tradition. Yet, on the other hand, it is often conceded that Christianity has had a significance in parts of nineteenth- and twentieth-century Africa comparable with that which it possessed in Northern Europe a thousand years earlier. By itself this indicates the extent to which the serious historical study of Christianity in Africa is still in its infancy. The history of the early medieval Church and its social impact has long ceased to be the preserve of solely Christian historians, and as research into African history develops we can confidently expect that this neglect will cease, and that the ring will be broken. This development would be heartily welcomed by a Christian who helps to teach the subject to undergraduates in London. Not only would it provide a pleasant respite for those students who find the more pious aspects of the subject somewhat antipathetic, but it should also contribute to the astringent, penetrating criticism which must develop before we can deepen our understanding of the subject.

Even more regrettable is the relative absence of African contributions. Fortunately some of the most distinguished recent research has been undertaken by Africans and certainly we stand on the brink of a major breakthrough in this respect; but for the present nearly all the published studies have been written by outsiders, who remain in varying degrees inevitably alien to African Christianity. All aspects of the subject have suffered from this lack of African participation; let us begin, however, with that sector where its consequences have perhaps been least serious. Belloc's dictum that 'Europe is the Faith, and the Faith is

Europe' contains one of his wildest heresies; yet it remains true that a study of Christianity in Africa since 1800 must involve an analysis of the outside forces which produced so massive an intervention in the life of Africa. The aims and assumptions, both theological and secular, which shaped missionary activity; the concentration on one area rather than another; the fluctuating financial resources and uncertain reinforcements; the nature and limits of missionary dependence on other intrusive forces, both official and commercial: all these are aspects which demand an intimate understanding of the 'home base' interpreted in its widest sense.

Accounts of the development of individual missionary societies provide a starting-point for the examination of these background issues. Despite some notable omissions, there seems to be, at first sight, a reasonable provision of standard histories on the comprehensive pattern set by Stock and Lovett.[1] The omissions are most evident on the Catholic side: the White Fathers, the Society of African Missions, the Verona Fathers, and the Holy Ghost Fathers are all obvious candidates with almost exclusively African interests.[2] But there are also the Baptists, the missions of the Church of Scotland,[3] the Scandinavians, the Paris and the Swiss Romande Missions, and some of the Anglican Religious Orders who have worked in Africa—the Cowley Fathers, the Community of the Resurrection, and the Community of the Sacred Passion. Yet much as these gaps need to be filled, a fresh look at many of the standard histories is perhaps as urgent a necessity. It is not merely a question of supplying the twentieth-century picture, of bridging the gap since they were written, vital though this is as Mr. Norman Goodall has demonstrated.[4] It is also the familiar fact that history must be rewritten by every generation. The issues and problems which interest scholars today are significantly different from those which concerned Stock and

[1] Stock, 1889–1916; Lovett, 1899.

[2] Useful though they are, none of the following is a substitute for a full, scholarly treatment: Todd, 1962; Goyau, 1937; Bouniol, 1929.

[3] Here again the only recent study, Hewat, 1960, is too brief to do more than raise some of the principal problems.

[4] Goodall, 1954.

his contemporaries. Developments in missiology have, for example, led to an increased awareness of the changing emphases in missionary aims and methods. There is a greater interest in vocation and motive. We would like to examine far more closely the factors influencing the missionary approach to African thought and institutions, or the role of missions in shaping the European image of Africa and their influence on metropolitan policy, or the varying degrees of influence exerted by the home-based officials of the societies on missionaries in the field. We find ourselves therefore increasingly trying to read between the lines of these older works and to quarry scraps of information which could often best be won by going again direct to their sources. Most missionary societies recognize the importance of recording, publishing and rewriting their history: it is for scholars to demonstrate how essential can be their collaboration in this task.

Yet histories of missionary societies cannot by themselves lead to a thorough understanding of the background forces which shaped the missionary intervention in Africa. Decisive advances in this study await increased attempts to investigate the relationships between the missionary societies and the Churches and nations of which they were a part, to view the home base as a facet of ecclesiastical, and even secular, history. In the first place there is the need to know more concerning those institutions which cut across the various missionary societies. There is already a pioneer account of the development of the International Missionary Council,[5] but little is known of its precursors. Bianquis' intensive study of the origins of the Paris Missionary Society[6] demonstrated *inter alia* the international and interdenominational character of the early nineteenth-century missionary revival; there remains, however, a notable gap between this era and Edinburgh 1910. Even more is there a need to study the extent to which the Churches attempted to control the activities of the societies which represented them on the mission field, the methods employed in this attempt and the repercussions it caused within the Churches themselves. Dr. Cnattingius' work on the early relationship between the Anglican Church and the

[5] Hogg, 1952. [6] Bianquis, 1935.

S.P.G. and C.M.S.[7] has demonstrated the potentials of such a study. Unfortunately his work stops short of the second half of the nineteenth century when the careers of both Bishop Crowther and Bishop Colenso raised fundamental issues for Anglicans, while the later confrontation of the U.M.C.A. and the C.M.S. in East Africa illustrates the need to carry a study of this theme into the twentieth century. Without a clearer understanding of the relevant currents and forces within Anglicanism, of Keswick and the Churchmen's Union, of the development of the Lambeth Conferences and the policies of Canterbury, one cannot grasp the significance of these events in Africa either for African Anglicans or for the Anglican Communion as a whole. Dr. Hewat's book is a pointer to the work which also remains to be done on the Churches' control of the Scottish missions, and the importance of this aspect of the home base is clearly seen in the case of Rome.

The dominant influence of the Sacred Congregation of Propaganda Fide, more perhaps than any other factor, sharply distinguishes nineteenth-century Catholic missionary activity in Africa from that of earlier centuries. The aftermath of the French Revolution reduced Catholic missions to their lowest level since the fifteenth century; but it also seriously weakened the control previously exercised over the missions by the *ancien regime* and the Portuguese *padroado*. Propaganda was, therefore, at last enabled to intervene effectively, and to supervise in a direct and intimate fashion the new societies and organizations which developed in the second quarter of the nineteenth century, and which were to play so notable a role in the evangelization of tropical Africa. Few over-simplifications, however, could be more misleading than that which depicts a monolithic organization effortlessly enforcing its will on its workers scattered throughout the world. Father Janin and the Rev. Dr. Storme have illustrated aspects of this story which impinge on Africa,[8] and they have begun to delineate the complex balance of power between Rome and the leaders of the new societies. The full nature of this relationship has, however, still to be investigated: the contacts of the great fund-raising instruments, in particular *l'Oeuvre de la*

[7] Cnattingius, 1952. [8] Janin, 1935; Storme, 1951.

Propagation de la Foi, with Propaganda and the missionary societies would be an important starting-point; the materials for such a study are available, and one suspects that it would do much to clarify the changed and inner tensions of the Catholic home-base. It is astonishing, also, that there is as yet no authoritative account of the missionary initiative of Bartolomeo Cappellari who guided the crucial period of reconstruction, first as Cardinal Prefect of Propaganda and then as Gregory XVI (1831–46). No less regrettable is the lack of scholarly studies of the development of Propaganda under his successors Pius IX and Leo XIII, although it is unfortunately idle to hope for these while the hundred-years' closure-rule is applied to the Congregation's archives. Until a far more detailed picture can be constructed, we shall not be able to assess satisfactorily the influence of Rome on mission policy in Africa. Nor shall we fully understand the fortunes of the new societies in Africa, the impact of Cardinal Lavigerie, or the missions' relations with the imperial powers. Indeed we have hardly begun to appreciate the gradual mobilization of the peasant and professional resources of Catholic Europe and their encounter with tropical Africa.

So far merely the European home-base has been considered. That of North America seems even less adequately investigated, yet it is of at least comparable importance for twentieth-century developments. A disadvantage for someone working in London is that several of the major works have proved to be inaccessible;[9] a fortunate exception is Mr. Barclay's work on Methodist missions, whose detailed analysis of the interaction of the home-base with the foreign fields is opening-up in an exemplary fashion this rich and largely unexamined theme.[10] A recent survey of missionary archival material in the United States relating to Africa should do much to draw the attention of American research to this field.[11] One hopes that the more conservative, fundamentalist wing—including the Brethren missions and international bodies such as the Africa Inland Mission and the Sudan United Mission—will not be neglected, and that particular attention will also be

[9] I have for instance been unable to see Brown, 1937; Strong, 1910.
[10] Barclay, 1949.
[11] Collins and Duignan, 1963.

paid to Pentecostal influences, the Seventh Day Adventists, and American Negro Churches. Only when this work has been done will the variety and breadth of the build-up of American missionary interest in Africa become apparent and its predominance in certain aspects of the contemporary situation be more explicable.

One other base, lodged within Africa itself, must also be considered. By the last quarter of the nineteenth century the Christian denominations of European stock settled in South Africa were exerting powerful direct and indirect influences on the evangelization of the continent. The oldest of these groups, the Dutch Reformed Churches, although relatively slow in starting, was then thrusting up into Central Africa, had crossed the Zambesi and was soon to stretch out to Nigeria. Dr. Van der Merwe has surveyed this movement,[12] and his thesis points to the many aspects of this story which remain to be examined more deeply. The stormy early history of the Anglican Province has been well-served,[13] but the influence of these events on its missionary outreach needs to be considered, and one suspects that the interactions of pastoral work for the European congregations and evangelism among Africans is a theme that would repay investigation for all denominations. In comparison to the contribution of settlers to the work of evangelism, the indirect results of the deteriorating racial situation in South Africa and its impact on the Christian image throughout Africa are far less susceptible to scholarly examination. Yet diffuse and intangible though they may be, their pervasive significance calls for a careful and thorough analysis.

Yet however vital the study of the home bases may be for an understanding of the development of Christianity in Africa, it remains but a relatively minor prerequisite to the investigation of the work of the missionaries in Africa and the analysis of the reception, propagation and interpretation of the Faith by Africans. Much of the secondary writing on missionary activity is still only to be found in the standard accounts of the societies. For Africa,

[12] Van der Merwe, 1936.

[13] Lewis and Edwards, 1934; Gray, 1876; Cox, 1888.

even more than for the home base, these are unsatisfactory in many respects. Here it is not just a question that for the most part they have become dated, and that the shift of our contemporary interest has been even greater in the case of developments in Africa. A more enduring disadvantage is the fact that, on the one hand, these works in most cases are inevitably concerned with a wider field, and hence their sections on Africa tend to be briefer and more superficial than an Africanist would like, while, on the other, confined to the work of one society, their view of a particular African field is restricted and partial, even where their presentation of events transcends mere apologetics. The experience gained over the whole range of a society's activities undoubtedly possesses a relevance for Africa, and scholarly accounts of a society's work have of course still much to contribute to an understanding of their African labours; yet this approach is surely no substitute for a study of the missions in their African environment and for a focus centred directly on the interplay of the forces which they encountered there. Biographies, another traditional genre of mission literature, are in their narrower field often more rewarding, and sometimes provide an unrivalled insight into the personal world of the missionaries, their motives, attitudes and methods.[14] They have, however, obvious limitations, and in fact most missionary biographies are probably best used as source material. In this respect the student can only regret that the substantial two-volume biographies of the last century have been largely discontinued, though the publication of correspondence has sometimes more than offset this loss.[15]

Regional studies surmount the limitations of these more customary forms of mission literature, and for the moment they seem likely to yield the highest dividends in the study of missionary development in Africa. J. Du Plessis' *A History of Christian Missions in South Africa* (1911) was an early attempt to survey a region, though somewhat vitiated by the denominational divisions perpetuated in his chapters. The possibilities of a more thematic treatment were explored on a far larger scale, and for the continent as a whole, by Professor Groves.[16] The pro-

[14] Northcott, 1961; Smith, 1939. [15] Schapera, 1961. [16] Groves, 1948–58.

duction of a standard work of this magnitude places all of us in his debt, though here the comprehensive scope of the undertaking precluded that investigation in depth that the subject now demands. Intensive studies of smaller areas, pioneered by Professor Oliver and his pupil Dr. Slade,[17] have illuminated many of the major problems facing missionaries in Africa. They have been particularly successful in examining the relations of the missions with colonial policy during the Partition and the colonial period. A great deal of work along these lines, however, still remains to be done. Recently a Marxist historian has written what is unlikely to be the last word on the Rhenish Mission in German South-West Africa,[18] and this debate should be extended to embrace German enterprise in the rest of Africa. Research now in progress should throw light on the frontiers of settlers and missionaries in the South African Protectorates and Barotseland, but gaps remain, notably in Southern Rhodesia. Leopold II and Lavigerie is proving a theme of abundant dramatic interest;[19] but someone has still to take up the question of the imperialism of French missionaries from where it was left by Father Perbal,[20] and also to examine the influence of anti-clericalism during the French colonial period. Yet while a beginning has thus been made on the question of missions and colonial policy, many major themes of missionary methods and policy, and of their impact in the fields of education, medicine, and social welfare, still await detailed investigation.

So far, however, one might be in danger of assuming that Euro-American initiative dominates the history of Christianity in Africa, and that the African role has merely been one of passive receptivity. The principal distinction of recent research has been to rectify and radically transform this picture, and in so doing it has opened up a new dimension for the subject as a whole. This reorientation was first achieved in the study of Separatist and Independent Churches, and from the many outstanding works which have been published two perhaps are of especial interest for historians, on account of the sources which they used.

[17] Oliver, 1952; Slade, 1959.
[18] Loth, 1963.
[19] Storme, 1957; Perraudin, 1958.
[20] Perbal, 1938 and 1939.

Professor Shepperson and Mr. Price[21] combined the use of oral memories with an exhaustive and most rewarding search of the literature and archives of the American background influences, while Dr. Webster[22] has revealed the neglected potentials of the Churches' own archives and the private papers of leading African Christians. The study of this field of African initiative has in fact been so thorough and so convincing that some writers have been led to believe that Separatists and Independents alone have spoken with the authentic voice of Africa.[23] Recent reassessments of West African mission history have, however, begun to expose the extent to which Christian evangelism was a joint Afro-European undertaking, in which Africans often held the dominant role. Not only did African ministers and evangelists supply a leadership and continuity which a rapid mortality prevented most Europeans from providing, but African Christian traders and craftsmen were also often the effective pioneers far beyond the radius of European missionaries, creating Christian nuclei and arousing a demand for teachers and an interest in their message. The formation of Creole Christianity in Freetown, so fundamental to this whole story, has been touched on magisterially,[24] and two studies by African historians, recently published, have triumphantly recalled from near-oblivion the achievements and initiative of Africans in the Anglican mission to the Niger and in the origins and growth of Methodism among the Fante.[25] These outstanding examples, which will assuredly be followed by others, have already altered the whole focus of the early modern history of Christianity in West Africa, and they raise the question of whether Bantu Africa awaits a similar transformation. Here a variety of factors combined to enhance the European contribution; but one wonders whether the work of the European leaders, even in the pioneer period, reduced the African role to the insignificance which it at present enjoys, and throughout the subsequent phase of rapid expansion the emphasis should certainly be reconsidered. So far this process of reassessment has

[21] Shepperson and Price, 1958.
[22] Webster, 1964.
[23] Davidson, 1964, p. 34.
[24] Fyfe, 1962; see also Porter, 1963.
[25] Ajayi, 1965; Bartels, 1965.

been practically confined to Buganda, with two detailed accounts of the conversion and sacrifice of the Baganda martyrs,[26] an intensely interesting preliminary analysis by Canon Taylor,[27] a biography,[28] and two first-fruits of research which has yet to be published in full.[29] Elsewhere there are as yet little more than a few published indications[30] of this vast field of African activity which historians have still to investigate, and which can alone complement and fulfil a study of the missionaries' contribution. If this dimension is to be studied at all adequately, a large-scale salvage operation is an immediate priority, and the efforts of the Society for African Church History and others to encourage the preservation of Church records and private papers should be welcomed and intensified. For if the diaries, letters, and minute-books of the first generation of African Christians and their successors continue to lie exposed to destruction, and if the oral sources remain unrecorded, the essential evidence will soon be lost, and the possibility of a balanced understanding of the African, European, and American contributions to the development of Christianity in Africa will disappear. Yet the African contribution to this story has by no means been confined to the efforts of dedicated African Christians, and a further dimension of our study must embrace an attempt to assess the developing relationship between Christianity and the total African environment. This implies surely that, for the pioneering period and in many cases for a long time afterwards, the unit of study will be confined to the relatively restricted horizon of the local ethnic and cultural group. For it is only at this level that one can begin to examine in detail the interaction between Christianity and the specific network of tribal belief and social institutions, though an inherent aspect of the story is the expansion and merging of these horizons. For the historian this raises the problem of finding adequate sources at this level, and underlines yet again the

[26] Thoonen, 1941; Faupel, 1962.
[27] Taylor, 1958.
[28] Luck, 1963.
[29] Low, 1957; Rowe, 1964.
[30] Rauscher, 1953. See also the account of the Union Church of the Copperbelt in Taylor and Lehmann, 1961; and the references to the work of African catechists in Ross, 1964. Cousins, 1897, has remained an isolated study of the rich field of African leadership in the mission denominatious of Southern Africa.

urgency of rescuing the local records and memories before they finally vanish. Recently, however, a sociologist and an anthropologist have demonstrated the possibilities of examining this interaction through successive periods of contact;[31] and where the historical process is involved, Clio must soon reassert her authority.

REFERENCES

Ajayi, J. F. A.
(1965) *Christian Missions* in *Nigeria* 1841–1891. London.

Barclay, W. C.
(1949) *A History of Methodist Missions. Part I. Early American Methodism 1769–1844*. New York. (In progress.)

Bartels, F. L.
(1965) *The Roots of Ghana Methodism*. Cambridge.

Bianquis, J.
(1935) *Les Origines de la Société des Missions Évangéliques de Paris*. Paris. 3 vols.

Bouniol, J.
(1929) *The White Fathers and their Missions*. London.

Brown, A. J.
(1937) *One Hundred Years: A History of the Foreign Missionary Work of the Presbyterian Church in the U.S.A.* New York.

Bureau, R.
(1962) 'Ethno-sociologie religieuse des Duala et apparentés', *Recherches et Études Camerounaises*. Yaoundé.

Cnattingius, H.
(1952) *Bishops and Societies*. London.

Collins, R. and Duignan, P.
(1963) *Americans in Africa: A Preliminary Guide to American Missionary Archives and Library Manuscript Collections on Africa*. Stanford.

Cousins, H. T.
(1897) *Tiyo Soga*. London.

Cox, G. W.
(1888) *Life of John William Colenso*. London.

Davidson, B.
(1964) *The African Past: Chronicles from Antiquity to Modern Times*. London.

Faupel, J. F.
(1962) *African Holocaust*. London.

Fyfe, C.
(1962) *A History of Sierra Leone*. Oxford.

Goodall, N.
(1954) *A History of the London Missionary Society*. London.

Goyau. G.
(1937) *La Congrégation du St. Esprit*. Paris.

Gray, C.
(1876) *Life of Robert Gray, Bishop of Capetown*. London. 2 vols.

[31] Bureau, 1962; Horton, 1964.

Groves, C. P.
(1948–58) *The Planting of Christianity in Africa*. London. 4 vols.
Hewat, E. G. K.
(1960) *Vision and Achievement, 1796–1956: A History of the Foreign Missions of the Churches United in the Church of Scotland*. Edinburgh.
Hogg, W. R.
(1952) *Ecumenical Foundations: A History of the International Missionary Council and its Nineteenth Century Background*. New York.
Horton, R.
(1964) 'A Hundred Years of Change in Kalabari Religion.' Paper prepared for the Conference on The High God in Africa, University of Ife, Nigeria, 1964.
Janin, J.
(1935) *Le Clergé Colonial de 1815 à 1850*. Toulouse.
Lewis, C. and Edwards, G. E.
(1934) *Historical Records of the Church of the Province of South Africa*. Cape Town.
Loth, H.
(1963) *Die Christliche Mission in Südwestafrika*. Berlin.
Lovett, R.
(1899) *A History of the London Missionary Society*. London. 2 vols.
Low, D. A.
(1957) *Religion and Society in Buganda 1875–1900*. Kampala.
Luck, A.
(1963) *African Saint: The Story of Apolo Kivebulaya*. London.
Northcott, C.
(1961) *Robert Moffatt: Pioneer in Africa 1817–1870*. London.
Oliver, R.
(1952) *The Missionary Factor in East Africa*. London.
Perbal, A.
(1938) 'Le nationalisme de Mgr. Augouard', *Revue d'histoire des Missions*, pp. 385–407.
(1939) *Les Missionnaires français et le nationalisme*. Paris.
Perraudin, J.
(1958) *Le Cardinal Lavigerie et Léopold II*. Rome.
Porter, A. T.
(1963) *Creoledom: A Study of the Development of Freetown Society*. London.
Rauscher, F.
(1953) *Die Mitarbeit der Einheimischen Laien am Apostolat in den Missionen der Weissen Vater*. Munster.
Ross, A. C.
(1964) 'The Foundations of the Blantyre Mission, Nyasaland', *Religion in Africa*. Edinburgh.
Rowe, J. A.
(1964) 'The Purge of Christians at Mwanga's Court', *Journal of African History*, V, pp. 55–72.
Schapera, I. (ed.)
(1961) *Livingstone's Missionary Correspondence 1841–1856*. London.
Shepperson, G. and Price, T.
(1958) *Independent African: John Chilembwe and the origins setting and significance of the Nyasaland native rising of 1915*. Edinburgh.
Slade, R. M.
(1959) *English-speaking Missions in the Congo Independent State 1878–1908*. Brussels.

Smith, E. W.
(1939) *The Mabilles of Basutoland.* London.
Stock, E.
(1899–1916) *The History of the Church Missionary Society.* London. 4 vols.
Storme, M. B.
(1951) *Evangelisatiepogingen in de Binnenlanden van Afrika gedurende de XIXe eeuw.* Brussels.
(1957) *Rapports du Père Planque, de Mgr. Lavigerie et de Mgr. Combini sur l'Association internationale Africaine.* Brussels.
Strong, W. E.
(1910) *The Story of the American Board: An Account of the First Hundred Years of the American Board of Commissioners for Foreign Missions.* Boston.
Taylor, J. V.
(1958) *The Growth of the Church in Buganda.* London.
Taylor, J. V. and Lehmann, D.
(1961) *Christians of the Copperbelt.* London.
Thoonen, J. P.
(1941) *Black Martyrs.* London.
Todd, J. M.
(1962) *African Mission: A Historical Study of the Society of African Missions.* London.
Van der Merwe, W. J.
(1936) *The Development of Missionary Attitudes in the Dutch Reformed Church in South Africa.* Cape Town.
Webster, J. B.
(1964) *The African Churches among the Yoruba 1888–1922.* Oxford.

Résumé

PROBLÈMES DE PERSPECTIVE HISTORIQUE: L'IMPLANTATION DU CHRISTIANISME EN AFRIQUE AUX XIXème ET XXème SIÈCLES

Le nombre relativement réduit d'œuvres écrites par des Africains et par des non-chrétiens indique la mesure dans laquelle les recherches historiques sur le développement du Christianisme en Afrique depuis 1800 en sont encore à leurs débuts. Une analyse des caractéristiques de l'organisation-mère des missions ayant eu une incidence sur leur travail sur le terrain constitue un des aspects d'une telle étude. L'histoire des diverses sociétés missionnaires peut fournir un point de départ pour ces recherches. Certaines sociétés missionnaires, particulièrement celles d'obédience catholique, ne disposent pas encore d'une histoire écrite selon des principes d'érudition et beaucoup d'œuvres anciennes doivent être considérées à la lumière de nouveaux centres d'intérêts. Des progrès réels dans cette étude des organisations-mères, ne seront réalisés que lorsque l'on aura étudié plus avant les rapports entre les sociétés missionnaires et les Eglises et pays dont elles faisaient partie. Il est particulièrement important de procéder à des recherches approfondies sur le contrôle exercé par les églises métropolitaines sur les sociétés qui les représentaient en terrain missionnaire. Ce problème, tout en ayant affecté toutes les sectes à des degrés variés, a joué un rôle particulièrement important dans le cas de l'église catholique, car c'est l'augmentation de l'influence effective de la Congrégation de la Propagande qui, peut-être plus que tout autre facteur, a différencié très nettement les activités missionnaires catholiques du XIXème siècle en Afrique de celles des siècles précédents. La nature exacte de l'équilibre des pouvoirs très complexe établi entre le Vatican et les dirigeants des nouvelles sociétés et organismes missionnaires reste encore à étudier. Le développement et les contacts des grands organismes destinés à trouver des fonds, surtout la Congrégation de la Propagande, l'initiative missionnaire du Pape Grégoire XVI (1831–1846) constituent deux domaines prioritaires pour la recherche pour lesquels nous disposons maintenant de sources.

Cependant, à moins qu'il ne soit procédé à une modification profonde de la règle de clôture de 100 ans qui est encore applicable aux archives de la Congrégation de la Propagande, il sera impossible à la présente génération d'historiens d'évaluer de manière satisfaisante l'influence catholique en Afrique pendant la période cruciale du partage de l'Afrique et de l'établissement de la domination coloniale. Cette étude de l'interaction des organismes européens et des travaux missionnaires en Afrique devrait également être développée et comprendre deux autres facteurs qui ont amené des missionnaires chrétiens en Afrique. Il s'agit du développement graduel et de l'augmentation des intérêts missionnaires nord-américains vers l'Afrique, tout particulièrement au vingtième siècle, fait qui est d'une importance remarquable ainsi, également, que de l'influence directe et indirecte exercée par les églises de caractère européen établies en Afrique du Sud.

Néanmoins, l'étude des organismes métropolitains n'est qu'une condition d'importance relativement secondaire pour les recherches à entreprendre sur le travail des missionnaires en Afrique et sur la façon dont les Africains ont accueilli, propagé et interprété la Foi qui leur était présentée. Il existe deux formes traditionnelles de littérature missionnaire—les biographies et les histoires des diverses sociétés—qui peuvent encore beaucoup contribuer à une meilleure compréhension des activités missionnaires en Afrique. Cependant ces deux formes littéraires présentent certains défauts de par leur nature même. Les histoires des sociétés missionnaires la plupart des cas traitent d'un domaine dépassant le seul continent africain et, part conséquent, les sections qui en traitent sont en général trop brèves et trop superficielles pour satisfaire un africaniste. D'autre part, puisqu'elle ne décrivent que le travail d'une seule société, leur conception d'une zone africaine donnée est forcément limitée et manque d'impartialité. C'est par des études régionales intensives que l'on arrivera sans doute à surmonter ces difficultés. Des études de ce genre ont déjà donné beaucoup d'éclaircissements sur les rapports des missions avec le gouvernement colonial pendant l'époque du partage et celle de la colonisation mais beaucoup d'aspects essentiels des méthodes et politiques missionnaires ainsi que l'influence des missionnaires en matière d'éducation, de médecine et d'œuvres sociales doivent encore être analysés en détail.

Cependant, si toute l'attention des chercheurs devait se limiter aux organismes métropolitains et aux activités des missionnaires non-africains, on courrait le risque de supposer que ce sont des initiatives euro-américaines qui ont dominé l'histoire du Christianisme en Afrique et que le rôle joué par les Africains eux-mêmes s'est limité à une acceptation passive. Le principal mérite des recherches récentes a été de transformer cette conception et, ce faisant, ces études ont permis de donner une nouvelle dimension à la discipline dans son ensemble. Cette ré-orientation a tout d'abord été réalisée grâce à l'étude des églises séparatistes et indépendantes pour laquelle on a fait un usage assez extensif de sources orales et de documents et écrits de chrétiens africains importants. Des réévaluations de l'histoire missionnaire ouest-africaine ont également commencé à exposer la mesure dans laquelle l'évangélisme chrétien a été une entreprise afro-européenne commune dans laquelle ce sont souvent des Africains qui ont joué un rôle dominant. Ce n'est pas seulement les pasteurs et évangélistes Africains qui ont permis au travail missionnaire d'avancer alors que la mortalité très élevée empêchait les Européens de poursuivre leurs efforts, mais c'est également les commerçants et les artisans Africains Chrétiens qui souvent ont été des pionniers de la religion qu'ils allaient faire connaître bien au-delà des sphères d'influence européennes. Des études récentes traitant de la formation du Christianisme créole à Freetown, des réalisations et initiatives purement africaines au sein de la mission Anglicane du Niger et du développement du Méthodisme Fante ont déjà beaucoup altéré les concepts d'ensemble de l'histoire du Christianisme en Afrique Occidentale au début de la période moderne. Ceci nous amène à nous demander si l'histoire Chrétienne en Afrique Bantoue devrait être revue dans le même sens. Dans cette région, un certain nombre de facteurs ont contribué à un renforcement de l'influence européenne; on peut néanmoins se demander si, même à la période des pionniers, le travail des dirigeants européens avait réduit le rôle des Africains au peu d'importance qui lui est actuellement accordé. Il est certain que pour la période d'expansion rapide qui a suivi il faudrait réexaminer le problème. Jusqu'à present ce processus de réexamen s'est limité au Buganda mais d'après certaines indications dispersées il semblerait qu'il y ait là un vaste domaine d'activités africaines qu'il appartient aux historiens d'étudier. Si ces nouvelles perspectives doivent faire l'objet d'une analyse sérieuse, il faut qu'on leur accorde une très haute priorité car il s'agit d'une veritable opération de sauvetage. En effet, si les documents de la première génération de Chrétiens Africains et de leurs successeurs continuent à être exposés à la destruction et si on ne recueille pas les sources orales, les données de base seront bientôt anéanties et la possibilité d'arriver à une compréhension équilibrée du développement du christianisme en Afrique disparaîtra.

II. RELATIONS BETWEEN CHRISTIAN MISSIONS, EUROPEAN ADMINISTRATIONS, AND TRADERS IN THE GOLD COAST, 1828–74

I. TUFUOH

THE BACKGROUND

In December 1828 the first Basel missionaries arrived at Christiansborg, the Danish headquarters in the Gold Coast; six years later, the first Wesleyan missionary reached Cape Coast. Though they attracted little attention at the time, these two events turned out to be as important as some of the more stirring events of European contact with the country. With them Christian missions first struck root in the Gold Coast.

Behind the Basel and Wesleyan enterprise lay more than three centuries of sporadic attempts to convert the peoples of the Gold Coast to Christianity. These attempts began with the state-inspired missionary ventures of the Portuguese period. Off and on, between 1482 and 1576, Catholic missionaries, operating from the Portuguese headquarters at Elmina, made efforts to convert people in the neighbouring districts. In 1576 this work came to an end with the massacre of practically all the missionaries working in the Komenda area.[1]

After a break of more than sixty years, there was a last brief flicker of Catholic missionary activity in the Gold Coast. In 1638 two French Capuchins settled near the Portuguese factory at Axim. At about the same time, another group of French Capuchins started work in Komenda. Between them these two groups of missionaries collected a large following, and made converts of a number of the Efutu nobility.[2] But by 1640 friction with the Portuguese authorities had forced them to abandon their work.

Between this and the arrival of the Basel and Wesleyan Missions in the nineteenth century, attempts to evangelize the

[1] For these early Catholic attempts see Wiltgen, 1956, and Bane, 1956.

[2] Wiltgen, op. cit. p. 45.

country became less frequent and less enthusiastic. The decline set in with the elimination of Portugal from the keen European competition in the Gold Coast. In the third decade of the seventeenth century, this coast was drawn into the struggle against Spain in which the new Protestant power of the Netherlands had been engaged for the last half century. Portugal, conquered and annexed to the Spanish Crown in 1580, became the target of the economic warfare with which the Dutch sought to bring down the Spanish Empire. In 1637, São Jorge Castle, the Portuguese headquarters, capitulated to the Dutch. Five years later, the Dutch captured the last Portuguese fort at Axim, and expelled the Portuguese from the Gold Coast. In terms of missionary effort the expulsion from the coast of the only Catholic power which had operated there on a large scale was a loss to the country. It is true that under the Portuguese, the missions had not achieved much on this coast. But the desire to use the opportunity for evangelization had been there, and efforts had been made to make converts. This could not be said of the Dutch who had replaced them, nor of the English and the Danes who became their main rivals. In fact, before the evangelical rivalry, indifference was general in the areas under the control of these Protestant powers.

The English, Danish, and Dutch establishments on the coast usually had a chaplain on the list of officers; but when there happened to be chaplains on the coast, they limited their ministrations to the Europeans, their mulatto wives, and children. It would appear that nothing more was expected of them, for, as late as the beginning of the nineteenth century, C. H. Monrad, the Danish chaplain at Christiansborg, could say that it was not right to regard the chaplain as a missionary, and that as far as he could ascertain it had never been the object of his appointment to work for the conversion of the natives.[3] The Dutch took a similar line. The Directors of the Dutch West India Company, the authority responsible for the Gold Coast settlements, declared quite firmly that they could not make the teaching and baptism of heathens their concern.[4] Neither the Danish nor the Dutch Church showed the slightest interest in the matter. In

[3] Bartels, 1949, p. 78. [4] Ibid.

Britain the cultured, worldly, and sceptical upper clergy regarded 'enthusiasm', the mainspring of all missionary enterprise, as bad form.[5] It is hardly surprising then that the English authorities on the coast showed only the mildest of interest in efforts to take the gospel to the wider community outside the forts. This lack of interest is strikingly illustrated by the missionary career of Philip Quaque who worked at Cape Coast Castle from 1765 to 1816.[6] During his long career, he managed to baptize some fifty persons only. His general lack of success is to be explained partly by the actions and attitudes of the English authorities and merchants in and around Cape Coast. Though they never directly opposed his ministrations, they appear to have made things as difficult as they could for him. In the late seventies, the Governor used every conceivable excuse to cancel church services at the Castle for long periods together.[7] From start to finish, Quaque had to fight against the demoralizing effect of indifference and even hostility among the garrison to all a missionary stood for.[8] Their rejection of the missionary's persuasions went with a manner of life marked by brutality and debauchery.[9] Their example could not but act as a drag on Quaque's efforts to convert the people to a religion with which the European was identified. This general attitude of indifference to missionary effort remained substantially unchanged until the time of Maclean.

THE BASEL AND WESLEYAN MISSIONS 1828–74

In the period up to 1850 (when the Danes were bought out of the Gold Coast by the English) the Basel and Wesleyan missions worked in the Danish and English spheres of influence respectively, and their relations were primarily with the specific local authorities and merchant communities in their respective areas.

The Basel Mission had an extremely difficult start. They came into a heritage of indifference and neglect. The last appointment to the Danish chaplaincy on the Gold Coast had been that of C. H. Monrad, who worked at Christiansborg between 1805 and

[5] Mellor, 1951. [6] Bartels, 1955. [7] Lawrence, 1963, p. 64.
[8] Bartels, op. cit., pp. 168–9. [9] Ibid., p. 173.

1809. True to the tradition of the chaplaincy, Monrad had not gone out of his way to undertake evangelization among the heathen, but the garrison community for whose benefit he had been appointed resented his presence. Some of them, in open defiance of the law, dealt in slaves;[10] many indulged in a life of debauchery,[11] and, if they needed spiritual consolations, sought them from fetish priests.[12] A chaplain's persuasions were out of tune with their manner of life, his presence a source of embarrassment. They either treated Monrad with open scorn or left him severely alone.[13] In despair of achieving anything among the Danish expatriates and adult half-castes, Monrad devoted almost all his time to teaching the youth in the Castle School.[14] When Monrad's term was over, the Danish authorities on the coast did not ask for a replacement.

In 1823 Major Johan Christian von Richelieu became Governor of the Danish settlements. He was unusual as a Govenor in the concern he showed for religious matters. He himself conducted divine service and taught the youths in the Castle School. When in June 1826 he was on the point of going home on leave, Richelieu was asked by some of the mulattos, who cherished warm memories of Monrad, to bring them back a chaplain.[15] Influential religious circles in Denmark were appalled to learn that for nearly twenty years there had been no chaplain on the Gold Coast and when the Basel mission applied to be allowed to send missionaries to Christiansborg, the Court Chaplain, Roenne put in a plea for them.[16] Permission was granted, and in 1828 four missionaries, Holzworth, Salbach, Schmid, and Henke, were sent out to Christiansborg.

At Christiansborg the climate of opinion was far from favourable to missionary enterprise. The Danish governors who followed Richelieu had none of his enthusiasm for religion. Henke wrote of Lind, Governor of Christiansborg between 1828 and 1831, that he had many good points but that unfortunately he was a rationalist.[17] Between Henke and the Governor a disagreement

[10] Debrunner, 1956, p. 14. [11] Ibid., p. 21. [12] Ibid.
[13] Ibid., p. 20. [14] Ibid., p. 24. [15] Ibid., p. 25. [16] Ibid.
[17] Henke to Kissling, 11 March 1830, B.M.A. Africa (1829–39).

arose over the content and treatment of religious instruction in one of the schools, which led to the subject being dropped for some time from the curriculum.[18] For Hein, Lind's successor, Henke had not a single good word; he was, wrote Henke, a combination of pride, ambition, greed, and sensuality, a man who did not care for religion.[19] Governor Ahrenstorff who came after him was no better.[20] Henke described the Europeans at Christiansborg in this period as a dissolute crowd. With the exception of the Governor and two others, the Danish expatriates practised polygamy. Though all but one attended services regularly, each had his own faith, none the true faith.[21] Their manner of life seems to have brutalized many of the Europeans. Monrad wrote of the European of his day: 'He treats his Africans and wives in a way revolting to human nature.'[22] In the 1830s Riis noted the same harshness and lack of restraint in their dealings with Africans, but he conceded that in many cases the harshness was provoked by criminal practices.[23] Such people were certainly not the best advertisement for a civilization with which the Africans generally identified Christianity.

From the time of Maclean a striking change took place in the relations between the English authorities and missionaries. The arrogance and indifference of governors and other members of the ruling set towards missionaries gave way to respect, sometimes friendship, and enthusiastic support of their efforts. Within a year of association with Maclean, Freeman reported to his headquarters: 'The deep interest which the President takes in the prosperity of the work in which I am engaged as well as in my own personal welfare lays me under a lasting obligation to him.'[24] At the end of Maclean's term as President of the merchant administration Freeman wrote: 'Our present Governor has always been to us a warm and steady friend.'[25] Maclean clearly saw that

[18] B.M.A. Henke to the Inspector, 30 January 1831.
[19] Henke to the Inspector, 31 October 1831.
[20] Ibid.
[21] B.M.A. Henke to Inspector, 20 May 1830.
[22] Quoted Debrunner, op. cit., p. 21.
[23] B.M.A. Riis to Inspector, 6 June 1832.
[24] M.M.S. Freeman to General Secretaries, 16 January 1839.
[25] M.M.S. Freeman to Beecham, 23 November 1843.

for a system of government like his in which influence counted for everything, administrative action could find no better ally than missionary enterprise. But his enthusiastic support of missionaries did not rest entirely on calculations of this kind. Son of a Presbyterian minister, Maclean was brought up to take his religion seriously. The understanding and sympathy for missionary endeavour which many of his predecessors were by inclination and tradition of service incapable of, came naturally to him. And in Freeman he found a model missionary. Cruickshank, who knew the man well, said of Freeman that he combined 'the wisdom of the politician with the active zeal of the missionary'.[26] To immense tact, unfailing courtesy and shrewd appreciation of men, he added a passion for getting things done. In many ways he was very much like Maclean and a close relationship based on mutual respect and understanding developed between the two men. On potentially explosive issues like domestic slavery and the relations of the protectorate with Ashanti they held broadly similar views. There was thus no room for that clash of opinion which elsewhere so often set missionaries and administrators at odds. Their enthusiastic co-operation established a pattern of relationship between government and mission which, but for a brief interruption between 1844 and 1846, remained unbroken for a decade.[27] In the period up to 1857, when Freeman was Chairman of the District, these relations were kept smooth by Freeman's close personal contact with successive governors. For nearly a quarter of a century after Maclean's death (1847) Freeman was indisputably the most outstanding expatriate on the Gold Coast. By the fifties he had not only had long experience of the country, on which alone many expatriates were wont to base

[26] Cruickshank, 1966, Vol. I., p. 117.

[27] The reasons for this interruption will be found in: C.O. 96/6 Hill to Stanley, 27 February 1845; C.O. 96/6 Hope to Beecham, 21 May 1845; C.O. 96/6 Hill to Stanley, 7 March 1845; C.O. 96/6 Hope to Maclean, 17 May 1845; C.O. 96/6 Maclean to Hope, 21 May 1845; C.O. 96/6 Stanley to Hill, 20 August 1845; C.O. 96/4 Hill to Stanley, 6 August 1844; Stephen's minute to Hope, 23 November 1844.

M.M.S. Brooking to General Secretaries, 1 March 1845; Martin to Beecham, 7 March 1845; Freeman to General Secretaries, 10 December 1845.

Also, Metcalfe, 1962, pp. 311–15.

claims to be consulted on matters affecting the administration, he had also by his integrity and unflagging interest in their affairs won the confidence of many of the protectorate chiefs, among them the influential Otu of Abrah.[28] He was one of the very few men in the 'protectorate' in whom the King of Ashanti had implicit trust.[29] His prestige was equally high on the Slave Coast, where his negotiations with the wily Gezo of Dahomey for the abandonment of the slave trade were a source of disquiet to the slave merchants of Lagos, Badagry, and Whydah, and of hope to the officers of the squadron.[30] It is hardly surprising that one Governor after another sought his opinion on sundry matters affecting the administration.

Winniett (1846–50), who ended up by offering Freeman a post in the government, indeed made no attempt to keep his consultation private. In March 1848 when he decided to visit Abomey, the Dahomean capital, to follow up the negotiations for the stoppage of the slave trade and the reoccupation of the English fort at Whydah begun unofficially by Freeman five years before, he took the missionary along as his aide. Later that year he again chose Freeman as his companion and adviser on a journey to Kumasi, in an attempt to clear suspicion and misunderstanding which had clouded relations with Ashanti in recent years, and to persuade the King to give up the practice of human sacrifice.[31] In both cases, it is true, the Governor merely asked Freeman to come in publicly on projects with which he was already privately associated: in Dahomey he was the initiator of the policy the

[28] For Freeman's relations with Otu see: M.M.S. Freeman, 'Reminiscences and incidents of travels and historical and political sketches in and of the countries bordering on the Gold and Slave Coasts and in Ashantee, Dahomey etc.' (unpublished manuscript) pp. 13–16. C.O. 96/41, Pine to Labouchere, 31 August 1857; Enclosure Freeman to Pine, 27 June 1857.

[29] This trust would seem to have been created by a feeling that unlike the traders and administrators Freeman was not out to get something for himself. In 1842 the King told one of his courtiers, 'he has come to Kumasi bringing no trade palaver. He is not come to make arrangements for sending slaves down to the coast. It is evident that he is come here to do us good.' M.M.S. Freeman, Journal of Second Visit to Ashantee, 22 January 1842.

[30] M.M.S. Freeman to General Secretaries; Enclosure Gezo to Queen Victoria, 13 March 1843.

[31] C.O. 96/11 Winniett to Grey, 22 February 1847; C.O. 96/13 Winniett to Grey, 6 November 1848.

Governor sought to pursue; in Kumasi Freeman personally and the Wesleyan mission in general had since 1842 taken on the task of trying to establish clear intelligence between the King and the British authorities, and of weaning the court from the practice of human sacrifice.[32] But no such explanation can be offered for Winniett's action in February 1850 in asking Freeman to accompany him on a tour of the Danish possessions which had just been transferred to the British Government.[33] The reason for this would seem to be the obvious one that, having tested and found Freeman's advice sound, Winniett decided to avail himself of the missionary's services whenever he could. So much indeed did Winniett wish to avail himself of Freeman's experience that in May 1850 he took the unusual step of offering a full-time missionary a post in the administration as clerk of the newly established Legislative Council.[34] What change, if any, would have taken place in the relations between the mission and the government as a result of this move, it is impossible to say, for Grey refused to sanction the appointment on the grounds that the small volume of Council business could well be handled by the Colonial Secretary in addition to his normal duties.[35] Winniett's failure did not stop his successors from continuing to call on Freeman's services. In April 1853 during an Ashanti war scare Freeman reported to his headquarters: the Ashanti crisis 'has naturally led to my having much to do at the castle. His Excellency the Governor having some time back expressed a wish that I would in all cases of importance act with him as a member of the Executive Council in offering any advice which my long connexion with this country may at any time enable me to give.' Though he had fallen in with the Governor's wishes, Freeman felt it necessary to make a reservation: 'Any advice that I may give I offer not of course publicly in the capacity of a member of Council but *privately*.'[36] This reservation was probably made

[32] M.M.S. Freeman to General Secretaries 30 July 1838. M.M.S. Maclean to Mycock 9 April 1840. Beecham, 1841, p. 341.

[33] M.M.S. Freeman to General Secretaries, 9 April 1850.

[34] C.O. 96/18 Winniett to Grey, 30 April 1850. M.M.S. Winniett to General Secretaries, 22 May 1850.

[35] C.O. 96/18 Winniett to Grey, 3 April 1850; Minute by Grey, 2 August 1850.

[36] M.M.S. Freeman to General Secretaries, 13 April 1853.

because of recent developments in local politics. In 1849–50 the merchants had made a bid to secure control of the government through a council dominated by merchant representatives; this had failed when Grey gave the settlements a Legislative Council on which the merchant representatives were outnumbered by officials; the result was resentment, sometimes even open hostility to the government, among the merchants.[37] Freeman may have felt that too open an association with the administration would set him (and the mission) at odds with the merchant community.[38] If merchant discontent made it prudent for Freeman to seek the anonymity of giving advice in private it appears at the same time to have increased the demands of administrators on him. Smouldering discontent made the merchants grudging in their co-operation and gravely suspect in the eyes of the administration at a time when, with the contradictions and other weaknesses of the protectorate system becoming increasingly apparent, the government stood most in need of informed advice and support.[39] Where governors could only hope to get merchant support at a price, they could count on Freeman to give counsel and bring his influence to bear without attaching political strings. Thus even an administrator like Sir Benjamin Pine, who was prepared to go some way to conciliate merchant opinion and give the merchants a greater voice in the government,[40] turned to the missionary when he needed advice on important issues. In 1857, when Sir Benjamin decided that the protectorate system needed drastic surgery, he called upon Freeman to help to pinpoint what had gone wrong and suggest remedial action. His long and forceful dispatch on the proposed operation, which so shocked the phlegmatic officials of the Colonial Office by the open display of

[37] Metcalfe, 1955.

[38] Writing in October 1850 about the financial difficulties of Winniett's administration and his own decision to back out of his provisional undertaking to take the post of Clerk of the Legislative Council, Freeman stated; 'There is much unpleasant difference and contention existing now betwixt some of the merchants and the Government here and it would be unpleasant and injurious for me in connexion with my position as a missionary, to run the risk of coming into collision with the merchants as a Government official.' M.M.S. Freeman to General Secretaries, 23 October 1850.

[39] Metcalfe, 1955, p. 183.

[40] Ibid., p. 182.

emotional involvement, was firmly grounded on Freeman's observations, communicated both verbally and in a letter.[41] Where others were suspected of having a particular axe to grind, Freeman was accepted without reservation as a dispassionate observer, who intervened only when asked to do so. Indeed, one explanation of Freeman's success in acting as the confidential adviser to a long line of administrators without arousing the hostility of the extremely touchy displaced merchant ruling set, must be sought in the fact that he never attempted to play the role of *éminence grise*, though he was well placed to do so. For a man who was so often called upon to take on tasks of a political nature and who was so close to the centre of decision, Freeman was remarkably reluctant to force his opinion on administrators. This is the more surprising since most expatriates in those parts seemed to have blueprints for good government and kept up a steady flow of letters and memoranda with the object of keeping Governors and the Colonial Office on the right course. Moreover, in this community of small cliques and narrow interests, where political influence was apt to be used for the promotion of this or that specific interest,[42] Freeman never sought through his close relations with Governors to advance interests exclusive to his missionary society. The impression grows that for him it was enough that his co-operation with Governors in political matters kept the government and his mission in step and served to underline the essential interdependence of missionary activity and administrative action on this frontier of influence. The years 1838–57 saw relations between the government and the Wesleyan mission at their closest. Freeman, in joint harness with Maclean, tried to create a new accord with Ashanti[43] and strove to convert the Court of Dahomey to the new humanitarian programme; Winniett sought to add the persuasions of the Governor to the

[41] C.O. 96/41 Pine to Labouchere 31 August 1857; Enclosure Freeman to Pine, 27 June 1857.

[42] There was a running feud between the representatives of the firm of Forster and Smith and the other English firms which permeated the politics of the settlements. One episode in this running battle provoked Cruickshank to write: 'The pettiness and absurdity of their warfare is truly Lilliputian.'—See Swanzy, 1956, pp. 97–102 and 106.

[43] See pp. 45–46 below.

efforts of the Wesleyan mission to get the King of Ashanti to abolish the practice of human sacrifice;[44] and the local government made the first real effort through the measures culminating in the Education Ordinance of 1842[45] to share with the missions the burden of education. During this period dealings between the government and the mission were characterized by a candour and informal ease[46] which were soon to be replaced by a frosty politeness. This close accord was largely Freeman's personal achievement, and when he resigned from the chairmanship of the mission in September 1857, the personal link was removed and with it much of the ready understanding on which it had been built.

When the Wesleyan mission began its operations on the Coast the forts and settlements were under a merchant administration and the small community of merchants were virtually the sole legatees of what British influence there had been in the protected territories. The reaction of this small but influential group to evangelical activity was a factor of no little importance in the initial development of the mission. As has already been pointed out, a constant source of frustration for those who had attempted evangelization in these parts before the Wesleyans had been the indifference, sometimes hostility, displayed by the merchants towards an activity which all too often stood as a silent reproach to their manner of life. The Wesleyan mission did not have to face this difficulty. The change-over from the slave trade to legitimate commerce would seem to have brought to the settlements a new set of British merchants more inclined than their predecessors to maintain some of the standards of decency which would have been expected of them at home. The first Wesleyan missionaries, who were not particularly disposed to view the foibles of their

[44] C.O. 96/11, Winniett to Grey, 22 February 1847.

[45] C.O. 96/25, Hill to Packington, 1 December 1852; Enclosure Ordinance (passed 25 November) 1852.

[46] In a comment on an address of thanks from the Wesleyan missionaries, Winniett stated, 'The support and countenance I have invariably given to the Wesleyan ministers have proceeded from a sincere regard for their frank and honest dealings with me.' C.O. 96/15 Winniett to Grey, 3 January 1849; Enclosures (i) Address of Wesleyan missionaries 1 January 1849, (ii) Winniett's reply, 2 January 1849.

fellow men with tolerance, found little wrong with the merchants beyond their excessive indulgence in food and drink. There are several entries in Dunwell's journal in which he notes with some distress the frequency and lavishness with which the Cape Coast merchants entertained. 'Hitherto,' he wrote, five months after his arrival on the Coast, 'I have almost entirely refused attending the frequent parties here; which indeed (some) have been disgraceful [*sic*]; my refusals appear to give offence and cause suspicion in some; but be that as it may I cannot hold friendship with the world; the mouth of God hath declared that it is enmity with him.'[47] From his journal Dunwell emerges as a man of intense and brooding disposition, who had a puritanical distrust of the good things of life. His strictures on the merchants may therefore have been more severe than the nature of their pleasures deserved. At any rate, though the merchants may have been lacking in the austere virtues of plain and sober living, they seem in other respects to have stood up well under critical scrutiny. The missionaries were particularly impressed by the readiness with which the leading merchants went out of their way to help the mission with counsel and encouragement.[48] And their journals provide ample evidence of the generosity of the merchants to which sometimes, as in Dunwell's case, they made an ungracious response because of a personal quirk. Indeed, such difficulties as there were at the start in the relations between the mission and the merchants appear to have been due largely to the unwillingness or inability on the part of some of the early missionaries to fit themselves into a community which did not share their strict nonconformist views. When in 1838 the mission came under the direction of Freeman, a broad-minded man of gregarious instincts, the last trace of reserve disappeared. Within a year of his arrival on the coast Freeman wrote to his headquarters: 'I am glad to say that the European gentlemen are becoming daily more and more interested in the welfare and prosperity of our mission and I sincerely hope that should I fall in the field or be

[47] M.M.S. Dunwell, J., Journal, 27 May 1835.

[48] M.M.S. Dunwell, Journal, 16 February 1835. Wrigley G.O., Diary, 30 September 1836.

absent from the station ere the person you intend to send arrives he will endeavour to keep up that friendly feeling which now exists between the merchants, the Government, and the Society.'[49] Clearly in the twenty-odd years since Quaque's death merchant attitude towards missionary enterprise had undergone a remarkable change.

The gradual replacement of the hardened traders of the pre-abolition period by new men apart, two main factors seem to have brought about this change: an external factor, namely, the impact on the British community on the coast of the pressures generated by humanitarians in Britain; and a local factor, namely, the transformation under Maclean of the local administration from a mere agent of British trading interests into an instrument of social reform in the adjacent territories. The long humanitarian agitation in Britain affected changes on the coast in two main ways: first it subjected this, as other areas under British influence where the traffic in slaves and the institution of slavery still flourished, to close official and unofficial scrutiny and thus created in the merchants a feeling that their activities might at any moment become a matter for public comment in Britain.[50] This consideration had certainly been a strong factor in the feverish attempts of the Company of Merchants in its last days to present a new image to the public. Secondly, the humanitarian agitation in the late thirties became a sustained plea for the adoption by the British Government and the public of a programme of reconstruction in Africa, one of the main planks of which was missionary enterprise. As with most causes the humanitarians championed in these years, missionary enterprise in Africa acquired a new and enhanced stature which made it difficult to ignore and politically rash to oppose. Merchant rule on the Gold Coast had been a grudging concession from the Colonial Office, and the merchants could only hope to hold their mandate if they

[49] M.M.S. Freeman to General Secretaries, 10 October 1838.

[50] The African Institution, the Anti-Slavery Society and the African Civilization Society, one after the other, had a host of correspondents 'on the spot' in Africa—administrators, traders, explorers, etc.—who fed their journals with first-hand information and enabled them to keep a close watch on the African scene.

showed themselves sensitive to those changes of mood in Britain which were leading the Imperial Government to search for a new and more humane relationship with African peoples. For this, if for no other reason, the merchants would have had to show a departure from the indifference and hostility of their predecessors once missionary enterprise in Africa had become a pet scheme of the humanitarians. There was another factor, however, which helped to change the attitude of the merchants towards missionary effort. Maclean, disregarding the instructions of the Colonial Office, had committed his administration to the gamble of trying to initiate a social revolution by persuasion and fiat over an extensive area of non-British territory.[51] Though their approach was essentially pragmatic, and boiled down to making decisions as problems arose, the general drift of the policy of the administration was the modification of native law and custom by excision of practices repugnant to them and the grafting of English ideas and practices on to the existing system; and the interposition between the traditional rulers and their subjects of a new authority, namely, the administration, which would deal impartially between ruler and subject.[52] For the assault on native law and custom the administration had no legal authority; neither had it the physical force which could cow the people into accepting unpopular innovations. To be safe and also to obtain enduring results the operation had to take the form of bringing the people round to see the case for changes in their customary law and practice. To achieve its second objective, which in its levelling tendencies had revolutionary implications for the ordering of native society, the administration needed the support of a new group disposed by their training to favour some re-distribution of power in the society and sufficiently influential to carry the ordinary people with them. In effect, for the gamble to come off, the administration needed to create in the protected territories a substantial body of men who shared its assumptions

[51] For the authoritarian element in Maclean's system, see Metcalf, 1962, Chapter 8 *et passim*.

[52] The exalted position Maclean claimed for his administration in the new order is clearly seen in his dealings with Kweku Aka, the chief of Apollonia. See Metcalfe, op. cit., pp. 166–7.

and prejudices. The key to this lay in evangelization and the provision of Western education on a generous scale. But kept in near penury by the cheese-paring policy of the Colonial Office, the administration was not in a position to take on these burdens itself. It was natural for the merchant government to welcome the efforts of independent and self-supporting bodies like the missionary societies who were equipped for these tasks.

For their part the missionaries had good reasons for wishing to maintain friendly relations with the merchants. It is no discredit to the missions to say that material considerations influenced their attitudes in this matter. Finance was always a problem for the missions; and though one missionary secretary in a moment of stress declared, 'it is not by a baptism of money, but by a baptism of the Holy Spirit that the work is to be permanently advanced',[53] even he could not have denied that the quality and scope of missionary work depended in some measure on the funds available to the missions. As their needs were hardly ever adequately covered by the annual grants made by the parent societies, the missions treasured unexpected windfalls in the shape of donations from the merchant houses, and it would have been less than human if missionaries had made no attempts to cultivate their potential benefactors, especially as their indebtedness to the merchants went far beyond the occasional contributions to their funds. Here, as in Nigeria, the mercantile establishments performed an invaluable service for the missions by acting as their bankers.[54] The Basel Mission, which from small beginnings in 1850 soon developed a vigorous trade section as an integral part of its work, stood less in need of this service than the other missions on the coast. For the Wesleyans, however, this service was indispensable. The bulk of their business was done through credit facilities provided by the merchant houses, especially those of Forster and Smith and Hutton and Sons. From these establishments the missionaries took provisions and other goods on 'drafts' or bills of credit which the houses in England presented for payment at the society's headquarters.

[53] M.M.S. Hoole to Freeman, 10 July 1856.
[54] Ajayi, 1958, p. 137.

Though it had a profit angle in that it facilitated the sale of their wares, this business involved considerable inconvenience for the merchant houses. Not infrequently missionaries issued drafts in excess of the annual grants made by the parent society, and months of wrangling between mission and headquarters would pass before the bills were settled. An instance of this occurred in 1848 when two drafts for £500 and £120 made out to Messrs. Hutton and Sons became the subject of heated correspondence between Freeman and the General Secretaries.[55] A protracted wrangle over finance towards the end of Freeman's superintendency caused a mighty pile-up of bills in which the firm of Forster and Smith alone had an interest of some £1,470.[56] Even more serious were causes in which missionary headquarters refused outright to honour drafts which were not covered by the yearly grant. When this happened, the merchants had no option but to hold the bills over until the local mission could settle from their next grant.[57] It was no small sacrifice on the part of the merchant houses to tie up their money in this way. Lastly, it was merchant activity that enabled the missions, in the beginning at any rate, to operate in this area. As Dr. Ajayi has pointed out, till the establishment of the West African mail boat in 1853 every missionary depended for passage, freight, and correspondence on the trading vessel.[58] 'Passengers and freight,' he writes, 'were taken as a favour because it was more profitable for the traders to carry trade goods than missionary houses and gift boxes and equipment. They were quite often taken free.'[59]

Though considerations of this kind played a part in drawing missionaries and merchants together, they were by no means the most important in the growth of a *rapport* between the missions and the merchants. It is doubtful whether the links forged by the dependence of missionaries on merchants for many essential services would have held if there had been sharp differences of

[55] M.M.S. Hoole to Freeman, 22 November 1848.

[56] M.M.S. Freeman to General Secretaries, 11 September 1857.

[57] In some cases the firms wrote off the debt. For example, when in November 1848 a draft of £50 made out to Forster and Smith was dishonoured, the firm presented the sum as a donation to the mission.

[58] Ajayi, op. cit., p. 136.

[59] Ibid.

purpose between them. The bond which most firmly held missionary and merchant together was a common interest in providing through specific activities and institutions a foundation for the spread of Christianity and Western culture in the protected territories. In the thirties, both as individuals and through the collective action of their council, the merchants backed to the hilt the Wesleyan mission drive to bring Western influence to bear through the establishment of schools and churches.[60] The missionaries for their part were some of the stoutest defenders of the instruments and methods which Maclean and his council were using for the same purpose.[61] The understanding born of the pursuit of a common purpose drew strength from another source. The concentration in a handful of towns of a small expatriate community,[62] set apart from the larger community by the same manner of life, with the resulting opportunity for personal contact, discussion, and consultation, could not but result over the years in something of a common outlook on many issues. The sense of belonging together, of being in joint harness, pervaded relations in the expatriate community until the fifties, when merchant disaffection with the administration destroyed the basis of co-operation. Writing in 1875 in reply to queries about the continuance of human sacrifice raised by the Aborigines Protection Society, Freeman observed:

> In former times, say twenty or twenty-five years ago, the intercourse between the governors of these settlements, and the principal Residents, both merchants and missionaries, who then mainly constituted the upper class of civil society, was more free, close, and genial than it is in the present day; and in consequence such delicate and intricate questions as the present one could be freely discussed, and local experience could be brought to bear on the minds of Governors and other Rulers, and modes of action planned, and

[60] In his letter of 2 August 1838, Freeman reports that William Topp, the acting President, 'has given a larger sum than anyone for the building of the chapel'. In January 1840 Maclean informed the African Committee of the establishment of schools in Anomabu and Accra for whose maintenance the administration and the Wesleyan mission were to be jointly responsible.

[61] M.M.S. Freeman to General Secretaries, 1 January 1842. Freeman here defends Maclean against the strictures of Dr. R. R. Madden, perhaps the harshest of the President's critics.

[62] There were forty Europeans on the Gold Coast in 1847, the year of Maclean's death. C.O. 100/3 (Blue Book).

measures taken, calculated to result in practical benefit in dealing with the numerous pagan and despotic surroundings of these regions, where moral influence must necessarily be the basis of political action; but of late years, things here on the coast, have, in that respect, changed greatly for the worse; and beyond the ordinary gentlemanly courtesy between stranger and stranger, there is very little intercourse, so that delicate questions of this nature cannot be dealt with as they could formerly.[63]

The crisis of confidence between the merchants and the administration of the fifties was primarily responsible for straining relations between those who constituted the 'upper class of civil society'. Suspecting the merchants of trying to get them to dance to their tune, the governors tended to keep them at an arm's length and to rely increasingly on the advice of officials and a few hand-picked confidantes. Discontent on the one side and suspicion on the other were hardly calculated to ease social intercourse between merchants and administrators. The tension between them communicated itself to the missionaries, who were caught between a desire to stay out of it all and an uneasy feeling that it was their duty to state the rights and wrongs of the matter, as they saw it, if the need arose.[64] Since, initially at any rate, their sympathies lay with the administration, relations between the missionaries and the merchants could not have been particularly comfortable. Though Freeman's tact saved an awkward collision between the mission and the merchant community, the coolness which set in at about this time never quite disappeared from their relations. With the government the mission continued to maintain a link while Freeman was still in control. After his resignation in 1857 relations with the administration became much less genial. And in the sixties and seventies a new factor appeared to set mission and government even farther apart. This was a fundamental lack of sympathy among the administrators for the things

[63] Rhodes House (Oxford)—MSS British Empire S 18, C 134/225. Freeman to Chesson, 14 October 1875.

[64] Ibid. Freeman states bluntly, 'I consider that the existing Government here is suffering much injustice from certain parties connected with the country; and my Brethren here are of the same opinion as myself.' In the paragraph immediately preceding this he refers to 'much unpleasant difference and contention between some merchants and the Government here'; so there can be little doubt about the identity of the 'parties' referred to.

evangelization stood for. In 1874 Freeman, who had returned to the mission two years previously, wrote that the prospect of getting the government to help provide better education was pretty dismal. His reason was that 'the greater number of the officers who now come out to the coast, to fill appointments here, are Rationalists, who do not believe in Divine Revelation, and who consequently, to say the least, have few earnest sympathies with us in our labours.'[65] By the end of our period, then, the sense of involvement and unity of purpose between various sections of the expatriate community of the Maclean period had become nothing more than a faint memory.

To the Basel mission the state of affairs in the seventies was nothing new. For the twenty-odd years of its association with the Danish authorities on the Gold Coast, the mission was never really in accord with the administration. The frustrations of the early years, when first Henke and then Andreas Riis came up against the indifference and capricious authoritarianism of the Danish establishment, gave the relations between mission and government an undertone of unease from the start. In the late thirties this uneasy relationship deteriorated into open conflict, the effects of which continued to be felt to the end of the Danish connexion with the coast. The quarrel arose from a disagreement over a political issue; but its course appears for the greater part to have been shaped by the intransigence of the two persons involved. Andreas Riis, the sole survivor of the early batch of missionaries and indeed the effective founder of the Basel mission on the Gold Coast, was not an easy person to get on with. A choleric man with a biting tongue, he could brook no contradiction.[66] In the forties he quarrelled with practically all his colleagues, including his own nephew, H. N. Riis.[67] He had the unfortunate habit of making damaging remarks about his colleagues in public.[68] Clearly, tact was not his strongest point. The other protagonist was Frederick Siegfried Morch, who became

[65] M.M.S. Freeman to General Secretaries, 2 June 1875.

[66] B.M.A. Windmann to Inspector, 7 January 1846. B.M.A. Windmann to Inspector, 1 September 1842.

[67] B.M.A. H.N. Riis to Inspector, 29 December 1845.

[68] B.M.A. Windmann to Inspector, 7 January 1846.

Governor of the Danish settlements in December 1834. Riis portrayed him as a man driven by a desire to lord it over all and sundry.[69] Riis can hardly be considered an impartial judge, but his assessment of his opponent's character is borne out by other evidence.[70] A man of inordinate ambition, Morch was also temperamentally incapable of working slowly towards his ends.[71] It was this desire to win great prizes quickly that led him into the political decisions which started the quarrel.

The general situation from which the conflict arose consisted in a series of disputes closely connected with Morch's attempt to transform the vague connexion between the Danes and the peoples of the eastern districts of the Gold Coast, particularly the Akwapim and the Krobo, into effective Danish paramountcy; the specific issue with which it was connected was the Akwapim reaction to Morch's energetic but ill-advised policy. By the beginning of 1836 Morch's headlong intervention in a long-standing quarrel between Akwapim and Krobo had generated so much ill-will in Akwapim against the Danish establishment that the idea began seriously to be entertained of transferring Akwapim 'allegiance' to the English, who had long disputed Danish claims to exclusive jurisdiction in the eastern districts.[72] By March 1836 Ado Dankwa, the King of Akwapim, had been won over to this decision, and early that month a formal offer of 'allegiance' was made to Maclean in Accra.[73] Always cautious in his approach to things, Maclean suggested a solution which in effect rejected this radical re-alignment of forces on the coast, but kept the door open for negotiation between the English and the Danes, and the Danes and the people of Akwapim.

From this point the course of events came to be influenced by a recent family feud. Just before Morch arrived on the coast one of the King's sons was convicted of the crime of poisoning another member of the royal family, a crime which carried the death penalty. In a desperate bid to stave off a double tragedy from the family, the King had offered the next of kin of the

[69] B.M.A. A. Riis to Inspector, 28 May 1836.
[70] See Metcalfe, 1962, pp. 198–9. [71] Ibid.
[72] Metcalfe, op. cit., p. 199. [73] Ibid., p. 201.

deceased monetary compensation in return for his son's life.[74] In that branch of the royal family anger provoked by this event still rankled, and it seems clear that from the beginning of 'the English affair', the aim of this group and their supporters was to encompass the ruin of Ado Dankwa by embroiling him with the Danes. At the time of Maclean's interim decision this group was already in touch with Morch, and had agreed to work for the overthrow of Ado Dankwa and his replacement by his nephew Adum.[75] The secret plot envisaged the capture and detention of Ado Dankwa and the subsequent enstoolment of Adum. The attempt to seize Ado Dankwa in June 1836 failed, and he sought asylum in Jamestown; with the result that until the old King's death in exile six years later there were two rulers of Akwapim, each at the head of a powerful faction.

The differences between Riis and Morch came to the surface fairly early in the dispute, but it was not until the abortive coup in June and the subsequent division of Akwapim into two bitterly opposed camps that the breach between them became complete. Riis's stand in the early stages of the dispute would seem to have been influenced by two things: his disgust with the Danish community at Christiansborg and his great regard for Ado Dankwa.[76] To escape the debilitating influence of the Danish colony and the petty annoyances of officialdom, Riis had moved to Akropong in March 1835. Since then his relations with the King had been very close. There are indications that in the period before the crisis Riis was in fairly constant touch with the King. From his position away from the pressures of the small expatriate community and right in the centre of the Akwapim unrest, Riis could enter, as far as it was possible for an outsider to do so, into the frustrations and resentments behind the mounting hostility towards the Danish establishment. While there is no real evidence for the accusation that Riis set Ado Dankwa and his chiefs against the Danes, there can be little doubt that he gave

[74] Reindorf, 1895, pp. 311–16. [75] Metcalfe, op. cit., p. 202.

[76] B.M.A. Riis to Inspector, 1 April 1836. 'I find no consolation in the company of my country people, since their moral life is bad.'—Debrunner's translation. Of Ado Dankwa he wrote, 'He knew how to rule, was loved and respected by many and feared by all.'—quoted by Metcalfe, op. cit., pp. 196–7.

them his moral support in what he conceived to be a quarrel which would be settled by negotiation. Their defection to the English seems to have taken him by surprise, and, for some time, put him in a quandary. It was during the three months after this event, while he was kicking his heels at Christiansborg, that his involvement in the affair began to take on the colour of personal opposition to Morch.[77] After the abortive coup in June, when the duplicity of Ado Dankwa's enemies became clear, this opposition drew fuel from a sense of outrage at an action which set members of the same family at each other's throats.[78] In factional strife which followed, Riis never disguised his opposition to Adum's party which was supported by Morch. The conflict between them became so bitter that in 1838 Morch declared that there was no room for both of them on the coast, and that if Riis was not made to leave he would leave himself.[79] Morch in fact asked for and received an edict from the King of Denmark authorizing him to send Riis home whenever he chose.[80] But for some reason he had not acted upon it when he died in 1839. Morch's death did not result in any immediate lowering of the tension between the government and the mission. As late as 1846 Riis was still being presented in official dispatches as a mischief-maker and the cause of the administration's embarrassments in Akwapim.[81] Even after Riis's departure from the coast in 1845 the memory of the bitter disagreements in the thirties continued to intrude upon the relations between the mission and the administration. The slow and difficult task of mending fences between them was hardly under way when the Danes sold out to the English in 1850.

By the time the eastern districts came under the English sphere of influence some of the factors which created strains in the relations between the merchants' community and the administration, and between the administration and missionaries in the sixties and seventies were already operating.

[77] Morch threatened to have him brought back and imprisoned if he returned to Akropong. B.M.A. Riis to Inspector, 28 May 1836.

[78] B.M.A. Riis to Inspector, 14 April 1845. Riis claims here that he opposed Adum 'for moral and Christian reasons'.

[79] B.M.A. A. Riis to Inspector, 3 February 1838. [80] Ibid.

[81] B.M.A. H.N. Riis to Inspector, 8 January 1846.

REFERENCES

The following abbreviations have been used in the footnotes:
B.M.A. Basel Mission Archives, in Basel, Switzerland.
M.M.S. Methodist Missionary Society, London.

Ajayi, J. F. A.
(1958) 'Christian Missions and the Making of Nigeria.' Ph.D. thesis. London.
Bane, M. J.
(1956) *Catholic Pioneers in West Africa.* Clonmore and Reynolds.
Bartels, F. L.
(1949) 'The Provision and Administration of Education in the Gold Coast. 1765–1865.' (Unpublished M.A. (Lond.) thesis.)
(1955) 'Philip Quaque, 1741–1816', *Transactions of the Gold Coast and Togoland Historical Society*, Vol. I, Pt. V.
Beecham, J.
(1841) *Ashantee and the Gold Coast.*
Cruikshank, Brodie
(1966) *Eighteen Years on the Gold Coast of Africa.* 2nd edition.
Debrunner, H.
(1956) 'Notable Danish Chaplains on the Gold Coast', *Transactions of the Gold Coast and Togoland Historical Society*, Vol. II, Pt. I.
Lawrence, A. W.
(1963) *Trade Castles and Forts of West Africa.* London.
Mellor, G. R.
(1951) *British Imperial Trusteeship (1783–1850).* London.
Metcalfe, G. E.
(1955) 'After Maclean', *Transactions of the Gold Coast and Togoland Historical Society*, Vol. I, Pt. V.
(1962) Maclean of the Gold Coast: the Life and Times of George Maclean, 1801–1847.
Reindorf, C. C.
(1895) *The History of the Gold Coast and Ashante.*
Swanzy, H.
(1956) 'A Trading Family in the 19th Century Gold Coast', *Transactions of the Gold Coast and Togoland Historical Society*, Vol. II, Pt. II.
Wiltgen, R. M.
(1956) *Gold Coast Mission History* (1471–1880).

Résumé

RAPPORTS ENTRE LES MISSIONS CHRÉTIENNES, LES ADMINISTRATIONS EUROPÉENNES ET LES COMMERÇANTS EN GOLD COAST 1828–74

LE CONTEXTE

C'est en décembre 1828 que les premiers missionnaires de Bâle arrivèrent à Christiansborg, le quartier général danois en

Gold Coast; six ans plus tard, les premiers missionnaires wesleyiens atteignirent Cape Coast. C'est ainsi que les missions chrétiennes prirent racine en Gold Coast.

Les efforts des missionnaires de Bâle et des Wesleyiens avaient été précédés par plus de trois siècles d'essais sporadiques pour convertir les populations de la Gold Coast au Christianisme.

Il est vrai que sous la domination portugaise, les missions n'avaient pas réalisé grand chose sur la côte. Mais le désir de saisir cette occasion d'évangélisation existait et il y eut quelques efforts de conversion. On ne peut en dire autant pour les Hollandais qui remplacèrent les Portugais ni pour les Anglais ou les Danois qui devinrent leurs rivaux. En fait, avant l'époque du renouveau évangélique l'indifférence en matière d'évangélisation était de règle dans les régions placées sous la domination des Puissances Protestantes.

Un exemple frappant de ce manque d'intérêt généralisé est la carrière missionnaire de Philip Quaque qui travailla à Cape Coast de 1765 à 1816. Pendant toutes ces années il ne baptisa qu'une cinquantaine de personnes. Du début à la fin, Quaque eut à lutter contre les effets démoralisants de l'indifférence et même de l'hostilité que manifestait toute la garnison à l'égard du travail missionaire. Cette attitude d'indifférence ne se modifia pas avant l'époque de Maclean.

LES MISSIONS BÂLOISES ET WESLEYIENNES DE 1828 À 1874

Pour ses rapports avec la communauté européenne de la Côte, la Mission Wesleyienne, dans les premiers vingt ans du moins, se trouva nettement favorisée. A l'époque de Maclean un changement très frappant se produisit dans cette région: l'arrogance et l'indifférence des gouverneurs et des autres membres des milieux au pouvoir à l'égard des missionnaires céda la pas au respect et quelquefois même à l'amitié et à un appui enthousiaste de leurs efforts. Ce changement fut dû en grande partie au caractère, au jugement et au tact de deux hommes: Maclean, président de l'administration des Marchants de 1830 à 1844 et Freeman, président de la Mission Wesleyienne de 1838 à 1857.

Maclean se rendit compte que pour un système de gouvernement tel que le sien où l'influence était ce qui comptait, avant tout gouvernement dont l'objectif ultime était l'introduction d'une culture étrangère, l'administration ne pouvait trouver de meilleur allié que les missions. Mais son appui enthousiaste aux efforts missionnaires ne provenait pas uniquement de calculs de ce genre: Fils d'un pasteur Presbytérien, Maclean avait été élevé dans le respect de la religion. La compréhension et la sympathie pour les missionnaires dont beaucoup de ses prédécesseurs avaient été incapables lui venaient naturellment. De plus, il trouva en Freeman un missionnaire modèle. En plus d'un très grand tact, d'une courtoisie parfaite et d'un jugement très sûr des hommes, Freeman possédait de surcroît une passion pour le travail bien fait. Les deux hommes devinrent très liés se respectant et se comprenant l'un l'autre. Il avaient en gros des opinions semblables sur des questions qui auraient pu devenir explosives telles que celles de l'esclavage et des relations entre les Ashanti et le Protectorat. Il n'y avait donc pas entre eux de possibilité de conflit d'opinion qui existait ailleurs entre les missionnaires et les administrateurs. Leur coopération enthousiaste établit ainsi des rapports excellents entre l'église et le gouvernement qui durèrent pendant vingt ans à l'exception d'une brève interruption entre 1844 et 1846.

Pendant cette même époque les rapports entre la mission et les commerçants dans les rangs desquels les membres du Conseil gouvernemental étaient élus ne furent plus marqués par les tensions et l'hostilité des années avant 1830. Ils devinrent des rapports de compréhension et de coopération. Ce changement provenait de trois facteurs essentiels: d'abord l'abandon du commerce des esclaves qui fut remplacé par un commerce légitime semble avoir amené sur la Côte de nouveaux commerçants anglais plus enclins que leurs prédecesseurs à y maintenir des normes de décence comparables à celles de la métropole. La présence de missionnaires ne constituait pas pour ces hommes nouveaux la même source de gène que pour ceux qui les avaient précédés. Un deuxième facteur fut l'incidence qu'eut sur la communauté Britannique installée sur la Côte la pression exercée par les groupes humanitaires en Angleterre. Unrésultat direct de l'agitation humanitaire des années 1830 fut de renforcer et de renouveler le statut des entreprises missionnaires en Afrique qu'il devint alors difficile de laisser de côté et dangereux d'opposer sur le plan politique. Le troisième facteur, et peut-être le plus important, fut la transformation administrative qui eut lieu sous Maclean: les comptoirs cessèrent d'être simplement des centres pour le développement des intérêts commerciaux britanniques mais devinrent des instruments de réforme sociale dans les territoires adjacents Pour aboutir au succès, l'expérience de Maclean avait besoin de deux éléments avant tout: l'évangélisation du pays et l'éducation occidentale à grande échelle. Comme l'administration n'était pas à même de remplir ces deux tâches par elle-même, il était naturel que le gouvernement voie d'un œil favorable les efforts des groupes indépendants et auto-financés tels que les sociétés missionnaires qui étaient fort bien équippées pour mener ces tâches à bien. De leur côté les missionnaires avaient de bonnes raisons de vouloir maintenir des rapports amicaux avec les commerçants. (1) Les missions avaient toujours des problèmes financiers; comme leurs besoins n'étaient presque jamais couverts de manière adéquate par les fonds annuels fournis par les maisons -mères, elles étaient très heureuses de tout don inespéré pouvant leur être accordé par les maisons de commerce, et ce n'était qu'humain de la part des missionnaires de cultiver l'amitié de leurs bienfaiteurs éventuels. Deuxièmement, les maisons de commerce rendaient des services incalculables aux missions en leur servant de banquiers. Le plus gros des affaires des missions était rendu possible par le crédit qu'accordaient les maisons de commerce à la Mission Wesleyienne. Cette fourniture de crédit, par lettres de crédit, constituait un énorme risque pour les maisons de commerce ainsi que des sacrifices assez importants pour elles. Troisièmement, avant l'établissement d'un service de bateaux régulier sur la Côte en 1853, tous les missionnaires dépendaient des vaisseaux de commerce pour leurs voyages, et pour l'envoi de frêt et de correspondance. Mais il ne faut pas exagérer l'importance de considérations de cet ordre pour expliquer le développement de bons rapports entre les commerçants et les missionnaires. Il est peu probable que des liens établis sur la dépendance des missionnaires par rapport aux marchands pour beaucoup de services essentiels auraient tenu s'il avait existé des différences trop nettes dans leurs objectifs. Ce qui unissait le plus les missionnaires et les commerçants était leur intérêt commun dans l'établissement de bases solides pour le développement du Christianisme et de la culture occidentale dans les territoires du protectorat. Cet intérêt commun se poursuivait grâce à des institutions et activités différentes. Ce sentiment d'être attelé à un même travail continua à présider aux rapports entre les européens et les missionnaires jusque vers les années 1850 où la désaffection des commerçants à l'égard de l'administration (le territoire était devenu Crown Colony en 1844) détruisit les bases mêmes de la coopération. Lorsque Freeman donna sa démission de la Présidence de la Mission en 1857, les contacts personnels avec l'administration disparurent. Dans les années 1860 et 1870, un facteur supplémentaire vint éloigner plus encore la mission et le gouvernement. Il s'agit d'un manque de sympathie fondamental de la part de l'administration pour les principes mêmes de l'évangélisation.

III. MISSIONARY POLICIES AS SEEN IN THE WORK OF MISSIONS WITH THE EVANGELICAL PRESBYTERIAN CHURCH, GHANA

E. GRAU

The Evangelical Presbyterian Church has its roots in the North German Mission, Bremen, Germany. This Mission was organized in 1836, and sent missionaries to the then Slave Coast in 1847. Of the four sent, only Lorenz Wolf lived to begin mission work at Peki, the seat of the paramount chief of Krepi, Kwadzo Dei.

The early history was a story of death notices, meagre response to the Gospel, and tribal wars destroying stations. That today we can tell the story of a strong independent church where once there were only missionary graves, is a miracle of God's grace and man's devotion. Apart from the self-sacrifice of men and women, there were other factors which furthered the progress towards independence. First there was the statesman-like leadership of the head of the mission, Dr. Franz Michael Zahn, from 1862–1900. Famous as a missiologist in Europe and America, his ideas of mission theory and practice became a reality in Togoland. From the beginning, agricultural, educational, medical, and technical work were considered a normal part of evangelization. The aim to establish an indigenous Church was clearly expressed, and a Seminary for the training of pastors was established in 1864, when the mission could count only about one hundred Christians.

Another factor which helped to make the Church independent was the language work of the missionaries. In 1854, only one year after work was opened in Keta, Missionary Schlegel's *Key to the Ewe Language* was printed. By 1861 he had translated the four Gospels. By 1877 the whole New Testament had been printed, and in 1913 the whole Bible. A hymn book (1867, revised 1887, 1896, 1925), a catechism (1877, revised 1887, 1907, 1932), the Liturgy (1877, revised 1930), the Church Order (1887, revised 1933, 1958) and a church paper all helped to arouse the sense of 'church' among the scattered congregations.

A third major influence was the education of African young men in Germany. Before 1914, twenty had been sent. Not only was their influence on their own people very great but their training had been such that they were able to lead their Church well after the missionaries were removed.

The fourth great influence was the first World War. When the German missionaries were being interned, the African pastors and teachers came to the fore. In spite of the disturbed political situation and 'official' language changes (from German to English in British Togoland and to French in French Togo) the Church advanced. When the Scottish Mission finally responded to the appeals of the British Government to aid the Ewe church in the British area, the missionaries were immediately able to organize the congregations into a self-governing, and largely self-supporting Church. Since it was organized along Presbyterian lines, it eventually took the name, 'Ewe Presbyterian Church'. In 1954 the name 'Ewe' was replaced by 'Evangelical' because many people of other tribes had become members of it.

The other significant contribution of Scottish missionaries was in education. They were responsible for helping the German-trained, German-speaking teachers of the Church to become English-speaking teachers. After the German missionaries had been allowed to return (1923) the Scottish missionaries withdrew (1930), only to be recalled during the second World War. Again their main work was in education. One came to be Supervisor of schools in 1941, and then to open the first Teacher Training College in British Togoland in 1946 at Amedzofe. Another then became General Manager of Schools, but only until 1951 at which time an African was prepared to take over the post.

It was during the second World War that the eyes of the E.P. Church were turned to America. The last Bremen missionary to leave the Gold Coast was Dr. E. Voehringer, born in the Gold Coast of missionary parents, but raised in the U.S. after the first World War. He had then been allowed to stay after the internment of the other missionaries because of his U.S. citizenship.

The E.P. Church asked him to try to find help for them in the U.S., since the Scottish Mission had made it clear that they were not in a position to help further with men or money. The request for help went through the International Mission Council to the Board of International Missions of the Evangelical and Reformed Church (now the United Church Board for World Ministries of the United Church of Christ). It was through the efforts of the Scottish Mission that the Colonial Government granted permission to the American Mission for entry into the Gold Coast.

At the end of the 1963/4 school year, the Church had 300 primary schools with 1,393 teachers, 43,065 pupils, and 50 middle schools with 235 teachers and 8,363 pupils. In the field of higher education, the E.P. Church maintained its Seminary as a teacher-training institution until 1920. From then on, students were trained at Akropong, but when government instituted the four-year teacher-training course in 1925 and an additional year was added by the Church for the training of catechists, the lack of preaching practice in Ewe at Akropong caused the Church to reopen its own Seminary at Ho in 1929. It remained there until 1950 and then was reopened in Peki in 1952. The Church opened Mawuli School at Ho in 1950, a Secondary School in Hohoe in 1962 and a Training College in Bimbila in 1962. The E.P. Church joined with the Presbyterian Church of Ghana and the Methodist Church in establishing Trinity College for the training of the ministry in 1943. In 1950 the Church began its mission work in northern Ghana in the Yendi area, establishing an agricultural work scheme there in 1958, and an agricultural training school for young farmers in 1962. With the help of government, it established hospitals in Worawora (1952) and Adidome (1957), with a nurses training school at Worawora. Becoming a charter member of Christian Council in 1929, the E.P. Church has continued its support of the Council's activities, and is since 1957 one of the four Churches discussing Church Union in Ghana. It is a member of the All Africa Conference of Churches, the World Alliance of Reformed Churches, and the World Council of Churches. It has a total Christian community of 86,000 with about 27,000 communicant members being served by 40 African pastors in 32 pastoral districts, two Scottish missionaries (1 ordained), 27 American missionaries (5 ordained) and since October 1964, two German missionaries (1 ordained).

In order to understand the attitudes of the missionaries of the North German (Bremen) Mission towards their work and the people among whom they worked, it is necessary to understand the basic attitudes of the mission itself. While the Society stood within the Pietistic Movement of Germany, it cannot be accused of some of the failings usually ascribed to Pietistic missionary endeavour. The mission did not have the support of the Landeskirchen, but it did have devoted friends among the outstanding pastors of the North German Provinces early in the nineteenth century.[1] While it is true that its first missionaries normally did not go through the training expected of the German clergy previous to 1914, theological education was not despised, and the men in charge of the training of the missionaries (at Hamburg and later at Basel) were well qualified for the task.[2] In spite of the movement in Germany towards denominational missions, the Bremen Mission maintained a non-denominational position and insisted in its constitution and by repeated declarations that confessionalism was not to be taken to the mission field, and that the faithful presentation and teaching of the Word of God through the influence of the Holy Spirit would result in the establishment of a Church, able and qualified to reach its own doctrinal position and polity.[3]

THE CONGREGATION A WITNESS

In line with this position, the missionaries were given certain basic principles to be followed in their work.[4] While their task was the conversion of unbelievers, they were not to ignore Christians living in the area, and they were to unite these with the

[1] Schlunk, 1936, p. 10.

[2] *Bericht der Norddeutschen Missionsgesellschaft*, 1837, p. 11; 1841 in *Monats-Blatt der Norddeutschen Missionsgesellschaft* (from now on abbreviated *MB*), 1841, p. 410; 1842 in *MB*, 1842, p. 248; *Bausteine 1936*, p. 11; Brauer, 1851, p. 659.

[3] Zahn, 1864, p. 7; Diddo Wiarda, 1936, p. 138.

[4] Brauer, op. cit., pp. 660–72.

new converts into integrated congregations. The congregation was believed to be superior to the individual Christian in its power to witness. We see this principle at work in Andreas Riis, the Basel missionary who, although desiring to move inland, remained in Christiansborg until a chaplain was sent to minister to the Danes and other Christians in the castle.[5] There were practically no Europeans in the area where the Bremen Mission worked, but missionaries made every effort to minister to Christians from Nigeria and Sierre Leone who had settled in Keta.[6] In addition, as soon as there was a small congregation and a school, the members and school children accompanied the missionaries or African evangelists on preaching tours to neighbouring towns and, from all reports, these efforts were effective.[7]

THE STUDY OF LANGUAGE AND CULTURE

Great emphasis was laid on the missionary's duty to instruct, whether through sermons, school, conversation, or literature. Thus, the study of the local language became of primary importance, and the reliance on an interpreter was discouraged. The stress on language study was maintained, and while not all missionaries became fluent in the language, the encouragement for improvement was never lacking.[8] As a result, the linguistic work of the mission was unequalled and reached its highest level in men like Schlegel, Knusli, Dauble, Spieth, Westermann, and Wiegrabe, and in a Bible translation (completed in 1912) which is still considered excellent for use today.[9]

But instruction, to be effective, must rest upon the understanding of those instructed. The missionaries were therefore urged to learn to know the people among whom they lived: their way of life, beliefs, customs, attitudes, and relationships.[10] Through the years, almost all the missionaries who lived long enough to seize the opportunity, contributed to the understanding

[5] Schlatter, 1916, p. 27. [6] *MB*, 1884, p. 96. [7] Müller, 1904, p. 67.
[8] Brauer, op. cit., pp. 660 ff., Instructions par. 3.
[9] *Bausteine 1936*, pp. 263 ff.; *MB*, 1896, p. 88; 1897, pp. 69 ff.; 1903, p. 79; 1904, p. 44; 1906, p. 13 f., 52, 109; 1907, p. 112; 1908, p. 44; 1910, p. 118; 1911, p. 47; 1913, p. 3 f.
[10] Brauer, op. cit., pp. 660 ff., Instructions par. 4.

of the customs and beliefs of the Ewe people. Hornberger, Spieth, Westermann, and Spiess were outstanding along these lines.[11] After having been told repeatedly and dogmatically, that the early missionaries condemned all things African, it comes as quite a surprise to read that in 1846 Bremen missionaries were told that 'an inconsiderate damning or dismissal of heathenism is no way to win the trust of the heathen and to convince them of the truth of Christianity, but it will rather raise a spirit of stubbornness and obstinacy in holding on to the traditional beliefs, and will shut their hearts to the missionary. Much more useful will it be to find, in the faith and heart of the heathen, points of contact for Christian truth, and from there begin the work of conviction.'[12] While this sympathetic appreciation of customary practices is evident in the missionaries' writings, it would be wrong to conclude that it caused them to shut their eyes to what they thought to be wrong. So we find that Wolf (the first missionary in Peki), while speaking favourably of the yam festivals, condemned the traditionally accepted ritual murders, sexual immorality, and lack of concern on the part of fathers for their children. Missionaries were not to try to wipe out all customs and replace them with European practice, but Christianity was believed to have power to make customs more gentle and to create a worthy civilization among the people who embrace it.[13]

CONCERN FOR THE WHOLE OF LIFE

Christianity, therefore, was to have a full impact on the total life of the people among whom the missionary lived. Those who had benefited from it were to share its blessings. Early missionaries have often been accused of withdrawing their converts into a closed community, but this was certainly not the policy or the intention of the Basel and Bremen Missions. Christians were to be better farmers; they were to learn a trade; they were to take their place in 'legitimate' trading (as opposed to the slave and rum trade) and they were to make their presence felt in the

[11] Müller, op. cit., pp. 77–100; *MB*, 1914, pp. 66–68; 1906, p. 52; 1907, p. 112; *Bausteine 1936*, Book List.

[12] Brauer, op. cit., pp. 660 ff., Instructions par. 6.

[13] Ibid., pp. 653–7.

government of their towns and tribes. It was expected that the converts' Christian attitudes would influence the social and civil life of their people.[14] When a man became a Christian, he remained with his family and clan. But since the life of the family was centred in heathen customs, conflicts between the Christian and his heathen relatives became unavoidable. Because such conflicts could well end in the Christian surrendering to the demands of his relatives, church members asked the missionaries for permission to settle on or near the mission stations. This happened in Ho in 1881 and in Anyako in 1887. Under the influence of Zahn (the Bremen Mission Inspector, 1864 to 1900), the Bremen Committee at first refused to grant permission, but when Christians settled on the stations nevertheless, the Committee took no steps to prevent them. Their official position was that where there were some Christians in a town, they were to let their lights shine in the midst of their heathen surroundings.[15]

Among the conditions laid down for settlement were two of significance: (1) The civil organization of the Christian town was to be in the hands of the elders, and in no case in the hands of a missionary. (2) Settlers who returned to heathen practices could be immediately sent away from the town without compensation,[16] and Zahn did not want missionaries to take a hand in driving men 'out of house and home'.[17] According to his theological view, there was no such thing as a Christian state, and he thought the same of Christian settlements. Therefore, a missionary would be acting contrary to New Testament teaching were he to take civil authority upon himself.[18] His attitude made missionaries and African Christians aware of the fact that at best, Christian settlements were an emergency measure that should not become the accepted practice.

The family was considered to be the most effective unit for

[14] Müller, op. cit., pp. 73, 74, 77, 103.

[15] Norddeutsche Missionsgesellschaft, *Committee Protokol*, December 1881, p. 300; 14 February 1887, p. 110; 2 December 1889; 12 October 1891; Letter Zahn to Spieth, 14 July 1890.

[16] *Com. Prot.*, op. cit., 14 February 1887.

[17] Letter Zahn to Spieth, 29 May 1886.

[18] Letter Zahn to Spieth, 14 July 1890.

social change and therefore a great effort was to be made to establish Christian homes. The purpose of blessing a marriage was not to make a former marriage a real marriage but to consecrate a marriage as Christian and thus to relate the couple (and their children) to the Christian Communion.[19] It is often claimed that if only the early missionaries had permitted polygamists to join the church, there would have been many more converts. In fact, the Bremen Mission had quite an advanced view with regard to polygamy. They told their missionaries, 'Polygamy existed at the time of Christ and the apostles, but we do not find that monogamy was made a condition for acceptance into the Church. Therefore, a man who has several wives must be admitted to baptism and communion; however, all are always to be reminded that monogamy is the true marriage according to God, and that only in this way can the purposes of marriage be reached.' This position was reaffirmed again in the Church Order of 1876,[20] but was no longer thought necessary in the revision of 1933.

CIVIL AUTHORITY AND COLONIAL POWER

The missionaries were to set a good example to their converts in their attitude towards civil authorities. That at the beginning these were a number of chiefs made no difference; they were not to be belittled, despised, resisted, or overthrown by the missionaries.[21] It has often been said that Missions worked hand in hand with, or prepared the way for, colonial powers. This was certainly not true of the Bremen Mission. Before 1884, the colonial might of Britain was scarcely felt in the Slave Coast, the area of the Mission's work, and even during the Ashanti war of 1869–74 the Mission's contacts were with the Anlo, the Waya, and the Ashanti and not with British officers. When Germany acquired Togoland and Britain established firmer control over her territories the Mission was for the first time confronted by colonial pressures.[22]

[19] *MB*, 1874, pp. 1312, 1317, 1326; 1875, pp. 1357, 1358.
[20] *Church Rules*, 1876, par. 62. c.
[21] Brauer, op. cit., pp. 660 ff., Instructions par. 7.
[22] Trierenberg, 1914, pp. 1, 2; Calvert, 1918, p. 4; *MB*, 1886, p. 182.

Voices in Germany, which had never before spoken for missions, suddenly demanded that German mission societies should immediately put all their efforts into work in German colonies.[23] When the North German Mission Society was asked to expand its work into Togoland, Zahn, while admitting that this territory lay on the route of the logical extension of the Society's work, declared that he was not prepared to open stations, chiefly owing to lack of personnel and money but also because he did not believe that it was God's will to move African teachers from where the Ewe people needed them to where a white merchant wanted them. 'The German flag alone cannot be a signpost for mission work.'[24] Zahn further wrote to Spieth, the President of the Mission at that time:

> I am completely against colonies, and that is all one has to say today to be marked as an enemy of our Fatherland. But when a missionary becomes involved in politics and furthers the colonial acquisition of Germany through his influence, then I maintain, whatever else his intentions may be, that he has made a big mistake, if he has not committed a crime.[25]

Yet he did not advocate that missionaries should oppose the colonial governments under which they worked. He advised that they be always friendly and helpful to the officials in order that there should be no cause for complaints.[26] In spite of this, the complaints poured in, not because the missionaries caused trouble, but because of the effects of Zahn's policy. German officials looked with suspicion on the educational work of the mission. They did not agree with Zahn that English would be of greater help to a young West African than German. The accusation that the Mission was 'English' was repeatedly made, although only the final class of the middle schools studied English, all other classes being held in Ewe.[27]

A further attack on the Mission's language policy was made by Captain von Puttkammer in a report to the German Chancellor,

[23] *MB*, 1886, p. 115; 1887, p. 40.
[24] Zahn's report, 25 June 1886.
[25] Letter Zahn to Spieth, 15 February 1888.
[26] Letter Zahn to Spieth, 18 July 1894.
[27] *Com. Prot.* 2 December 1889; 15 May 1894; 21 October 1895, p. 370; Letter Zahn to Spieth, 17 May 1894; *MB*, 1903, p. 33.

in which he called the Ewe language 'a wild, extremely primitive Negro dialect' and in which he argued that the ideas of culture could therefore be transmitted to the Ewe people only through a cultural language, and that as a language of culture in a German colony only the German language could be considered.[28] It was only the excellent linguistic work done previously by the missionaries that caused the government to permit Ewe to be used in the schools.

So sensitive to government control was Zahn that he refused to accept grants for education on the bases that: (1) the mission school must maintain the character of a Christian school and thus emphasize Bible teaching, to which government is indifferent; such indifference would be easily manifest to the students, who would thus make light of Bible teaching; (2) that for the development of character, true understanding and learning, instruction in the vernacular was essential. Eventually, Zahn lost his battle, for his insistence on the teaching in the Ewe language was out of favour not only with the two governments but also with the people who wanted their children to study European languages.[29]

After Zahn's death, the mission, under W. A. Schreiber, took a more conciliatory position with regard to the government and soon reaped benefits not only in more generous grants for education but, on the German side, in aid of the publication of Spieth's valuable book, *Die Ewestamme*.[30]

When the Scottish missionaries arrived after the first World War, their main task became the adjusting of the Mission's educational practice to the new scheme introduced by the government in 1925. German-speaking teachers had to be given courses in English and British educational methods in order to be able to continue as teachers under the new government.[31] There was stricter control over mission schools for the sake of a unified educational system that depended on the missions for most of the education done in the country. While the Scottish missionaries

[28] Letter Zahn to Spieth, 18 July 1894.

[29] *MB*, 1904, p. 75 f.; 1903, p. 15.

[30] *MB*, 1905, p. 50; 1908, p. 48; 1910, p. 30.

[31] Letter Schlunk to Foreign Mission Committee, United Free Church, 15 February 1924.

regarded government grants as a natural response by government for such an arrangement, Schlunk (the successor to Schreiber) was aware of dangers involved in this co-operation. As a result of the new scheme, the mission, along with the Catholic Mission, was in charge of all primary education in the region. Soon the requests from chiefs and towns for schools poured in, and while government grants increased yearly, they were insufficient to meet the growing demand, so that the financial burden became too heavy for the Church, requiring too great a proportion of the total budget.

There were other dangers, too. Schlunk wrote:

> The carrying of school responsibility is a compromise, heavily loaded with difficulties. Some of these are of a temporary nature. New rules, accounting of them to the department, and introducing them to the teachers and to the school children, tend to make the supervising missionary a Government official, whose care for souls has been necessarily limited. Then there is a lack of teachers who consider it their highest ideal to serve Jesus Christ. They lack the deeper understanding of the subject they are to teach in religious instruction classes, and so lack the interest. Some do not have a thorough enough knowledge of their own language, and so prefer to teach in English. If the school work is done poorly, and the Government inspector drops the standing of the school, we must either close it, or maintain it at a cost too great, particularly in view of the meagre results.
>
> But there are other difficulties which are part of the very system. It makes the Mission a tool of colonialism. This is bearable as long as the colonial people accept the leadership and benefits brought by the colonial power. But as soon as anti-colonial feelings arise, it becomes very doubtful that it will then be possible to dissociate Christianity from European cultural expansion, and to have it accepted while the other is refused. It is doubtful whether the present school system, in spite of the inclusion of scripture knowledge, is able to deny its European emphasis. Yet, what can the Mission do? Only if we fall in line will we be allowed to work at all, and will it be possible for us to have any influence. It will be our task to exert our influence on Government for good, and secondly to train a thoroughly prepared Christian teaching profession.[32]

PREPARING CONGREGATIONS FOR SELF-GOVERNMENT

With regard to the establishment of congregations, the missionaries were to be very careful in receiving converts. Although

[32] Annual Report 1926 in *MB*, 1927, p. 62 f.

baptism was not to be too long delayed, it was to be preceded by instruction. In addition, a further period of instruction was to be given before the candidate was admitted to communion. Public worship was to be arranged on Sundays as soon as the congregation had two or three members. It was expected that missionaries would have to lead the congregation at the beginning, but they were to strive to make members capable of leadership as soon as possible. Elders were to be formed into a consistory. The purpose of the consistory was to make the congregation autonomous. However, the missionaries were reminded, for the congregation to be truly autonomous means also to be self-supporting, and so the consistory was to be taught to do as much as possible for the maintenance of its church and school. The first elders were to be selected by the missionaries to serve for a limited period of time. Thereafter elections were to be held by the congregation. From the very beginning, the congregation was also to be made aware of its responsibility for those in need. Deacons were to be elected to direct the congregation in this service.[33] This aspect of Christian service has become a part of the life of the average congregation, and gifts are regularly given to help the poor of the town. A more striking example comes from the period of the Ashanti war, and the wars of the Anlo, during which the local congregations within the battle areas organized themselves to treat and comfort the wounded and dying warriors, although, at times, these were their enemies.[34]

In 1899, Zahn asked that a financial report be given to the African Church yearly so that they would know 'how expensive everything is'. The report was to serve as an instruction and an encouragement to the people to contribute and thus meet in part their own financial needs. But Zahn also reminded the missionaries that in church financial matters not law but gratitude should be the motivating power. Church dues or church tax he could in no way support, but wanted instead only free-will offerings. While not denying the importance of financial independence, he did not wish it to be regarded as the only or the chief characteristic of an indigenous church. He said:

[33] Brauer, op. cit., pp. 660 ff., Instructions par. 5. [34] *MB*, 1866, p. 815.

It is not a question of money but of the necessity that every Christian be taught to do with all his might what is necessary in order that he, his people, and those yet far away may receive and cherish the Gospel. Once this idea has been implanted, not only money, but every other service necessary for the self-support of the church will come.

But when the African leaders did not agree with his position, he yielded. 'The Ewe Church must learn to raise the moneys necessary for church purposes' and as 'a fine, external discipline', as 'one of the good Christian virtues', he was willing to let a church tax be introduced 'although, it seems to be the most unsuitable form' of giving.[35]

Because the mission believed that the effective witness of the congregation depended on the quality of its life, a Church Order was to be drawn up so that new converts would know what is seemly. 'This is necessary, because it is hard for new converts to deny their old habits and misdeeds, and because the will needs a peg to which to cling.' Down through the years, therefore, the mission emphasized the importance of rules, while at the same time guarding against a formal legalism, believing that discipline would aid the self-development of the Church.[36]

The intention to prepare the new converts for self-government in the local congregation, and eventually in the Church, was kept in view throughout Zahn's inspectorship. The first Liturgy was to be revised by Africans. The Church Order was to be revised every three years, and more power was to be placed into the hands of teachers and pastors. However, slow progress was made in the actual implementation of the intention until the first World War caused the removal of the missionaries. Yet, when self-government came, the African leaders and people were not willing to take it. They wanted nothing more than to get their missionaries back.

TRAINING CHURCH LEADERS

When, in 1922, the United Free Church of Scotland was finally persuaded to take over the Bremen stations in the Gold

[35] Letter Zahn to Missionaries, 1899 (no other date); 21 February 1899; *Allgemeine Missions-Zeitschrift*, 1890, pp. 289 ff., p. 314; Letter Zahn to Spieth, 29 May 1886, 2 June 1886.

[36] *Com. Prot.*, 13 September 1875; 28 February 1876.

Coast and British Togoland, it became the task of the Scottish missionaries (A. W. Wilkie and T. L. Beveridge primarily) to organize the church and to train the African leaders in taking over control. That they were doing a good job was acknowledged by Schlunk when, in 1923, he wrote of the three German missionaries, returning to the field to work as members of the Scottish Mission (although supported from Germany):

> They will have to recognize the independence of the congregations and pastors which was won during the war. They will have to, more than previously, be advisors and spiritual leaders. They will also have to be able to keep their hands off a number of things.[37]

The returning missionaries were told not to touch the organization of the Ewe Church and its African leadership. They were not to do jobs which Africans could do.[38]

Wilkie continued to strengthen the hand of the African leadership. He wrote to one of his Scottish colleagues:

> You need only make it quite clear that the authority of Synod Committee must be recognized and that its decisions will not be changed by any threat from any agent, whether pastor or teacher. The members of the Committee will be a bit flustered at first, but they will very quickly understand that their only way to establish authority and confidence is to make decisions with careful deliberation and thereafter abide by them.[39]
>
> I think you will find it strengthens the Synod Committee to get the Synod Clerk to write to the pastor of a district in regard to any transfer. This should be done rather as a Committee concern than as a secretarial. And the authority of the Synod Committee must be supreme. . . . Of course, everyone knows quite well that I am behind the scenes, but I am exceedingly anxious to train the Clerk to act in the name of the Church. In some very difficult cases lately, by request, I have written the letters but they have been signed by the Clerk and not by me.[40]

When German missionaries disagreed with the decisions of Synod Committee and appealed to Schlunk to get a reversal through the Foreign Mission Committee of the United Free Church, Ashcroft, the Africa secretary, wrote:

[37] *MB*, 1923, p. 8 f.

[38] Duplicated copy, *Ergebnisse der Besprechung der Missionare-Konferenz am 5. Juni 1923*, Bremen.

[39] Letter Wilkie to Watt, 21 February 1924.

[40] Ibid.

Unfortunately, there is no court of appeal or review in the case of Church matters on the Gold Coast. The Synod is supreme, and although we and you sometimes feel that this results in decisions being reached with which we are out of sympathy, it is better that the decision of the local Church should stand rather than be overturned by a foreign body.[41]

Wilkie clarified the function of missionaries of Synod Committee. He explained that they were full members of the Committee, at liberty to express their views and cast a vote. Although the African members may look to the missionaries for advice and guidance, they are not forced to accept that advice. Wilkie objected strongly to protests being made against Synod Committee decisions to the home society, when no such protests were made to Synod Committee at the time the case was discussed. He also objected to the presenting of facts to the home society, while withholding such facts from Synod Committee which required them for making wise decisions. He felt strongly that such actions would quickly wreck the constitution of the Church, and would make it impossible to train leaders for self-government by thus keeping them subject to external authority.[42]

The type of missionary needed also concerned Wilkie in his efforts to strengthen the young Church. In writing to Schlunk he stressed the necessity of appointing men of adaptability in view of the growing sense of nationalism among the African people. 'Some frankly disbelieve in it. Such men had better be in their own homeland where they can render other forms of service; but I would ship such misfits home by the earliest steamer.'[43]

Although Wilkie was not completely successful in persuading the German missionaries of the necessity for a change, he did have the satisfaction of gaining the support of Schlunk and Stoevesandt (Inspector of the Mission). Both men saw their task to be that of establishing an indigenous Church. Schlunk wrote:

We are building, in the first instance, an Ewe Church, but we are building it as a member of a large West African Protestant Church. And we know exactly that the most important part of the work will have to be on the field,

[41] Letter Ashcroft to Schlunk, 9 December 1924.
[42] Letter Wilkie to Ashcroft, 13 March 1925.
[43] Letter Wilkie to Schlunk, 1 August 1925.

that the most important decisions will have to be reached there, and that the ever-growing costs will have to be met, in ever larger proportions, by the field.[44]

Stoevesandt reported:

The natural development of the Ewe Church leads to a larger unit. The division of the separate churches is strongly felt, but more so the necessity for united action. The churches cannot remain in isolation. Church discipline, schools, training of pastors and many other things force into awareness the necessity for unified standards and closer fellowship.[45]

T. L. Beveridge continued the defence of African leadership in the Church. The Secretary of the Bremen Mission and the Church, although determined to do his best to prepare African Christians for self-government, did not believe that the time for self-government had come as yet. 'If we allow our pastors full authority and self-government now, we shall get a caricature of the Christian Church.' He feared that although the form of Christianity might be there, the spirit would be lacking. He was not of the same opinion as Beveridge with regard to the ability of the Synod Clerk to maintain the development of the Church without the presence of a missionary as member of the Synod Committee. He was sure that the Ewe Church, being twenty-five years younger than the Church in the Gold Coast, could not be expected to reach that stage of development in two years.[46] Beveridge replied:

The difficulties of the pastors and people on your side are not so much greater than over here, where the burden of responsibility has not removed their old disabilities altogether, but has encouraged them to faithful and self-sacrificing effort for their own Church and its great Master and Head.[47]

The pastors on the Ewe side soon learned to overcome some of their disabilities, and as their number grew, so did their ability to lead and to take responsibility. When the second World War once again reduced missionary aid to one man, African leaders were ready and able to continue the work of the

[44] Annual Report 1925 in *MB*, 1926, p. 52.
[45] Annual Report 1927 in *MB*, 1928, p. 99.
[46] Letter Schosser to Beveridge, 4 July 1926.
[47] Letter Beveridge to Schosser, 21 August 1926.

Church. In 1951, the schools came under the management of an African. No agitation for Africanization had been necessary, for back in 1946 the Scottish Mission had given notice of its withdrawal from the management of the Church's schools.

But there remains one more test of the soundness of mission policies with regard to this indigenous Church. What of its life? Perhaps this evaluation ought to be left to one of her sons, who has had more opportunity than most men to see churches throughout the world. In writing about Dr. Karl Hartenstein, a former Director of the Basel Mission, the Rev. Dr. C. G. Baëta also gives a picture of his Church:

> I always regarded him as a typical modern representative of Swabian Pietism, that particular expression of Christianity which so successfully combined fervent earnestness, deep humility, enthusiasm curbed by sober and realistic self-restraint, distaste for fuss, display, exuberance or extravagance of any kind, and simple, straightforward faith in God, the Bible and sound doctrine. It is a combination difficult to describe, but those of you who are familiar with what is understood among us as the 'old Basel-Bremen type' of religiosity and way of life, will know exactly what I mean. If one way of getting at something hard to describe is to tell its results, then we may say that it is the sort of ethos which produced what an old inspector's report on our schools characterized as 'everywhere the same general atmosphere of simplicity and wholesomeness'. We in the Presbyterian Churches of this land are a direct offshoot of Swabian Pietism, and please God, this type of Christian witness may never be wiped out from the earth.[48]

REFERENCES

The following abbreviations have been used in the footnotes:

Bausteine 1936. A. W. Schreiber (ed.) *Bausteine zur Geschichte der Norddeutschen Missionsgesellschaft*, 1936.

MB. *Monats-Blatt der Norddeutschen Missionsgesellschaft.*

Baëta, C. G.
(1953) 'Dr. Karl Hartenstein', *Christian Messenger*, Accra, p. 8.

Brauer, Johann Hartwig
(1851) *Die Missions-Anstalten und Gesellschaften der evangelischen Kirche des Europäischen Vestlandes*, Part 2.

Calvert, Albert F.
(1918) *Togoland.*

Müller, Gustav
(1904) *Geschichte der Ewe Mission.*

[48] Baëta, 1953.

Schlatter, Wilhelm
(1916) *Geschichte der Baseler Mission 1815–1915.* Vol. 3.
Schlunk, Martin
(1936) 'Die Geschichte der Norddeutschen Mission im Lichte der Bibel', in *Bausteine 1936.*
Trierenberg, Georg
(1914) *Togo.*
Wiarda, Diddo
(1936) 'Mission und Konfession', in *Bausteine 1936.*
Zahn, Michael
(1864) *Die Arbeit der Norddeutschen Missionsgesellschaft.*

Résumé

LES MÉTHODES MISSIONNAIRES EXAMINÉES DU POINT DE VUE DU TRAVAIL DES MISSIONS AVEC L'ÉGLISE PRESBYTÉRIENNE ÉVANGÉLIQUE AU GHANA

L'Église Presbytérienne Évangélique est issue de la Mission Nord Allemande établie à Brême, Allemagne. Cette mission s'organisa en 1836 et commença à envoyer des missionnaires sur la Côte des Esclaves en 1847. Sur les quatre premiers missionnaires, seul Lorenz Wolf survécût et pût entreprendre des activités missionnaires à Peki, capitale du grand chef de Krepi, Kwadzo Dei. L'histoire des débuts de cette mission n'est qu'une longue liste d'avis de décès, de guerres tribales et de très faibles réactions à l'enseignement de l'Évangile.

Un certain nombre de facteurs facilitèrent des progrès vers l'indépendance et les facteurs suivants méritent un examen attentif: premièrement, le chef de la mission de 1862 à 1900, l'inspecteur Dr. Franz Michael Zahn, dirigea les travaux de manière très éclairée. Respecté comme missiologue en Europe et en Amérique, il mit en œuvre au Togo ses théories et pratiques missionnaires. Des le début, le travail agricole, technique, médical et éducatif fût considéré comme faisant partie des activités normales de l'évangélisation. L'établissement d'une église indigène devint l'un des objectifs clairement définis et un séminaire pour la formation de prédicateurs fût établi dès 1864 alors que la Mission ne comptait qu'une centaine de Chrétiens.

Le travail linguistique des missionnaires fût un autre facteur qui contribua à l'émancipation de l'église. Les Écritures (l'Évangile en 1861, le Nouveau Testament en 1877 et toute la Bible en 1913), un livre de cantiques, un catéchisme, la liturgie et le règlement de l'église ainsi qu'un journal de l'église permirent de créer un sens de l'église parmi les congrégations éloignées.

Le facteur le plus décisif peut-être qui conduisit vers l'indépendance fût les deux guerres mondiales. Après la première guerre mondiale, la Mission Écossaise vint remplacer la Mission de Brême. Elle pût organiser les diverses congrégations en une église dont la structure fût conservée après le retour de la Mission de Brême en 1925 et le retrait des missionnaires Écossais en 1930. Après la seconde guerre mondiale, l'Église Presbytérienne Evangélique demanda son concours au 'United Church Board' (à l'époque évangélique et réformé) par le truchement du Conseil Missionnaire International.

Il est vrai certes que la Mission de Brême s'inscrivait dans le mouvement piétiste en Allemagne mais on ne peut l'accuser de certaines des fautes généralement imputées aux efforts missionnaires piétistes. La Mission ne méprisait pas l'instruction théologique et quoique la plupart des missionnaires n'aient pas suivi les cours de formation normaux menant au pastorat, ils recevaient néanmoins une instruction à un niveau élevé (d'abord à la Maison des Missions à Hambourg et ensuite à Bâle).

En dépit des tendances 'dénominatives' prévalentes en Allemagne la Mission de Brême maintînt sa position 'non-dénominative' et, dans sa constitution ainsi que dans des déclarations répétées, insista pour que le confessionalisme ne soit pas transmis aux missions. De plus, elle estimait qu'une présentation et un enseignement fidèles de la Parole de Dieu par l'intermédiaire de l'influence du Saint Esprit auraient pour résultat l'établissement d'une église valable et bien qualifiée pour arriver à fonder ses propres positions et politiques doctrinales.

On dit souvent que les premiers missionnaires condamnaient tout ce qui était africain. Pourtant ce n'était absolument pas l'intention de la Mission de Brême qui avertissait ses missionnaires en ces termes: 'Une condamnation ou un refus inconsidéré du paganisme n'est certes pas la voie permettant de gagner la confiance des païens et de les convaincre des vérités du Christianisme . . . il sera beaucoup plus utile d'essayer de trouver dans la foi et le coeur des païens des points de contact pour leur apporter les vérités chrétiennes et de là commencer le travail de conviction.'

Il est possible que certaines missions aient eu pour politique d'attirer les convertis dans des 'communautés chrétiennes' fermées, mais la Mission de Brême encourageait ses convertis récents à devenir des témoins de l'influence du Christ sur l'ensemble de la vie de leur société. Ainsi les chrétiens se devaient d'être de meilleurs paysans. Ils devaient apprendre un métier. Il leur fallait prendre leur place dans la commerce 'légitime' (et non pas celui des esclaves ou du rhum) et ils devaient faire sentir leur influence dans le gouvernement de leurs villes et de leurs tribus.

La Mission estimait que la famille constituait l'unité la plus efficace pour le changement social et par conséquent fît de gros efforts afin d'établir des foyers Chrétiens. La bénédiction du mariage n'avait pas pour but de légaliser une union pré-existante mais de consacrer le mariage comme étant chrétien et ainsi de mettre en rapport le couple (et ses enfants) avec la communion chrétienne.

On a souvent prétendu que si les premiers missionnaires avaient permis aux polygames d'adhérer à l'église, il y aurait eu beaucoup plus de conversions. En fait la Mission de Brême ne refusait pas l'accès à l'église aux convertis polygames. On disait aux missionnaires:

> la polygamie existait au temps du Christ et des apôtres et la monogamie n'était pas exigée pour être accepté dans l'église. Par conséquent, un homme qui a plusieurs épouses doit avoir le droit au baptême et à la communion; néanmoins, il faut toujours rappeler à tous que la monogamie est le seul mariage vrai aux yeux de Dieu et que ce n'est qu'ainsi que l'objectif du mariage peut être atteint.

Cette position fût affirmée encore par l'ordonnance de l'Eglise de 1876, mais dans la version révisée en 1930 on ne l'estima plus nécessaire.

L'attitude de la Mission vis-à-vis du colonialisme fût clairement définie quand l'Allemagne s'établit au Togo en 1884. Zahn écrivit à cette époque:

> Je suis complètement opposé aux colonies et il suffit de dire cela aujourd'hui pour être considéré comme un ennemi de notre pays. Mais lorsqu'un missionnaire commence à s'occuper de politique et par son influence développe les acquisitions coloniales de l'Allemagne, je maintiens, que, quelque puissent être ses intentions, il commet une erreur grave, sinon un crime.

Lorsqu'un fonctionnaire allemand s'attaqua à la politique missionnaire d'enseignement dans la langue Ewe, qu'il qualifiait de 'dialecte nègre sauvage et extrêmement primitif', Zahn alla défendre sa position auprès de l'Office Colonial à Berlin et finit par refuser les subventions gouvernementales accordées pour l'éducation afin d'éviter qu'un contrôle gouvernemental ne soit imposé aux écoles missionnaires. Même pendant les années d'après-guerre, après que le Gouvernement Britannique ait subventionné les écoles de la Mission de Brême et qu'il les ait amenées dans son système éducatif grâce au travail des missionnaires Écossais, Schlunk, inspecteur de la Mission à l'époque, y voyait un certain danger et écrivit:

> Il existe des difficultés inhérentes au système lui-même. Il fait de la Mission un accessoire du colonialisme. Ceci est supportable aussi longtemps que le peuple colonisé accepte la direction et les avantages de la puissance coloniale. Mais dès que des sentiments anti-colonialistes émergeront, il est fort douteux qu'il soit possible de faire une distinction entre le christianisme et l'expansion culturelle européenne et qu'il soit accepté alors que cette dernière sera refusée. Il est peu probable que le système scolaire actuel, quoique l'étude des Écritures soit inscrite au programme, puisse renier son influence européenne. Néanmoins, que doit faire la Mission? Ce n'est que si nous nous conformons à la politique gouvernementale que nous aurons la possibilité de travailler et ainsi d'avoir de l'influence. Il nous appartiendra d'exercer notre influence sur le gouvernement dans le bon sens et ensuite de former des enseignants chrétiens très qualifiés.

L'intention de la Mission était de préparer les nouvelles congrégations à l'autonomie. Ainsi less missionnaires se devaient de s'efforcer de rendre leurs fidèles capables de se diriger eux-mêmes le plus rapidement possible. Des anciens, élus parmi les fidèles, devaient se grouper en un consistoire à qui on devait enseigner à faire le plus possible pour l'entretien de l'église et des écoles. La congrégation devait également prendre conscience de la responsabilité qu'elle avait envers ceux qui étaient dans le besoin. En 1899, Zahn demanda qu'un bilan financier soit remis chaque année à l'église africaine afin que ses membres puissent se rendre compte 'de la cherté des choses'. Ceci devait servir d'enseignement et d'encouragement pour que les fidèles apportent leur contribution et assument une partie de leurs besoins financiers. Zahn n'était pas en faveur d'impôts ou de cotisations à l'Église ne voulant accepter que des dons. Lorsque il fût amené à modifier sa position surtout à cause de la pression des dirigeants africains, il accepta ces contributions comme constituant 'une bonne discipline extérieure' mais continua de dire qu'il s'agissait là d'une 'extrêmement mauvaise façon de donner'.

C'est aux missionnaires Écossais que dévolut la formation de dirigeants pour l'église qu'il aidèrent à établir en 1923, Il fallût déclarer l'autorité du synode (organe exécutif de l'église) en dépit de l'opposition des agents ecclésiastiques, des missionnaires et même des missions. L'église telle qu'elle est aujourd'hui est la preuve du succès de ces efforts.

La vision qu'avaient les missionnaires Écossais d'une Église de l'Ouest Africain fût reprise par les missionnaires Allemands mais elle n'est pas encore réalisée. Cependant, grâce à l'établissement du Conseil Chrétien et de 'Ghana Church Union Committee' en 1957, le but est en vue.

IV. CATHOLICS AND PROTESTANTS IN THE CONGO

RUTH SLADE REARDON

Unlike the evangelization of the Congo coasts by the Portuguese in the sixteenth century, the nineteenth-century missionary movement into the Congo interior was undertaken by both Protestants and Roman Catholics simultaneously. Three hundred years of separation, polemic and indifference had gone by since the Reformation, and it was not surprising that on both sides there was a very one-sided view of the other's faith and practice. Protestant missionaries arrived at San Salvador in 1879 to find that all that remained of the Portuguese efforts were the ruins of a Christian cathedral, a crucifix among the King's other fetishes, and confused memories of the earlier teaching. They were quite prepared to attribute this disappearance of Christianity solely to the fact that it had been introduced into the Congo in a Catholic form. They needed to seek no other reason, since they regarded '... Popery as a corrupt and corrupting religion ... only a baptized paganism'[1] and were firmly convinced that the 'light, even in good and devoted Catholic missionaries', ... was dimmed by false doctrine and superstition.[2] Whereas the Catholics, on the other hand, were ready to warn African rulers about the errors of Henry VIII, Luther, and Calvin,[3] and turned their attention to the need for a speedy advance up the Congo river partly because of their fear of being outdistanced by the Protestant pioneers.[4] Indeed, this sense of need to arrive first at each strategic point and thus be able to choose the best site for a mission station, was reflected often enough in the appeals to subscribers which appeared in both Protestant and Catholic missionary magazines.

[1] Guinness, 1890, p. 179.
[2] Bentley, 1900, I, p. 40.
[3] Ibid., p. 161.
[4] Carrié, 1890.

THE EUROPEAN POWERS AND THE MISSIONARIES

The arrival of Henry Moreton Stanley at the mouth of the Congo in September 1877 effectively placed the Congo river upon the map of Africa and proved the immense possibilities of the opening up of the Congo basin. By the end of 1878 European governments were becoming interested in the region. Portugal had begun to realize that if her ancient claims to the area were to be justified, they must be supported by a display of activity. France was represented on the coast by her traders and missionaries, and both groups were eager to press inland once the way was opened up. Stanley himself had accepted service under Leopold II, King of the Belgians, and was about to set off in charge of the King's first expedition.

The English missionaries sent out by the Baptist Missionary Society and the Livingstone Inland Mission (an offshoot of the undenominational Regions Beyond Missionary Union, largely supported by Baptists) were vitally concerned in the question of which European power was to rule in the Congo basin. Great Britain herself had decisively refused to take an interest in the acquisition of the region.[5] With Portugal, France, and the *Association Internationale du Congo*, which was under the patronage of Leopold II, all in the running of the sovereignty of the Congo basin, the Protestant missionaries came out in favour of the King of the Belgians. This was largely because they feared that France and Portugal, as Catholic countries, were likely to favour Catholic missions at the expense of the Protestants, whereas Leopold II was loud in proclaiming that his Association intended to protect and assist all Christian missionaries, irrespective of denomination.[6]

Early in 1881 three Catholic missionaries had arrived in the Congo accompanied by a military and a naval officer. They had brought presents and a letter from the King of Portugal to the King of Kongo, and a Portuguese gunboat was to be sent monthly to watch over their interests. It was obvious that for Portugal the presence of her missionaries was intended to confirm her ancient rights in the Congo.

[5] Crowe, 1942, pp. 202–3.

[6] Slade, 1954.

So far as the Holy Ghost Fathers were concerned, their links with the French explorer Savorganan de Brazza were very close, and a man like Prosper-Philippe Augouard, one of their most dynamic missionaries, was ready to think in terms of a double allegiance: 'Pour Dieu! Pour la France!'[7] Thus with the Catholic missions so closely connected with the political ambitions of France and Portugal, it was not surprising that the Protestants were on the side of Leopold II. They had received considerable assistance and protection from Stanley during their early efforts to establish their mission stations between the coast and Stanley Pool, and Leopold II himself had expressed a friendly interest in their work. They were thus ready to help him in his campaign to win English public opinion to the support of the political claims of the *Association Internationale du Congo*.

The situation at the court of the King of Kongo was something like that in Buganda, where the French Catholics and the Anglican missionaries were in close competition for the royal favour, and where this rivalry coloured their political outlook. It was hardly surprising that at San Salvador Pedro V found the presence of two competing sets of Christian missionaries confusing in the extreme. He wanted to offend neither the Baptists, who had arrived first and were teaching and healing his people, nor the Catholics who were supported by the authority of the King of Portugal. There seemed to be only one solution; as each Sunday came round he pleaded sickness and thus attended neither Mass nor the preaching of the Word.[8]

LEOPOLD II AND THE MISSIONS

The final delimination of African territory at the Conference of Berlin in 1884–85 left San Salvader under Portuguese rule, but the majority of the Baptist mission stations were in territory which was to be administered by the *Association Internationale du Congo*—in effect by Leopold II, who was proclaimed 'Sovereign of the Congo Independent State' in July 1885. Once secure in this coveted position, he no longer needed the support of English public opinion—and therefore of the English missionaries—as

[7] Bentley, op. cit., I, p. 379. [8] Slade, 1959.

he had done prior to 1885, and his main concern was to imprint a Belgian character upon Christian missionary work in the Congo. It was obvious that he could not replace the English Protestant missionaries there by Belgian Protestants, who were too few in number to support such a missionary enterprise. So far as the Catholics were concerned, however, he made great efforts to ensure that foreign missionary personnel should give way to Belgians. After considerable pressure from the King, Pope Leo XIII decided early in 1886 that the territory of the Congo Independent State should be reserved for Belgian missionaries as soon as the personnel became available. Leopold II had already persuaded Cardinal Lavigerie to recruit a number of Belgian priests to work with his White Fathers in the eastern part of the Congo State, and by 1888 he had succeeded in getting the Flemish Scheut Fathers to take an interest in the Congo. In the west the Scheutists were thus able to replace the Holy Ghost Fathers, who gradually withdrew to French Congo. Then in the eighteen-nineties Belgian Jesuits, Trappists, Sacred Heart Fathers, and Premonstratensians all started to send missionaries to the Congo at the King's request.[9]

Thus up the main Congo river and its chief tributaries went a double stream of Christian missionaries—the Catholics who were also Belgians, and the English, American, and Scandinavian Protestants. The Scheutists followed the Baptists up the main river as far as Nouvelle Anvers, and then turned their attention to the Kasai in 1891, the year in which the American Presbyterians began a mission there. The Jesuits took up the lower Congo and the Kwango as their field, and worked side by side with Swedish Protestants and American Baptists. In 1897 a Sacred Heart mission was planted at Stanley Falls, where the Baptists had been working for some years. In his anxiety to attract Belgian missionaries to the Congo, King Leopold facilitated their settlement in every possible way. They were freely given large concessions of land, while their personnel and goods were often transported in the State steamers. So much State favour was shown to the Catholic missions that the Protestants

[9] Storme, 1951, pp. 557.

began to feel themselves at a considerable disadvantage by comparison.

THE CONGO REFORM CAMPAIGN AND THE MISSIONARIES

At the turn of the century English and American public opinion became aroused by reports of the ill-treatment of Africans by white officials in the Congo. It was when the Protestant missionaries began to take part in this Congo reform campaign that they came into direct conflict with the State authorities. Prudence had made them very slow to speak out in public criticism of the administrative methods of the Congo government, but once they had decided that this was the right course for them, their eye-witness atrocity stories figured largely in the literature of the campaign.[10] The Catholic missions, on the other hand, pursued a policy of private representation rather than public criticism—their situation *vis-à-vis* the State was considerably more delicate than that of the Protestants in view of the subsidies and State help which they were receiving—and Leopold II did all that he could to use them in combating the propagandists who were attacking the State regime. He even invited a Catholic mission from England—the Mill Hill Fathers—to take up work in the Congo in an attempt to answer the campaign which was being conducted in the English press; in order to mobilize English and American Catholics in support of his cause he tried to persuade them that the entire agitation was Protestant in origin, directed against Catholic Belgium. His efforts were not without success,[11] but Catholic opinion had comparatively little influence in Great Britain and the United States, and it was largely the force of the Congo reform campaign which eventually led to the annexation of the Congo Independent State by Belgium in 1908.

'FOREIGN' AND 'NATIONAL' MISSIONS

The State authorities had done their best to ensure that Catholic and Protestant missions should be planted at a certain distance from each other, so as to avoid friction as far as possible.

[10] Slade, 1955.

[11] Slade, 1957.

This could not always be arranged, however, and at times local rivalries had flared up into open conflict when Catholic catechists and Protestant evangelists found themselves in competition in the villages. During the Congo reform campaign individual Protestant and Catholic missionaries had engaged in polemics against each other, respectively attacking or defending the Congo State government for its administrative policy. The Protestants continually felt themselves at a disadvantage due to the fact that they were treated as 'foreign' missionaries, unwanted intruders, while the Catholic Belgians always seemed to have the support of the administration. In fact, there were times of sharp divergence between Catholic missions and the State; these differences blew over, however, while the distinction between 'foreigners' and 'nationals' remained. After the annexation of the Congo by Belgium, the *Ministère des Colonies* set on foot a scheme whereby it was hoped that the English, American, and Scandinavian Protestant missionaries in the Congo would gradually be replaced by Belgian Protestants. Inevitably this plan was doomed to failure from the beginning, since Belgian Protestants were quite unable to support such a burden.[12] Eventually a very small Belgian mission came to swell the ranks of the Protestants, but this was all.

TOWARDS UNITY AMONG THE PROTESTANT MISSIONS

Before the turn of the century, the Protestant missions had become troubled by their diversity of outlook and practice, it was clear that they needed to come together to discuss how they could prevent their work overlapping and achieve a common policy towards African Protestants who moved from one region to another, a common approach to their relations with the State, and so on. A conference held at Leopoldville in 1902 was the first of a series of General Conferences which drew representatives from most of the Protestant societies working in the Congo. These conferences were called at two-yearly intervals, until in 1911, following the proposal of the World Missionary Conference which had met at Edinburgh the year before, a Continuation

[12] Slade, 1959, pp. 348–61.

Committee replaced the temporary one which had previously organized these General Conferences.[13] This Committee had no executive powers,[14] but it was an expression of the belief of the Congo Protestant missions in their essential unity, a unity which could be obscured, but not denied, by their differences of organization and practice. In 1924 the Congo Continuation Committee became the Congo Protestant Council, a responsible body which within four years was supporting a full-time secretary. Ten years later the Protestant Churches in the Congo took a common name, the Church of Christ in Congo, and enjoyed a common membership, so that a Protestant who moved from one area to another could present a membership certificate and be accepted on a testimony of the Church from which he had come.

DIFFICULT RELATIONS BETWEEN CATHOLICS AND PROTESTANTS

However, the influence of the ecumenical movement which was drawing the Protestant missions closer together, had no effect upon their relations with the Catholics. Catholics were standing apart from the ecumenical movement; the fear that it would only lead to a vague indifferentism was expressed in the encyclical *Mortalium Animos* in 1928. So far from relations between Catholics and Protestants in the Congo improving, in the course of the nineteen-twenties Protestants began to complain of serious discrimination against themselves. At that time a great impetus was given to Catholic missionary expansion by the 'missionary Pope' Pius XI, who realized that the Congo presented a unique opportunity for advance, and Belgian missionary effort concentrated increasingly upon the Belgian colony. Medical missionary work was developed a great deal, partly in an effort to counteract Protestant influence in this sphere.[15] Protestants complained of close identification of the Catholic Church with the government in the Congo, and pointed to the fact that the Mill Hill missionaries from England were subsidized by the

[13] Carpenter, 1952, p. 35. [14] Stonelake, 1937, p. 61.

[15] *L'Aide Médicale aux Missions*, 1928, pp. 13, 16 ff.; *Pie XI et la médicine au service des missions, 1928*, p. 38 ff.

government in the same manner as the Belgian Catholic missions, while Protestant Congolese were treated in various ways as foreigners. Administrators, of course, differed in outlook, so that at various periods and in particular localities a great deal depended upon the attitude of the individual on the spot; and the Protestant missionaries recognized that, apart from the subsidies given to 'national' missions, official instructions ordered impartial treatment.[16]

The question for the Protestants was how best to get these official instructions carried out. In the late twenties the secretary of the Congo Protestant Council began to gather precise information and complaints from Protestant missionaries all over the Colony, in the expectation that if necessary the International Missionary Council would take up the matter, and bring the weight of its influence to bear upon the Belgian Government. In the Katanga both the American Methodists and the Garanganze Evangelical Mission complained that they were having the greatest difficulty in obtaining sites for new stations, particularly in the mining camps, although land was granted freely to the Benedictines. The Protestants in the Katanga began to complain directly to the Provincial Government in 1928, while at about the same time the Catholic missionaries began a pamphlet warfare in which they did not hesitate to point to 'the identity between the political programme of the American missions and the political programme of Moscow', both aiming at the overthrow of the Belgian colonial regime.[17] In the lower Congo the English and American Baptists and the Swedish missionaries gathered exact information about reports of the ill-treatment of Protestant women and children by Catholic missionaries, and a joint protest was made in the spring of 1931, when Dr. Emory Ross, secretary of the Congo Protestant Council, together with several other missionaries, met the acting Governor-General.[18]

The Secretary of the Congo Protestant Council had already written to Dr. J. H. Oldham of the International Missionary

[16] Stonelake, op. cit., pp. 133–6. [17] de Hemptinne, 1929, p. 30.
[18] From the archives of the Bureau des Missions Protestantes du Congo Brussels.

Council about the situation in the Congo, suggesting that affairs were sufficiently serious to warrant the intervention of this international body.[19] Oldham visited Brussels late in 1931, and had a number of unofficial discussions with high officials in the *Ministère des Colonies*. During 1932 the Congo Protestant Council continued to collect evidence of concrete cases of religious discrimination in various parts of the Congo, and in February 1933 presented the Colonial Minister in Brussels with a detailed memorandum. This complained of the persecution of Protestants by Catholic missionaries, of the inability of the government to check the excesses of the Catholic missions, of the minute subsidies accorded to Protestant medical work, and of the complete lack of any subsidies for Protestant educational work. In March Oldham arrived in Brussels to discuss these complaints at the *Ministère des Colonies*. He had secured the backing of the English Free Churches and hoped for the same in the United States; he had interested the Archbishop of Canterbury in the issue, and declared himself ready to threaten a public campaign in England and America if the Protestant missions were not freed from persecution and if the distinction between 'national' and 'foreign' missions was not abandoned. It was only very slowly that the situation improved, but by 1939 the tension had relaxed, and after the war the Belgian Government decided to give subsidies to foreign Protestant missions for their educational work in the colony.

It is clear that in the pre-war years, when Protestants were complaining of the lack of religious liberty in the Congo, the relations between the government and the Catholic missions had been very close. Humanly speaking, it would have been exceedingly difficult at this time for the Catholics not to have given way to the temptation to use their political influence against their rivals when the government itself was so anxious to limit the activities of the non-Belgian missionary element, especially since at that period their seminary training could hardly have led them to see any very clear theological reason why they should do so—

[19] From the archives of the British Conference of Missionary Societies, London.

rather the contrary. They had no real knowledge of Protestants, and no contact at all with them on the religious level, so that they were only too ready to identify all Protestant missionaries with the extreme sub-Christian sects which were as great a trouble to the Protestants as to themselves.

At the same time, many Protestant missionaries had tended to bring anti-Roman prejudice with them to the Congo, apart altogether from the situation which they found when they arrived. By 1939 there were more than forty Protestant missions at work in the Congo. After the first groups of English Baptists other missionaries had followed, Scandinavians and a number of Americans—Presbyterians, Baptists, and Disciples of Christ. But later again had come a host of smaller missions, most of them American and some English, representing the smaller denominations (the mission of the American Episcopal Methodist Church is an exception) and undenominational missionary societies, many with an approach which may loosely be described as 'fundamentalist'. Certainly they would expect to have nothing in common with Catholics.

THE POST-WAR SITUATION

After the war, the political situation was more favourable to the beginning of Catholic–Protestant *rapprochement*. In 1946 a Liberal Belgian Colonial Minister decided to subsidize foreign Protestant educational work, provided that the Protestant missionaries fulfilled the requirements and reached the standards laid down by the colonial authorities. Later, the fact that a Liberal Socialist coalition government was in power in Belgium between 1954 and 1958 meant, in Africa, the end of the long period during which the colonial government and the Catholic missions regarded their interests as identical.

At the same time there was a gradual change in the general climate of opinion among Catholics in Europe; Protestants began to be regarded not as mere heretics but as Christian brothers. In Belgium itself there were several centres devoted to the promotion of ecumenism, and the Week of Prayer for Christian Unity began to be widely observed. This general change of climate affected the younger Belgian missionaries, and in some cases personal exchanges and friendships developed between Catholic and Protestant missionaries. It became possible for the two groups to begin to become acquainted with one another before they arrived in the Congo, since one of the requirements of the Belgian colonial authorities when they subsidized the educational work of foreigners was that all foreign missionaries should spend one year in Belgium before going to the colony. A joint meeting for prayer for unity between the Protestant missionary group and Catholics with a special interest in missionary work in Africa was arranged for the first time in Brussels during the Week of Prayer for Christian Unity in January 1958, and this led to further contacts, both in Belgium and in the Congo itself. Some missionaries began to lament the fact that Catholic–Protestant hostility had been transferred by the missionaries to the African clergy and people, and appeared to have become very deeply rooted in them. The change of climate has of course been amazingly speeded up in the Congo as elsewhere since Pope John XXIII announced the calling of the second Vatican Council in the perspective of Christian unity. To give but one example of this change: in January 1964 the preacher at a recollection held for the Catholic clergy of Leopoldville was a Protestant pastor.

Catholic intolerance is lessening, although it has not altogether disappeared. On the Protestant side, however, there has remained a great deal of fear and suspicion during the post-war years. The older-established Protestant missions come from Churches which belong to the World Council of Churches, but many of the newer missions—which sometimes display greater vitality—tend to be suspicious of the ecumenical movement. This attitude received concrete expression when the Congo Protestant Council withdrew from the International Missionary Council over the issue of its integration with the World Council of Churches; this happened not because all the missions desired the break but because those who did not, hesitated to make a stand which would risk endangering that degree of internal unity already achieved among the Congo Protestant missions themselves. In this climate it is easy to understand that these more ecumenically-inclined missions are equally reluctant to show themselves as over-anxious for contact with Catholics.

Independence in 1960 inevitably affected the ecumenical situation. The transition from 'mission' to 'Church' which had been proceeding at very different rates among the Protestant groups, was suddenly speeded up on all sides. African Church leaders were placed in positions of responsibility. When the All Africa Conference of Churches was established at the Kampala Assembly in 1963, the Congo Protestant Council sent an African delegate, nine Congo 'Churches' and one 'mission' sent African delegates, and one 'Church' sent a European missionary. The Congo Salvation Army sent an African observer. (There were also ten European or American missionaries from the Congo, representing nearly a quarter of the Assembly staff, presumably so high a proportion because Congo missionaries have to speak both English and French, the two Assembly languages.) The delegates from the Congo participated with enthusiasm in an Assembly whose general climate was one of impatience with the 'imported divisions' which Christian missionaries had brought to Africa, and in the Congo itself it does not seem to be the Africans who want the existing divisions among Protestant 'missions' and 'Churches' to continue. In fact, they often complain that at least in certain localities Christian missionaries have broken up a unity which existed in African society before they arrived. This pressure for unity seems to stem more from practical than from theological reasons, and some missionary observers have the impression that they want 'African' unity as much as, or more than, 'Christian' unity. How far is this attitude being carried over to relations between African Protestants and Catholics? It is impossible to generalize, but one may safely say that this seems to be the direction in which relations are moving. Many missionaries fear they will move too quickly in this direction in the coming years, and that problems of 'faith and order' may not be given enough serious examination by Africans.

Meanwhile, however, there appears to be very little organized effort to 'think together' the immense problems which face

Christians in the Congo today—the political responsibility of a Christian, the 'indigenization' of Christianity, and so on. (Here we have not discussed the question of the growth in the Congo of African messianic movements whose existence reproaches both Catholics and Protestants for continuing their 'western' approach longer, perhaps, than necessary.) The opening of the Protestant university at Stanleyville for the academic year 1963–64 just as the Catholic university of Lovanium (Leopoldville) was celebrating its tenth anniversary, testified to the deep cleavage which persisted in the educational system, right to the highest level. Because of the troubled situation in the Stanleyville region, however, the Protestant University was given shelter at Lovanium at the beginning of the academic year 1964–65; the fact that the two universities have been living and working together on the same campus has led to many ecumenical contacts and activities.[20] There are two fields also in which organized collaboration is going ahead. One is that of practical relief work, where Protestant and Catholic bodies are working together to do something to alleviate a situation which must sometimes tempt to despair. The second is that of Bible translation; there is more than one scheme of revision or translation in the Congo on which Catholics and Protestants are working together.

The Congo is vast, and Catholic–Protestant relationships differ a great deal from region to region. Something like a third of the Congolese are Christians; of these Christians about a third are Protestants. The pressing problem for both Catholics and Protestants today seems to be that of the quality of Church membership rather than its numerical strength. And in the Congo as elsewhere, if there were a deepening of the Christian faith within the divided groups and a more profound awareness of what the Christian mission involves in the local situation, this would inevitably lead to a greater awareness of unity in Christ, a unity which would seek its visible expression across those divisions.

[20] Vanneste, 1965.

REFERENCES

Bentley, W. H.
(1900) *Pioneering on the Congo*. London. 2 vols.
Carpenter, G.
(1952) *Highways for God in Congo*. Leopoldville.
Carrié, P.
(1890) Quoted in *Missions Catholiques*. Lyons. XII, p. 65.
Crowe, S. E.
(1942) *The Berlin West African Conference*. London.
de Hemptinne, Mgr., Préfet Apostolique du Katanga
(1929) *La Politique des Missions Protestantes au Congo*. Elisabethville.
Guinness, F. E.
(1890) *The New World of Central Africa*. London.
L'Aide Médicale aux Missions, 1928.
Pie XI et la Médicine au Service des Missions, 1928.
Slade, R.
(1954) 'L'Attitude des missions protestantes vis-à-vis des puissances européennes au Congo avant 1885', *Bulletin de l'Académie Royal des Sciences Coloniales*, XXXV, pp. 684–721.
(1955) 'English missionaries and the beginning of the anti-Congolese campaign in England', *Revue Belge de Philologie et d'Histoire*, XXXIII, 1, pp. 37–73.
(1957) 'King Leopold II and the attitude of English and American Catholics towards the anti-Congolese campaign', *Zaïre*, XI, 6, pp. 593–612.
(1959) *English-speaking Missions in the Congo Independent State*. Brussels.
Stonelake, A.
(1937) *Congo Past and Present*. London.
Storme, M. B.
(1951) *Evangelisatiepogingen in de binnenlanden van Afrika*. Brussels.
Vanneste, A.
(1965) 'Catholic-Protestant relationships at Lovanium University, Leopoldville', *One in Christ*. No. 2, pp. 166–8.

Résumé

CATHOLIQUES ET PROTESTANTS AU CONGO

C'est vers les années 1880 que simultanément des missionnaires catholiques et protestants firent pénétrer la foi chrétienne à l'intérieur du Congo. Ce fut une époque remplie de polémiques et de préjugés. Les missionnaires protestants ne trouvant à leur arrivée que de très légères traces de l'évangélisation portugaise du XVIe siècle sur la côte congolaise étaient prêts à attribuer cette disparition du Christianisme au fait qu'il avait été introduit au Congo sous forme de catholicisme. Les catholiques, pour leur part, avaient l'intention de mettre en garde les chefs africains contre les erreurs d'Henri VIII, de Luther et de Calvin et se décidèrent à avancer rapidement vers l'intérieur en remontant le Congo en partie parce qu'il craignaient que les pionniers protestants ne les gagnent de vitesse.

Les premiers missionnaires protestants au Congo étaient des anglais appartenant à la Société Missionnaire Baptiste (Baptist Missionary Society) et au groupe de l'Union Missionnaire pour les Régions étrangères (Regions Beyond Missionary Union). Après eux arrivèrent des Scandinaves et un certain nombre d'Américains—Presbytériens, Baptistes et Disciples du Christ. Plus tard encore arrivèrent de nombreuses petites missions, la plupart d'entre elles américaines et quelques-unes anglaises, représentant les petits groupes protestants et un certain nombre de sociétés missionnaires indépendantes. On pourrait décrire la plupart de ces missions comme ayant un caractère 'fondamentaliste'. En 1939 il y avait au Congo plus de 40 missions protestantes.

La grande majorité des missionnaires catholiques au Congo par contre était Belge. Lorsqu'en 1885 Léopold II, roi des Belges, devint souverain de l'État Indépendant du Congo, il voulu donner un caractère Belge à l'évangélisation du Congo; l'année suivante il s'arrangea pour persuader le Pape Léon XIII de déclarer que le territoire de l'État Indépendant devrait être réservé aux missionnaires Belges dès qu'il y en aurait suffisamment de disponibles. Le Roi avait déjà convaincu le Cardinal Lavigerie de recruter un certain nombre de prêtres Belges pour travailler avec ses Pères Blancs dans la partie orientale de l'État du Congo. A l'Ouest, les Pères du Saint Esprit Français se retirèrent au Congo Français à l'arrivée des pères Scheutistes Flamands et graduellement les Jésuites, Trappistes, Pères du Sacré-Cœur et les Prémonstratoriens commencèrent tous à envoyer des missionnaires au Congo sur la demande du Roi Léopold.

Il n'est pas surprenant qu'il y ait eu une longue période d'hostilitiés ouvertes entre les missionnaires protestants et catholiques. Il arriva par exemple qu'il y ait de véritables batailles entre cathéchistes catholiques et évangélistes protestants en concurrence dans un même village. Les missions catholiques étant des missions 'nationales' étaient favorisées et subventionnées par le gouvernement. Pendant la période de la campagne pour la réforme du Congo au début du siècle, les missionnaires protestants étaient entrés en conflit ouvert avec les autorités en publiant en Angleterre et aux États-Unis des rapports donnant des renseignements de première main sur la mauvaise administration du Congo. En tant que missionnaires étrangers, ils étaient traités comme des gêneurs indésirables. Un plan visant à remplacer les missionnaires protestants étrangers par des Belges, établi par le Ministère des Colonies, peu après que la Belgique ait repris le Congo en 1908, fût voué à un échec dès le départ du fait qu'il n'y avait pas en Belgique suffisamment de protestants pour assumer un fardeau aussi lourd. Néanmoins, des protestants Belges établirent une petite mission au Congo. Il eût été extrêmement difficile aux missionnaires catholiques de ne pas succomber à la tentation d'user de leur influence politique contre leurs rivaux alors que le gouvernement lui-même était très désireux de limiter les activités des éléments missionnaires non Belges et que, de plus, la formation reçue à l'époque dans les séminaires ne les incitait aucunement à trouver des raisons théologiques valables à l'encontre de cette attitude, bien au contraire.

Il est assez naturel que les missionnaires protestants aient été mécontents du manque de liberté religieuse au Congo. Le Conseil Protestant du Congo fût formé en 1924 quelques années après le Conseil Missionnaire International, mais l'influence du mouvement œcuménique qui rapprochait les diverses missions protestantes les unes des autres n'eût aucun effet sur leurs rapports avec les catholiques. Au début des années 1930, la tension était très forte. Ce n'est qu'après que le Conseil Missionnaire International soit intervenu auprès du gouvernement belge et qu'il y ait eu menace d'une campagne publique en Angleterre et aux Etats-Unis si les persécutions à l'égard des missions protestantes ne cessaient pas, que leurs conditions d'améliorèrent graduellement.

Après la guerre, la situation politique devint plus favorable à un début de rapprochement entre catholiques et protestants. Un ministre des colonies Belge décida en 1946 de subventionner les efforts menés par les étrangers pour l'éducation au Congo. De plus, le fait qu'un gouvernement de coalition libéral–socialiste ait été au pouvoir en Belgique entre 1954 et 1958 eût pour conséquence de mettre un terme en Afrique à la longue période pendant laquelle le gouvernement colonial et les missions catholiques avaient considéré leurs intérêts comme étant identiques.

En même temps, on assistait à un changement graduel dans l'atmosphère et l'opinion générale des catholiques en Europe: on commença à considérer les protestants non plus comme des hérétiques mais comme des frères Chrétiens. En Belgique même, plusieurs centres consacrés au développement de l'œcuménisme fûrent créés et l'observance de la semaine de prières pour l'unité Chrétienne se généralisa. Lorsque le Pape Jean XXIII annonça la convocation du Deuxième Concile du Vatican ce changement d'atmosphère s'intensifia beaucoup encore. Ceci eût une incidence sur les jeunes missionnaires Belges et, dans certains cas, des amitiés et rapports personnels prirent place entre missionnaires catholiques et protestants. Certains commencèrent à déplorer le fait que l'hostilité entre catholiques et protestants ait été transférée par les soins des missionnaires au clergé et à la population africaines.

Néanmoins, beaucoup de protestants continuèrent à craindre et à se méfier des catholiques dans les années d'après-guerre. Certaines des missions récentes tendent à être soupçonneuses du mouvement œcuménique dans son ensemble; en fait, le Conseil Protestant du Congo se retira du Conseil Missionnaire International sur la question de son intégration au Conseil Mondial des Églises. Les missions ne désiraient pas cette rupture à l'unanimité mais celles qui voulaient rompre n'hésitèrent pas à prendre une position qui aurait menacé l'unité déjà acquise au sein des missions protestantes du Congo.

En 1960, l'accession du Congo à l'indépendance eût évidemment une influence sur la situation œcuménique. Des dignitaires ecclésiastiques africains se virent confier des postes importants. Certains d'entre eux participèrent à l'assemblée de Kampala en

1963 qui institua la Conférence Pan-Africaine des Églises. Une atmosphère d'impatience généralisée à l'encontre des 'divisions importées' par les missionnaires chrétiens en Afrique présida aux délibérations de cette assemblée. Il semble que le désir d'unité exprimé par beaucoup des dirigeants des missions protestantes africaines provienne de raisons plus pratiques que théologiques; cette attitude, dans une certaine mesure, se reflète dans les rapports entre africains catholiques et protestants.

Il existe encore une division très nette dans le système d'éducation. L'université protestante de Stanleyville ouvrit ses portes pour l'année académique 1963–64 alors que l'université catholique de Lovanium célébrait son dixième anniversaire. Néanmoins, une collaboration active et organisée entre les catholiques et les protestants se poursuit dans deux domaines: d'une part les activités charitables de secours, et, de l'autre, les traductions de la Bible.

V. THE MISSIONARY STRUGGLE WITH COMPLEXITY

T. PRICE

The Protestant missionary enterprise which accompanied the upsurge of European industrialization was complex in its origins, and various in its effects. Rising as it did in churches which existed to maintain the right of private judgement in religion, it regarded liberty as a good to be advocated and established; and this, combined with an ethic which demanded goodwill to all men and particular consideration for the impoverished and powerless, directed it against the institution of slavery. On the other hand, productive economic labour was also a good in itself, a defence against sinful activity, and a necessary support for the material organization of the churches. Christian knowledge was referred to metaphorically as 'light', a usage founded on the Lord's reported saying, 'I am the Light of the world'; and by deduction, where this light was lacking there was only darkness. But the light was conceived as a beam on the path out of the world into eternity, rather than an illumination of the world around. When Dr. David Livingstone said that he was going to open the interior of Africa to commerce and Christianity, he was outlining his strategy first for strangling the slave trade, in the interest of the bodily survival of the Africans; and then for making the life thus obtained for them worth living.

The problem of ignorance, which offered no ground for the exercise of responsible private judgement, did not come to the attention of concerned Christians only with their turning to look out to the non-European world. They had already seen it in their own peasant and proletarian fellow-countrymen; and had encountered the language barrier, in Britain, among the Welsh and Gaelic-speakers of the western coasts and islands. They attacked these obstacles by establishing Bible Societies, which subsidized printing and distribution of suitable portions of Bibles, and where they would be fully used, complete Bibles, so that poverty and ignorance of a metropolitan language should not prevent anyone from seeing the need to commit himself to the fellowship of a properly-enlightened Church. The Bible, unlike the Jewish and Islamic scriptures, had never been confined to one sacred language and a proud part of the Protestant tradition was that the Roman Catholic lapse into that priestly notion had been remedied by great translators whose courageous lives had been worthy of their vocation as God's mouthpieces. The directors and supporters of the Bible societies were ready and able to support and encourage new translators as missionary ventures revealed communities who knew none of the languages of historic Christendom.

The Protestant doctrine of individual responsibility and private judgement notoriously produced a great number of differences between the individuals who became church leaders. Differences tended to become oppositions, and the record of contention between users of English Bibles with and without the apocryphal books, the Douai and the King James translations, suggests that different translations made by different missionaries might readily have become nuclei of separate sects. The Bible societies, however, by adopting particular translators or translation centres, were able to throw such material weight behind a particular version for each language, that missions in the same language area had to use the same Bible text. This in turn meant that the form of the language used in the Bible was given currency outside its original area; and while few 'Bible-dialects' escape criticism and some are rejected to be replaced by new versions, the prestige, permanence, and ubiquity of print held the chosen dialect to be regarded as standard. Common agreement on the value of Bible society work, and contribution to its support, also linked otherwise unfriendly people, as is noted in the 24th (1833) Report of the Edinburgh Bible Society: 'A Bible Society permits Christians, without any sacrifice of principle' (later described as 'the ordinances which the Lord has enjoined for the observance of his disciples', and meaning ritual and church government) 'cordially to co-operate for the circulation of the word of God'. Four years earlier a letter from 'Demerary' enclosing proceeds of a collection taken there from 'many large proprietors of slaves' indicates that the range of co-operation was indeed wide; while notes in 1826 that Bibles were supplied for convicts transported to Australia, and for free but illiterate and unbaptized settlers in maritime Canada, balance the racial picture of those who benefited by Bible Society benevolence.

The Bible Society term for their publication was 'the Word of God'. It is retained in the spine title of the Nyanja Bible to this day; instead of the usual 'Biblia' it has a rendering of 'The Sacred Book, which is the Word of God'. This is exactly what the pioneer missionaries held that they had to take out into the world. It was not only what God, not men, wanted to communicate to man; it was the only source of that communication. This conviction among Bible Society directors was the root of bitter dissension over publishing anything but the plain text of the Bible, excluding the Apocrypha. Like most limited convictions, it was a powerful spring for action, which united individuals who otherwise differed in interests and capacities in missionary enterprises. Some were inspired by pity for unbelievers doomed to hell for all eternity, who could only be saved if they knew of, and accepted, the work of Christ. Some were in revolt against the corruption and self-satisfaction of their fellow-Christians at home, and trusted that new Christians would display purity and primitive virtue. Some, notably the artisan missionaries, sought a sphere in which they could do the work which they had mastered, not for the profit of an employer but as an offering to their unseen Lord. And some, judging from their subsequent careers as traders and transporters, were seeking escape from the pressures of rigid convention and over-crowding in their own society.

They were all, however, people of the Book. Everyone who could read and had a Bible was in communication with God, and no human office conferred any specially close relation with Him. Livingstone, in this as in much else a type and an example, found in the last clause of the Gospel according to St. Matthew a person to person promise: 'Lo, I am with you even unto the end of the world.' When enduring physical frustration and moral agony in Manyema, on his last journey, he read through the Bible four times. He was not reading for information, but finding comfort in conversation with God. The Bible could bring this to every literate believer, and one undisputed purpose of all missionary work was to provide translated Bibles and teach the people to read them.

Indeed, until they were able to put a locally comprehensible version of the Book, or at least key extracts from it, into the hands of the people, the missionaries could not properly account for themselves. African culture, however, embodied wide use and great interest in respect of curative (and the opposite, destructive) substances which corresponded in effect to the medicines to European physicians. Missionary doctors accordingly were readily received and apparently understood; and this acceptance of practitioners of a science encouraged the missionaries to assume that their whole culture, developed from a state not unlike that of the Africans by advances in various physical sciences and their application, was recognized by Africans as wholly imitable and admirable. They were encouraged in a natural ethnocentrism, and regarded divergence to African ways as not only desertion from the good life, but denial of a good example which the Africans had a right to expect. Whatever their doctrinal divergences, they stood together on this view of missionary responsibility. Physically they went out to Africa, psychologically Africans had to come to them, spiritually such coming over was valid only if it was the result of intellectual conviction and personal decision; and it needed a place to come to.

Mission stations were founded in response to many converging needs. While pioneer missions were prepared to recognize African political authorities and were not deliberately agents of imperial annexation, the survival record of those who were dependent on day-to-day favour of tribal chiefs, and had no place of their own within the country, was disastrous. If missionaries were to have sufficient span of life to establish communication and show an example, they must have some choice of location and control of their living conditions. Sometimes they were granted land, as they thought by gift; sometimes they, as they thought, bought a tract. They had no means of recognizing that there was very little difference from the African point of view, and that in fact they were being received as adherents to the African community around them, with no idea that their presence was a seed that would develop in ways of its own. From their point of view they had obtained concession, within which their principles would have predominance and their way of life could be established and maintained. On the station they could accumulate equipment, initiate new modes of land usage for their own sustenance and as example to the people, and keep out such elements of the local culture as they judged to be undesirable. It was regarded as good rather than bad, at that stage, that within the station boundaries missionaries could live with the least possible change from the way of life in which they had grown up at home, and with the least possible adjustment to the land and people into which they had come. It was axiomatic that sound adjustment would be to their standards, and that those standards only needed to be displayed.

The missionaries in fact became settlers, thus fulfilling the hope that Livingstone had expressed that some of the spacious tracts that he had discovered would be occupied by godly and industrious fellow-countrymen of his, whose example would show the Africans how life should be lived. Like other settlers, they needed the help of labourers, and they had modest means to pay for it. The relation of employer and employee was a simple and intelligible one, in which collaboration was satisfied by tangible results, and disagreement was made plain in terms of too few bundles of thatching grass or too short a measure of cloth. Some of the missionary enterprises, in house building and gardening, showed that they had useful new ideas; and the fact that even these were not rapidly adopted in common practice was a salutory warning that change would be equally slow in coming in behaviour and belief: it was fourteen years after the founding of the mission at Blantyre that adjacent villagers were noted to be 'now building good square, sensible huts'.

In this sphere the artisan missionaries were able to enter at once on the work for which they had enrolled, without the frustrating period of initial impotence which preachers had to endure while they learned the language. Yet there was no caste separation of occupations. The first grammar of the Nyanja language was compiled by the gardener with the Livingstonia Mission; and the artisan John Buchanan of Blantyre, later a sugar and coffee planter, translated the Gospel of Luke into Yao, and had it published. As departments built up special responsibilities, this admirable omnicompetence died out.

The station boundaries did not exclude Africans from residence. They simply marked the point at which value judgements changed, without the values being clearly recognized. Outside the station, virtue was to support what the others of the community said and did. Vice was to weaken the common strength. When mission doctors went beyond physic and took to surgery and amputation, they were regarded as destroyers, and individuals who submitted to surgery as traitors to their fellows. The Blantyre Mission publication *Life and Work in British Central Africa*, February 1898, mentions a patient whose leg was amputated, and none of his people came from the adjacent village to nurse him and cook for him, as relatives did for patients under medical treatment.

In fact the adherents of the first missionaries were mainly individuals whose social bonds had already been cut by effects of the slave trade: people whose communities had been annihilated, runaway or rescued slaves. Livingstone's 'Faithfuls', the ideal Africans in the eyes of missionaries and their supporters, had this background. They were willing to take risks and make adjustments in order to establish new social bonds, and on the mission stations they found patrons in whom their past experience aroused pity and a will to repay them for their undeserved misfortunes. Psychology has now taught us that such experience of social disruption does not make stable personalities capable of easy reintegration into communities. In the nineteenth century it led to a great deal of mutual disillusion and resentment, within the bounds of the stations on which the missionaries felt that they had full authority and responsibility. Outside those bounds, the African slave-holders who had so far no reason to have moral doubts about their relations to slaves, resented the existence of settlements where their ideas of justice and injustice were overturned. Missionary benevolence did not seem to extend to them, and when opportunity offered, they made what profit they could from the missionaries when they emerged from their stations, by demanding tolls for passage through their territories. Before long all missions were forced into agreement with Livingstone's conclusion that direct action against slavery would simply make any effective widespread work of conversion impossible. In the end this policy built up such frustration that the missionaries welcomed the imposition of imperial rule, which dealt summarily and irresistibly with slave raids and slave-holding.

Meanwhile, on the stations, the adherents were anxious to learn the language, and ready to learn the skills, of their patrons; and the missionaries were equally anxious to inform their adherents of the gospel of salvation, while also teaching them what was required of a Christian whose whole life should witness to and commend his belief. The European means to both these ends was the school, in which the teacher was conceded parental authority for the time in which pupils were under instruction. In a boarding school, the authority covered all the activities of twenty-four hours a day, for months at a time. The religious teaching on the mission stations impressed on the pupils their right and their responsibility to choose the Christian way for themselves, irrespective of what others, however closely associated with them hitherto, might regard as wrong about it. So long as they were on the mission station, and with the lack of background in many of their lives, it was in fact conformist to become Christian; and for many this reflected enduring convictions, and, they themselves and their teachers said, the work in them of the Spirit of God. For others, however, the warning of the parable of the Sower in their gospel was justified. When they recrossed the boundaries of the mission stations, and found other communities living on different principles, they were prepared to exercise their private judgement again, and conform to less restrictive codes. By that time many Europeans who did not share the missionary commitment to teach the way of salvation had come to Africa with enterprises which could profitably employ literate African agents, and rebels against missionary discipline found that they could not only avoid return to social repression but could live prosperously and independently of all restraint but that imposed by the interests of their employers. In this situation they did not always observe even that limitation, and drunkenness and dishonesty in handling money were made a reproach to the mission education which had given them their original qualifications for employment.

Discipline can always be represented as oppression by those who suffer under it, but nobody has found how to reconcile the principle of individual responsibility and private judgement with the needs of a community, without some more summary discipline than that of argument and persuasion. When the initiators of a new community differ completely from those they are to mould, in language, in moral standards, and in philosophical assumptions about the nature of the world and human society, the conflict between individual and community rights must be scarcely reconcilable. Education undertaken as a simple attack by Christian enlightenment on a range of evils rooted principally in ignorance became simultaneously a service demanded by people who were becoming conscious of incapacity, through lack of education, to resist aggressions, and a process which turned submissive associates into deserters and assailants. It was this which contributed largely to the abandonment of a promising beginning in providing Africans with first-hand experience of Europe. A number of those who had adopted a good deal of the European culture of the mission stations accompanied missionaries who were going home on furlough. There they were presented and accepted as typical of the best who had turned to salvation. It was all the more embarrassing when later inquiries by people whom they had met had to be answered in some cases by report that they had lapsed from missionary standards of behaviour. This did not mean that they had been rejected by all reputable Europeans: one of those in Nyasaland, Thomas Cheonga, was in his later years the valued informant in the anthropological investigations of Dr. H. S. Stannus on the Yao tribe. It however did mean that missionary interest in providing wider experience for adherents was discouraged.

Meanwhile another interest had directed some of the most competent and authoritative missionaries beyond the limits of their stations. In order to translate the Bible, it was necessary to learn the language much more deeply than was needed for giving orders to workers and servants, and to understand the requests and complaints of people on the station. The stock villager's answer to any inquiry not concerned with what is under his eyes at the moment: 'I don't know, it is the old people who know,' inevitably directed the inquirers about language to the seniors who had no reason to seek out the missionaries. They were secure enough in their own society. To them the missionary had to come as an inquirer, not a teacher; a learner who could make mistakes and must expect to be put right; one who could not override their assertions. Those missionaries who entered on this relationship found themselves making friends and coming to admire men who showed no indication of becoming converts—though frequently they were prepared to send junior members of their family to learn in the schools conducted by the mission. In the prefatory guide to his Dictionary of the Nyanja language Dr. Clement Scott recorded his conclusion from his studies, that 'this language and this people declare the genius of Africa to be broad and courteous', adding the comparative observations that 'the formulas of civilisation, theological, social, political, like a veil conceal the truth'. It is reminiscent of what acquaintance with the Zulu did for Bishop Colenso; but this was printed in Edinburgh 'for the Foreign Mission Community of the Church of Scotland', a very substantial mark of the respect which Dr. Scott and his views commanded among his own people.

The association of missionaries who earned the respect of their colleagues by their attainments in the local language, and tribal elders who held a traditional respected position in their own society, brought the Christian communities as they developed at first into a socially prestige-carrying position. Other factors contributed. Members were all literate, and the degrees of literacy among them were not strikingly apparent to the mainly illiterate non-Christians who regarded it as a source of power. The social pattern which the missionaries brought with them regarded age as an honourable personal attribute and many churches employed 'elder' as a functional designation for particularly responsible members. Thus while the majority of the pioneer missionaries' associates and adherents were youthful, the Christian community fitted into the social category of dignified seniors from the first, without thinking to question the attribution. It was in fact advantageous in the period when tribal and national authorities still held power.

The dialects of the languages which the Bible translators learned were those used by the senior members of the local community, and while few were so extremely divergent from vulgar usage as the Court Bemba into which R. D. MacMinn translated the New Testament, the sought-for dignity in the Bible language was in fact the overtones of old men's speech. When radicalism and revolt, youthful energy and fresh thinking came to be fashionable values, people could still read the Bible in their local language for information, but the livelier new Christians hear the tones of what they hope is a dead local past. The translators are forgotten by those who have the mental capacity to be interested in them, if they felt that they owed them anything.

But whatever the side-issues which emerge from consideration of the historical circumstances of the work of translation, to do it was an immediate necessity, and once it was done, the printing of sufficient numbers of copies brought the missionaries into relation with the Bible societies. These societies were quite prepared to undertake publication, and harnessed their considerable and growing organizations to the task of providing funds to meet the costs. For the best use of their funds, they adopted only one text in any given language, and thus prevented the divisions between the missions from being reflected in different versions of the Bible for any single language field. Orthography was stabilized for all writers in the language, and dialectal variation much reduced when people came to write their own notes and letters. It was and is a principle of the Bible Societies that while Bibles destined for impoverished groups may be sold at less than cost price, only the helplessly destitute may be given free copies. Probably the first introduction of many Africans to the working of industrial production and monetary economy beyond the transactions of the local market has come through explanations why, though the grace of God is free, the book which is for Protestants the principal means of grace is withheld until money is found to pay for it.

The missionaries, however, did not wait helplessly until the Bible Societies were supplied with acceptable manuscripts and had stocks of Bible portions to send out to them. Printing like so much else in their day had not developed much beyond a handicraft. The apparatus could be transported in small packages which could be managed even by porters, and many stations had printing presses from which they were able to provide themselves with school primers and short Bible portions to meet local needs and test experimental versions. Some like the Morija Press in Basutoland have proved to be worth maintaining into the period of easy transport of books printed by the great presses in Europe and America.

African apprentices were soon enrolled and proved capable learners of the craft of printing, thus contributing considerably to African morale in the face of the many mysteries claiming wonder in the white men's settlements. The local presses also published small sheets of news and comments, in which Africans were mentioned by name, and sometimes had contributions printed. This all contributed to a sense of symbiosis in the neighbourhood of the stations. In spite of the fact that the stations were purposely developed to enable European standards and sometimes mere conventions to be maintained in the African environment, and to this end excluded more and more of the African culture around them, the African culture kept in contact through more and more individuals adjusting themselves to the European standard. The difference between this development and that envisaged by the founders of the stations was that the adjustment was apt to be made in a spirit of defiant response to a challenge rather than obedience to a commanding call.

It was observed by a Livingstonia missionary that when the period of peril to life and liberty from slave-raiding had passed, the people around him gladly accepted the right they were assured they had of self-determination, and became 'every man a chief'. They rejected social discipline and were not very amenable to missionary direction. Over the same period, on the stations, schoolboys went on strike ostensibly in protest sometimes against the food provided for them as boarders, sometimes against the garden work required of them. Apprentices bound by indentures absconded in considerable numbers, and when found and brought before a magistrate, complained that an apprentice now was just what a slave had been. All this exasperated and to some degree puzzled the missionaries. They might have been enlightened had they been able to hear a speaker to the Royal Commonwealth Society in October 1964 tell of a young delinquent explaining a theft he had committed as protest against 'being done good to and laboured among'. This is an obvious borrowing of now outmoded missionary language, which was however commonly used and widely published over a long period of mission history. It was quite accessible to any African who could read English, and the attitude could be felt by those who could not. They no longer needed patrons, and could express their dislike of being patronized.

For those who read this as simply lawless rejection of discipline, the episode of the Prophet Harris movement in West Africa at about the same time should have provoked thought. It was admitted that in a mission lasting about two years he brought more people to profess Christian faith than all the orthodox missions in the area had done over two generations. His inspiration was a conviction that he had received the Holy Spirit; accordingly he spoke with a conviction of immediate authority which few or no missionaries of the older churches would claim. His preaching was apparently orthodox but simple, but his baptismal formula and ritual included laying his Bible on the head and saying, 'This is God's Book, you must obey it.' When he was taken into detention by political authorities during the war in 1915, his hearers continued to spread the doctrine of abandoning animistic beliefs and brutal rituals, and obeying the Bible, which not many seem to have been able to read. The Prophet himself read portions in a vernacular translation, but his movement survived and spread on the distribution among the congregations of English and French Bibles.

It seems that the effective element in his movement was his authoritative command 'Obey'. He did not call for obedience to himself, he made no personal profit from the obedience. He founded no station, he built up no material going concern which had to be kept going. Nor, apparently, did he argue and demonstrate reasonableness. He did not establish schools to enable illiterates to read the Book which they had to obey. They had to follow his pattern of obedience as they saw it or heard of it. It may be suggested that this simplification, unintended but implicit in the nature of the preaching and its background, gave liberty from the unmanageable complexities of historic Christianity making demands on new adherents; while the demand to obey within the narrow limits of what they learned offered a safe outlet for active aspiration. The fact that the principal command was to turn against the powerful and fear-inspiring animistic practice of local religion, and so was a demand on courage, invoked an element not prominent in the station-based religion of the missions.

One may say in fact that Christianity in Africa was a soft religion, dispirited under a vast inheritance of alien, even if intellectually supported, tradition. Protest, when it began to be made, designated this inheritance as Westernism, and linked itself with general reaction against white men's arrogant complacency in the possession of power. In fact the deficiency is more exactly described in a statement coming from a meeting of the All Africa Church Conference in 1962: 'The main approach (by missions of the older churches) has been largely intellectual and catechetical.' This was based on St. Paul's requirement that the Christian should be able to give a reason for the faith that was in him. In practice the reasons smothered the faith, or rather preceded and inhibited it, in some missionaries as well as in African hearers.

As the habituation of Africans to European culture grew

through education and social contact with rapidly increasing numbers of European immigrants, it became apparent to them that they could choose what they wanted from the vast complexity of that culture. This choice, involving rejection of control, is being exercised with different results by different individuals and common interest groups. Some in the Christian field have accepted the possibility of being 'younger churches', taking over the mission stations and expressing desire to have European teaching members made available to them by what were originally missionary sending churches. These continue up to the present in the intellectual and rational tradition of the missions. Others have abandoned the burden of alien tradition and made their own new start from particular Biblical passages. So long as these groups have a self-confident prophet they share his spiritual confidence; but when they lose such a leader, their responsible members tend to return to what the conference already quoted called 'the heritage of centuries of Christian thought and experience'; but they now seek the theological college when they have one available, not the mission station where the attempt was made to bring all life into a rounded Christian discipline.

To the pioneers of Protestant missions it would have been inconceivable that there should be a fear of freedom, and they did not recognize how far this was responsible for such success as they had in imposing godly discipline. They regarded a community as the convergence of like-minded individuals exercising free choice and sound judgement, and did not realize that their teaching to that end was wrecking existing communities most of whose members would not attain the judgement to form immediately new ties. They overestimated their own acceptability, not giving enough weight to the fact that friendship with some Africans would alienate others. We have seen the end of a stage, in which the cumulative effect of all these overtook the field missionaries, while their central directors devised policies to meet principally the political rise of independent Africans. It seems doubtful whether any constructive approach has been made to the contradictions which spoiled the missionaries' dream of a new early church rising on the foundations of the Bible in the language of the people, and the free expression in word and deed of Christian goodwill.

SUGGESTIONS FOR FURTHER READING

Reports of Commissions of the World Missionary Conference, 1910.
Reports of subsequent Missionary conferences at Le Zoute, 1927; and Tambaram, 1938.
The Planting of Christianity in Africa. Vol. 3, by C. P. Groves (Lutterworth, 1955).
The Shire Highlands as Mission and Colony, by J. Buchanan (Blackwood, Edinburgh, 1885).
The Rise of our East African Empire, by F. D. Lugard (Blackwood, Edinburgh, 1893).

Résumé

LA LUTTE MISSIONNAIRE CONTRE LA COMPLEXITÉ

Les activités missionnaires des églises protestantes européennes s'inspirèrent des principes de l'éclairement intellectuel et de la liberté personnelle. Ces principes se heurtèrent très gravement en Afrique à l'institution de l'esclavage et à l'ignorance des révélations et des découvertes connues ailleurs dans le monde. L'ignorance la plus déplorable était celle des Écritures Chrétiennes.

Pour remédier à cette situation il fallait mettre au point des commentaires bibliques et former la population à lire de façon compréhensive. Des besoins existants en dehors de l'Afrique avaient déjà suscité la création de sociétés bibliques capables de surmonter les problèmes techniques de la reproduction et de la distribution bénévoles de la Bible. Sa nécessité de s'en remettre à ces services permit d'éviter le développement de sectarianisme entre des groupes de missionnaires isolés et pleins de zèle pour les principes auxquels l'exercice de leur propre jugement les avaient menés. En fait la participation des sociétés bibliques aux activités missionnaires assura, même si cela n'était pas intentionnellement, que dans chaque zone linguistique un seul texte de la Bible et une seule orthographe de la langue écrite soient utilisés.

Mais la Bible n'est pas seulement quelque chose qui doit être transmise aux ignorants. Elle constituait pour tous les missionnaires, quelles que soient leurs différences d'interprétation externe, une source de puissance et de réconfort fréquemment consultée. Les missionnaires en brousse de même que les éditeurs considéraient que la Bible pouvait indiquer directement à tout lecteur compréhensif ce dont Dieu savait qu'il avait besoin. Cette conviction les liait les-uns aux autres et justifiait leurs prétentions à la direction de sociétés qui leur étaient étrangères.

Le travail médical des missions concordait avec l'un des intérêts et domaines d'activités des Africains. Leur acceptation de ces efforts donna aux premiers missionnaires l'impression qu'il y avait plus de points communs entre leurs valeurs et celle des Africains que ce n'était le cas en réalité. On supposait que les Africains allaient accepter avec reconnaissance tous les éléments de la culture religieuse européenne si on leur montrait l'ensemble du système de vie. On établit des stations missionnaires non seulement pour fournir des conditions de vie saines en refusant une partie du milieu local mais aussi pour donner un exemple. Le contrôle fût obtenu par l'acquisition de parcelles de terrain. On ne comprit pas immédiatement que la conception du droit de propriété n'était pas la même chez les acheteurs que chez les vendeurs. Mais au début les stations constituaient entre les étrangers et les indigènes un lieu de contact en termes de patrons et employés ce qui permit de mettre à l'épreuve la confiance des deux côtés. Les activités auxquelles prenaient part les employés à la station étaient en général compréhensibles par rapport à leur propre culture mais ceci tout en utilisant des outils plus perfectionnés et en travaillant à une plus grande échelle. A cet égard les membres artisans de la mission exercèrent une autorité qui resta identifiée à la station missionnaire.

Les Africains qui vivaient à l'intérieur des limites de la station adoptèrent les caractéristiques externes de la vie européenne: costume, conventions et langue dans une certaine mesure. Ceux qui étaient prêts à subir le choc d'une telle adaptation étaient pour la plupart des gens qui ne se sentaient pas en sécurité au sein de la société tribale: esclaves réfugiés ou survivants de communautés dispersées ou encore des personnes accusées de sorcellerie. Ils voulaient à la fois essayer de s'identifier à une communauté forte et s'opposer à la discipline, alors que leur adhérence à la mission discréditait cette dernière aux yeux des autorités indigènes établies. Le gouvernement impérial reprimait toute tentative d'hostilité ouverte de la part de ces autorités et était accepté comme un collaborateur des efforts missionnaires.

Dans les écoles qui constituaient le moyen essentiel de remodelage de la vie et la pensée africaines, but de l'action missionnaire, l'autorité missionnaire s'exerçait sans s'excuser ou se cacher. Mais une bonne part de cet enseignement impliquait que chaque individu a le droit et le devoir de décider par lui-même de ses croyances et de sa conduite. Lorsque des entreprises européennes laïques commencèrent à offrir des emplois lucratifs à ceux disposant de la culture nouvelle acquise dans les écoles, beaucoup d'élèves des missions se virent à même de rejeter les directives missionnaires. Certains adoptèrent une attitude de défiance offensante pour leurs nouveaux patrons également et attirèrent à l'égard des efforts missionnaires des critiques européennes. Néanmoins, les stations missionnaires et leurs écoles étaient la seule voie permettant de quitter la sphère de plus en plus étroite de la vie traditionnelle pour se lancer dans la vie moderne et les écoles continuèrent à instruire ceux qui le demandaient. La perte de confiance de la part des missionnaires se refléta dans le fait qu'ils cessèrent d'emmener en congé avec eux leurs meilleurs éléments car ils n'étaient plus sûrs de leur stabilité.

Parallèlement à ces activités des stations, certains des missionnaires les plus estimés sortirent des limites des stations et commencèrent à s'associer avec des africains très proches de culture africaine. Les catéchumènes des stations n'étaient pas suffisamment mûrs ou dignes de confiance pour servir d'informants sur les langues locales: cependant les traductions de la Bible exigeaient une connaissance profonde et étendue de la langue alors que les habitudes ecclésiastiques demandaient un style solennel. Et c'étaient les anciens de la communauté africaine qui détenaient la dignité et la connaissance, ou du moins le savoir ancestral véritable. C'était à eux que devaient s'adresser les missionnaires. Ils venaient les écouter et apprendre avec patience. C'est ainsi qu'ils apprirent beaucoup de choses qui leur firent estimer la culture africaine et émoussèrent quelque peu leur zèle destructeur. Mais les traductions de la Bible copièrent le style des anciens et lorsque l'énergie et la fraîcheur de la jeunesse devinrent populaires, en lui-même, le fait qu'il n'existait qu'une seule version de la Bible assura sa dévaluation.

La compréhension de ce qui avait été un mystère au début incita les jeunes à se révolter. L'expérience pratique révéla qu'en fait beaucoup de soi-disant mystères n'étaient que le produit de techniques qu'il était possible d'apprendre. L'un des mystères les plus impressionnants était celui du livre imprimé. Même lorsque l'on avait appris à le lire, le mystère de son origine demeurait. Mais beaucoup de stations missionnaires avaient dans leur matériel une presse à imprimer. Quoique cette technique n'ait eu aucun fondement dans la culture africaine, ces apprentis parvinrent à s'en servir et, à partir de cela, l'idée germa que les africains pourraient arriver à produire et à posséder tout ce que les européens avaient.

Ceci impliquait la fin de la soumission aux maîtres qui leur avaient enseigné le rejet de la soumission aux autorités traditionnelles.

Les espoirs des missionnaires qui pensaient qu'une simple soumission à la puissance serait remplacée par une conformité raisonnée aux idéaux chrétiens tels qu'ils étaient exprimés au sein de l'organisation missionnaire se trouvèrent déçus. Des grèves dans les écoles et des engagements rompus de la part des apprentis fûrent certaines des manifestations de ce désir d'indépendance. Néanmoins on avait encore besoin d'écoles et d'apprentissage et il fallait imposer l'obéissance.

En Afrique Occidentale à l'époque, le prophète Harris avait suscité la création d'une communauté importante, fidèle mais dispersée qui fondait sur une promesse d'obéir 'au Livre de Dieu'. Il ne semble pas qu'il ait exigé que les membres de la communauté examinent les Ecritures ou même soient suffisamment instruits pour le faire. L'essentiel de ce culte semble en fait avoir été de refuser de s'engager dans les rites des religions animistes locales: une exigence positive demandant du courage et forçant les membres du groupe à s'entr'aider. Le prophète ne vivait pas au sein d'un groupe donné agissant comme un censeur ou incitant les fidèles à des efforts de plus en plus durs. De plus, il est peut-être important de noter qu'il ne vivait pas de manière plus prospère que ses adhérents et ne profitait aucunement de leur obéissance. Contrairement à la majorité des missionnaires, il était conscient de la révélation de l'Esprit Saint et n'éprouvait pas le besoin européen de justifier sa position par des raisonnements logiques. La présentation de la religion de Harris ne demandait que très peu de réflexion.

La situation dans les stations missionnaires était tout autre. La préparation évangélique était longue et intellectuellement ardue, la supervision et le contrôle rigides. On exigeait l'obéissance à un code de conventions détaillé. Les résultats que l'on peut observer ont amené beaucoup d'observateurs à suggérer que les exigences étaient trop fortes.

L'autorité étrangère européenne s'est retirée dans une très grande mesure des 'églises nouvelles' qui ont cependant des rapports bien établis avec les églises orthodoxes à l'étranger. Cette autorité n'a jamais été officiellement admise par les 'églises indépendantes'. Une nouvelle ère s'est ouverte pour la réconciliation de la liberté et de l'obéissance.

PART TWO

THE ANALYTICAL PERSPECTIVE

INTRODUCTORY REVIEW: THE ENGAGEMENT OF CHRISTIANITY WITH AFRICAN CONCEPTS AND WAY OF LIFE

(a) THE 'WHY' AND 'HOW' OF CONVERSION

In introducing Dr. Gray's paper for discussion Professor Low suggested that a new starting-point in the consideration of the modern history of Africa might be found in recognizing, as one of its basic features,

> the fact that it has witnessed the impact of an industrialised high culture upon a vast area with no industry and no indigenous high culture of its own, and has seen this area making a highly creative response to this impact and to the new situation and the new opportunities which it has opened up. Africa in this respect is unique among the continents of the world. Other areas which have made such a response have had high cultures, or borrowed high cultures, of their own: no other area *without* a high culture has made a positive response—the Australian Aborigines have not, nor have the North American Indians.
>
> These considerations are of great importance for Christian history. Usually a great deal is made of the astonishing spread of Christianity in the last two thousand years into every continent and country. Nowhere, however, has Christianity as yet made a decisive invasion of the strongholds of the other world religions. Christianity, indeed, has nowhere been as successful against them as some of them have been against each other, and as one of them has been against Christianity. There is no Christian parallel to the Buddhist victory over Hinduism; Hinduism's victory over Buddhism; Islam's success in India against Hinduism, or in the Middle East against Christianity. Christianity had a great triumph in the Roman world, and from there spread to the rest of the Western world. Outside the West, however, it is only in Africa that Christianity has known major success in another major cultural area; and this means that the spread of Christianity to Africa is a topic of far greater importance in Christian history than is generally recognised.

M. Bureau's theory of a 'crisis of disillusionment' following upon the first wave of evangelization and the penetration of Western administration, trade, and ways of life in general, of which evangelization formed part, received much interested discussion. The 'crisis' was characterized by a lessening of the practice of Christianity and a return, at a deeper level, to pagan culture. How did this 'crisis' manifest itself: in the loss of faith itself or in a certain lassitude in practice only? Is it always accompanied by actual defection to animism, Islam, or materialism? When does it set in: with the second or third generation of Christians, and is it the old or the young who are most affected? Is the crisis precipitated by inadequate Christian training or the resurgence of repressed traditional practices or any other forms of religious pressure? Are similar phenomena observable in animism or Islam? Does the rapidity of christianization bear any relation to the intensity of the crisis when it comes? Can this crisis be seen as part of the inevitable disintegration of any closed society on the impact of an aggressive higher culture? Is it possible to construct a typology with reference to the length and rhythm of evangelization, missionary methods, and the psychology of the people evangelized?

Some relapse must be expected after a period of mass conversions, or a time during which to get baptized was regarded as more or less fashionable, but it must be noted that considerable numbers always remained faithful to the newly-adopted religion. More remarkable still is the fact that this 'disillusionment' following evangelization need not only result in movements away from Christianity and the Gospel, what one might call 'reversionary' or backward-looking crises, although it apparently describes the situation found by M. Bureau among the Duala. 'Disillusionment' can also result in specifically Christian movements seeking to arrive at the satisfaction which, it is felt, is actually present in the Gospel but has somehow not been passed on by the missions. The 'crisis' came among the Luo (Western Kenya) in 1940–50, i.e. in the second generation of evangelization (which began in 1902). After some forty years of rapid church growth there were twenty years of revivalism and independent church formation. The East African Revival, which first came to Luo country in 1937, is the best example. Luo members of this Revival are now thought to number 10,000, and their whole organization is based on the truth summed up in their daily greeting *Yesu romo* ('Jesus satisfies'), which is also a widespread greeting among Revival members in other parts of East Africa, i.e. they claim to have recovered the *satisfaction* inherent in the Gospel that was not manifest in the missions' presentation of it.

It must be remembered that, in any case, historical study is always *ex post facto*, permitting conjectures and hypotheses to be developed to explain what happened in psychological and sociological terms. Professor Low's paper on the first conversions to Christianity in Buganda affords an excellent example of how unpredictable and *ad hoc* some of the determinative factors in the evangelistic situation may be. His thesis that the earliest Buganda conversions were not merely the result of faithful missionary work (or else why was this not equally successful in Muslim or Hindu societies?) but of sociological change was supported by Mr. Welbourn who had come to a similar conclusion working along different lines. The story of Muslim martyrdom ten years prior to the Christian underlined the centrality of political issues in the whole matter of conversions. In fact it was almost a historical accident that Buganda became a dynamic Christian instead of a dynamic Muslim Kingdom. While it was not unlikely that the Baganda drew a distinction between Arab slavers and Christian missionaries, the assumption that ethical values and relations of the religious system to political needs were qualitatively different in Islam and Christianity could not be maintained. If Islam had had a longer period in Buganda it might have struck deeper roots, and it must be remembered that Christian missionaries were professionals in a way the Arab Muslims were not.

The basic role of politics in this religious change is further emphasized by the fact that 'religion' does not occur in the Ganda vocabulary except as an Arabic word introduced to describe the imported religions. Mr. Welbourn sees Buganda life as being concurrently defined in empirical and mythological terms. In the mythological statements 'I am Allah's' or 'I am Christ's' some Baganda found a phantasy structure and an identity which harmonized with the new political structure, and when faced with the alternative of death or of denying Allah/Christ, they chose death because only so could they affirm their identity. This thesis is further discussed in Mr. Welbourn's book *Religion and Politics in Uganda 1952–1962*. But Dr. Mbiti recalled that upon questioning, some of the earliest Ganda Christians had given such reasons as the following for their conversion: 'We saw that the missionaries loved us; they came to us; they visited us; they ate with us', or 'we were told that if we believed we would go to Heaven where there is no death or suffering'. The question was therefore whether sociological or political considerations alone provided an adequate explanation of the facts. What was their religion to these young men who preferred to die rather than give it up: simply the way of the white men as distinguished from that of the Arabs? Or a more efficacious spiritual power than that of traditional religion? Was it perhaps that they believed the Christian missionaries to be better and more powerful men than the Arab slavers? What evidence is there that they hoped to gain personal advancement or national expansion? Did they not have an inner religiosity which found fulfilment in Christianity? What does a historian do with such facts as the Resurrection and the empty tomb which have been such potent factors in history?

(b) CHRISTIANITY AND AFRICAN CULTURE: SOME PSYCHOLOGICAL IMPLICATIONS OF THE ENCOUNTER

The discussion introduced by Father Schuyler emphasized at the outset the extreme difficulty of scientifically assessing the complex relationship of two concepts which in themselves are very far from clear or unequivocal. Not only the perennial controversy over the authentic interpretation of its essence but also its extremely variegated historical presentation makes 'Christianity' a term without precise connotation. In the African context it has been associated with, *inter alia*, mixed motivations, strange alliances, concern for earthly gain (even if for apostolic purposes), involvement with political, economic, and other social interests; the world has known Christian slavers, exploiters, racists, bribers, prostitutes, murderous mercenaries, polygamists, etc.

As to African culture, whether such a definable entity could be said to exist at all was the subject of debate. Mr. Welbourn in particular felt strongly that at best the term could only signify an unwarrantable turning of scholars' analyses of specific societies into basic features applicable to all. 'We still need particular studies of particular societies. There is not one "African Personality" but *many* African cultures. We dare not talk of "African Culture", "African Theology", "African Life and Thought". These are all things which may develop as particular Africans try to discover a truth which is independent of Africa . . . but the pan-African *eschaton* is not yet here. . . . Any conscious attempt to be African will fail; only by being man will the African be African.' Again while on the one hand some very general features of African cultures can be distinguished, e.g. extended family and the sense and values of family continuity, pre-eminence of communal concerns, institutionalized subordination (in the moral and socio-political senses), tribalism, relatively closed societies, importance of bodily expression, symbols, etc., on the other hand there is wide variety and constant change resulting from education and social mobility, from different levels of cultural growth and of community aspirations and such other factors as urbanization, industrialization, diffusion of western techniques, political power and ideologies, etc. Thus it is not easy to obtain conceptual clarity in such a discussion or to determine which of the many voices is the authentic African voice. However, it was agreed that the terms represented identifiable entities obviously inter-related in the African scene. Some older works such as Edwin Smith's *The Golden Stool* and Mary Kingsley's writings have usefully discussed the relationship and are still most helpful in introducing outsiders to an understanding of the situation as a whole.

Recent productions in African literature and art have been stimulated by Christianity: for example, Christ has been represented as a coloured man contemplating the modern African scene. A large number of poems on Christian themes has already been published in Swahili, and novels are exploring areas of African life within the context of Christian training and ideals ('mission boys', etc.). Church music is also developing in African idioms as, for example, the 'Missa Luba'; in Ghana the Methodists have made very effective use of Fanti lyrics, i.e. simple Christian statements set to traditional dirge music.

Efforts to discover suitable African forms have been in progress also in architecture for Christian use. Is there in all this a danger that the Church in African might become an inward and backward-looking community unable to speak with knowledge and convincing authority to the present and the future? Surely, for example, the question in Christian architecture is not whether church buildings are African or European, but whether their style fits their use? Some even take the stand that, since African cultures are crumbling anyway before the advance of technology and industrialization one must abandon all efforts to preserve them in order to concentrate on preparation for the age of science.

It must be borne in mind that the present ways of expressing Christianity in Africa were first developed at a time when the rule was for Africans to seek to become like Europeans. The result is that forms, which have now become traditional features of the Christian milieu, are plainly alien to the general environment and strike observers more or less forcibly as such. But, unless a Christian happens also to be consciously an Africanist, African forms are likely to be strange and unattractive to him. Objection has been raised by Africans to the use of African symbolism in church architecture, dress, decorative art, and liturgy. Missions have been censured as much for trying to preserve African cultures as for destroying them. The highly successful indigenizing efforts by thoughtful leaders such as Bishop Lucas of Masasi were not generally welcomed, neither has the enthusiasm of many missions to work in the local languages been universally appreciated.

What is here at stake really is the very important question of the identity of the African Christian. Is he a black Westerner or, if not, what is he? In order to become a Christian must the African cease to be African? India has been in a similar quandary. After wrestling with the problem of whether, because of his entire upbringing and the manner of living which he had adopted and in which he felt at home, he had become a brown European, Nehru discovered, as in a flash of inspired insight, that his real identity was that of an heir to the whole marvellous cultural heritage of India. This realization unleashed in him the deep satisfaction and release that are reflected in his book *The Discovery of India.* Japan did not encounter this problem of uncertainty about its own identity because the period of its modernization or westernization coincided with the restoration of its traditional emperorship.

The difficulty for Africa is of course that it has never had a general high culture of its own. Thus the attempt to be consciously African must be understood as a rejection of a previous attempt to be European as well as being a reaction against the European-imposed sense of African cultural inadequacy, or of guilt for the sin of Ham inculcated by fundamentalist Bible interpretation. The 'Négritude' movement has taken the line of seeking sympathetic understanding and appreciation for the characteristic features of African life and its folkways, and appears to have spent itself in evolving a 'deep', intricate, and rather wordy literary style. 'The African Personality' has (at least in Ghana) been employed as an expression of self-confidence that admits no need to apologize to anybody for things and manners African. The Yoruba attitude was reported to be that those who had lost their culture might need to parade it; Nigerians had not and so had no such need. However, the necessity to accept much that is obviously not of African origin evokes a reaction and there is continuing tension with Europeans who are ambivalently regarded with admiration and as an influence to be eliminated by Africans (see, for example, G. Jahoda: *White Man*). Probably this is a fertile seed-bed for guilt feelings.

The search must continue for an identity which ensures to all African Christians, Africanist and non-Africanist alike, a satisfying self-consciousness and dignity in social and inter-racial relations. If the definition of this identity has so far been predominantly in nationalistic terms, probably reflecting the Protestant emphasis upon personal freedom from external control, this must be supplemented by the reflection that a Christian comes from God and goes to God; his citizenship is in heaven, i.e. his total and final value systems extend well beyond those of his own culture. Full realization of the potentialities of genuine Christian culture within the African context will involve both the working out of a clear Christian mind regarding this context and of an equally clear African mind concerning Christian values and ideals. If the last named are to be generally acknowledged and made fruitful for personal and social development, there would need to be co-operation with compatible secular forces, with fellow Christians of all denominations and with sound non-Christian religious and moral influences. On the part of evangelists at all levels there is need for understanding and sympathetic appreciation as well as for a more competent and relevant communication of the Christian faith and all that it implies.

Mr. Welbourn's paper introduces a fresh point of departure in the consideration of these matters, namely the whole area of the unconscious, and invites examination of the unconscious motivations of some Christian preachers, the unconscious level of receptivity of African hearers, and some observable results that may be attributed to the interaction of these unconscious factors. Are traditional (or 'tribal') societies psychologically equipped to enter into understanding relations with either religious missionaries preaching individual salvation from an oppressive sense of guilt or administrative missionaries who impose a physically sanctioned dogma of individual responsibility for social order and prosperity? Can the gospel of cleansing from guilt be intelligibly preached to people who know only shame? Can Christian teaching create, or promise, a society in which no person will be ashamed and the society find life eternal? Father Mulago criticized the denial to Africans of a sense of guilt, stating that in Bashi speech there were words for 'sin' and 'contrition'. M. Bureau reported that in Cameroon the word for 'sin' meant 'to go against custom', and that a person believed to have brought trouble on his group accepts this judgement even though consciously innocent.

Father LaRoche has come to the conclusion that guilt was consciousness of offence against the One God, which Africans distinguished from social offences expiated by sacrifice, and that the latter tended to stifle the former. Dr. Grau, agreeing, was of the view that guilt was related to sin, and not all were sensible of it; shame concerned the self and a sense of humiliation. Dr. Mbiti said that his people regarded as 'sin' offences against the 'living' (familial) dead, by injury or negligence; they did not feel they could offend God. M. Bureau suggested that clarity might come by applying the notion of intention to 'sin'. Dr. Freeman-Grenville drew attention to Arabic reports of long exhortations to repentance in medieval East Africa, but it was not clear whether they were addressed to Africans. The only non-Arabic Swahili word for misdoing covers offences from sin to slips of the tongue.

Mr. Price, who opened the discussion on Mr. Welbourn's paper, had remarked that people busy with pressing conscious demands and opportunities were a little out of their depth in matters relating by definition to the unconscious; they had to depend upon psycho-analytic specialists for estimates of the nature and importance of these issues, and did not find all that is said convincing. With regard to the question whether 'grace' is available only to the guilt-conscious, it would seem that here we are in a different universe of discourse and that if this term signifies the remedy for the humanly irremediable, then the stated limitation is invalid.

(c) A NOTE ON TYPES OF RELIGIOUS SOCIETY, BY THE REV. F. B. WELBOURN

Prompted by Professor Shepperson's paper (pp. 249–68) Mr. Welbourn prepared this note which seeks to relate Ethiopianism in Africa to a wider perspective and a more comprehensive analysis of the forms of religious movements:

I

Professor Shepperson is, it seems to me, making a plea for a terminology in relation to independent churches, which is at least consistent. There are several factors which have to be taken into account in attempting this. There is, first, the existing terminology which was rehatched, as Professor Shepperson says, at Mindolo in 1962. It is based on independency in Africa (as is already implied by the name 'Ethiopianism'), and I want to ask whether any terminology—indeed, any study—of independency is adequate which confines the phenomena to Africa. I cannot myself be happy with a schematization which omits the early schisms in the Church, the millenarian movements described by Cohn in Europe of the eleventh to sixteenth centuries, the Reformation, and the contemporary multiplication of sects in England and America—let alone the rest of the 'undeveloped' world. Separatism is, perhaps paradoxically, one; and I think this means that we must at once drop the term 'Ethiopianism' except as a description of one set of local varieties.

Secondly, I cannot be happy with a scheme which ignores the essential connexions, within Africa itself, between religious separatism and political nationalism or tribalist movements such as Mau Mau. It is not only (as Hodgkin has pointed out) that political discontent may find its first expression in religious symbolism. It is also that there is a direct connexion, in the slogan 'Africa for the Africans', between the ideas of pure Ethiopianism and of political pan-Africanism; and direct connexion also through particular persons who were leaders of religious independency before passing into a political party. Discontent, like separatism, is one. Some movements may be more obviously the concern of political scientists, others of Church historians. It is for the latter that we are seeking a terminology; but it must be a terminology which recognizes no ultimate divide.

Thirdly, we have to take into account Professor Low's emphasis on the possibility of finding conviction and enthusiasm in orthodoxy in Africa as well as in separatism. With this I would want to link his recognition that an ardent Christianity is not just a reflection of the vitality of the faith, but is often a vehicle for political yearnings. Not only independency, but orthodoxy too may be both enthusiastic and politically orientated.

Fourthly, we have to ask why Roman Catholicism is so much less prone to separatism than Protestantism. It is possible that now at last we have in Maria Legio among the Luo a large-scale African schism from Rome, M. Bureau may be able to give us an answer in his forthcoming study.

Fifthly, Maria Legio draws attention to the fact that African separatism may still occur in the post-colonial period. One has to be careful here, for an important motive of Maria Legio is the expulsion of expatriate missionaries. It may be a delayed bubble from the colonial cauldron. Similarly, Professor Shepperson mentions that Lumpa in Zambia and African Jehovah's Witnesses in Malawi have embarrassed independent African governments. But their institutional origin was in colonial days. So far as I know, only the Religion of Jehovah and Michael among the Chunya of Tanzania has actually come into being since independence and is said to be a challenge to the authoritarianism of local TANU officials. But this is enough for my purpose. We must have a formula which does not suggest that independency *as such* is a product of colonialism. Lanternari holds this view uncritically. Even Sundkler, who is in a sense the master of us all, has given it support. It may, indeed, be true that African separatism in the last hundred years has been due precisely to colonialism; and it may be that African separatism is such a large-scale phenomenon that it should be isolated and given a terminology of its own. But this seems to me to be once again the heresy of Africanism. I have pleaded for particular studies of religion in Africa over against the eschatological vagueness of the African Personality. Only so, it seems to me, can particular Africans, who are still after all primarily Yoruba or Akan or Ganda, find their proper place in the community of men—find, that is, by being men, what it is to be African men. At the same time I ask that each independent movement—gaining its particular characteristics from the fact that it is a movement among particular African men in particular African towns and villages—should be set against the background of independency in the world at large.

II

I should like to try to do this by setting up five ideal types of religious society, recognizing quite clearly that we are never likely to find them concretely except in mixed form.

The first is that of a simple unitary society, such as traditional African societies are often said to be, in which every empirical event has a mythological co-ordinate. Life is lived not only in the horizontal dimension of secular relationships but in the vertical dimension of relationship with the living dead (or whatever is equivalent to them). It is this vertical dimension which gives stability and meaning to the whole three-dimensional social structure. If I were speaking psycho-analytically, I should want to put the same thing by saying that, in the ideal type I am describing, the same social structure provides not only the best empirical means available for getting things done but also, through its mythological overtones, provides a means of acting out the unconscious phantasies. (Perhaps I can illustrate this from a traditional English merchant ship, where the first mate is not only the efficient executive through whom work is organized; he is also a 'shit' and knows that he must accept this mythological role so long as he holds this particular empirical position. He thus makes it possible for the captain to be mythologically wholly good and elicit the empirical obedience demanded of a ship's company at sea.) It is clear, I think, that totalitarian societies are attempts to return to a unitary experience of this character. But the interdependence of the mythological with the empirical, of unconscious phantasy with conscious rational behaviour, or religion with politics, is a reality in *every* society and may become overt unexpectedly. An independent church may turn overnight into an active nationalist movement. A political party may discover the need for churchgoing.

The second ideal type is described in Saint Peter's first epistle, when he speaks of Christians as strangers and pilgrims—men who are committed to full participation in an earthly society but whose citizenship is in heaven—whose total value system, if you prefer it, is derived from outside the particular culture in which they live. This is the peculiarly Christian version of the unitary state which inevitably involves tensions. If it is not to lead to wholesale persecution of Christians on grounds of sedition, it must also mean compromises—and these may be of an individual or an institutional nature. The most obvious institutional compromise is that which sets up separate institutions to deal respectively with phantasy and rational needs. We get Church and

State as separate, even if interdependent, institutions. It is not a satisfactory solution, since the Church soon claims the right to interfere in empirical affairs, and the State begins to develop its own secular mythology. But as a solution it has been tried in at least two forms.

One of them is the third ideal type—what I want to call the Catholic type which, to invert Luther, believes that *cuius religio eius regio*. In any dispute, the Church must always have the last word. But it retains the idea that the Church is for all men, irrespective of empirical boundaries which may divide them. Identity is defined in eschatological terms: 'I come from God and go to God.' The fact that I live in a particular country under a particular ruler is entirely secondary to the fact that both I and my ruler are subject to God.

In Europe this type of solution broke down. We got instead the fourth ideal type—the Protestant type. The role of the two institutions is reversed. It is now *cuius regio eius religio*. Identity is defined empirically in terms of nationality. I want to suggest that this is the fundamental character of Protestantism. In its Anglican, Calvinist, and Lutheran forms it insisted that to be truly Protestant was to be at the same time truly Catholic. It wanted to retain the world-wide character of Christianity but to be free of alien control. Of course, a lot of other things were happening in Europe at that time: developments in rationality, in empirical science, in capitalism, in the whole scale of mobility and intellectual experience. Nationalism and Protestantism got mixed up in them all and cross-fertilized them all. Therefore the Counter-Reformation was negatively involved with them all. But, if I am right in thinking that the essence of Protestantism lies precisely in the rejection of alien control, in the principle *cuius regio*, then it is a term which can also be applied, for instance, to the Monophysites in Egypt, the Donatists in North Africa *and* to the Ethiopian movement of modern Africa. Moreover, it is important that, when they moved into a colonial situation, the European Protestant missions and nations reverted to the Catholic—if not indeed to the unitary—type. Once more *religio* determined the right to *regio*. But this time it was the religion not of Christ but of the white man's burden. The dominant myth of both Church and State (and this applied as much to Catholic as to Protestant missions) had become the superiority of white civilization and the obligation to impose it on even unwilling savages. Ethiopianism is a 'Protestant' response to an alien church of 'Catholic' type; and we must not be deceived by the fact that most of the alien churches concerned continued to proclaim their uncompromising Protestantism. They were deceiving themselves. Similarly, in a different situation, the Religion of Jehovah and Michael is a Protestant response to TANU 'Catholicism'.

The fifth type has been called the sect type. I want here to call it the Healing type, whether the healing is spiritual or physical. (In Hebrew and Greek there is no distinction.) Against the large changes of which Protestantism was a part, it is legitimate to suppose that men were losing identity rather alarmingly. Short of finding a new identity—and, the more complex society becomes, the more difficult is it to find anything better than a number of interlocking roles—one possible accommodation is to let the superego take over the functions of the ego and develop the driving Anglo-Saxon conscience. If this fails, there is the possibility of an evangelical conversion—of becoming a member of a sect which offers healing from guilt. But the symptoms of a lost identity may not be sense of guilt. They may be psychosomatic, or persecutory illusions. They may simply be loneliness. Healing is still required; and one or other Healing sect sets about offering it. Thus we get most of the fundamentalist sects of England and America, the Zionist and Aladura churches of Africa—and, of course, those Christians who revert to more traditional types of healing.

III

Once we get a Healing group, it would not be surprising if it showed some of the same characteristics as W. R. Bion[1] has observed in therapeutic groups established by psycho-analysts. He thinks that such groups, in addition to their acceptance of the

[1] 'Group Dynamics: a Re-View', in M. Klein, ed., *New Directions in Psycho-Analysis*, Tavistock Publications, 1955, Chap. 19.

rational purpose of healing for which they have come together, are motivated by three wholly unconscious, mutually incompatible but spontaneously interchangeable, patterns of behaviour, whose origins he traces to basic levels of psychological organization.

(i) The first he calls the 'dependent' pattern, in which the whole group looks to the leader to get things done. The 'leader' may be a written constitution—in religious terms, a bible—which the group itself creates in order to avoid the responsibility of taking decisions.

(ii) The second pattern he calls 'messianic'—the appearance of a tremendous hope involving a leader, or an idea, yet unborn. Because it is the hope that matters, it is important that it should not be fulfilled; and the group may find endless excuses for not attempting to do so.

(iii) The third pattern is that of 'fight-flight', in which the whole group either becomes violently aggressive *or* panics and will pay no attention to a leader who tries to lead in any other direction. (It is a pity that Corfield had not read Bion before he wrote about Mau Mau.)

It is not difficult to fit Zionist and pagan regressive movements into these alternating patterns of behaviour; and Bion has some intriguing ideas—which I do not pretend to understand—as to when schism and coalescence may be expected. I suggest that, by combining the well-established terms, Catholic and Protestant, with a psycho-analytic approach to therapeutic groups, we may have all the terminology necessary to describe African separatism in a world-wide context. Apart from purely local usage, the labels Ethiopianism, Zionism, and the rest can be discarded.

IV

Does this suggested schema account for the apparent lack of separatism among Roman Catholics? One easy answer is that Protestants provide sufficient independent alternatives for dissident Roman Catholics to join without having to take the initiative of forming their own. There is also the 'all or nothing' answer given by Jung; a discontented Protestant joins a sect, a discontented Roman Catholic becomes an atheist. But there is also another answer in the terms I am using. Because European Protestantism became deeply involved both in contemporary rationalism and in Puritan morality, it tended to become a group concerned with the rational solutions of problems of right belief and right conduct. It ignored the needs of unconscious phantasy which find expression in Catholic sacrament and ceremonial and myth. To swallow the Catholic pill was, as it were, to get a balanced diet—for those who could digest it. The Protestant pill may have been more digestible; but it lacked the spiritual vitamins; and these had to be supplied in other ways. I have a feeling that the magnificent liberalism of the Vatican Council and of this seminar may be, from one point of view, a sign that Rome is losing nerve, trying to develop a more digestible pill. In that case Maria Legio may be only the first sign of what Rome can really do once she starts on the path of separatism.

V

Finally, I want to ask what happened to orthodoxy when it first came to Buganda. I suggest that both Anglican and Roman Catholic missions became from the start Protestant-type churches—churches, that is to say, which provided the mythological element for a resurgent nationalism. Why Christian monotheism should have been the mythology appropriate to Buganda's particular needs at the time is a question which should be discussed. But, because it provided the new identity which Ganda at that point needed, it was seized with conviction and enthusiasm and the blood of the martyrs became the sap of the political kingdom.

(d) RESPONSES TO THE GOSPEL

When considering differences that had been noted concerning responses to the Gospel in Africa, the question was raised whether the basis of the inquiry reported by Father Schuyler in his paper had been broad enough to afford an adequate reflection of these. While university students as future members of an elite are an important element among the people, the overwhelming number of African Christians are to be found among the peasantry; there are, besides, other elites, such as politicians without university or even secondary school education, and the well-established cadres of professional men and civil servants, some already of a second or third generation. Moreover, at their age many students may be merely reacting against their upbringing. Some doubt was cast on the suitability of the concept of Nigeria itself as a unity in this context, since, while being correct as a political expression, it failed to take account of the great variety of peoples, 'tribes', linguistic, and religious groups which constitute that nation. Thus, to yield results of full and permanent value such inquiries need to be greatly extended to include a much wider selection of social categories, admittedly a complex undertaking.

Dr. Freeman-Grenville, in opening the discussion on this topic, drew attention to the fact that response to the Gospel in tropical Africa was usually thought of exclusively in terms of that coming from previous followers of indigenous African religions. Christian missionaries have as a rule avoided an approach to Muslims on the presumption that few, if any, conversions would be forthcoming. While this might be so in lands where orthodox Islam is entrenched it appeared to be worth considering whether such was really the case in many parts of Africa. The great expansion of Islam in East Africa seems to date only from around 1907 and, particularly among the peasantry (who form the majority of Muslims as they do of Christians), it seems clear that the profession of Islam is but the thinnest veneer shrouding the persistence of ancient beliefs and in many cases even of traditional pagan cults. The Ahmadiyyah sect had made attacks on Christianity its speciality as part of its own programme for the reform of Islam. While orthodox Islam rejected this sect its own attitude to Christianity was hardly less antagonistic. All this was part of the background to the Christian impact in Africa and should be included in any systematic survey.

With regard to separatist movements in Africa, it was noted that while there were many ex-Roman Catholics among the Kimbanguists in the Congo, the incidence of breakaways from this church was negligible. Was this the result of Rome's suppression of the Bible and would the new emphasis on biblical theology therefore lead to separatism? Was it possible to use for comparison the High Church Anglican missions which combined the Catholic respect for tradition and ceremonial with the Protestant insistence on the Bible? Was the admission to the Gospel ministry of men of low formal education one reason for divisions? Bearing separatism in other religions in mind (e.g. in Islam, Buddhism, and Hinduism) was this a phenomenon of religion in general or is African separatism a peculiarly African manifestation?

It was felt necessary, in the first place, to develop a clearer and more comprehensive typology of separatism. Its expression across the continent had naturally been differentiated and while for example such terms as 'Ethiopianism' and 'Zionism' were accurate as describing the types prevalent in Southern Africa, they were not necessarily transferable to other areas of Africa. At present it was perhaps best to accept the typology worked out at the Conference on Independent Church Movements held at Mindolo, Zambia, in 1962,[2] but efforts must be continued to reach one which would be still more comprehensive.

While being in agreement with Ruth Benedict's dictum (quoted by Mr. Welbourn) that if one wants to understand race conflict it is more important to understand conflict than to understand race, the seminar was generally of opinion that in separatism we were confronted with very closely inter-related and interdependent psychological and sociological factors. It would appear that the background to African separatism does contain some specifically African elements. For example, the distinctive content of Ethiopianism has been determined by race conflict which, owing to the historical fact of the slave trade and its consequences, is quite different in its nature from race conflict elsewhere. On this basis there is a sense of not only continental but also racial solidarity.

There appeared to be among separatists a common reaction to the Bible as susceptible of use for strengthening Africanist

[2] Research Pamphlet No. 11, Edinburgh House Press, London, 1963.

ideology. The view was also expressed that a study of the African conception of ministry, as displayed by its African incumbents, might be found rewarding and that probably African Anglican bishops, for example, were putting an entirely new content into the episcopal office. Professor Low pointed out that, since colonialism was often named as a cause of separatism, it was now necessary to coin some such new phrase as 'an authoritarian, bureaucratic state' to cover the common features of colonialism and some newly-independent governments. Taken as a whole, the separatists across the continent seemed to be offering African solutions to problems as yet unresolved in the mission-related churches. These problems arose from the points of sharpest conflict between Christianity as it has been preached and the traditional African way of life: polygyny, ancestor worship or veneration, religious therapy, forms of worship involving drumming and dancing, and other activities emphasizing physical self-expression. There was a good deal of pamphlet literature by separatist leaders dating from 1880 onwards, and theological analyses of them should be undertaken to throw more light on the roots and the ways of thinking of independent Churches.

Much discussion was given to the methodology adopted by Dr. Barrett in the wide-ranging, cross-cultural study presented in his paper. In opening the discussion on it Dr. Long drew attention to three possible criticisms concerning: (*a*) comparability of phenomena studied (e.g. is the ancestor cult among South-Eastern Bantu comparable with that found among certain West African peoples?) (*b*) The over-simplification which arises from the need to categorize (e.g. What is a 'complex' political system? What is 'general polygyny' or 'limited and restricted polygyny'? What is a tribe?) (*c*) Unevenness and unreliability of the source materials used, bearing in mind the fact that, in spite of impressive bibliographies, very little really is known of the full range of movements and that much of what is known was gathered by biased or even hostile recorders. Did we indeed have sufficient data on the two hundred and sixty-two tribes involved to be able to compare them?

Dr. Long also pointed to some difficulties regarding the

selection of Dr. Barrett's eighteen variables included in the scale of religious strain. If, as the latter has written, 'movements tended to occur in nations of high literacy, with a high ratio of white to black population, with a large number of mission bodies at work, in tribal units with a complex political system', then it was surprising that these factors were not used in the scale of religious strain.

Dr. Long likewise discerned some overlap of categories resulting in a built-in bias in favour of the factor of the translation of the Scriptures, which is then regarded as of major importance. Again, the association between the factors singled out for special attention is not demonstrated, the argument being framed solely in terms of the 'logical' association between polygyny, ancestor cult, the earth goddess, and certain missionary and 'colonial' factors. But in conclusion he commented as follows:

> Having made several rather critical remarks about the paper, I would like to finish by suggesting that large-scale comparative study may in fact lead to a better understanding of independency in Africa, by examining a whole range of qualitatively different factors. Dr. Barrett's paper thus shifts the emphasis away from the isolation of certain kinds of factors as being the primary ones (see e.g. Kuper, who relates it to the breakdown of tribal structures, Shepperson who in his early writings treats the political factor as the major one, and Lucy Mair and Balandier who suggest that economic and political factors are the key ones). Instead, Barrett's analysis examines the relationship between a whole range of variables, tribal aspects, missionary and 'colonial' factors and religious features. To conclude I would like to quote from a recent review article by Professor Shepperson,[3] who makes a similar point: 'the association of independent African churches and politics ought not to become a conditional sociological reflex. . . .'

Dr. Barrett contributed the following further comments on the future importance of independency in Africa:

> It is possible to study in some detail the numerical increase of separatism among the Luo of Western Kenya. They now have at least eight major separatist bodies, including those from the Anglican Church and the Church of Rome. The Church of Christ in Africa, which separated from the Anglican Church in 1957 with seven priests and some 10,000 worshippers, solely

[3] 'Church and Sect in Central Africa', *Rhodes-Livingstone Journal*, No. 33, June 1963, p. 87.

among the Luo tribe, now claims fifty-three clergy, three bishops, and 60,000 members in fifty-six different tribes in East Africa. Similarly, there is the recent formation of the East African Churches' Association, by some 40 independent bodies not admitted to the Christian Council of Kenya, one of whose criteria for membership is the absence of any Western affiliation.

It is interesting that the Church of Christ in Africa is not interested in the spread of 'independency in Africa' as a concept or as a policy; it remains primarily concerned with the task of the evangelisation of East Africa. A strong ecumenical interest is also now emerging, with the invitation to its senior bishop, Matthew Ajuoga, to join the East African consultations on Church reunion between the Anglican, Presbyterian, Methodist, Lutheran, Moravian and other Churches.

The clear link between independency and the publication of the Scriptures can be illustrated from numerous areas. Along the West African coast all the large tribes from the Ivory Coast to Cameroon are somewhat heavily involved in independency, with the sole exception of the Edo-speaking Bini (some 400,000 people, centred on Benin City), who have resisted its spread, and who also (despite the current importance of the Edo language) are the only such people still without the vernacular translations of the New Testament or the Bible, though translators are now at work on them. This imparts to independency a definite biblical, even reformatory, character.

(e) AFRICAN THEOLOGICAL INTERPRETATION

Speaking on the long-discussed question of the possibility of an 'Africanization of Theology', Fr. LaRoche underlined the distinction between revelation and theology. If God manifests Himself in Jesus Christ, the Word made flesh, the work of the theologian consists in endeavouring to secure such deeper understanding, awareness, and assimilation of the revealed truth as should lead to commitment, i.e. the response of the entire man to the self-revealing God. This reflection by faith on the revealed truths naturally and necessarily uses the means and methods of human knowledge and science (such as logic and philosophy) and is also influenced by the historical situation of the theologian. Thus theologians have made varying contributions in the unravelling of the inexhaustible riches of revelation. In the New Testament there is a Pauline and a Johannine theology; within Christian philosophy there have been widely different theological traditions: Greek theology constitutes a different tradition from

Latin theology, while within the theology of the Latin Church the Augustinian tradition is distinct from the Thomistic and the Scotistic. There are also different approaches to theology (i.e. biblical, systematic, scholastic, etc.), endless varieties of stress and accent, and different schools of spirituality. Cultural elements obviously play here a decisive role and there is no reason why an authentically African theological tradition should not in due course emerge.

In Fr. Bell's opinion such a tradition would have to start from some sort of African philosophy, metaphysic, cosmology, or psychology. Up to the present the point of departure for attempts towards African philosophical reflection upon divine revelation has been traditional religious beliefs and ritual practices. Fr. Alexis Kagame, in his *La Philosophie Bantu-Rwandaise de l'Être*, uses an analysis of language structure as a starting point for a metaphysic. If language is the expression of thought patterns then important indices to the particular genius of a people must lie hidden in language. The first Western European metaphysician, Boetius, started out as a grammarian.

Fr. Bell further drew attention to the promise for African initiative in the field of exegesis, in which the rich world of African symbolism might yield invaluable new insights into the Word of God, and offer particular help in the presentation of revealed truth to Africans. While considerable time must elapse before the results of such work could become available, it is certainly very worthwhile work and ought to be taken up.

Dr. Barrett was greatly impressed with Fr. Mulago's elaboration, in his paper, of the Bantu philosophy underlying ancestor worship, and felt that it made a real 'African' contribution to theology dealing, as it did, with a subject rarely, if ever, considered in European theology. If Fr. Mulago as a Christian theologian would be prepared to endorse (possibly in a somewhat modified form) this aspect of Bantu philosophy it ought to go a long way towards reversing the traditionally negative attitude adopted by missions in respect of this cult.

Professor Shepperson said that one of the influences which might help to precipitate African theology was Marxism which was now, in all its varieties, spreading rapidly in Africa. The recent trend in Marxist studies in the West had been to focus attention on Marx's philosophical manuscripts written before 1848. In these appeared the concept of 'alienation' which, however defined, would seem to be of value for the study of theology in Africa today. Kwame Nkrumah's Consciencism and the writings of L. S. Senghor provided interesting examples of African attempts to cope with Christianity and Marxism together. Marxism was therefore obviously highly important for the future of Christianity in Africa.

Professor Idowu remarked that a most unsatisfactory element in the African Christian situation was that the theology in use was one prefabricated and introduced without any African involvement. In considering the two basic theological notions of grace and life within the African context particular attention should be given to the sacraments and their symbolism. The notion of covenant and alliance with God should be stressed. African marriage, as an alliance between two families of which the spouses are the representatives, as well as the entire clan system in general, would then fall squarely within this framework of covenant. In this connexion it would be good if the marriage service were to be regarded as incomplete without Holy Communion.

Professor Low suggested that with reference to Christian teaching systematic study might be undertaken of the quite considerable literature already in existence on African thinking: the writings of African philosophers and theologians, anthropological, psychological, and linguistic literature, the apologetic publications of separatism or Islam or Orthodoxy or secular ideology, in Africa. The reference to Islam drew from Fr. Martin the comment that a Christian dialogue with this religion had not as much as even started yet; in Senegal the way was being prepared for such dialogue by giving instruction to Christians on Islam.

Regarding the question of elements of African religion which were better described as superstition Fr. LaRoche considered the essence of superstition to consist in attributing to creatures and things honours and powers which they did not possess and which were really attributes of God alone. In summing up the discussion he concurred in the view that the cult of the ancestors could not be simply and completely rejected since it contained such positive values as filial love, gratitude, reverence towards one's forebears, and the desire to remain united with them. It ought rather to be christianized by being purified of those elements that were unacceptable to Christians.

(f) COMMUNICATING THE GOSPEL

In introducing Dr. Mbiti's paper, Dr. Gray said that it would be of great assistance to all those concerned with the strategy of evangelism in Africa. As befitted a representative of the Queen of the Sciences, Dr. Mbiti had cast much of his paper in the imperative; Dr. Gray was tempted to translate some of it into the imperfect and even the interrogative: to try to see what had been achieved already in the task of adaptation and to question the relevance of some of this work in the light of historical perspective. He suggested that one of the major aims of the seminar should be a review of research already accomplished in the various disciplines and fields, and an examination of the urgent research priorities. The developing appreciation and understanding of African religious thought, the foundation which underlay any attempt at adaptation, was surely one of the most fascinating themes for the student of the history of ideas in and concerning Africa. A study of the Christian contribution in this field was greatly needed. Such a study should not only assess the missionary contribution in the work of pioneer studies from Junod to Tempels, but, if it was to embrace anything like the total reality of the Christian encounter with African religious ideas, would also have to include, as Dr. Barrett had suggested, a hard and close look at the theological training of missionaries.

The second great theme in such a study would be the work of African theologians in elucidating their religious heritage and in confronting the problems of adaptation. One thought not only of such a master as the Abbé Kagame, but also of the large number of doctoral dissertations which were now being written. The volume of essays entitled *Des Prêtres noirs s'interrogent* had merely whetted an appetite without satisfying it by subsequent substantial publications. There were two practical problems in this respect. The first was the difficulty experienced in finding a publisher for these theses. Dr. Gray suggested that this was particularly true for students in Rome, and instanced the case of a study of Igbo sacrifice and the Mass, which although completed five years previously had still not found a publisher. Was there not a need perhaps for a series which would undertake to publish competent and scholarly work in this field? Secondly there was the urgent need to compile a bibliographical guide to this literature, particularly of the large number of local studies and pamphlets which were being printed on small mission presses, and which often contained valuable information. It was greatly to be hoped that the new journal *Religion in Africa* would assist in such a task, and would help to make both Catholics and Protestants aware of what the others were doing in this field.

Dr. Gray considered that one of the most valuable aspects of Dr. Mbiti's paper was his insistence that the Church was now operating not only in the old, nineteenth-century Africa rooted in particularist traditions, but also in skyscraper Africa which shared in large measure the problems of the ferro-concrete way of life, where the challenges of materialism and secularism were at least as relevant as those of ancestral cults and polygamy. It was indeed this fact that distinguished the problem of evangelization in Africa in the mid-twentieth century from that of previous periods: for the first time the problems facing the Church in Africa were increasingly becoming identical in many respects to those which faced it elsewhere.

This awareness of the current of history was linked in Dr. Mbiti's paper with an Anglophone suspicion of the generalizations and excesses sometimes associated with the search for *négritude*, with the feeling that a preoccupation with the somewhat abstract problem of reconciling Thomist and Tutsi ontology should not be allowed to obscure the more practical concrete problems of pastoral theology. In this respect Dr. Gray drew attention to one notable omission. Dr. Mbiti had argued persuasively for the use of the drum in worship, and suggested a particular application of this to the rite of adult baptism; he did not however mention the dance. One should perhaps consider the case of the oldest Church in Tropical Africa for, however much the Ethiopian Church owed to Semitic theology and ritual, the persistence and prevalance of the ritual dance was surely a witness to its African heritage. And during this seminar, while watching a Palm Sunday procession at Larteh, Dr. Gray's sympathies had been wholly enlisted on behalf of one or two of the older schoolgirls who, albeit somewhat surreptitiously or unconsciously, were importing traditional rhythmic movements into the more sober rendering of the processional hymn.

Much of the subsequent discussion was concerned with the possibility of the development of an African theology. Fr. Mulago strongly criticized those who argued that since theology was a universal an African theology was *ipso facto* an impossibility; all too often those who upheld the concept of a universal theology were in fact upholding their particular tradition, be it Belgian, French, etc. M. Bureau maintained that one should speak of African contributions to theology, rather than a specific African theology. Theology was a universal science, and one could not contrast African with Western theology. Theology had started in Palestine with Jewish thought, subsequently being influenced strongly by Greek ideas which had provided foundations for the universal, technological civilization of which we were all increasingly a part. One must distinguish sharply between this modern civilization and various local cultures within it. Local adaptation could be concerned only with forms of expression such as the liturgy. Fr. Schuyler agreed that it was the modes of communication which could be Africanized, and suggested that it was as unreal to talk of an African theology as of a lay theology. Dr. Reardon, however, argued that the Second Vatican Council, by recognizing the tradition of Eastern theology, had in fact accepted the concept of a plurality of theologies. Different theological schools and traditions could exist within the defined Catholic dogma. Professor Shepperson wondered whether one was not in danger of over-stressing the distinction between Western and African theologies; he reminded the seminar that

J. B. Horton had stressed the contribution of St. Augustine and the North African Church, and also that the medieval scholastic tradition owed an immense debt to Muslim philosophy. Professor Forde suggested the relevance of theological differences introduced into Africa by differing missionary societies as a subject for further research. How far and in what ways had Africans responded to the various theologies to which they had been exposed? In reviewing the discussion Dr. Mbiti regretted that his use of the term 'an African theology' had suggested difference in fundamentals. He expressed the conviction that it was impossible to plan in advance the contribution of Africa to Christian theology. But a place for that contribution should be found. Personally he was concerned with the relevance of the Christian revelation for Africa and the means by which this could be realized.

Several other points were raised during this discussion. These included the significance of new trends in linguistic studies for theologians in Africa. Professor Shepperson hoped that there would be an increasing co-operation between theologians and linguists in considering the translation of terms and ideas into African languages, and Dr. Freeman-Grenville reminded the seminar of the considerable work currently being undertaken by Catholics in connexion with the translation of the liturgy. He hoped that the opportunity would be taken to report on the various problems which arose in this task. Dr. Freeman-Grenville also stressed the importance of introducing African forms into Christian rites, and referred to a discussion of the Holy Saturday rite in a recent number of the *African Ecclesiastical Review*. Finally, Professor Shepperson called attention to the problem arising with the introduction of an historical religion, such as Christianity, into African societies in which there had not traditionally been a developed sense of chronology and historical process. It was worth noting in this connexion that the Seventh Day Adventists and the Jehovah's Witnesses had, with their elaborate time-charts based on their interpretations of the Book of Revelation, achieved a considerable impact.

VI. CONVERTS AND MARTYRS IN BUGANDA

D. A. LOW

In 1886 some fifty or so young Baganda were put to death by their ruler, the Kabaka of Buganda, and numbers of others were cut down in the highways and byways around his capital. The majority were Christian converts who had refused to renounce their new-found faith. In 1964 Pope Paul VI canonized twenty-two of them. Recognizing that there were a number of others among them who were not of his Church, he invited the Anglican Archbishop of Uganda to be present at the canonization ceremony in Rome.

The story of the burnings at Namugongo has been told often enough before.[1] Some of the central issues in it, however, have still to be faced. Most existing accounts proceed on the assumption that once the ardour of the converts' faith has been demonstrated, no further explanation of their heroism is necessary. But will this do? When faced with formidable challenges have Christians always courted death as these men did? Why, precisely, was their faith so unwavering?

Once these questions have been asked, others soon spring to mind. The Martyrdoms took place in 1885–86. The first Christian missionaries had arrived in Buganda in 1877–79. How was it that there were Christian converts in Buganda, let alone Christian martyrs, within such a relatively short time of their arrival? More than that; in other places in East Africa there were conversions to Christianity at this time; but elsewhere they were from among the detribalized—from among freed slaves, refugees from tribal wars, and so on. In the whole of East Africa it was only in Buganda that there were at this time converts from within the heart of a flourishing tribal society. Moreover, before the conversions to Christianity in Buganda there were conversions to

[1] The most recent accounts are Faupel, 1962; Rowe, 1964.

Islam.[2] There had been too a serious persecution of Muslims and a large number of Muslim martyrs. What was in train here?

It is not very easy to say. It is by no means certain that existing intellectual procedures are adequate to handle such issues; and particularly in this instance there are serious difficulties in marshalling enough meaningful evidence. All one can do is to advance certain hypotheses; but perhaps this is the right way to proceed.

It is reasonably clear that some of the issues were specific to Buganda, since the events with which we are concerned had no counterparts in its neighbouring kingdoms, and it is in the light of a quick glance at the history of Buganda that some explanations may be offered.

A hundred years ago Buganda was within sight of the apogee of its power. Standing upon the north-west shore of Lake Victoria it had come to over-awe its weaker neighbours and challenge its stronger ones. But it had not always been so. Three or four centuries earlier Buganda had been one of the weakest kingdoms in the area. In the interval, however, it had effected a marked territorial expansion and internally there had also been substantial changes. At the beginning of its ascertainable history Buganda seems to have consisted of a congeries of localized clans, which had become subject to a ruler, the Kabaka. This, however, had only served to engender a basic tension at the heart of the political order in the kingdom. For while the Kabaka was head of all the clans (or Sabataka as he was called) he was at odds with the Bataka, or the heads of each of the clans. He wished to control the whole; they to control their own parts. Several developments in the ensuing struggle gradually enabled later Kabakas to prevail over the Bataka. The combination of a number of originally localized clans within a single kingdom was politically successful; a substantial political order was created. In consequence (or so it would seem) the inevitable tendencies within localized clans towards fissiparation were given an outlet, and the clans became dispersed. This seems to have given subsequent Kabakas their opportunity. In due course they gradually took steps to enhance

[2] Katumba and Welbourn, 1964.

their own royal authority at the expense of the Bataka more particularly by establishing their own personal appointees to important territorial chieftaincies in the country at the expense of those provided primarily by the clans. These chiefs were called Bakungu. By the nineteenth century they were being supplemented by a further echelon of directly appointed chiefs, the Batongole, who were more like personal stewards of the Kabaka, but like the Bakungu had responsibilities scattered across the countryside. They too acted as a curb upon the Bataka; but they also provided a curb upon the Bakungu, who, but for this and other measures, might well have become as great a check upon the Kabaka's autocratic authority as the Bataka had been. In the end, by the middle part of the nineteenth century the Kabaka was sitting at the centre of a carefully contrived and artfully balanced network, and from this vantage point exercised a remarkable royal supremacy over his kingdom.[3] It is fairly clear, however, that he was still subject to serious challenge from the tribal gods.

The traditional focus of religious attention in Buganda was a pantheon of instrumental gods—of war, of health, of thunder, and so on. According to Baganda tradition these had been mainly taken over from the people of the neighbouring Sesse islands in Lake Victoria at some early period in the history of Buganda when it needed supernatural support against Bunyoro-kitara, its much more powerful neighbour to the west. The gods apparently did their duty. They seem indeed to have played a very prominent part in giving Buganda its earlier cohesion in the first two or three centuries of its history. But in a way which was typical of that earlier phase, each of these gods became the particular responsibility of one of the originally localized clans. One clan became responsible for providing the priests and the mediums of one particular god. And in this way each god became intimately linked with a particular clan, even while performing a tribal-wide function as well.[4]

However, with the development of the Kabaka's autocratic authority, the need to turn to the gods to give the kingdom

[3] The most useful account of all this is Southwold.

[4] Roscoe, 1911, Ch. X.

cohesion became less and less, and this seems to have given later Kabakas the opportunity to challenge the old gods directly. By the nineteenth century this had, in any event, become particularly important. For by this time the gods seem to have been the last serious obstacle to the establishment of the Kabaka's complete supremacy over everybody and everything in his kingdom. Through the mouths of their priests and mediums the gods could still curse a Kabaka, and even hound him to death. What was more, such powers now appear to have been used to support the rearguard action against the Kabaka's growing authority which was being conducted by the Bataka (with whom through their association with the clans the gods were intimately linked). In other words, the inherent conflict between the Kabaka and the Bataka was being aggravated by and conjoined with a conflict between the Kabaka and the traditional gods. All of which touched an issue of great moment in the history of Buganda—the conflict between centre and periphery which in a rural polity like Buganda could only be resolved in favour of the former after very considerable effort. On such issues, of course, the Kabaka could be assured of the support of the men who clustered about his court, and it was apparently here that one finds the background to such reports as this of a scene at the Kabaka's court in July 1874:

> There was an unusual assemblage at the palace, and some great question evidently engaged M'tesa's attention. I leaned feebly against the post behind me, and suddenly there were cries and confusion without, and the fatal cords of the executioners were encircling the necks of seven men, who had just been by turns addressing M'tesa. These were the spirit-guardians of the lake, a terror to all Uganda supposed to exercise control over the lake and river. The terror they have inspired, the murders they have committed, are a matter of tradition. M'tesa had broken the chain of this superstition in order that his men might take me far out upon the lake. M'tesa said to me: 'It pains my bowels (*batn*) to do this, but they have done me and my people great injury, and I do this for you as well.' This execution was followed by a rush into the palace of a large number of officers of the Army, headed by the Kongowee (General in chief) with clubs in their hands. With wild gesticulations and loud vociferations they rushed towards M'tesa, shouting: 'You are the great M'tesa, we are your faithfuls.' Said and Abdul stood by the door and witnessed with their own eyes these executions.[5]

[5] Long, 1877, pp. 61–62.

It is important to try and see what was happening here. Into this society secular values had not yet intruded. The supernatural could not, therefore, be ignored, and what was evidently required was a new cult over which the ruler himself would have complete control instead of one which was closely associated with his opponents. Yet such a change could not be easily effected. There was obviously very little the Kabaka could do to reform the traditional gods. There were, as it happened, no more gods belonging to neighbouring peoples whom he could satisfactorily borrow. All Baganda traditions were against the Kabaka turning himself into a god, and there was very little to be said for turning the royal ancestors into gods; their priests and mediums could be as troublesome as the priests and mediums of the existing gods.

Such being the position which had been reached by the middle of the nineteenth century, one can begin to understand how extraordinarily timely it was for the Kabaka that Arab traders should have arrived about this time at his court, and that they should, among other things, have spoken about Islam. For here was a ready-made religion with immense potentialities which he could not only adopt as his own, but whose use he could also hope to control.

There were now other considerations as well. First—and most important—the Arab penetration heralded the arrival within the relatively closed circle of Baganda existence of a vast new world. To meet such a fearsome threat, many African peoples have sought to conjure up some greatly increased supernatural support; and one of the obvious things for them to do has been to develop quite markedly their own existing religion. (The Nuer of the southern Sudan for example, as Professor Evans-Pritchard has told us,[6] developed in response to the Egyptian and European advent a wholly new series of prophets.) Yet to develop his own religion was precisely what the Kabaka of Buganda could not do. But there has always been an alternative. It has always been possible to adopt the formula of the invaders; and this is what the Kabaka of Buganda did, it would seem, in his day with Islam. As it happened a bold step like this fitted in very well

[6] Evans-Pritchard, 1958, pp. 116, 308–10, 319.

with the adventurous proclivities of the Baganda which from time to time they display in a quite dramatic way. In this connexion and in others it is of enormous importance to recognize that for the Baganda the golden age lay in the future. For most of their neighbours, who over the centuries were losing territory and importance (not least to the Baganda) the golden age lay in the past. But for a good deal of their history the Baganda have had their eyes fixed on the future. Something like Islam therefore which was at once purposive and creative had a very good chance of procuring from them a favourable response. Certainly once its initial impact had been carefully considered, it came to be seriously entertained by the Kabaka and his court. To adopt Islam looked like solving the religious problem which he faced internally. It looked like helping him with his external problem by giving him access to the spiritual supports which the Arabs possessed. And it accorded very well with the forward-looking approach which held a very prominent place in Baganda thinking. At all events by the mid 1860s the Kabaka was encouraging his courtiers to adopt Islam. Many of them were becoming circumcized. He himself had adopted the Arabic calendar, started to wear Arabic dress, and for ten years after 1866 annually observed Ramadan. He supervised, moreover, the building of mosques not only at his court but in the countryside (was he once more invading the rural strongholds of the Bataka, and, this time, their associated gods?). At the same time he periodically took it upon himself to expound the Koran to his court, and thus displayed not merely his intellectual interest in its doctrines but, one may suppose, a desire to be closely associated with their promulgation. Nothing comparable occurred in any of the neighbouring kingdoms in East Africa; but then, I would argue, none of them saw quite the same complex of developments which took place in Buganda.

By the mid 1870s, however, some of Kabaka Mutesa's own initial excitement over Islam was beginning to die down. Muslim converts, for example, were now starting to refuse to obey his orders to eat the meat he sent to them, on the grounds that it had been killed by his royal butcher who had not been circumcized.

The decretals of Islam were apparently beginning to take precedence over the orders of the Kabaka. If such insubordination were to become rife among his own closest associates, all the efforts of himself and his predecessors to establish their ultimate supremacy over their kingdom would be brought to nought. And the trouble now was that these Muslim courtiers were becoming so deeply attached to their new-found faith that they were not to be easily put off. Accordingly, in about 1875–76, Kabaka Mutesa had a hundred or more of them put to death to teach the others to mend their ways; but they met death boldly, and, at best, the survivors were only temporarily cowed.

There was now a further matter: by the mid-1870s it was becoming clear that the giants of the new world which was now increasingly impinging upon Buganda were not the Arabs who brought the new wonders to the country, but the Europeans who manufactured them; and the Europeans were not Muslims at all.[7] If therefore one was to make a successful *rapprochment* with this second and mightier alien invasion, Islam was unlikely to be of very much assistance. It is scarcely surprising therefore that when a number of Europeans came to Buganda in the mid-1870s the Kabaka should have insisted upon having urgent discussions with them about Christianity; nor that he should have ended one of these (with the explorer Stanley in 1876) by announcing to his court:

> I say that the white men are greatly superior to the Arabs, and I think, therefore, that their book must be a better book than Mohammed's.[8]

The Kabaka did not there and then become a Christian, any more than he had in the end become a circumcized Muslim; no wise Kabaka would jump so rapidly to such conclusions. But he did give the missionaries who arrived in his country during the next few years a very warm welcome, and he was careful to oversee the formal worship they conducted, which suggests that once again he was anxious to secure control over the new religion and become its foremost exponent.

[7] Here, and elsewhere, see Kagwa, 1927; Zimbe, 1939; and Mukasa, 1938.
[8] Stanley, 1890, p. 206.

But for the rest the previous story of the conversions to Islam was not repeated. For when in 1879 Roman Catholic missionaries arrived hard on the heels of Anglican missionaries, it soon appeared that there was not just one kind of Christianity in which the Europeans believed, but two; and their respective adherents were soon denouncing each other at court with often uncontrolled vehemence. This presented the Kabaka and his courtiers with a most baffling problem. For if it was important, as many of them thought it was, to secure access to the same spiritual supports which the Europeans enjoyed, how were they to know which version of Christianity they would best be advised to adopt? The answer could not be given quickly. The whole situation was complicated because there was some strong resistance to the Kabaka's readiness to entertain Christianity from the Arab traders in the country, and from those about his court who still adhered strongly to Islam. The ensuing confusion, moreover, was soon made very much worse, when, early in 1880, the adherents of the old gods took the opportunity to launch the most serious counter-attack they had ever mounted against this tampering with alien gods by bringing the medium of the most important of them, Mukasa, the God of the Lake, to the Kabaka's court amid the cheering of crowds and the beating of drums.

Amid this mounting confusion, the more cautious minds at the Kabaka's court began to ponder deeply whether all this upheaval might not have very serious consequences for their kingdom—might not, indeed, undermine both the integrity of its social order, and its ability to meet any external danger, the latter being throughout this period an especially serious consideration in view of the Egyptian attempt in the mid 1870s to annex the kingdom to their Sudanese empire. It was not long indeed before these further thoughts became major points for discussion, along with all the others, in the interminable debates which from 1879 onwards, week in week out, month in month out, year in year out, regularly took place at the open meetings of the Kabaka's court, for the most part in his presence.

As the confusion increased, the Kabaka himself did nothing to resolve it, but made it all very much worse by swinging in every possible direction in swift and bewildering succession. This was not only because he was beset by genuine intellectual confusion. It was also, it would seem, because he was afraid that if he took a decisive step in any one direction he might break his court apart into deeply divided, and perhaps even bitterly warring factions. He seems in short to have anticipated very clearly the rifts which eventually overtook his court a few years after his death when a less circumspect man presided over its fortunes. But his non-committal attitude had some very serious implications; for in effect it meant that upon these now momentous issues he was abdicating his leadership—something which no Kabaka in living memory had ever done before—and that was to leave his courtiers floundering.

One of the consequences was that the missionaries were left free to proselytize, if they did not proceed too openly. (The Kabaka evidently felt that if he took any decisive action against them he might well lose the support of the more forward-looking elements at his court whose vision of an expanding future for the Buganda kingdom—which they saw as being brought within their reach by the teaching of the new religion—he personally shared to the full.) The missionaries made excellent use of their opportunities. They were often devoted men, and whether Roman Catholic White Fathers, trained, as these were, under the fervent eye of the great Cardinal Lavigerie of Algiers, or evangelical Anglicans of the Church Missionary Society from Britain, they radiated a profound faith in the rightness of their creed. At the same time they displayed many of the skills of western civilization. The leading Anglican missionary, for example, was at once an engineer, and an expert blacksmith, printer, and house-builder, and the gospel which he and his colleagues preached was typical of its time in stressing the intimate connexion between Christianity and civilization. 'The book,' one missionary told the Kabaka in presenting him with the Bible, 'is the source of England's greatness.' As it chanced no 'godless' European traders ever came to Buganda at this time to throw doubt on such claims. And in all the circumstances, it is not altogether surprising that these claims should have been accepted in a somewhat uncritical manner by some of the young men about the court, who, in the intervals between military expeditions and running errands for their lords, had time on their hands to cluster about the missionaries, to listen to their teaching, and to talk about it among themselves. They were plainly anxious for enlightenment. They had fallen by this time into a quite fearful intellectual confusion. For close followers of the Kabaka there could be no going back to the old gods. The supernatural, however, could not be ignored. Some might still find satisfaction in Islam. But this might not be the royal road to the great future for themselves and their kingdom for which as earnest, forward-looking, young Baganda many of them were still aspiring. For some of them, in the end, the adoption of Christianity seemed to be the only way forward. They appear to have been struck by various facets of Christian doctrine. In Africa the supreme God is usually a very distant being: Christianity brought Him within reach. The young men were greatly impressed by the missionaries; by their teaching, personal kindness and self-assurance, and by their mechanical skills. It could very well be that they held the open sesame to the great new order for their kingdom (and for themselves as its future leaders) which they claimed.

In due course the only question which had still to be answered was, to which version of Christianity should they adhere? Some eventually solved their dilemma by visiting each mission station in turn, and then opting for the one which, for some personal reason, they found most congenial. Most, however, took the rather different course of talking the whole problem out with their closest friends—given the dangers of life at an autocrat's court this was an elementary precaution—before deciding to attach themselves to one mission station or the other as a group. As a result of both processes, by the early 1880s the first baptisms were taking place at the two mission stations, and by 1884 the Roman Catholics and the Anglicans had each baptized about 200 members of the Kabaka's court, many of whom were already formed into closely linked small clusters. These baptisms were sincerely meant. Personal names have immense symbolic importance in Africa. One prominent convert, whose name was Mukasa and had taken the good Old Testament name of Ham, was soon telling a missionary, 'Do not call me Mukasa: my name is Ham.'

There were, of course, grave issues at stake here. The first converts were leading where the Kabaka had not gone before. The first conversions to Christianity took place, therefore, in very different circumstances from the first conversions to Islam, which had been mainly at the bidding of the Kabaka. They arose out of many personal and collective decisions to resolve the intellectual, spiritual, and psychic confusion which had overtaken the Kabaka's court by the early 1880s. At the same time it is no coincidence that many of the first converts were young men who were either still bachelors or at most possessed one wife; they found it easier to resolve the difficulties that were entailed in the missionaries' insistence on monogamy. It is not impossible indeed that if either mission station had been willing to relax its position on this issue the Kabaka himself would have become baptized. They refused to do this, however, as he would not give up his wives, because, as he pointed out, to do so would be to undermine considerable areas of the existing political, social, and economic order in his kingdom. His readiness, however, to consider in the end the possibility of following where his young courtiers had gone before—a most remarkable course for any nineteenth-century Kabaka to contemplate—gives some idea of the momentum which Christianity was beginning to enjoy at his court by about 1884.[9]

In that year the old Kabaka died, still unbaptized, and was succeeded by his young son, Mwanga. Mwanga, like any new occupant of a traditional throne, was in an unenviable position. He was a man of the same generation as the majority of the Christian converts. He shared their hostility towards the old gods and their traditionally-minded supporters. He sympathized with the ambitions of the young men about his court for a great new future for his kingdom, and in the nature of things, he was soon looking to them to rid him of the incubus of his father's old

[9] I hope to detail all this elsewhere: but on the aspirations of the Baganda see Mackay to Wigram, 10 August 1882, C.M.S. Archives, CA6/016; and on Mutesa's thinking see O'Flaherty to Wigram, 28 February 1883, ibid., CA6.

chiefs. But in a very short time, in large part because the European scramble for Africa was now getting under way, he began to share the concern of the more cautious minds at his court about the Christian converts. He was worried lest they might become, in view of the overall circumstances of the mid-1880s, and in particular because of their close association with the European missionaries, traitors to the long sought, and hard won, autonomy of the Buganda kingdom. Indeed, this soon became a further major issue of controversy at the Kabaka's court. In due course, in June 1886, there was a breach; but it occurred only when some of the young converts interfered with his practice of sodomy, which he had learnt from the Arabs. The Kabaka's sudden anger was fanned by his father's old chiefs, and together they set on foot a severe persecution of the Christian converts, during which (among other things) thirty-two converts were burnt alive on a single pyre on a single day.

Many of the converts went into hiding. But some of them deliberately courted arrest, and went to their funeral pyres singing hymns as they died. It is important to try to see why. Life, of course, was still relatively cheap in Buganda. Execution was an occupational hazard at the Kabaka's court, and its members had no illusions about the possibility that a sudden change in the Kabaka's humour could quickly bring them to mutilation or death. It is conceivable, of course, that like both the Christians and the Muslims in Buganda two years later, the converts could have rebelled. At this stage, however, they seem to have had little of the organization and few of the guns they were to employ in 1888. But in any event, amid all the vituperative accusations which were levied against them at this time for insolence and treachery, they were evidently determined to display their loyalty. But if so why did they not apostatize? Part of the answer would seem to lie in the fact that in their ranks there were a number who had solved the immense spiritual and intellectual confusion into which the Kabaka's court had been thrown in the last years of the previous reign by becoming baptized Christians; men who had found great comfort and strength from the assurance which that had given them; and for some of whom at least retreat presented greater problems than advance. There is certainly every reason for thinking that their Christian convictions had now become profound and far-reaching, and there can be no doubt at all that they had arrived at a peak of devotion and fervour. The same, however, had been true of the Muslims who had been martyred a decade previously; and in all the circumstances of the time, it is difficult to reach a satisfactory understanding of what was afoot without taking a further consideration into account as well. This is, I believe, that these men saw—like the the Muslim martyrs before them and like later groups of Baganda in various other situations after them—that there had come a point when it was vital for the future of the society to which they felt themselves to be no less loyal and responsible than the Kabaka himself, that someone should make a stand against the existing order in the country for that greater order towards which for so many centuries of continuing effort Buganda had been striving. In the terms available to them in the 1860s and 1870s that new order looked like finding its consummation in Islam and through Islam in the culture which the Arab traders were bringing; in the 1880s it found its hope in Christianity and through Christianity in that new civilization which the Europeans were bringing. In the Buganda martyrs we must, I think, recognize that their own interpretation of the urgent requirements of their very profound patriotism played a large part in enhancing their new-found religious enthusiasm. In 1875–76, and again in 1885–86, this involved some of them in mutilation and death. In 1888—for reasons which are beyond the scope of this paper—the remainder took another road (partly because for the first time they were able to do so)—that of rebellion and revolution.

If all this is anywhere near the mark, it has at least three implications. It emphasizes that religious conviction and enthusiasm in Africa may be found in Christian 'orthodoxy' as well as in Christian separatism. Among academics the tendency has been to doubt this. It is time it was righted. Secondly, it suggests that the origin of any story of widespread conversion requires some much more extensive investigation than it usually receives. We have, for a start, to ask the question why conversions occur in place A and not in place B, and we must now expect that the search for the answer may take us in all sorts of unexpected directions. And then thirdly, we must, I think, recognize that an ardent Christianity is not necessarily just a reflection of the vitality of the faith. It may be—indeed I suggest it often is as well—a vehicle for the almost apocalyptic yearnings which have patently overtaken large parts of Africa as it has undergone the disruptive creation which has marked its dramatic transformation during the past century and more. If we can take such considerations into account, we may be able to take the study of Christianity in Africa somewhat further.

REFERENCES

Evans-Pritchard, E. E.
(1958) *Nuer Religion*. Oxford.
Faupel, J. F.
(1962) *African Holocaust; The Story of the Uganda Martyrs*. London.
Kagwa, Apolo
(1927) *Bassekabaka be Buganda*. London.
Katumba, Ahmed and Welbourn, F. B.
(1964) 'Muslim Martyrs of Buganda'. *Uganda Journal*, XXVIII, 2.
Long, Colonel
(1877) *Provinces of the Equator: Summary of Letters and Reports of H.E. the Governor-General, Part I, year 1874*. Egyptian General Staff, Cairo.
Mukasa, H.
(1938) *Simuda Nyuma*. London.
Roscoe, J.
(1911) *The Baganda*. London.
Rowe, J. A.
(1964) 'The purge of Christians at Mwanga's Court', *Journal of African History*, V, 1, pp. 55–72.
Southwold, Martin
(n.d.) *Bureaucracy and Chiefship in Buganda*. East African Studies, No. 14, Kampala.
Stanley, H. M.
(1890) *Through the Dark Continent*. New edn. London.
Zimbe, B. M.
(1939) *Buganda ne Kabaka*. Mengo.

Résumé

CONVERTIS ET MARTYRS AU BUGANDA

Ce chapître décrit, avec plus de détails que n'en donnent les études antérieures, les raisons des premières conversions au

Christianisme et le martyr des premiers Chrétiens au Buganda. Les raisons profondes pourraient en être les changements sociaux-culturels intervenus au Buganda au 19e siècle, en rapport avec les premiers contacts avec Zanzibar et les Européens de l'extérieur. A cela venait s'ajouter le pouvoir autocratique du roi, le Kabaka (et celui des chefs nommés par lui) s'opposant au pouvoir des clans et des chefs de clans, ce qui amena un conflit entre les deux systèmes qui constituent la société Ganda. Comme les prêtres et devins traditionnels s'étaient ralliés aux clans, le Kabaka et ses alliés furent amenés à s'opposer à la religion traditionnelle, ce qui les rendait particulièrement réceptifs aux appels d'une religion nouvelle. C'est à ce moment, au milieu du 19e siècle, que l'Islam s'implanta pour la Ière fois au Buganda. Son adoption par le roi lui apparut un moyen de résoudre un problème interne particulièrement grave, et favorisa les approches de plus en plus précises du monde extérieur. Aux environs de 1870, cependant, il devint clair que l'Islam ne pouvait aucunement constituer une religion royale et qu'elle ne procurait aucun *modus vivendi* envers l'avance des Européens. En face de cette situation nouvelle, le Christianisme, religion des Européens, en vint à être sérieusement pris en considération, mais la rivalité entre missionnaires Protestants et Catholiques, entre Chrétiens et Musulmans, entre adhérents des nouvelles religions et de l'ancienne, entraina de tels conflits à la cour du Kabaka que, pendant près d'une décade, ces faits provoquèrent une confusion intellectuelle et spirituelle profonde et perturbante.

Afin de s'en préserver, certains courtisans du Kabaka en vinrent peu à peu à opter pour une religion de préférence aux autres—option le plus souvent prise tout à fait arbitrairement. Comme le démontrèrent les évènements (conséquence surtout de la division des Européens en Afrique de l'Est aux environs de 1880), quelques Chrétiens furent persécutés pour leur foi nouvelle. Plusieurs, cependant, surent s'y maintenir, même si cela impliquait pour eux la torture et la mort, car, dans l'effrayante confusion où ils se trouvaient, elle leur apportait une grande sécurité spirituelle et semblait leur promettre cet 'âge d'or' auquel les Baganda aspiraient ardemment, tournant le dos au passé.

VII. INFLUENCE DE LA CHRISTIANISATION SUR LES INSTITUTIONS TRADITIONNELLES DES ETHNIES COTIÈRES DU CAMEROUN[1]

R. BUREAU

L'évangélisation protestante a commencé il y a plus d'un siècle chez les Duala, l'évangélisation catholique il y a environ 80 ans.

Nous ne chercherons pas à reconstituer cette histoire mais nous tenterons de mettre en lumière ce que nous pouvons appeler le 'dialogue' qui s'est institué entre l'action missionnaire et les formes de la vie sociale des groupes évangélisés. Il nous semble en effet que l'étude de l'impact chrétien doit se situer dans une double perspective: perspective 'dynamique' et perspective de 'mise en situation':

Perspective dynamique. L'état actuel des structures sociales est le fruit d'une histoire complexe. Les tensions et les crises successives entraînées par l'évangélisation ont, pour une bonne part, forgé les comportements sociaux et religieux d'aujourd'hui.

Perspective de mise en situation. L'évangélisation n'est pas, bien entendu, un phénomène isolé; il est banal de le dire mais la tentation est grande de l'oublier.

En ce qui concerne l'évangélisateur, il convient de tenir compte des déterminations historiques qu'il a subies. D'une part, les missionnaires étaient tributaires de la mentalité et des idées de l'Occident d'où ils venaient et de l'époque qui était la leur. D'autre part, ils se sont trouvé impliqués sur place dans la situation coloniale dont, par la force des choses, ils faisaient partie intégrante.

En ce qui concerne les groupes sociaux évangélisés, la situation politique, économique, religieuse antécédente à la présence missionnaire a conditionné les types de réactions aux valeurs, idées et croyances importées par les missionnaires étrangers.

[1] Cf. *Ethno-sociologie Religieuse des Duala et apparentés*, Recherches et Études Camerounaises, B.P. 193, Yaoudé, 1962, 350 p.

Un point de vue objectif sur l'influence de la christianisation doit donc envisager, d'une manière ou d'une autre, les éléments suivants:

— Les valeurs humaines et religieuses des missionnaires à l'époque de l'impact.

— L'état de cohésion interne et les relations externes du groupe évangélisé.

— Le contexte politique et économique dans lequel se déroule le dialogue.

— L'enchaînement des phénomènes, c'est-à-dire la suite des actions et réactions des deux réalités en présence: la mission et le groupe ethnique.

Ces questions de méthode ainsi brièvement exprimées, nous pouvons entrer dans le cas précis qui nous occupe. Pour ne pas nous perdre dans l'ensemble complexe des multiples traits culturels qui constituent le patrimoine social des Duala, nous choisirons, pour illustrer notre exposé, deux institutions exemplaires à plus d'untitre: le culte des génies de l'eau et le prix-de-la-fiancée. Le projet des premiers missionnaires, les Pallotins allemands, se présentait sous un double aspect:

(1) déraciner la religion traditionnelle et les modes de vie qui y sont liés;
(2) implanter le culte chrétien et les institutions chrétiennes.

Le réalisation de ce projet ne supposait pas, dans l'esprit des premiers prédicateurs, la connaissance approfondie de la culture qu'ils affrontaient, en raison d'une conjoncture sensiblement différente de celle d'aujourd'hui:

— D'une part, l'intérêt pour les 'sauvages' né au 16ème siècle s'était éteint dans une Europe toute préoccupée par ses problèmes intérieurs (Révolution, Empire . . .)

— Depuis le Concile de Trente, d'autre part, le souci principal des théologiens catholiques était de conserver l'intégrité de la doctrine, de préciser les éléments d'un droit ecclésiastique rigoureux, d'entretenir des formes d'expression religieuse estimées universelles. La grande querelle des Rites Chinois au terme de laquelle les traditions des pays non-chrétiens sont devenues à priori suspectes est à l'image de cette période de trois longs siècles de repliement, dont le Concile actuel fait à peine sortie l'Église catholique. (En 1600, les missionnaires étaient autorisés à célébrer la messe tout entière en langue chinoise . . .). Le 19° siècle européen marque en effet une ouverture sur le monde fort différente de celle du 16° siècle où les missionnaires avaient suivi les navigateurs et les commerçants de la Renaissance. Il y a cent ans, le militaire venait en tête, suivi par l'administrateur, mûs tous les deux par des visées impériales et civilisatrices; la percée politique était ensuite utilisée par le commerçant et le missionnaire.

Ce dernier pouvait donc, pour réaliser son projet, compter sur la puissance coloniale. Le missionnaire bénéficiait du prestige que lui offrait le fait d'appartenir à la race des chefs, détentrice de la puissance des armes (le 'primitif' ne peut-il pas se définir comme l'homme qui ne peut tuer qu'un homme à la fois?) et maîtresse d'un instrument administratif efficace. Bien plus, le missionnaire pouvait compter sur l'appui effectif de l'appareil mis en place par le colonisateur, puisque le projet de 'civiliser' les colonies rejoignait en bien des points celui de les christianiser.

Les débuts de l'œuvre missionnaire sur la côte camerounaise, à la fin du siècle dernier, ont donc été marqués par deux sources d'ambiguités:

(1) une ignorance tranquille de la civilisation africaine lié à une conviction de la supériorité radicale de l'ensemble des valeurs occidentales;

(2) une collusion des pouvoirs civil et religieux. Ce dernier point est aggravé par le fait que les missionnaires français viennent surtout de régions où l'évolution des rapports entre l'Église et l'État est retardataire.

Ces préambules nous ont semblé nécessaires pour rendre compte des modalités de la transformations de la société Duala sous l'influence chrétienne.

I. L'AMORCE DU DIALOGUE

A.—Le missionnaire en face des traditions païennes

(1) *La tactique générale. Établissement d'une sphère chrétienne*

Il fallait 'planter' l'Église, c'est-à-dire faire reculer le paganisme. Les adultes étaient trop enfoncés dans leurs pratiques pour qu'il y eût espoir de les en sortir. Par contre les enfants représentaient une matière encore informe que l'on pourrait modeler pour constituer la base de la société chrétienne de demain. La tactique missionnaire ne fût pas celle que l'on est convenu d'appeler 'de la table rase'. Ils tâchèrent plutôt de planter un arbre vigoureux capable d'étouffer, à plus ou moins brève échéance, l'arbre du paganisme. Il fallait mettre en place une sphère sociale chrétienne qui empièterait petit à petit sur la sphère ancienne jusqu'à la faire disparaître. La formation des enfants, *à l'abri* dans un internat, semblait convenir éminemment à l'entreprise. *L'école* était donc le moyen privilégié pour amorcer la transformation de la société Duala.

Il importait par ailleurs d'éviter toute ambiguité dans l'enseignement chrétien. La religion ne pouvait être prêchée directement à des gens qui n'avaient que des concepts païens dans l'esprit. Un soubassement de culture occidentale, rationnelle, était considé comme nécessaire pour permettre la greffe du christianisme. On se défiait par exemple de la confusion qui pouvait naître entre certains rites d'initiation et l'entrée dans l'église par le baptême.

Cette attitude trouva un accueil rapidement favorable. Le Blanc était reconnu comme disposant de 'forces' plus puissantes, puisqu'il réussissait de plus grandes choses. Le secret de ces forces devait certainement résider dans la science du Blanc. Pour rejoindre le Blanc, il fallait donc acquérir ses connaissances, humaines et religieuses. Le catéchuménat et l'école tendaient à se confondre.

L'école ne constituait cependant qu'un élément parmi d'autres de la tactique d'isolement de la sphère païenne. Les postes de mission s'installent de façon à pouvoir vivre en autarcie. Il s'agit d'organiser l'action missionnaire de manière à créer des *pôles d'attraction.* Les stations sont volontairement éloignées des centres européens et des agglomérations villageoises. Cette méthode d'investissement de l'espace permet d'isoler les 'lieux' chrétiens de tous les autres centres sociaux et de ménager des aires de culture agricole importantes pour assurer la subsistance des missionnaires et embaucher à cet effet des travailleurs parmi les familles converties. La construction des églises exige par ailleurs la présence d'ouvriers qui finissent par se fixer aux alentours de la concession missionnaire. La station constitue un microcosme à l'intérieur duquel gravitent les membres d'un groupe socio-professionnel nouveau: les 'employés de la mission', catéchistes, instituteurs, ouvriers . . . et leurs familles. Ces conglomérats doivent jouer le rôle de *pilotes* dans l'enracinement de l'ordre chrétien.

L'école avait surtout du succès chez les garçons. Les missionnaires réalisèrent vite qu'il n'y aurait pas de mariages chrétiens sans que les filles soient éduquées. On fit venir des religieuses d'Allemagne, et c'est ainsi que naquîrent les 'écoles de fiancées' communément appelées 'sixa'. Les jeunes filles destinées à épouser des chrétiens étaient invitées à séjourner plusieurs mois ou même plusieurs années à la mission pour y recevoir un enseignement moral et religieux.

Les supérieurs donnaient d'autre part la consigne suivante: 'Il faut inviter les chrétiens à se regrouper.' Des zones chrétiennes se dessinaient dans les villages.

Ces méthodes portèrent leurs fruits. Les convertis, considérés dans les débuts comme des originaux, devînrent assez nombreux pour que les 'païens' irréductibles soient à leur tour jugés comme des individus marginaux. Comme le notait un missionnaire, le christianisme était devenu 'à la mode'. Entre les deux guerres mondiales, la quasi totalité de la population fut baptisée.

(2) *Attitudes particulières vis-à-vis des 'coutumes'*

Les missionnaires, catholiques ou protestants, ont rapidement cherché à déceler les 'coutumes' jugées 'sauvages', et de ce fait incompatibles avec une vie chrétienne. Les fonctions sociales de ces modes de vie particuliers n'étaient perçus d'aucune manière. On leur appliquait l'étiquette 'diabolique', et tous les moyens étaient pris pour les extirper. On ne songeait pas plus à fournir des équivalents chrétiens puisque l'on ne se rendait pas compte de leur importance culturelle. Les coutumes indifférentes pour la foi n'étaient pas prises en considération. Ainsi, parmi les nombreux remèdes utilisés par les Duala, les missionnaires avaient distingué les rites 'magiques' et l'emploi légitime des plantes et autres thérapeutiques. Le problème consistait donc à opérer des distinctions entre les éléments 'diaboliques' et les autres. On ne se rendait pas compte à quel point tous les traits culturels étaient liés entre eux; on ne prévoyait pas que la destruction de certains éléments culturels entrainerait nécessairement des perturbations dans le reste des institutions.

(*a*) *Les 'sociétés secrètes'*. Les associations de culte constituaient la bête noire des premiers missionnaires. Les baptistes anglais s'en plaignent comme d'un fléau: 'ils rendent un culte aux esprits de la rivière, qu'ils appellent miengu; c'est à l'action de ces esprits qu'ils attribuent les évènements qui favorisent ou compromettent la prospérité de la tribu. La société qui organise ce culte aux rites compliqués, est toute-puissante.'

La société '*jengu*' (plur.: *miengu*) correspond assez bien à ce que Marcel Mauss appelle 'un phénomène social global'. Elle remplissait, sur un plan 'horizontal', des fonctions multiples et contrebalançait en bien des points l'autorité de la hiérarchie verticale. Nous allons énumérer rapidement ces fonctions afin de pouvoir montrer ensuite le processus de transformation des structures sociales.

Les *miengu*, génies de l'eau, entretiennent avec les hommes des relations complexes, ambivalentes. Dans cette société dont l'économie tourne autour des produits des rivières et de la mer, il importe avant tout de se concilier les maîtres de la vie aquatique. Chaque membre de la tribu a son jengu protecteur auquel il convient d'obéir, sinon le châtiment est inévitable: noyade ou possession.

Les spécialistes du *jengu* constituent une société dont la première fonction est celle *du culte*: les rites de fécondité (fécondité des femmes, fécondité de la pêche) sont assurés par les membres de l'"isango' (nom de la société de culte). La principale cérémonie consiste à descendre dans l'eau des présents offerts aux génies de l'eau. La fonction *thérapeutique* est également importante: les spécialistes de la guérison sont les membres du jengu; les maladies de langueur notamment sont guéries par des séances de danses qui reproduisent les conditions de la possession par les esprits.—L'association joue un rôle primordial dans le maintien de la *paix* entre les divers clans, le règlement des litiges, etc. Elle concourt en permanence à l'unification des divers groupes.—La fonction *pédagogique* est peut-être la plus importante: l'initiation est en effet assurée par les responsables de l'association. Il faut noter que les filles sont initiées selon des rites plus complexes et plus riches: le jengu donne aux femmes des rôles importants qu'elles n'auraient pas par ailleurs; le chef de l'association est souvent une femme; l'autorité masculine est ainsi fortement équilibrée. La *divination*, spécialité des femmes particulièrement douées pour les transes, leur permet de jouer parfois des rôles déterminants. L'initiation est assurée dans une case particulière, la *pamba*, qui sert par ailleurs à l'exercice du culte des miengu.—*La justice* est également exercée par les membres du jengu en de nombreuses circonstances; l'autorité des nobles est renforcée par cette fonction pénale, car les initiés sont recrutés exclusivement parmi les aristocrates.—La fonction *économique* du jengu enfin est déterminante: les lots de pêche sont attribués par les chefs de l'association; un impôt est prélevé sur chaque expédition et le montant de la compensation matrimoniale est fixé par les responsables de la société de culte.

On se rend compte ainsi de l'importance de cette société dans la société et du rôle qu'elle joue dans la totalité des domaines de la vie sociale.

Les missionnaires n'avaient pas idée de cette complexité. Pour eux, le culte des génies de l'eau était avant tout condamnable, et, sur le plan de la moralité, les danses entretenues par l'association étaient incompatibles avec une vie chrétienne. L'initiation qui assurait la tradition du culte devait être supprimée.

L'influence des pasteurs et des prêtres fût rapidement suffisante pour que la destruction des '*pamba*' fût obtenue. Les masques des membres du jengu fûrent brûlés. Les convertis s'abstenaient entièrement des danses traditionelles. Aujourd'hui le souvenir de ces traits culturels est perdu. La destruction obtenue par la tactique exposée plus haut a été presque complète. *Les fonctions non-cultuelles de l'association disparûrent par le fait même.* Nous verrons plus loin qu'il fallût du temps pour que les répercussions de cette disparition se fassent sentir.

(*b*) *Le prix de la fiancée.* Les dons fournis par la famille du fiancé à l'occasion du mariage n'avaient aucune raison d'inquiéter les premiers missionnaires. Effectivement, ce symbole juridique de l'union garantissait le mariage comme institution naturelle. Un missionnaire note le soulagement exprimé par les parents lorsqu'ils apprirent que leurs filles en stage dans les sixa pourraient se marier à la fois chrétiennement et dans le respect du principe de la compensation matrimoniale.

Pourtant, quelques dizaines d'années plus tard, la 'dot' est dénoncée comme un 'fléau', constituant le principal obstacle au mariage chrétien. Tout dernièrement cette dot est interdite sous peine de péché. Que s'est-il passé?

Les influences conjointes de l'administration et de la mission ont déclenché une série de phénomènes incontrôlables dans le domaine des structures sociales.—La source principale du prestige traditionnel réside dans le contrôle des alliances et plus généralement dans ce que G. Balandier appelle les 'investissements sociologiques'. Ce sont bien entendu les aînés qui détiennent ce contrôle. Or, l'action missionnaire a ébranlé cet édifice hiérarchique par un certain nombre de pressions indirectes:

(1) La lutte contre la *polygamie*, très vigoureuse, a supprimé l'un des principaux moyens pour les anciens d'accroître leur prestige et leur pouvoir. La capitalisation des femmes devenue de plus en plus difficile a obligé à rechercher d'autres formes de capitalisation.

(2) Le savoir d'un type nouveau dispensé aux jeunes gens

précipite l'émancipation des éléments traditionnellement contraints de la société. De *nouveaux emplois* prestigieux sont réservés à la jeunesse qui échappe ainsi au contrôle des anciens; des sources de revenus en monnaie leur permettent une autonomie grandissante par rapport à la hiérarchie sociale.

(3) Dans le mariage lui-même, l'action engagée pour favoriser le rôle du *consentement* personnel dans les processus d'union a fortement diminué le rôle traditionnel des chefs.

Ces trois types de pression évoqués parmi d'autres expliquent, nous semble-t-il, l'inflation de la compensation matrimoniale. L'introduction de la monnaie offrait aux parents la possibilité de rattraper, par une sorte de jeu d'enchères, le contrôle des alliances qui leur échappait par ailleurs. Les déviations de la dot, contre lesquelles les missionnaires se sont élevés à juste titre, constituent pourtant le résultat, indirect, de leur action dans le domaine des structures sociales. Un tel processus est difficile à prévoir, bien entendu; mais une analyse plus poussée des transformations dûes à la christianisation permettrait au moins de ne pas accuser les sociétés des déviations causées par l'action étrangère elle-même.

Ce texte, extrait du Rapport officiel adressé à la S.D.N. en 1922, rend bien compte, semble-t-il, des déséquilibres inévitables entrainés par la prédication chrétienne:

L'action des missions, qui précède dans ces régions l'action administrative, s'est exercée au détriment de l'autorité des chefs. Ce résultat n'a pas été cherché, mais il a découlé normalement de la lutte contre le fétichisme et les abus de la société noire. La plupart des chefs sont féticheurs, les missions ont condamné le fétichisme; tous les chefs doivent leur autorité à leurs richesses, c'est-à-dire au grand nombre de leurs femmes, les missions ont condamné la polygamie; les chefs usaient de ceux qui ne pouvaient se soustraire à leur autorité comme d'esclaves, les missions ont introduit la notion de dignité et d'indépendance de la personne humaine. A côté du chef, la mission a placé le catéchiste dont l'autorité morale s'appuie sur l'autorité du Blanc et qui ne peut qu'enseigner le mépris du chef féticheur, polygame, esclavagiste. . . . Au fond, nous sommes près du moment où, dans cette population de la forêt, nous n'aurons plus affaire qu'à une poussière d'individus.

B.—Les réactions de la société Duala

L'attitude des missionnaires trouvait des correspondants dans certaines aspirations des groupes côtiers ou de certains éléments de ces groupes.

(1) Dans le contexte de la situation coloniale, le missionnaire apportait *protection* et *sécurité*. Le prêtre ou le pasteur se comportaient en effet dans une certaine mesure comme des 'anti-blancs', en ce sens qu'ils dénonçaient les abus du commerce et de l'administration. Au cours d'une rébellion par exemple, un Père Pallotin obtint la vie sauve aux chefs révoltés. D'autre part, les ilôts chrétiens mettaient relativement à l'abri des tracasseries administratives.

Vis-à-vis des abus de la coutume, les catégories sociales traditionnellement soumises (les jeunes, les femmes, les esclaves) trouvaient dans l'église une 'reconnaissance' inattendue de leur dignité sociale et de leur égalité devant Dieu avec les catégories supérieures. Les jeunes filles par exemple pouvaient échapper au mariage forcé avec un vieux polygame.

(2) Ces mêmes catégories contraintes acquérraient, par l'école et par la foi nouvelle, un *prestige* inespéré. La conversion remonta ainsi lentement la hiérarchie sociale. Les notables en vinrent petit à petit à accepter d'entrer dans la communauté chrétienne; leur prestige traditionnel se trouvait en effet menacé par les nouveaux responsables (catéchistes, maîtres d'école). La conversion du chef donnait généralement le signal de la conversion du groupe entier.

(3) L'acquisition de la '*puissance*' (force vitale), élément primordial dans les civilisations africaines et particulièrement bantu, joua en faveur de la conversion. Lorsqu'il fût admis que les Blancs disposaient de 'forces' supérieures à celles des Noirs pour dominer la nature, on en attribua naturellement l'origine à la foi et aux rites chrétiens. Les moyens traditionnels d'acquisition de la force tombèrent petit à petit en désuétude. Les 'medecine-men' devinrent des personnages marginaux ou anachroniques.

Ces divers mobiles permirent donc à la presque totalité des Duala et apparentés de recontrer le projet missionnaire. Le mouvement de conversion entraîna, pour de longues décades, les attitudes suivantes:

(1) Les jugements des missionnaires sur les coutumes fûrent adoptés pratiquement sans arrière-pensée. Le slogan '*le païen est sauvage*' servait de base aux idées que l'on se faisait des traditions. En ce qui concerne le mariage par exemple, on répétait que 'la femme est traitée comme une chèvre par la coutume'; 'la dot est versée dans un sac sans fond'. Une confrérie fût fondée pour l'élimination de la compensation matrimoniale.

(2) *Un très grand nombre de traits culturels disparûrent*, du moins apparemment. Les techniques de divination fûrent progressivement oubliées. Les danses fûrent, d'une certaine manière, remplacées par les cérémonies religieuses; les chorales se développèrent et les Duala devinrent vite des spécialistes du chant religieux. La définition du chrétien la plus courante était celle-ci: 'l'homme qui a abandonné les coutumes'.

Comme nous l'avons dit, la disparition du culte des *miengu* entraîna celle de l'association de culte elle-même. L'initiation disparût même des mémoires: l'école européenne la remplaçait. La médecine européenne était censée guérir plus efficacement les maladies soignées autrefois par les spécialistes du *jengu*. La justice et la paix étaient prises en charge par l'administration coloniale. L'économie obéissait à des règles nouvelles.

Mais on imagine que la liturgie, le droit, la médecine et l'école étaient loin de remplir exactement les fonctions assurées par l'ancienne association de culte. Un grand nombre de besoins se trouvèrent insatisfaits par les formes importées. L'école européenne n'enseigne pas les valeurs et traditions sociales propres à la tribu; elle n'intègre pas à la société car elle ne procure pas cette maturité et cette reconnaissance qui sont le fruit de l'initiation. On pourrait en dire de même des autres rôles de l'association. La messe chantée selon les mélodies grégoriennes n'a pas le rôle cathartique des danses rythmées par le village entier. La place dévolue aux femmes n'a pas trouvé son équivalent et les hommes tendent à reprendre leur hégémonie. Les grandes réunions destinées à rétablir la paix n'ont plus de raison d'être mais l'unité des clans apparentés n'est plus ressentie par l'ensemble.

Cet amoindrissement des formes culturelles propres aux Duala ne fût pas jugée comme un manque pendant de nombreuses années. La crise qui devait naître se déclencha à l'époque des grands mouvements d'opinion consécutifs à la dernière guerre.

II. LA CRISE. RUPTURE DU DIALOGUE

Il était dans la logique des choses que, d'une part, les ambiguités des motifs de la première conversion se fassent sentir un jour ou l'autre et que, d'autre part, la disparition des formes culturelles entraîne une crise interne.

Les premiers convertis sont devenus adultes; leurs enfants ne sont plus des convertis mais des fils de chrétiens. A première vue, le christianisme est définitivement implanté; le paganisme est un souvenir. Pourtant bien des indices révèlent le malaise: la confiance dans les missionnaires est moins grande, les jeunes sont moins attachés à la mission, les pratiques magiques reviennent à la surface.

A.—Les éléments de la crise

(1) La *force du Blanc* n'a été acquise ni par l'instruction ni par le baptême. Dans le contexte de la situation coloniale, les 'évolués' ont été déçus de voir que la science qu'ils avaient acquise dans les écoles de la mission ne leur a pas procuré les avantages matériels qu'ils attendaient. Plus ils avaient brisé les liens de dépendance avec l'ancien ordre social, plus ils étaient livrés à eux-mêmes.

Il en est de même pour la *sécurité* qu'apportait la mission. Ceux qui détiennent traditionnellement l'autorité ont été intégrés dans la communauté ecclésiale et les plus contraints des membres de la société n'ont plus contre ces derniers les mêmes recours que dans les débuts.

Les anciens maîtres de la société ont également perdu leur *prestige* séculaire et n'ont rien trouvé d'équivalent. Le privilège de la séniorité basé en partie sur le savoir est contesté par le nouveau type de savoir des couches cadettes de la société. Les aînés se plaignent de l'arrogance des jeunes et ces derniers refusent l'autorité des vieux. L'ancienne cohésion tribale se dégrade, et c'est le Blanc, missionnaire compris, qui en est rendu cause.

Une vague de déception se fait donc jour dans la société: le 'secret' des Blancs n'a pas été percé. La tactique missionnaire qui avait donné des résultats étonnants se retourne contre elle-même. Un évêque peut dire alors: 'nous faisons des chrétiens, la vie nous les enlève'; ce qui indique que la culture traditionnelle n'est pas réellement entrée en dialogue avec les éléments de la foi chrétienne; le paganisme n'a pas été étouffé et il n'est pas non plus intégré dans les formes nouvelles; l'osmose ne s'est pas réalisée.

(2) Une impression générale de *dépossession culturelle* se manifeste. On se plaint de ce que les Blancs ont supprimé tout ce qui permettait autrefois de survivre: les danses, les cérémonies de purification collective, la divination, les rites de fécondité.... Les professionnels de la guérison, individuelle ou communautaire, ont oublié leurs anciennes techniques. On ne sait plus conjurer le malheur, lutter contre la stérilité des femmes, assurer des pêches et des chasses suffisantes, etc.... La société se trouve saisie par une angoisse collective.

B.—Les réactions du groupe duala

Cette crise sociale entraîne le développement d'attitude destinées à récupérer, autant que faire se peut, le patrimoine perdu.

(1)—La société se cramponne d'abord à ce qui constitue le *noyau* de sa culture: le système de parenté. Ce qui a été lâché dans les autres domaines est rattrapé sur le plan de la structure clanique et particulièrement sur le plan des alliances matrimoniales. La mise en valeur du couple conjugal souhaitée par le christianisme est très lente. La grande difficulté des chrétiens réside dans le respect du mariage chrétien: on recule devant l'engagement exigé par le sacrement. La 'dot' augmente considérablement, contrairement aux prévisions et aux exhortations: elle apparaît de plus en plus comme un moyen de résistance des anciens contre la désagrégation du système de parenté; elle reste en effet le seul moyen de maintenir la hiérarchie traditionnelle. Les structures économiques n'ont pas évolué suffisamment pour que la famille élémentaire trouve les moyens de subsister par elle-même.

(2)—Le '*retour aux sources*' s'inscrit dans le mouvement qui mit les intellectuels en quête de la 'négritude'.

Certaines pratiques avaient plus ou moins survécu à la christianisation; elles sortent de la clandestinité. Ainsi on recommence à descendre solennellement de la nourriture dans les fleuves et la mer pour s'assurer la faveur des miengu.

Une grande place est donnée aux techniques magiques importées d'Europe.

L'un des phénomènes les plus révélateurs de la crise est sans doute celui de la reviviscence très généralisée des accusations de 'sorcellerie'. Il faut trouver des coupables: les collaborateurs du régime colonial, les catéchistes, et, d'une manière générale, les individus qui profitent de l'ordre nouveau, sont rendus responsables des morts, maladies, épidémies, de la stérilité du sol et de la pêche, etc.

Les valeurs traditionnelles sont ainsi recherchées de façon désordonnée; on tente de redonner vigueur à de vieilles formes désormais vides. Les missionnaires ont toujours dit qu'elles étaient opposées aux valeurs occidentales et aux valeurs chrétiennes: on les croit. La quête est donc menée au détriment de la vie religieuse. Les chrétiens en viennent ainsi à mener deux vies parallèles. En même temps que l'on reçoit les sacrements, on va voir les medecine-men pour conjurer les sorts et guérir les maladies. L'hétérogénéité des conduites, des droits et des croyances permet de jouer sur tous les tableaux en fonction des divers besoins. Ainsi se développe une certaine mauvaise conscience.

La mutation des valeurs escomptée par les missionnaires ne pouvait faire fi d'une certaine continuité avec la culture originale du groupe tribal. La crise est sans doute nécessaire pour que les institutions nouvelles retrouvent un fondement véritable dans les valeurs religieuses traditionnelles décantées. Le Noir s'aperçoit qu'il n'a pas été 'blanchi' par le christianisme; la puissance du

Blanc, il doit la conquérir lui-même, et par d'autres voies que celles qu'on lui avait proposées. Il va donc chercher à se poser lui-même en s'opposant au Blanc, selon la 'négritude'. Mais il s'aperçoit qu'il a perdu sa manière de penser comme Noir. Il revient donc à sa 'culture' païenne. La retournement dont nous avons parlé montre que l'on a converti la masse peut-être, mais *pas la conscience commune.* Une super-conscience chrétienne s'est développée à côté d'une infra-conscience religieuse qui n'est plus païenne, mais qui n'a pas non plus été baptisée: elle reste là comme une forme vide; c'est elle que l'on cherche maintenant à remplir.

Il n'est donc pas aisé de dresser un bilan, puisque le processus d'acculturation religieuse est en cours. La prise en charge des églises par des pasteurs autochtones permettra d'assurer des institutions sociales fidèles à la fois aux valeurs chrétiennes et aux valeurs traditionnelles. Ce mouvement de depassement de la crise est en cours et va s'intensifiant.

Summary

THE IMPACT OF CHRISTIANITY ON THE TRADITIONAL INSTITUTIONS OF THE COASTAL ETHNIC GROUPS OF THE CAMEROONS

The purpose of this paper is to outline missionary methods and the reactions of the Duala and related groups to these methods, taking into account the ideas prevailing in Europe at the time on foreign civilizations and the colonial situation in which the missionaries found themselves involved.

In the first period the missionaries faced with 'pagan' traditions found it necessary to establish points of Christian influence where the converts would be sheltered from heathenism. The founding of schools was the perfect answer to this problem: the young people were to form a new society so that the Faith could be grafted on to a basis of rational knowledge. The young girls trained in the 'écoles de fiancées' (schools for future wives) would

N

ensure the setting up of Christian families. Families of converts were gathered around the mission stations to constitute a pilot zone, the influence of which was eventually to eradicate paganism completely.

Many traditions were labelled 'savage' or even 'evil' and their social functions were not understood. The new converts were required to give up all their traditions. The cult of the water goblins (*jengu*) provides a good example of the process of cultural transformation through missionary action. The priests and ministers struggled against the cult itself—fertility rites, belief in spirits, and divination. However, the other functions served by the *jengu* association remained vacant; the *jengu* took care of initiation rites, made peace among various clans, insured obedience to the law of the clan, apportioned fishing grounds and so on.

The example of bride price is similar. At the beginning, the missionaries did not object to this, but the struggle against polygamy, the emancipation of the educated young, the reaction in favour of the young couple's consent to the marriage all contributed to a progressive decrease in the authority of the elders. The elders then tried to recapture the social control they had lost by increasing the amount of the bride price. Then the missionaries complained of an abuse which they themselves had indirectly brought about.

The missionary set-up offered new security to the traditionally submissive categories in the society. Education provided new prestige available to all. The new Faith was to give greater power than that obtained from ancient rites. When conversion became general, the Duala adopted the missionaries' judgements on their own civilizations, 'the pagan is a savage'. Many cultural traits disappeared and religious ceremonies replaced dancing. The school took over from the initiation rites, etc. A Christian was defined as 'one who has abandoned the customs' and particularly those pertaining to the water goblins' cult.

Logically the ambiguous nature of the first conversions became apparent: the power of the white man was not acquired and the society found itself disappointed. On the other hand, many traditions were forgotten and not replaced: the impression was that of a cultural vacuum which could, to a large extent, be attributed to evangelization. A bishop could say at this point: 'We manufacture Christians but life takes them away from us.' This amounts to saying that the cultural substratum was not converted. The methods used at the beginning made it possible to baptize most people, but the traditional institutions, more or less maimed, remained. The Christians lived two lives concurrently; their behaviour was divided and doomed to duality. Society first held on to its cultural focus, the kinship system. The inflation of bride price was the means and external sign of resistance. Accusations of sorcery, becoming more and more numerous, betrayed the increasing anxiety. A return to the old traditional ritual practices became general. Fertility rites were revived as well as offerings to the water goblins, and so on. The period of the break of the society with its own culture, however, made possible a process of maturation which was necessary for the implantation of new Christian institutions. The native clergy will now be able to re-integrate the original common religious consciousness into today's Christian life.

VIII. SOME PROBLEMS OF AFRICAN CHRISTIANITY: GUILT AND SHAME

F. B. WELBOURN

The object of this paper is to ask whether Protestant Christianity —preached largely in terms of salvation from guilt—could be understood by members of traditional African societies: or whether they had first to undergo an Anglo-Saxon type of education before they could appreciate the fundamental assumptions either of the missionaries or of colonial administrators.

My attention was first drawn to the problem by Erikson (1950), who suggests that, while shame and guilt are readily confused in western society, they arise out of different levels of individual development. *Shame* is the obverse of *autonomy*—the feeling which a child experiences when, at the appropriate stage, he fails to control his bowel-movements, to co-ordinate his muscles sufficiently to stand up and walk. Because failure at such points raises questions as to his acceptability to his parents, it is closely associated also with doubt. Klein (1948), using a different frame of reference, describes the experience of one of her patients:

> one of the first traumata of her experience: the heavy blow her narcissism received when she imagined that the measures taken to train her [bowel habits] meant the loss of the excessive affection bestowed on her in her infancy.

Guilt, on the other hand, is felt when a child uses his newly-found autonomy to display *initiative*. Anxious to please his parents, to show them what he can do, he pulls the books out of the shelves and incurs a prohibitive 'Don't'. In trying to please, he has invoked displeasure. He has hurt those whom he loves. This is the basic origin of guilt-feelings; and Klein (1953) finds them at a still earlier stage (the 'depressive position') when the baby, first experiencing its mother as a whole person, recognizes that the loved one—the source of all comfort and security—is identical with the object of its fierce aggressions.

Erikson finds the paradigm of the distinction in the experience of Adam and Eve (Genesis 3). If I may slightly develop his presentation, his first crisis of infantile growth ('Trust *versus* Basic Mistrust') is to be found in the story of Creation. There is complete confidence between man and God. Moreover, 'the man and his wife were both naked and were not ashamed'. Insisting on their autonomy, 'the eyes of both were opened, and they knew that they were naked; and they sewed fig-leaves together and made themselves aprons'. They had discovered shame. But they discovered also that they had exercised initiative displeasing to God. They heard the voice of God walking in the garden. For Erikson this is the internalized voice of the superego. The excuse of shame is not allowed. The fear of what others see is replaced by inner acceptance of responsibility, the recognition of guilt. Erikson's fourth crisis is 'Industry *versus* Inferiority'. It is the stage at which children learn the use of tools and of reason. Without the prior surmounting of both shame and guilt, it cannot be successfully negotiated; and it is at least interesting that Adam proceeded from the discovery of guilt to the tilling of the soil.

This paper is concerned with the subjective feelings of shame and guilt, and it is necessary to distinguish them from actions which may be judged by others to be shameful or guilty. It is possible to 'feel that I have let myself down', to 'feel ashamed of myself', not only in the presence of others but when I have committed an action which others would regard as shameful if they were present. Benedict (1947) has discussed this aspect of shame among the Japanese. It may also occur, as Lynd (1958) has argued in her full discussion, because I have failed to live up to my own ideals in circumstances where others would say, 'There's nothing to be ashamed about. You've done all that you could.' Equally, it is possible to feel no shame about, for instance, nakedness, which public opinion would judge as deeply shameful; and a distinction is made between those who have achieved such shamelessness either through moral turpitude or through an inner conviction of values overriding those of public opinion. Although it may not be easy to distinguish their objective effects, there is a recognized difference between 'I couldn't care less' and the typical Anglo-Saxon injunction, 'Don't mind what others think. Do what you yourself believe to be right.'

In the same way there is a clear distinction between legal or moral guilt, as judged by others, and the subjective feeling of guilt. The former assume that the agent was capable of conscious control over his actions; and it is possible for him to feel innocent, either because he genuinely believes that he did not act as alleged or because, admitting his legal guilt, he believes that, in the particular circumstances, it was a morally right action. Guilt-feelings, on the other hand, are under no conscious control. They may be caused by the disapproval of others, even if the agent believes himself morally right. They may be a response to simple ill-will towards others, or to choice between incompatible loyalties. They may rise from the deep unconscious with no known object.

Both shame and guilt, therefore, may have an internal or an external reference, and it is difficult to accept the Freud–Benedict distinction between guilt as based on an internalization of values and shame on disapproval coming from others. But the two are different; and it is proposed to adopt Piers' (1953) definition of guilt-feelings as arising from knowledge of a prohibition touched or transgressed, and of shame-feelings as response to a goal not reached.

In testing Erikson's scheme in East Africa, it became clear that in many societies language does not allow for the distinction. It is extremely difficult to express the idea of guilt-feelings as opposed to the wholly externalized fact of losing (whether actually guilty or not) a case at law. Among Lugbara of north-west Uganda *drinza* is now used to translate both 'guilt' and 'shame'. My educated informant could find no traditional sense in which it must be translated 'guilt'. In order to use it in this sense he had to take examples from an overtly Christian—and largely a 'Revival'—context. The East African Revival (Taylor, 1958; Ogot, 1966), characteristically evangelical in form, represents an interiorisation of the Puritan ethic with a radical emphasis on personal responsibility and guilt; and my Lugbara informant was able to distinguish clearly, in his own conversion experience, between the *guilt* of 'refusing entry to Christ, who stands at the door and knocks' and the *shame* of admitting to his previous associates that he had become one of the 'saved'. But he had to do so in English.

Of the Gusii of western Kenya the LeVines (1963) write that they consider 'the *ensoni* feeling of sexual shame . . . to be at the very core of their morality'. Taking 'sex' in a broad Freudian sense, *ensoni* is expressed in avoidance between generations and sexes and 'is not merely a matter of formal etiquette but a feeling experienced by individuals'. One of these avoidances (of free argument with kin of the parental generation) 'is sometimes considered separately as "respect" (*ogosika*)'; and, in general, the attitude of respect is more important towards males of this generation, of sex-avoidance towards females. Psycho-analytically, there is a beginning of deliberate training in fear of the father, on which guilt and later responsibility may be based. But in general there is discouragement of initiative till after initiation. From the age of three, children are expected to dress themselves; but 'once you let a child walk about freely, that means he is old enough to be initiated'. This pattern of encouraging the growth of *autonomy* but discouraging *initiative* in childhood, occurs in other African societies; and the relation of adult cultures to child-rearing deserves detailed investigation.

Among the Ganda, for instance, sitting is marked by a simple rite at the home of the paternal grandmother; and, after this, babies taken by their mothers to the gardens are firmly sat in a hollow in the ground. On the other hand, when a child first learns to walk, 'you mustn't let him get away from you. He might do all sorts of damage.' 'Shame' is translated *ensonyi*, etymologically identical with the Gusii *ensoni*. Probably because of the more highly developed political structure of Buganda, it is used in a far wider context; and Richards (1964), though with a purpose different from mine, quotes a number of examples where shame, and desire to humiliate others, play an important part in the political and social fields. The word *okuswala*, 'to be ashamed', means also 'to be out of proportion' and may be used of a mis-proportioned cow. It suggests the emphasis on preserving social equilibrium, which is probably central to the behaviour-code of many African societies. On the other hand, the idea of 'guilt' can be expressed only by the phrase *omusango gunsinze*, 'the judgement has defeated me', which is not traditionally an admission of actual guilt. The judge might well have been bribed; and there was always the possibility of appeal to a higher court. My wife well remembers receiving language-instruction from a missionary who used this traditional meaning of *omusango* to show that, since Ganda had no sense of sin, they were self-condemned as the worst of sinners.

It is, therefore, of some importance to discover that, in Teutonic languages also, the distinction between shame and guilt is a relatively recent development. The Oxford English Dictionary (1933) states that, while *shame* appears in some form in all early Teutonic languages, Old English alone has a root for *guilt*. Moreover, there is no quoted example earlier than 1593 in which 'guilt' must be interpreted subjectively. The date is surely significant. It corresponds, in Riesman's (1950) terms, to the transition from a 'tradition-directed' society motivated by shame to an 'inner-directed' society motivated by guilt. It marches with the rise of the Puritans, of whom Benedict (1935) has written:

> a sense of guilt as extreme as they portrayed and demanded both in their own conversion experiences and in those of their converts is found in a slightly saner civilisation only in institutions for mental disease.

Co-dependent with Capitalism, Protestantism, and the Scientific Revolution lay the attempt to find justification (to atone for the infantile breaking of parental trust) through worldly success, through the blood of Christ or through the empirical demonstration of God's glory in creation. Only in Protestantism did the motive become explicit. (Perhaps it is part of the essential function of religion to reveal the roots of the culture in which it flourishes). It was left to Freud and his followers to give it secular definition. As he wrote (1930):

> The sense of guilt is the most important [factor] in the evolution of culture . . . the price of progress . . . is . . . forfeiting happiness through heightening the sense of guilt.

and Klein (1953):

> Feelings of guilt . . . are a fundamental incentive towards creativeness and work . . . any sense of joy, beauty and enrichment . . . is, in the unconscious mind, felt to be the mother's loving and creative breast and the father's creative penis.

That another school of psycho-analysts might have interpreted creativeness in terms of the pursuit of a positive 'ego-ideal', rather than the negative promptings of the superego, suggests that other, more ancient, stream in British culture, represented by the evangelical reformers of the anti-Slavery movement and the Factory Acts; by Livingstone's vision of Christianity, civilization, and legitimate commerce going hand in hand; perhaps, indeed by the early settlers of East and Central Africa, with their hopes of becoming the focus through which Christian civilization should spread throughout the dark continent.

But the two streams could never be wholly disentangled. Webster (1964) notes how Henry Venn's ideal of planting self-supporting, self-governing, and self-propagating churches overseas—focused in the consecration of Bishop Crowther—gave way to a new generation of evangelicals schooled in the guilt-ridden atmosphere of the Keswick Convention. With their strict consciences they were—if not born, at least—'born again' to dominate the consciences of others and to prove the continuing need of their supervision of the African Church by spying out the immorality of Africans. On the whole, it is this will to dominate—this rationalization in moral terms of an overweening superego—which most characterized the British impact on Africa. In East Africa, Lugard and Ainsworth among the administrators, Tucker and Owen among the missionaries, were rare examples of the other point of view, whose policies were too often overridden by men who knew what was 'right for the African' and were determined to get it. Mannoni (1956) has indeed argued that precisely those Europeans, who found in their homelands insufficient opportunity to dominate, sought service in the colonies.

Colonialism may have hidden roots in political and economic needs. It could be prosecuted only so long as there were sufficient inner-directed individuals anxious to direct the lives of others.

Delavignette (1950) has put it, for all the colonial powers:

> Man must put the world in order. This determination has the compelling power of a religion, and the European is its prophet.

It produced men who not only had driving consciences of their own and assumed that it was the highest goal of individuals to be 'responsible'—to be able to stand aside from the crowd and make decisions as their consciences directed. They had not heard that other sense of the word 'responsible'—the ability to respond sympathetically to what might be the wholly different needs of others. They assumed that the Protestant conscience—or at least the English public school conscience—and the ability to take individual responsibility were the birthright of every man. If they were 'religious', they assumed also that every man was conscious of his guilt before God. In Buganda they found a few of the political *élite* who, through their experience of centralized administration over a large unit, were perhaps already becoming inner-directed. There were Muslim Ganda in 1875 (Welbourn, 1964) and Christians in 1885–87 (Faupel, 1962), who in their martyrdoms must have come near at least to knowing the guilt of conflicting loyalties. And these characteristics made an immediate appeal to missionaries and administrators alike. But in the rest of Buganda—in the rest of East Africa (I must write of what I know)—there was no similar experience on which to draw.

It is characteristic of traditional society, as Lee (1944, 1950) has written of the Wintu, that they regard the individual as a differentiated part of society, while the west sees society as a plurality of individuals. It is inevitable in these circumstances that evil should be conceived as 'the victim's irremediable but involuntary failure to fulfil the roles and achieve the performance regarded as normal for his status in the social structure' (Fortes, 1959). This is a shame situation—the failure to reach a goal or, in Ganda terms, being 'out of proportion'; and Fortes comments on the lack of guilt-feelings among the Tallensi, since all responsibility is borne by the ancestors. If Klein is right, no child can escape the unconscious experience of guilt in its earliest development. It is dependent not merely on an Oedipus situation in relation to parents and siblings. This might be subject to cultural modification. But it arises from the primary biological relationship between mother and child. It is, therefore, possible that members of traditional societies are able to project on to mystical beings much that inner-directed men, whose guilt-feelings are much nearer to the surface, must take upon their own shoulders (Carothers, 1954). It is not that, unconsciously, there is no experience of guilt but that it can be more readily projected and that the Oedipal situation is institutionalized in avoidances between the generations (LeVine, Fortes) and perhaps in initiation. The penalty is loss of creativeness, the gain is in closer community not only with men but with the mystical world.

Shame is, in the first place, an emotional response to falling short of the social norm; and both my Lugbara and Nkore informants suggested that shame might not be felt unless the actions themselves became known to others. A liberal Lugbara husband might give his wife foods which were taboo for women; but this would not be felt as shameful unless it became known outside the family. On the other hand, when Richards writes that the Kabaka's deportation in 1953 was seen as Buganda's shame, she is referring not to the supposed attitudes of non-Ganda but to a deeply-felt shock that such a thing could have happened to them, a sense that they had lost all meaningful existence.[1] Something of the same experience was to be found in Gikuyu who felt that to abolish clitoridectomy was to destroy the foundations of the tribe (Welbourn, 1961). Shame, again deeply felt, and again related to unsuccessful conflict with an out-group, is felt by Maasai *moran*, to whom the treaty with the British—often quoted as evidence of equality—has denied their traditional pastures and the right to fight at will both men and beasts.

It may be said that shame, as a motive of conduct, is common

[1] Dr. Richards denies the view here apparently imputed to her. I think she describes the social structure, while I try to supply the concomitant individual psychology.

enough in western society. But—at least in the subculture from which came the majority of missionaries and colonial administrators—it was the inner-directed individual, impervious to the jeers of others, who was held up as the ideal; and the parental injunction, 'Don't do that. You'll put me to shame', was directed (however unintentionally) precisely at making the avoidance of shame into a filial duty and therefore a potential source of guilt. The moral condemnation, 'That's not how an Englishman behaves', is certainly an invocation of shame, a statement that an ideal is being betrayed. But at the same time it holds the suggestion that a frontier has been transgressed—'so far an Englishman may go, but no farther'—and is therefore also an invitation to guilt. On the other hand, Doob (1964) found that it was only the most highly educated leaders of Ganda society who tended to emphasize the importance of work, to suggest hostility towards their fathers, and to plan for the future. These characteristics, along with others, distinguish such leaders clearly from 'minor leaders' and 'followers'. Doob has obtained similar results among Luo and Zulu—peoples very different both from one another and from Ganda; and he says that they are associated with acculturation—to a society, that is, in which hostility to father, with its concomitant guilt, is the near-conscious motive of hard work and of planning for the future.

The early colonialists, therefore, were faced with a society which they did not understand—whose psychological roots most of them were unequipped to recognize. Missionaries bewailed the lack of a sense of guilt; administrators spoke of irresponsibility and indifference to work for its own sake. Lonsdale (1964) quotes Ainsworth's recognition that, if they were to play their part in the individualist society which was required by a modern economy, Luyia must be slowly weaned from their traditional dependence on small-scale societies. British missionaries—from differing motives, but overall because boarding schools were the only possible form of education at the time—were to play their part in providing that 'education for leadership' which was an essential part of their tradition. Government schools were later to continue the same Anglo-Saxon tradition of 'character-building'. Opportunities in Government and commerce were to provide an environment in which the guilt-potential of individuals could be sublimated to the needs of the new culture. In the end, enough inner-directed men emerged to lead nationalist political movements and to man at least the higher ranks of an independent civil service with very much more than competence. But the question remains whether the new leaders make assumptions, and talk a language, as different as those of their colonialist mentors from the tradition-directed outlook of those whom they rule. One of Webster's most suggestive observations of the 'African churches' among the Yoruba is the repeated failure of reforms introduced by junior leaders through majority votes; and the experience that, unless change had unanimous support, it was better avoided. This is surely an important comment on the psychological basis of a one-party state.

Doob lists thirty-nine points in a battery of tests at which 'Makerere-educated leaders' differed significantly from 'followers'; and twenty-nine, almost identical, at which they differed significantly from 'minor leaders'. 'Minor leaders' and 'followers' differed significantly only at twelve points. The important feature of this report is that, in a country where 78·5 per cent of the population over sixteen years of age are Christian (*Uganda Census, 1959*) the influence of church and school might have produced a higher degree of acculturation. But, whatever the convictions of the early Ganda Christian leaders, the great majority of Ganda became Christian because only so could they become fully Ganda (Low, 1957). Without baptism they fell short of their inner ideal of themselves. Elsewhere in East Africa children at school might be laughed at if they had no 'second' (i.e. baptismal) name. To become Christian was a response to shame, not to claim salvation from guilt. Men accepted taboos imposed by the missionaries, and might excommunicate themselves if they offended. For many Christ became a ticket to a 'happy land, far, far away'. But for few did he have any relation to the important events of life.

Perhaps only in the Revival, spread widely through the

Protestant areas of East Africa, is there any acceptance of the inwardness of evangelical religion. Perhaps it represents the point at which its members, having experienced the social and economic consequences of the dominant culture of the West, can enter into that culture mythologically also. Highly educated men have had other channels through which they might do so. Yet an elderly Nkore woman—coming from a culture in which women have to avoid a long list of 'shameful' actions—told how, in the Revival fellowship, she had found support from others who wished to break with tradition and was now able to perform such actions without a sense of shame. In areas such as Buganda, where the guilt-content of Revival is much more explicit, shame is still a powerful, if undeliberate, factor in ensuring that members recite 'victories over sin' at the fellowship meetings and observe the group *mores* outside them.

The question therefore arises whether there is a theology—or at least a *kerygma*—proper to a shame-culture: or whether men must pass through a 'natural' transition from shame to guilt before they can be open to grace. It is a question not only about missionary techniques but about secular education. Can the new Africa be built on the basis of a still largely traditional society? or must its members first pass through the largely inner-directed mode of the West? It is a question also for the West. Riesman thinks that contemporary 'other-directed' society is motivated by 'a diffuse anxiety'. Bradbury (1963) regrets that shame is replacing guilt. The Hausers (1962) recommend it as a more adult emotion. Lynd seems to confine guilt to specific acts and misses the pervading inwardness of its deep unconscious roots. (It might be said that she regards only the superficial aspects of Oedipal guilt and ignores its deeper origin in the 'depressive position'). But she makes a powerful claim for the importance of shame in a culture based on fulfilment of the ego-ideal rather than on the largely negative percepts of the superego. The distinction between shame and guilt must, therefore, be taken seriously; and it may be that the answer to the question was given by two scholarly and deeply Christian Anglo-Saxon women with whom I discussed it in Uganda.

L. C. CARD NUMBER →

Author: International African Seminar. 7th,
(Full Name)

Title: Christianity in tropical Africa
Baeta, C G ed.

Place: Publisher:

Date: 1968 Edition:

Series:

ACTION

Out
Pre
C
R
On
Oe
Ci
Rd
P
D
Np

One is a Roman Catholic, the other a moderately 'high' Anglican. Both—as I felt free to tell them—showed by their conscientious devotion to duty what would normally be regarded as a deep guilt-motivation. Yet neither of them *felt* any real sense of guilt. They knew sin as objective separation from God. But, equally objectively, they were restored by Christ through the sacraments. They thought that I laid altogether too much stress on the importance of guilt in the Anglo-Saxon tradition. They appear to be pre-Freudian. Guilt has not yet broken through into consciousness. For them—as perhaps for others of a similar culture—Christ is the Restorer and Fulfiller of all things. It may be that in these terms he should be presented to traditional societies—that, for instance, it was not only politically, but theologically, true that it was possible to be fully Ganda only by being Christian Ganda. In that case, he is the Fulfiller of guilt: but only because guilt is one aspect of the whole personality which needs fulfilment. He is fulfiller also of the Beatles.

It is impossible, at this point, to avoid a subject of which I am deeply ignorant—the particular contribution of Roman Catholicism (and of 'high' Anglican groups like the Universities Mission to Central Africa) to the change in African attitudes. I have discussed elsewhere (Welbourn, 1965) the stereotypes in which Ganda commonly characterize the products of their two major secondary schools—the one staffed by English Anglicans and educating for leadership, the other by French-Canadian Roman Catholics and educating for obedience. It might be said, in Erikson's terms, that one encourages initiative while the other stops short at autonomy. Doob found that *none* of his 'followers' suggested hostility towards their fathers, while 29 per cent of 'Makerere-educated leaders' did so. Perhaps a Catholic priest is 'father' in the former sense, while Protestant missionaries reject the appellation but become, in fact, father-figures of a much more authoritarian kind. It is they who provoke rebellion by their spiritual children.

The consequences for Ganda politics—and indeed for the whole of Uganda—have been profound; and a necessary criticism of Doob's findings is that they do not specify the religious denomination of his subjects. It may be that views expressed were characteristic not so much of social class as of religious affiliation; and, since 62·5 per cent of Ganda Christians are Roman Catholic, there is considerable possibility of statistical error. All over East Africa it was Protestant Africans who formed the first power-structure below the colonial administration. All over East Africa, with one exception, the leading nationalist politicians are either Protestants or Muslims or, being Roman Catholics, have passed through some form of secular education before entering politics. Just as Puritanism revealed the roots of European capitalist society, so Catholicism was the inner dimension of traditional Europe. It may not be a good nursemaid of nationalism; but, itself belonging essentially to one traditional society, it may well be the most effective means through which members of another can enter into the Christian heritage and, no doubt ultimately, through it into nationalism and the responsible society. It may be that its schools form a better basis for the new Africa than some politicians are inclined to think.

A more competent hand should try to assess how far guilt—understood in the psycho-analytic and Puritan sense—is necessary to the Biblical concept of sin. I have a suspicion that, bearing in mind the distinction between shame and guilt, the former might be found to have even greater relevance. Yet I have a sneaking feeling that guilt-consciousness has been integral to any form of monotheism which has been a dynamic force in history. Surely Erikson (1956) is only paraphrasing Saint Augustine when he writes (I also paraphrase from memory), 'Who would deny to the young the glorious stimulus of guilt?'.

REFERENCES

Benedict, R.
(1935) *Patterns of Culture*. London: Routledge and Kegan Paul.
(1947) *The Chrysanthemum and the Sword*. London: Secker and Warburg.
Bradbury, M.
(1963) 'The New Language of Morals', *Twentieth Century*. Summer, 1963.
Carothers, J. C.
(1954) *The Psychology of Mau Mau*. Nairobi: Government Printer.

Delavignette, R.
(1950) *Freedom and Authority in West Africa.* London: Oxford University Press.
Doob, L. W.
(1964) in Fallers, L.A. (ed.) *The King's Men.* London: Oxford University Press. (Ch. 8.)
Erikson, E. H.
(1950) *Childhood and Society.* New York: Norton.
(1956) *Young Man Luther.* London: Faber.
Faupel, F. J.
(1962) *African Holocaust; The Story of the Uganda Martyrs.* London: Chapman.
Fortes, M.
(1959) *Oedipus and Job in West African Religion.* Cambridge University Press
Freud, S.
(1930) *Civilisation and its Discontents.* London: Hogarth Press.
Hauser, R. and H.
(1962) *The Fraternal Society.* London: Bodley Head.
Klein, M.
(1948) *Contributions to Psycho-Analysis, 1921–1945.* London: Hogarth Press.
Klein, M. and Riviere, J.
(1953) *Love, Hate and Reparation.* London: Hogarth Press.
Lee, D.
(1944, 1950) Quoted in Lynd (1958).
LeVine, R. A. and B. B.
(1963) in Whiting, B.B. (ed.) *Six Cultures: Studies of Child Rearing.* London: John Wiley.
Lonsdale, J. M.
(1964) Unpublished Ph.D. thesis, University of Cambridge.
Low, D. A.
(1957) *Religion and Society in Buganda 1875–1900.* London: Routledge and Kegan Paul.
Lynd, H. M.
(1958) *On Shame and the Search for Identity.* London: Routledge and Kegan Paul.
Mannoni, O.
(1958) *Prospero and Caliban.* London: Methuen.
Oxford English Dictionary
(1933)
Ogot, B. A. and Welbourn, F. B.
(1966) *A Place to Feel at Home.* London: Oxford University Press.
Piers, G.
(1953) Quoted in Lynd (1958).
Richards, A. I.
(1964) in Fallers, L. A. (ed.) *The King's Men.* London: Oxford University Press. (Chs. 6 and 7.)
Riesman, D.
(1950) *The Lonely Crowd.* London: Oxford University Press.
Taylor, J. V.
(1958) *The Growth of the Church in Buganda.* London: S.C.M. Press.
Uganda Census, 1959. Entebbe: Government Printer.
(1963)
Webster, J. B.
(1964) *The African Churches among the Yoruba.* London: Oxford University Press.

Welbourn, F. B.
(1961) *East African Rebels*. London: S.C.M. Press.
(1965) *Religion and Politics in Uganda, 1952–1962*. Nairobi: East African Publishing House.
Welbourn, F. B. and Katumba, A.
(1964) 'Muslim Martyrs of Buganda', *Uganda Journal*, XXVIII, 2.

Résumé

QUELQUES PROBLÈMES DU CHRISTIANISME AFRICAIN: HONTE ET CULPABILITÉ

L'enseignement du christianisme protestant s'est fait dans le sens de la rédemption de la culpabilité en soulignant l'importance des sentiments de culpabilité subjectifs. La question est de savoir si cette présentation était compréhensible dans le cadre de l'expérience traditionnelle africaine ou bien s'il fallait d'abord que cette expérience soit repensée dans des catégories anglo-saxonnes.

Erikson suggère que la honte et la culpabilité subjectives, quoique souvent confondues dans la société occidentale, ont leur origine (dans l'ordre cité) à différents niveaux du développement infantile. La première est l'opposé de l'*autonomie* et la deuxième de l'*initiative*. Il voit un paradigme de cette distinction dans la honte d'Adam et Eve de leur nudité suivis par le voix de Dieu dans le jardin du Paradis—voix internalisée du super-moi donnant naissance à des sentiments de culpabilité. Klein estime que la culpabilité a des racines encore plus profondes dans la tension entre l'amour et l'aggressivité chez le bébé qui pour la première fois se rend compte de l'existence de sa mère en tant que personne complète.

Freud et Benedict font une distinction entre la culpabilité fondée sur une internalisation des valeurs parentales et la honte fondée sur la désapprobation externe des autres. Mais des sentiments de culpabilité peuvent être causés par une désapprobation externe; et l'on peut éprouver de la honte en trahissant ses propres idéaux dans des cas soit où il n'y a pas d'observateurs présents, soit où ces observateurs approuvent le comportement que l'on estime être honteux.

Beaucoup de sociétés traditionnelles Est-africaines accordent une importance considérable à la 'honte' mais ne disposent pas de mot pour la 'culpabilité' sauf dans le sens de 'perdre un procès' ce qui n'implique pas forcément une admission de culpabilité réelle et encore moins des sentiments de culpabilité. Il semblerait que dans ces sociétés les méthodes d'éducation des enfants encouragent l'*autonomie* et découragent l'*initiative*. Selon le système d'Erikson, ceci impliquerait donc plutût la honte que la culpabilité.

Dans les langues teutoniques primitives on trouve également le concept de 'honte'; mais c'est seulement dans le vieil anglais que l'on a une racine pour le mot 'culpabilité'. Le premier exemple en anglais où l'on doive entendre la 'culpabilité' de manière subjective date de 1593. Ceci correspond à l'émergence de la personnalité 'dirigée de l'intérieur' et à l'importance accordée par les puritains à la rédemption de la culpabilité subjective qui, pour eux, constituait le centre même du christianisme.

Le capitalisme, le Puritanisme et la révolution scientifique fûrent tous causés par la culpabilité (par opposition avec la 'honte' de la 'société guidée par la tradition'). Le Protestantisme seul exprima ceci explicitement. Sur le plan séculaire c'est à Freud qu'il dévolut d'établir que les sentiments de culpabilité sont essentiels au progrès social et culturel.

L'autre tendance de la culture britannique fondée sur la poursuite du 'moi-idéal' est représentée sans doute par les évangélistes britanniques du début du XIXème siècle. Mais c'est une génération accablée par la culpabilité qui leur succéda. Les membres de ce groupe jugeaient les autres en termes moraux rigides et avaient pour intention de dominer l'église africaine pour son propre bien. Le désir de domination est caractéristique de l'essentiel de l'impact britannique sur l'Afrique soit sur le plan missionnaire soit sur le plan administratif.

Les hommes de ce genre avaient des consciences énergiques et attachaient une grande valeur à la faculté de prendre des décisions en opposition avec la masse. Ils supposaient que la conscience et le sens de la 'responsabilité' protestants appartenaient à tous les hommes comme un droit de naissance. Les missionnaires avaient la même hypothèse pour la conscience de la culpabilité. Ce n'est qu'au Buganda qu'ils trouvèrent des Africains qui, dans certaine mesure, partageaient cette expérience.

Les sociétés traditionnelles considèrent l'individu comme une partie différenciée de la société. L'Occident estime que la société est constituée par une pluralité d'individus. La motivation du comportement dans la société traditionnelle est forcément la honte alors que pour l'Occident c'est très souvent la culpabilité. La honte peut être ressentie très profondément non pas comme une simple réaction à la moquerie des autres mais comme la trahison d'un idéal intime. On peut citer comme exemples les Ganda et la déportation du Kabaka, les Gikuyu vis-à-vis de la menace de l'abolition de la clitoridectomie et les *moran* maasai devant l'interdiction imposée par les britanniques des combats traditionnels. Il existe une honte de ce genre en Occident également évidemment. Mais la culture anglo-saxonne a tendance à souligner l'importance dominante de la culpabilité—comme motivation; Doob a observé la formation de ce genre de personnalité dans trois sociétés africaines différentes en résultat de l'acculturation au système occidental. Les premiers missionnaires et administrateurs se trouvaient en face d'une culture dont ils ne pouvaient comprendre les racines psychologiques. Ils l'abordèrent donc en se fondant sur l'hypothèse que si cette culture n'était pas déjà anglo-saxonne elle devrait l'être.

Les écoles missionnaires ainsi que l'emploi dans l'administration et le commerce permirent le développement de personnalités 'dirigées de l'intérieur'. Ces hommes devinrent des dirigeants nationalistes et occupèrent des postes dans les fonctions publiques indépendantes. Mais la majorité des africains devinrent chrétiens pour des raisons dûes à la honte. Ce n'est que le 'Revival' qui accepte l'intériorité de la religion évangélique; et même la honte est très largement évoquée.

Existe-t-il un *kerygma* propre à une *culture fondée sur la honte*? Ou bien, les hommes doivent-ils découvrir la culpabilité avant de pouvoir répondre à l'appel de l'évangile? Peut-on construire l'Afrique nouvelle à partir de la culture traditionnelle? Où est-il nécessaire d'avoir une expérience semblable sur le plan séculier?

Ce problème se pose aussi à l'Occident d'ailleurs, où une nouvelle forme de honte devient à l'heure actuelle la motivation d'une société 'dirigée vers ce qui est autre'.

Il y a des chrétiens qui n'ont que très peu la conscience de la culpabilité. Pour eux le Christ est le Réparateur et l'Exauceur. C'est peut-être ainsi que le Christianisme est le mieux représenté par le catholicisme romain: puisqu'il appartient lui-même à une culture traditionnelle il serait la meilleure façon de présenter le Christianisme aux autres. Néanmoins il reste bien fondé de dire que partout où le monothéisme a été une force dynamique dans l'histoire, il y a eu une profonde conscience de la culpabilité.

IX. CONCEPTIONS OF CHRISTIANITY IN THE CONTEXT OF TROPICAL AFRICA: NIGERIAN REACTIONS TO ITS ADVENT

J. B. SCHUYLER, S.J.

A concomitant of human ageing is frequently, though unfortunately not always, a certain kind of balanced wisdom. A universal characteristic of wisdom is humility. So it is that, as the social sciences move painfully towards maturity, a certain humility signalizes some slow growth in wisdom. Thus Robert Merton observes that:

> the growing contributions of sociological theory to its sister-disciplines lie more in the realm of general sociological orientations than in that of specific confirmed hypotheses. The development of social history, of institutional economics, and the importation of sociological perspectives into psychoanalytic theory involve recognition of the sociological dimensions of the data rather than incorporation of specific confirmed theories.[1]

Thus we have become wiser in looking for and recognizing the broader scope of variable factors which bear upon a given phenomenon; we have not achieved that scientifically certain and verifiable knowledge of the origins, elements, characteristics, and derivations of social phenomena in any generalized degree.

An example which comes to mind is the critical work which has been directed towards the theory of religious causation of economic development. Max Weber's pioneering study *The Protestant Ethic and the Spirit of Capitalism*, for all its scientifically cautious qualifications, inspired many empirical researches testing its validity. Many are still going on. Yet most are now seen to have misconstrued Weber's thesis, and to that extent to be relatively worthless. A sober reading of the carefully scholarly Weber shows that the Calvinist ethic can be established in some small limited degree as one cause, among other causes, of the spirit of capitalism.[2] This can hardly be called a monistic theory

[1] Merton, 1957, pp. 88–89.

[2] Conant, 1951, pp. 25, 32.

of religious causation of social development, though some of his less astute disciples have read it as such. Their efforts have suffered the same fate, deservedly, as all known monistic theories of social change.

But not only have we become very cautious about our theoretical propositions, including those of religious causation and impact. We have also become very wary about our concepts and their formulations. What is religion? What is social causation? What is cultural change? And so on.

This has relevance for our seminar. If we agree with the author of *Science and Common Sense*[3] that science begins with some distinct though unclear concept and seeks to clarify that concept as the basis of further clarifications, then we see that much work needs to be done in clarifying the concepts which trigger our discussions. For 'Christianity', 'impact', and 'tropical Africa' are terms which evoke quite varied, even contradictory images in both academic and lay minds. Our first objective in this essay is to summarize the main types of these varying images, particularly as manifested in the literature. Then I should like to report on a small study, informal but in some depth, of the attitudes of some contemporary Nigerians to our questions. I think our conclusion must be that unquestionably Christianity has had an impact on tropical Africa. The degree of its unique impact, and the degree of its impact in combination with other influences can be ascertained only by tremendous research efforts and sophisticated multiple factor analysis. I see our own discussions here as making some small contribution in that direction.

Our first concern must be an adequate conceptualization of Christianity. As W. I. Thomas would put it, much depends on who is defining the situation. Was Christianity the vision of Henry the Navigator in his plan to win Africans to Christianity? Or was it rather in the plan of merchants, his fellow Portuguese Christians, to capture Africans for the slave trade? We probably have strong convictions on the matter, but could one expect Africans, or any others, to distinguish when both plans seemed

[3] For the latest competent critical discussion on Weber's thesis see Greeley, 1964, pp. 20 ff.

to come from the same source? The quiet leavening work of many thousands of Christian missionaries offered one image of Christianity. But all Europeans were identified as Christians—the soldiers, the merchants and traders, the administrators. In fact, many made use of the Christian Bible. We would not identify the immoral sexual and economic traffic of the riff-raff among them as Christian, but to the newly impressed Africans diverse modes of Christian conduct could give a confusing image of Christianity.

This reminds me of the father of a Nigerian friend. My friend tells me that his father, though closely associated with Christian clergy and laity and even helpful in the building of a Christian church, steadfastly refused to become a Christian and died a pagan. His reason? That, among his people, the worst adulterers, cheats, and even murderers were to be found among the Christians. He positively preferred pagan virtue. My students have asked me often why the collapse of sexual morality among their peoples dated from the arrival and growth of Christianity. We might insist on quite proper distinctions here, but is a general populace —whether African, or any other—sufficiently knowledgeable, objective, and perceptive to make them?

To develop this theme further, we might look at the obviously enlightened, Christian-motivated 'Bible and Plough' policy. Livingstone had said, 'We ought to encourage the Africans to cultivate for our markets as the most effectual means next to the Gospel for their elevation.' This was the Christian missionary's brilliant antidote to the slave traffic with all its social, moral, and economic evils. Yet the policy motivated explorations of the continental interior, which came later to be identified with imperialistic explorations. It also motivated direct political manoeuvrings, both in the politics of African nations and in the politics of imperial nations, for the establishment, protection, and development of the plough economy. Quite understandably this came to be identified with, and undistinguishable from the economic and political interests of traders and administrators. It would certainly be asking too much for the victims of whatever politico-economic operation, mission contrived or supported as it was, to distinguish between the selfish interests of mere traders or administrators and the altruistically motivated interests of the Christian missionaries. Thus political and military manoeuvres, such as the king-making operation in Abeokuta (1852), the sacking of Onitsha (1860), the annexation of Lagos (1861), and so on, which necessarily produced sufferers as well as beneficiaries, were situations which had to be defined as not alien to missionary endeavours and purposes. The relevance for the impact of Christianity is evident, though muddied.

Thus the image of Christianity as a light to tropical Africa is marred by the shadow of Christian traffic in slaves; the image of Christianity as uplifter of African personal and social living standards is clouded by involvement in the allegedly worldly pursuits of economic gain and political power. We go a step further. 'The spread of Christianity has always been allied with the spread of civilization. . . .' So says Louise Creighton,[4] and most of us would agree, though making allowance for some less complimentary pages of history. But this raises the question of the identity of civilization. If it is not equated with better mousetraps, interior plumbing, and rocket ships, but rather with a satisfactory level of peaceful, prosperous, and even progressive life, there are those who challenge the thesis. Christian peoples have not been singularly free of war, poverty, or even regression. On the other hand, some Africans, particularly those who are trying to build a past, offer a not unpersuasive case for their claim that Christianity attacked and has been destroying African cultures. Despite their failings, the argument goes, these cultures provided peoples with satisfyingly integrated life-systems, values, norms, traditions, meanings. Christianity upset the balance in these ways of life, and confused peoples who, unable to choose between old and new, settled into a kind of anomie which characterizes much of changing African society today. Again we have here the definition of a situation. Whether a rosy African past can be scientifically verified or not, there are those who see it that way. Their view of Christianity is that of destroying, not saving angel.

[4] In *Missions: Their Rise and Development*, n.d. p. 7.

Another conceptualization of Christianity would identify it with westernization and modernization. Yet Christianity is out of the Levant, and it is strong today in some orthodox and uniate Catholic and other Christian Churches of the east. Christianity's life in the west has dovetailed intimately with the latter's modernization, its development of a scientific mentality and a technological industry. Yet it engages even now in mortal struggle with a secularistic spirit which claims for itself, as vigorously as does Christianity, a home in the modern west. The Rev. Dr. J. O'Connell, S.M.A., of the University of Ibadan, who argues persuasively against the identification of modernization with westernization, aptly lists the characteristic changes of modernization:

> . . . formal schooling replaces tribal initiation; age-old agricultural implements give way before tractors and fertilizers; distances are shortened by the fast speed of machines; by and large ascriptive or inherited status tends to give way before achieved status—the chief and his sub-chiefs bow out before the elected politician; sharper distinctions arise between work and leisure; salaried employment in industry and elsewhere starts to spread and more impersonal labour relations predominate; health improves through more varied food and better medical care; occupations become more skilled and specialized; civil services, established according to rational and universalist norms, replace the slow-going personal administration of royal courts and village elders; and endeavour is made to institutionalise the control of economic growth through planning agencies; self-sustained, diversified; larger political units become viable from the improved systems of communications and better methods of administration; and inter-dependence comes into being between communities that were previously separated from and independent of one another.[5]

He adds, what is now generally recognized, that 'rapidly changing societies face problems arising from the weakening of kinship bonds, family disorganization, excessive individualism in the modernising sectors, and a sense of uncertainty about social and cultural identity'.

Obviously none of these characteristics, whether considered in their constructive or problematic aspects, is peculiarly or typically Christian. Though a strong point could be made for identifying,

[5] 1964, pp. 25 ff.

in aspiration as well as achievement, what is truly Christian with what is truly human. The fact, that these features of the modernization process have been finding a home in Africa does not necessarily argue to Christianization, but modernization. Anti-Christian powers have been sharing in the same process. Only the fact that Christians have shared in the process makes them relevant, and then only if their purposes or means have been typically Christian or unChristian.

Might we identify Christianity with the lands from which it has come to Africa? We have already seen that Europe produced both missioners and slavers. But we might look further. Tropical Africa's persistent resort to superstition, even among Christians, is cited as proof of its shallow Christianity. Yet a recent survey showed that 20 per cent of France's presumptively Catholic population resort regularly to astrologers or other fortunetellers. Some Irish pastors in Nigeria insist, whether with exaggeration or not I cannot say, that superstition is more widespread in traditionally Catholic Ireland than in more recently evangelized Nigeria. In discouragement we see African tribalism as a denial of Christian universal fraternity. Yet after 300 years Canada's French- and English-speaking are still antagonists, and little Belgium cannot harmonize its Flemings and Walloons. We recognize this unChristian type of ethnicity to be so worldwide as to ignore Christian borders. Need anything be said of the Anglo-Latin, Sino-Filipino, and other ethnic and racial antipathies in lands which claim to have been Christianized? We blanche at the marital infidelity and sexual immorality among Africans, and read social psychiatrists' diagnoses that rampant divorce, infidelity, and sexual license in the west are functions of modern western culture. Indeed, some Christian leaders seem disposed to drop the bans against such conduct. We look at African conformity to western Christian standards in the matter of modesty in dress as an achievement, yet we read reports of inspiring Christian life among other peoples which do not conform to western standards of modesty at all. Meanwhile western standards seem to have become other than what they were. We seem still to be looking for the distinctive criterion of Christianity.

Perhaps the direct challenge of many Christian missionaries against the very core of African cultures—their tribal authorities and family structures, their festivals and dancing and drumming, their ancestor veneration and manifold gods—suggests essential Christianity. Not so, for many of the most authoritative leaders of Christian mission groups directed adaptation to, rather than destruction of, native cultures. The sociologically popular ideal types offer little help. To identify the virtuous with Christian and the vicious with pagan is so unrealistic as to be meaningless. For to say nothing of the frequent unChristian conduct of Christians, there are the many missionary reports of great-souled pagans, whom Diedrich Westermann likened to Tertullian's *anima naturaliter Christiana*.[6]

We have not yet suggested what is perhaps most obvious to the practising Christian, though little mentioned by the historians of Christianity in Africa, namely, the system of Christian revelation and scriptures, of sacraments and liturgy, of personal and social moral codes, and of church organization. Yet, to say nothing of the differences—sometimes minor, sometimes major—among the several Christian churches in this respect, one does not have the impression that depth of Christian understanding or breadth of Christian knowledge characterize the Christians of tropical Africa. So much rapid evangelization in the one century, and especially the last half century, has simply not allowed the development of a popular or advanced literature, nor a level of education to build an intellectually competent elite, nor a catechetics to energize adult minds. One is inclined to agree that the mere preaching of the Christian religion itself in whatever form, without any type of so-called 'rice-Christianity', would have had, naturally speaking, very few listeners and fewer respondents.

Yet the fact is that the response has been quite remarkable. Raw statistics can be misleading, even frustrating, for they say nothing of history or quality, provide no perspective in depth. But they can offer initial orientation. In just one century Christianity has grown in Africa practically from scratch (except in the rather sparsely Christianized north) till today when some 40

[6] 1937.

million Christians comprise 15 per cent of the continent's 275 million population. Just since the turn of the century, the Catholic figure has risen from a half million to over 27 million today. Whatever it is, Christianity has had some meaning for a large part of the African people.

Probably the least ineffectual conceptualization of Christianity is a kind of operational definition so much used in certain empirical researches. Just as intelligence is defined as that which is measured by intelligence tests, so we conceptualize Christianity initially as that which people have in mind when they speak about it. This involves all the logical *non sequiturs* and *culs-de-sac* already discussed, but at least we can get off dead centre. Perhaps we might even advance a step towards a clearer conceptualization.

The urban sociologist considers as part of his data the attitudes of people towards cities and city life. These attitudes spread across a continuum from deep disgust to zestful enthusiasm. Attitudes towards Christianity's impact on Africa are no less varied, and no less part of the data of that impact. The realities underlying these attitudes, both advantageous and disadvantageous, to the Christian image, are recorded with some unison by historians and social analysts.

On the positive side there seems to be agreement that the Christian, largely British Protestant campaign against the slave trade and all slavery was not only effective in itself, but motivated much exploration of Africa. This eventually gave West Africa an opening to the world on its seacoasts rather than through the overland Sahara routes. The 'Bible and Plough' policy, instigated and encouraged by missionaries, developed a legitimate commerce to replace the dealing in slaves. The elimination of human sacrifices or religious murders, of the destruction of twins and their mothers in some areas, of cannibalism, and of much superstition and religious deception is attributed largely to Christian missionary efforts. Whether in pursuit of the 'Bible and Plough' policy, or simply to develop basic skills necessary for a new kind of world, missioners began schools. One of the effects of these scholastic endeavours was the emergence of bilingualism among many Africans and a *lingua franca*, usually English or French, which was to be a condition of national unities. These schools and the very association with the missionaries both produced a new elite and stirred human longings for the good things of European life. The Christian teaching of equality of human dignity not only opposed slave practices and exploitative use of women, but stimulated the new elite to challenge imperialist powers for independence. Frequently missioners led or helped Africans in the defence of their interests against colonial pretensions. The words of Dennis Osadebay, formerly Prime Minister of Nigeria's Midwestern Region, are often quoted in this connexion:

> . . . the missionary has made the African soil fertile for the growth of imperialism . . . [but] he has equally helped to lay the foundations for the present spirit of nationalism. . . . When African historians come to write their own account of the adventure of Africa with imperialism, they will write of the missionaries as the greatest friends the African had.[7]

Rising levels of education and aspiration led to pressure for such facilities as roads, hospitals, and more numerous schools. These seemed to possess self-multiplying factors. Home mission offices pumped men, money, books, travel, and educational scholarships into African development. Missionaries produced first dictionaries, grammars, and translations in many languages. They undertook ventures in agricultural improvement, for example, the plantation at Topo near Badagri. Such formerly independent nations as Sierra Leone and Liberia derive from Christian efforts for freed slaves. Current educational and medical work is still dominantly undertaken and supported by Christian missionary groups. Fourah Bay College derived from the missionary policy of training a native clergy, and many seminaries of different denominations are regularly producing African sons for work in the ministry. Much mission effort and money provided the wherewithal for Africans to travel to Europe and America for advanced education.

Such are most of the benefits of the Christian efforts in Africa. It might be claimed that some derived as much from non-Christian humanitarian groups as from Christians. This may be

[7] In *West Africa*, April 5, 1947, p. 280, cited by Coleman, 1958, p. 112.

so; but then we would have to investigate whether such humanitarianism itself had roots in Christian soil. Some of these benefits, some say, would have come sooner or later with or without Christianity. Probably, though certainly much later, at fabulously greater cost, and with little guarantee that human dignity and personal values would have been dominant concerns. We have not mentioned what many would consider to be the greatest of all values, which most of our historians and analysts do not cite, namely the tradition of a vision of truth and an understanding of life which the human heart most desperately seeks. No man has assessed the extent to which this factor has probably influenced the conduct of African personal lives and social relations.

The coin has another side, and analysts trace many negative influences to Christian origins. By and large European traders and merchants, though often nominally Christian, were no paragons of virtue, but rather selfishly principled worldings. Even the better ones were, as traders, naturally more interested in turning a profit than spreading the good tidings. Bengt Sundkler quotes Eiselen's observation that Bantu 'contact with a population of white Christians has raised the quantity and lowered the quality of Bantu Christians'.[8] This phenomenon, however, is nothing new in human experience.

More important, probably, was the missionaries' deliberate attempt, in their work of evangelization, to destroy the cultural patterns of the host peoples. I say deliberate, because statements of some early missionaries make it clear that they saw African religions and cultures to be so intermingled and unified that there could be no real religious conversion without cultural rejection. As a matter of policy cultural invasion was and is debatable. As a matter of fact this cultural invasion did result in some strong conversions, many compromised conversions, much antipathy, and much socio-cultural confusion. Surrender of their culture to embrace Christianity frequently resulted in the alienation of the individuals concerned as well as socio-cultural disorganization. The destruction of old tribal sanctions heavily

[8] Cf. Sundkler, 1961, p. 36.

supported by religious power led to a moral laxity among many who joyously subscribed to Christian freedom, but neither bothered about nor understood Christian law.

This opposition to all aspects of native culture and religion led towards a destruction of both, including many elements which probably could have and should have been preserved, for example, some aspects of the strongly knit family structures, much of the drumming and dancing, many art forms. Many rituals and prayers (connected with the major life events of birth, marriage, and death), quite compatible with Christianity and indeed quite beautiful, were abandoned, with resultant feelings of loss, diffidence, and homelessness among the converted. The very sharpness and completeness of the break between the incoming Christian cultures and the challenged host cultures contributed to the attitude which identified Christianity with the imperialism of the colonizing powers.

The Christian attack on slavery did contribute ultimately to the attack against imperial rule, but it also led to the breakdown of established social systems of authority and rule. And the preparation of students to work in colonial trade and administration contributed to the anomie of broken families, migratory labour, and the manifold evils of town and city life. Interference with the existing family system, including its sense of continuity in the veneration of ancestors, led to the weakening of parental authority. Clearly the sanctions of the Christian commandment on parental respect were not as compelling as tribally sanctioned punishments.

Christianity presented the scandal of diversity and opposition among the several Christian Churches. These were sometimes identified with different imperial powers, and always caused at least confusion if not actual anti-Christian hostilities. Christianity's uncompromising refusal to tolerate polygamy, except in some convert instances or among indigenous separatist Churches, has led to either a preference for Islam among some tribes or insincere professions of Christianity. Some Africans have simply taken the western ways which came with Christianity and not bothered with the latter, except to share in some of its material benefits. Some have responded with a kind of ethnocentric backlash, which rejects everything Christian and western—except what happens to be convenient at the moment. Some of the African nationalists and syncretist Churches manifest some of this reaction. The very feeling of inferiority engendered by the white Christians' rejection of almost everything African, black, and pagan also led to this reaction.

The foregoing is a more or less general summary, then, of analysts' appraisals of the impact of Christianity on tropical Africa. A book of pros and cons, denunciations and explanations, phenomenological evidence in support and denial could be written on every favourable and unfavourable claim. For example, despite the culturally destructive aims of some missionaries, a case could be made for the determined sincerity of many mission authorities who urged and directed adaptation of Christianity to local situations, without modification of Christian principles, and incorporation of local customs and values into Christian living wherever at all possible.[9] Whether a policy of acculturation would have been more successful than one of aggression is a question no less important than debatable. There is of course the sensationally though solidly successful pioneering effort of Matteo Ricci in sixteenth-century China. But there the host culture was already highly developed, and was able to respond appreciatively to this missioner who was a sympathetic intellectual and accomplished scientist.[10] His work was destroyed by successors who followed less sympathetic policies. On the other hand there have been the more paternalistically governed

[9] For example, Pope Pius XII said in 1950: 'Native custom has the privilege of *melior conditio possidentis*. Before in effect decreeing its eventual suppression the missionary must prove that it is indissolubly linked with error or immorality or absurd superstition. In so far as this proof is not made, custom holds. It has the force of law. It possesses legal right.' (Cited in Todd, 1962, p. 167.) See the same book's discussion of the attitude of the founder of The Society of African Missions, Bishop Melchior de Marion Bresillac, concerning directives for the development of native clergies well over a century ago. See also Pope Pius XII's two encyclicals on the missions, *Evangelii praecones* (Heralds of the Gospels), 1951, and *Fidei Donum* (On the Present Conditions of the Catholic Missions, Especially in Africa, 1957).

[10] For accounts of the missionary venture in China, see Cronin, 1955, and Dunne, 1962.

efforts in the Jesuits' Paraguay Reductions and in Dr. Albert Schweitzer's work in Gabon. The question arises whether a less educated populace would actually see much difference in a new religion which adopted many of the external observances of the old. This is the question in the minds of many Africans, both clergy and laity, who today strongly oppose Africanization of the Church's liturgy, language, and architecture—though not necessarily its personnel. Presumably owing to their foreign-educated tastes, they argue that European culture is far superior to the African, and claim that adaptation implies religious support for second class living and inferior standards in Africa.

Margaret Mead has argued strongly, even persuasively, for the quickness and totality of cultural change when technological civilization comes to technologically uninitiated peoples.[11] How realistic is this proposal in the secular version of the question of acculturation policy? Clearly the churches by themselves would not be able to dictate sudden and total change in the material and socio-political cultures of their mission peoples. But the Church has a history sometimes evident and sometimes not, of adaptation to and even canonization of many non-Christian cultural elements. It would seem that there has been and is room for a much more tolerant and flexible policy—including a willingness to adapt Christian principles to host cultures and to incorporate the latter into the Christian image where possible, and at the same time to encourage cultural rapport and exchanges. This sounds, perhaps, high-flown enough to qualify for the ivory tower; but conceptualizations of principle belong on high, though their application and testing belong in the valleys of daily living and prudential choices.

I asked my students at the University of Lagos, with almost two sessions of a course in sociology behind them, to aid in this assessment of Christianity's impact on their own country and people. These students are generally older and more experienced than most university students would be expected to be, many of them having spent several years in teaching, civil service, or industry before undertaking higher studies. They responded co-

[11] See Mead, 1956, Chapter XVIII, and especially pp. 445 ff.

operatively to the request that during vacation they answer, with the advice of their parents and elders in the villages, an open-end questionnaire. Introduced by a covering letter giving the historians' and social analysts' views as outlined above, the questionnaire sought unstructured answers on pre-Christian and Christian views and impressions on the following topics:

Value of life itself
Degree and freedom of choice and conduct
Concept of personal dignity
Level of conviction about religious tenets
Worth of one's own work and status
Respect for life and freedom
Satisfaction of religious ritual and liturgy
Care of the sick, underprivileged, accused, and guilty
Answers to life's major problems
Value of children, family reputation and unity, material prosperity
Christianity's divisions and divisiveness
Provision of material charity
Place of sex in personal and social life
Satisfaction of marriage.

Many of the forty responding papers were carefully and thoughtfully done. Several were lengthy and detailed.[12] For the most part they tended to support what the historians have told us, though their particular views fleshed out the skeletal development in the literature. Most manifested gratifying balance, though one had to notice subjective motivations behind their writing. Thus many were obviously *laudatores temporis acti* or *pro domo sua*, and some took the opportunity to be rhetorically and chauvinistically critical. Few made any distinction between Christian and western influences. Some made little attempt to reconcile apparent contradictions in their assessments of conflicting values. It was interesting, though not surprising in view of the foregoing, to notice that several papers could be seen to be in flat contradiction

[12] There has been neither time nor resources for either a statistically significant analysis or a multiple variable analysis.

with each other. All told, however, I think they express an authentic set of Nigerian views on an intimately Nigerian matter. Only 10 per cent came from Northern Nigeria; the others were quite broadly spread among Nigerians from west, mid-west, and east.

As we did previously with the historians, so we might here record consecutively positive and negative evaluations. At the same time we might attend to the opposite views on the very same matters. Often these views reflect an apparent degree respectively, of pro- or anti-Christian orientation.

Many of the more perceptive papers spoke glowingly of the broadness of life vision which Christianity introduced to the African. Though frequently confusing, its very pluralism provided scope for diversified views, and it elevated aspirations and expectations to levels of European achievement. Its vision of eternal life, and God as loving father rather than fearsome avenger and cause of all hardship and misfortune, introduced a hopeful purposiveness to human life. Love rather than fear became the criterion of godliness in human behaviour. (I might mention here that some respondents, reflecting the continuing debate among scholars today,[13] insisted that the concept of God as father was quite common in pre-Christian traditions.) This elevated understanding of God and His relationship with men offered a solution to life's problems and a balm for its ills, and put an end to shallow pre-Christian traditions and beliefs such as superstitions, witchcraft, fear of ancestors, and reincarnation. Thus living slaves were saved from the fate of accompanying their dead master to the grave and the life beyond. And there developed a sense of personal responsibility in view of the sanction of eternal life, which, according to one paper, is all the sanction which life should need!

Though some denied that it made any difference, several emphasized the value of prayer to the Father through Jesus Christ. Some few spoke of the value of personal prayer which

[13] Recall the Institute of African Studies' Conference on 'The High God in Africa' in Ibadan, December 1964; also the articles of James O'Connell and Austin Shelton in *Man*, 1962 and 1964 respectively, and of course E. B. Idowu's *Olodumare: God in Yoruba Belief*.

Christianity encouraged, as well as the personal opportunity and responsibility to achieve spiritual as well as other growth. Some appreciated the intellectually satisfying system of Christian theology as the foundation of an entire view of life, and several drew the connexion between it and certain principles of personal and social morality. These had to do with the personal dignity of every human being, the freedom of human choice, the rejection of slavery and imperialism, the responsibility for the weak and underprivileged, God's equal concern for rich and poor, and the denial of race as a factor of human worth. In short, these writers, and presumably their families and elders, saw the relevance of morality to Christian teaching on this life and the next, have integrated their life views around the core of Christian ideology, and have applied it, at least intentionally, to all phases of life.

Others have been far less concerned, at least in their expression, with Christian ideology than with the effects of the Christian presence. Thus many attributed to Christianity the diminution of witchcraft, though admitting that it still persists. This is represented as an attack on one of the established institutions of African life, and a victory over one of its more repulsive traditions. The victory is admittedly not complete, for witchcraft is still identified with many inconvenient or strange phenomena—illness, failure, sterility, twins (still in some places), misfortune, 'acts of God', and so on. The same favourable regard views the elimination of cannibalism and many forms of cruelty.

To judge from respondents' papers, the most favourable achievement of Christianity has been the revolution towards respect for the individual and his rights. Almost all referred to the elimination of human sacrifice, although some argued that Christianity alone could not have achieved it, but required the help of imperial military might. The ban on human sacrifice was identified with a less morphologically bloodthirsty view of the gods, and with the right of innocent persons to their lives. The principle came to be applied to the treatment of slaves, prisoners, twins and their mothers, the infirm, weak, and handicapped. A further application was the respect due to each person's soul, and even to the bodies of the dead, unimportant as well as important, that they be given decent burial. Another frequently mentioned application was the gradual rejection of inter-tribal wars with their slave-raidings and killings.

Almost universally recorded was Christianity's success in changing the attitude of certain tribes towards twins (one woman respondent included triplets!) and their mothers, although two respondents reported that the taboos still exist. It will be recalled that the earliest Christian groups included these twins and mothers rescued from tribal ejection and death.

Very often cited and developed, though sometimes challenged, was the increase of personal freedom which Christianity fostered. Many specified the right to freedom of choice in marriage, in occupation, in place and type of residence, in disposition of affluence, and in personal behaviour as definite gains over former socially sanctioned tribal conformity. Some saw this freedom, applied likewise to intellectual and religious growth, as a golden opportunity for exploiting hard work, for seeing the sky as the limit of personal endeavour and achievement. There was recognition that the right of the slave to be free implied the right of the colonial to be free from the imperial. Some applied it to the women's right to freedom from male domination, but more had severe reservations about this freedom. (Almost all respondents were male.) Only two papers made any application of this right to freedom to those Nigerians who have inherited some of the limitations of slave status within their respective tribes.

The matter of women's freedom came in for much discussion, though much was negative. Positive values were seen in the understanding of the natural causes for menstruation, sterility and the sex of children, in the woman's right to choice in marriage and her opportunity to opt for monogamous marriage. This freedom contributed to respect for the woman in the marital relationship, to an emphasis on her value as a person rather than on the dominantly functional role which she played. Many saw it as now possible for love to dominate marriage rather than mere contract or duty. Though not denying the serious dislocations which have accompanied women's freedom, several praised Christianity for preaching the equal dignity of woman and her equal rights in marriage. Some suggested that this was a cause of Christianity's early attraction for women. One wrote, rather astutely, that Christianity changed the dominant marital concern from interest in one's lineage to interest in one's wife.

Almost every respondent spoke favourably of the higher regard for the persons of the accused and the guilty. Again it was pointed out that such were among the earliest adherents to the Christian churches. There was further praise for the institution of law, law courts, and impersonal justice, as well as for the recognition of charitable forgiveness as a Christian virtue. Also for the Christian drive against traditional cruelties. On the other hand, there were denials that this caused much change in personal virtue or conduct. Many qualified their approval of the Christian treatment of the accused and guilty in that it contributed to lawlessness, deviance, and the destruction of social controls.

A comparable appraisal was made of the missionaries' work for the sick, underprivileged, and poor. Again praise was given for the establishment of medical and maternity clinics and the introduction of scientific medical techniques. There was less agreement that this represented improvement in personal care. Some insisted that the missionaries' hospitals tended to break a long tradition of familial responsibility and concern for the afflicted and needy. But most agreed that Christian charity for the sick did stimulate growing community responsibility, more equitable treatment and professional care.

Some few spoke of helpful instances of acculturation, for example the identification of St. Augustine's Day with the feast of the new yams, of the prevalence of some Christian songs and the idea of the Fatherhood of God even in some pagan circles. But it was also suggested that this cultural blending was sometimes a kind of syncretism in which certain familial, superstitious, tribal, and Christian elements were all wrapped confusedly together.

The bonds among early Christian communities were seen as the cause of co-operation among villages, particularly among similar denominational groups. This led to less isolated mentalities, a growing concern for personal neatness and respectability.

Some spoke very strongly of the influence of Christianity on habits of cleanliness, neatness, and hygiene. Frequently co-operative efforts among church groups expanded into co-operative civic enterprises.

As might be suspected, there was quite a difference of opinion on the subject of sex. Those seeing an advantageous influence in Christianity claimed that it made sex more than something merely biological while stripping it of its superstitious mysteriousness. Children have come to be desired more for personal than economic and lineal reasons. Monogamous marriage has brought more love into the family, more closeness between husband and wife, more marital satisfaction, and salvation of women and children from polygamous chaos, rivalry, and jealousy.

On the subject of politics, Christianity, despite its disintegrative effect on some tribal unities, was seen as contributing a re-integrative effect, a new focus for intra- and inter-tribal understanding. Its help in developing roads, commerce, education, a *lingua franca* helped to forge national ties beyond tribal boundaries. One respondent suggested that Christianity had given to states and statesmen standards of righteousness, moral support, loyalty to their objectives and policies, co-operation, permeation of the social milieu with a spirit of brotherhood, and a reminder to function as servants of God and His people. Moreover, today's political leaders received from their missionary education a common background and understanding.

Almost every respondent cited the Christian churches' contribution to education—from nurseries to scholarships for professional training in the ministry, law, medicine, science, and administration. Some 85 per cent of Nigeria's secondary schools are still run by voluntary agencies, mostly missionary groups. The very introduction and encouragement to learning, all the first schools, books, teachers, and funds, came from the Christian missions, and a little education developed its own thirst for more. For all the criticisms of over-Europeanization of educational methods and curricula, few Nigerians would question that the missionaries' education opened African doors to the outside world.

Much of the foregoing sounds like an unrelieved success story. Much of it is uncritically and imprecisely detailed. However, it does indicate that, in the minds of many Nigerians, Christianity has changed the map of Nigerian attitudes, objectives, and behaviour. In many respects the changes have been to Nigeria's benefit.

However, as we have seen, there is a strong other side to the argument. Most respondents charged Christianity with at least some negative impact on Nigerian life. The most serious charge is that Christianity disrupted a way of life which, by and large, provided satisfaction for its members. By destroying a religio-cultural integrity, without persuading Africans to accept an integral Christianity in its place, the missionaries introduced anomie on a wide scale into the lives of persons, families, and societies. Unwilling to work patiently and sympathetically for the peaceful evolution of African from pagan to Christian beliefs and ways, it stirred up antagonisms within and among families, villages, and tribes. It introduced an individualism of western stamp, as foreign to basic Christianity as it is to African communalism, which destroyed the bases of social integration and the balance between social stability and personal satisfaction. Its sponsorship of free choice as the basis of a new social order created instead widespread disorder. Because of its emphasis on book and European employment, Christianity has commercialized personal worth, made it a function of affluence and thus contributed to selfishness throughout the new Nigerian life. It broke the ties of stable authority in home and palace. Its own divided house has been a scandal and has led to further divisions. Its intolerant rejection of African experience and culture created in Africans a self-image of inferiority, which has erupted in a backlash of rejection of almost everything Christian and Western—even Christianity's most cherished spiritual teachings.

Every African custom and value which Christianity attacked had its place in the social structure—ancestor veneration and deference, family continuity and inheritance of wives, initiations and funeral festivities, polygamy and secret societies, tribal names and status structure, severe rejection of the immoral and unnatural deviate. When the parts crumbled, so did the whole structure. Lift women to monogamous equality; concubinage, prostitution, and promiscuity follow. Destroy belief in the gods; there is no need to fear their sanctions. Treat the criminal with love rather than punishment and disgrace; he continues his crimes. Supplant the supremacy of the tribe and family with personal importance; self-seeking aggrandizement takes its place. Children become liabilities, hence unwanted.

Though not in so many words, the foregoing analysis reflects the negative critics' views. Almost without exception the respondents reported severe decline in sexual morality—the loss of the value and observance of virginity, promiscuous conduct with the loss of divine and then social sanctions, increasing resort to abortion, and so on. Another frequent negative influence of Christianity was the destruction of local rituals. With their symbols, songs, and dances, they were meaningful, socially binding, and personally satisfying. They were psychologically fulfilling and socio-morally conformative. Christianity substituted rituals which were little comprehended or relevant, in which the people were more spectators than participants. People crowd Christian churches because of the social pressure to be modern, but without understanding of what they say they profess. Their young people go abroad to study and on their return they find, if they still have the faith, that the local religious community has little to satisfy their developed intelligence.

On this same score, Christianity has impressed many as being largely a social organization capable of worshipping God and mammon simultaneously, and demanding payment for the symbols of membership, the administration of the sacraments. Many conversions have been for material reasons, e.g. the avoidance of anti-mixed-marriage pressure, the opportunity of an education or a job, or even a less expensive funeral service. Thus for many Christianity is quite superficial, and so has no real answers to life's personal difficulties, nor any real influence on the people's social problems. This was Canon Stevens' observation in correlating the crowded churches in Lagos and Port Harcourt with the continuing serious problems of tribalism and economic injustice.[14]

[14] Stevens, n.d.

This negative picture, too, would seem to be over-drawn in some respects. But only in some. If we fuse the two pictures—of advantageous and disadvantageous impacts—together, and try to make allowance for what is Christian by merely extrinsic denomination, we are still possessed of a picture of pervasive influence on Nigerian life. We do not mean merely the public presence of Christian churches, and Sundays and other festivals, nor that all the influence has been helpful, or applied in a helpful way. There has been and is, however, enough of the beneficent and fruitful, to motivate further clarification of what Christianity might truly be said to be, how it might best be dissociated with its false images, and how it might more effectively and purely be adapted to well-intentioned African reception and development.

REFERENCES

Coleman, James
(1958) *Nigeria: Background to Nationalism*. University of California Press.

Conant, James
(1951) *Science and Common Sense*. New Haven: Yale University Press.

Creighton, Louise
(n.d.) in *Missions: Their Rise and Development*. London: Williams and Norgate (Home University Library of Modern Knowledge).

Cronin, Vincent
(1955) *The Wise Man from the West*. New York: Dutton.

Dunne, George, S. J.
(1962) *Generation of Giants*. University of Notre Dame Press.

Greeley, Andrew
(1964) 'The Protestant ethic: time for a moratorium', in *Sociological Analysis*, Vol. 25, No. 1 (Spring 1964).

Idowu, E. B.
(1962) *Olodumare: God in Yoruba Belief*. London: Longmans.

Mead, Margaret
(1956) *New Lives for Old: Cultural Transformation—Manus, 1928–1953*. New York: Morrow.

Merton, Robert K.
(1957) *Social Theory and Social Structure*. Glencoe: Free Press. Revised edition.

O'Connell, James
(1962) 'The withdrawal of the High God in West African religion: an essay in interpretation', *Man*, 62, 109, pp. 67–69.
(1964) 'The concept of modernisation', *Exiit*, Ibadan, No. 4.

Shelton, Austin J.
(1964) 'On recent interpretations of *deus otiosus*: the withdrawn god in West African psychology', *Man*, 64, 55, pp. 53–54.

Stevens, R. S. O.
(n.d.) *The Church in Urban Nigeria*, being a 'report on a visit of Canon R. S. O. Stevens to Nigeria during May and June 1963'. Birmingham.
Sundkler, Bengt
(1961) *Bantu Prophets in South Africa*. London: Oxford University Press. Second edition.
Todd, John
(1962) *African Mission*. London: Burns Oates.
Westermann, Diedrich
(1937) *Africa and Christianity*. London: Oxford University Press.

Résumé

CONCEPTS DU CHRISTIANISME DANS LE CONTEXTE DE L'AFRIQUE TROPICALE: ÉVALUATION NIGÉRIENNE DE CET ÉVÈNEMENT

Ce rapport est un essai d'orientation générale concernant les aspects conceptuels et pragmatiques de notre sujet. Le problème conceptuel dérive de la vaste imprécision qui règne dans les définitions du Christianisme et même d'une ambiguïté qui prête à confusion. Il est clair que cet état de choses rend souvent impossible l'accord ou la compréhension commune sur le sujet même de notre discussion. Il faut considérer, en outre, le problème des faits dans la mesure où ces faits eux-mêmes sont souvent observés à travers l'optique des idéologies personnelles préconçues. Cette contribution ne resoud aucun des deux problèmes mais elle a pour but de les clarifier.

Le première partie fait une revue des divers fondements pouvant servir aux différentes conceptualisations du Christianisme: son idéalisme humanitaire et sa participation à des poursuites de tout ce qu'il y a de moins humanistes; sa contribution à la promotion des peuples jusqu'au niveau de la civilisation européenne et sa collusion avec des aventures impérialistes; son intérêt pour le bien-être de ces néophytes et sa collaboration aux manoeuvres du pouvoir politique; sa prédication d'une vision spirituelle du monde et son engagement sur la voie du secularisme moderne.

Nous considérons ensuite le jugement généralement porté par

les historiens et sociologues en ce qui concerne l'impact réel du Christianisme sur l'Afrique tropicale. Il y a une liste d'influences soi-disant bénéfiques et une autre liste d'influences soi-disant blâmables. On trouve quelque indication dans la difficulté réelle de décider si telle influence particulière du passé ou en projet peut être jugée bénéfique ou non, mais le poids de l'évidence semble se trouver du côté affirmatif.

Nous résumons finalement les points de vue de quelque quarante étudiants universitaires et vraisemblablement de leurs parents et ainés vivants dans leurs villages respectifs. Après leur avoir donné une questionnaire extensif et simplement suggestif, on leur demandait d'exprimer leur propre pensée sur le sens de la venue du Christianisme en Afrique. *Grosso modo* ils fûrent d'accord avec les jugements des historiens en ajoutant souvent de la chaire au squelette de leurs appréciations.

Etant donné l'importance de la question, nous soulignons le besoin dans lequel nous sommes de faire des recherches pour une clarification plus précise du concept de Christianisme et une compréhension plus approfondie de ses succès et de ses échecs. Ainsi le Christianisme pourrait-il jouer dans l'avenir un rôle plus utile au sein de la vie et de la culture africaine.

X. ATTITUDES AND POLICIES OF THE YORUBA AFRICAN CHURCHES TOWARDS POLYGAMY

J. B. WEBSTER

From the first moment professional missionaries from Europe and America set foot in Africa they were confronted with the question of whether or not the marriage customs associated with polygamy were consistent with membership in the Christian church. A majority came to the conclusion that they were not. But once this decision had been taken the missionaries were faced with what many felt to be questionable alternatives—divorce, fatherless children, destitute women, and prostitution. Their dilemma was aptly expressed by one of the pioneers: 'It is true I have never baptized a polygamist, but I have never ventured to cause a divorce.'[1]

In the Anglican Church in the early and mid-nineteenth century, the bishops from India led by Bishop Milman of Calcutta and Bickersteth of Exeter were not prepared to set hard and fast rules, and advocated the baptism of polygamists under certain conditions.[2] In 1857 Henry Venn, general secretary of the Church Missionary Society and a powerful force among the evangelicals in the Anglican Church, issued a memorandum which laid down the policy that polygamists should not be accepted into membership in the Church. The bishops in Africa, with the exception of Colenso of South Africa, supported the C.M.S. view. Bishop Crowther and James Johnson, the two most prominent men in the Church in West Africa supported Venn's memorandum and opposed any compromise on the issue of polygamy.[3]

[1] Bowen, 1858.
[2] Stock, Vol. III, pp. 129, 642.
[3] For Venn's memorandum and the African Church rebuttal see Coker, 1915. For high church criticism of Venn see Stock, Vol II, p. 14. For the attitude of African bishops see Gray, 1958 and Stock, Vol. III, pp. 642 and 646. However, it appears that closer attention to Bishop Crowther's papers reveal that his position was not as rigid as Stock and Gray have pictured it.

There was no reference to polygamy at the first two conferences of the bishops of the Anglican Church held at Lambeth 1867 and 1878. The third Lambeth Conference (1888) adopted three resolutions: Baptized converts who took a second wife to be excommunicated, polygamists not to be accepted, and wives of polygamists might be baptized under certain conditions. From the voting it appeared that of the hundred and four bishops present, twenty-one were prepared to accept polygamists and thirty-four opposed any concession—even to wives.[4]

Prior to the Lambeth pronouncement, the debate on polygamy in West Africa had not been one in which the European missionary stood on one side and the African upon the other. In Lagos Professor M. T. Euler-Ajayi gave a lecture condemning polygamy on four counts and ended by calling it 'a cancer eating up and destroying our social system'. He upbraided those Europeans who advocated it for the Africans but themselves refused to practise it.[5] It can be argued that the Lambeth pronouncement came too early. The issue of polygamy had not been thoroughly discussed; Africa and Asia were not adequately represented in the episcopate, and no recommendations were made as to the alternatives.

The Wesleyan Methodist missionaries who had feared that the Anglican Church would compromise at Lambeth welcomed the resolutions in the interest of a united front. In 1895 Methodists passed a resolution in the Lagos synod that no man be recommended for membership or continued in full membership unless a monogamist. All missionaries were not in sympathy with this resolution. W. H. Findlay, secretary of the Missionary Society 1900–10, claimed that as a missionary in India he had baptized polygamists. In 1917 a schism in the Lagos Methodist Church provoked the synod to reaffirm its policy as laid down in 1895.[6]

[4] S.P.C.K., 1929, p. 133, and Stock, Vol. II, p. 646.

[5] Euler-Ajayi, *Polygamy* (Lecture delivered June 1882).

[6] Willington, 1890, p. 17: O. J. Griffin to Perkins, 18 April 1911, *Methodist Missionary Society Archives, London* [henceforth M.M.S. (London) Lagos District, original Papers, 1911]: 'Special Resolution Passed by the Synod', Lagos, 1918, *Oke Collection*, National Archives, Ibadan.

American Baptist missionaries were hampered in taking authoritative measures against polygamy by the essence of Baptist polity that such decisions should originate in the congregation. It was impossible to enforce such a ruling on individual and independent churches except through questionable procedures. Furthermore, the influential missionary, S. G. Pinnock, opposed the violation of the cardinal principle of Baptist polity in the interests of such a pronouncement. The first resolution of the mission executive in 1903 merely advised the local churches against admitting polygamists to membership. In 1910 the dependent churches were warned that, 'all financial aid shall be withdrawn from any church that has polygamous members'. In 1914 the independent churches agreed to a milder resolution: 'Believing that monogamy is the ideal state of family life, we declare our adherence thereto.' In 1916 the mission refused to build schools near independent churches suspected of tolerating polygamous members and in 1920 threatened to withdraw fellowship from these same churches.[7] Pinnock approved of the resolutions of 1903 and 1914 because they conformed to Baptist polity and placed the missionary in the proper Baptist relationship to the congregations. He felt that if the missionaries were unable through 'moral suasion' to influence the local churches to make their own laws on polygamy, they had no right to use 'the big stick' as they had in the resolutions of 1910, 1916, and 1920. In 1912 the missionaries asked Pinnock not to return to the Yoruba country but were overruled by the Foreign Mission Board in America. In 1922, after further complaints, the Board asked him to resign unless he was willing to conform to mission rules and take a definite stand on polygamy. Pinnock resigned.[8]

Thus the three protestant missionary societies maintained a solid front in their attitude to the custom of polygamy. Regard-

[7] 'The Mission Policy Regarding Polygamy', *The Nigerian Baptist*, Vol. 10 No. 4, April 1932, pp. 51–52; Constitution and Bye-Laws, Yoruba Baptist Association 1914; Minutes of the Baptist Mission Executive Committee 1850–1940, compiled by C. F. Roberson, *Baptist Seminary Library*, Ogbomoso.

[8] S. G. Pinnock, to the Foreign Mission Board (henceforth F.M.B.) n.d. 1921; Pinnock to Willingham, May 1912; Mission Executive Minutes, July 1922; F.M.B. to Pinnock, 14 October 1921; L. M. Duval to Pinnock; 14 January 1921; *Roberson Collection.*

less of the polity under which the missionaries worked, the weapon in the end was excommunication.

The year of the Lambeth pronouncement on polygamy coincided with the beginning of the African Church movement in Lagos.[9] Between 1888 and 1920 it developed into five major denominations—the Native Baptists 1888, the United Native African (U.N.A.) 1891, the African Church 1901, the West African Episcopal 1903, and the United African Methodist (Eleja) 1917. In 1913 some of these organizations set up the African Communion to provide for inter-communion and joint action on issues which affected the movement as a whole.

The African churches quickly realized that if they were to be more than external to Yoruba life, they must come to terms with the polygamous household, the first and basic unit of the society. Indigenization (often no more than the introduction of the drum into divine service) was the panacea for the ills of the Church. By it the missionaries and their African protegés meant the addition to the frills of worship of some quaint romantic touch of Africa—a slight reminder that one was worshipping in St. Pauls, Lagos, rather than St. Pauls, London. Indigenization did not mean a rebuilding of the structure of the Church, only the addition of an African curlicue to its already heavy gothic nature. By accepting polygamists into the Church through baptism, the African churches took a significant and vital step towards indigenization. As long as the Church ignored polygamy, it was forced to ignore discussion of social morality, for the majority of social bonds existed through polygamous relationships. Since it ignored the society, making only hostile references to it, the Church was charged with possessing little social conscience.

For forty years Africans grumblingly accepted the missionary doctrine on polygamy. But with the growth of independent

[9] The African Churches among the Yoruba are of a type classified as Ethiopian by Sundkler in his *Bantu Prophets*. Occasionally referred to as 'separatist' or 'independent' they have no connexion with prophet or syncretist movements. Some confusion arises since although all denominations of this group are collectively styled 'African Churches', one of the denominations takes the name 'The African Church'. In this paper 'African Church' refers to the denomination and 'African churches' to the group. For a fuller discussion of the historical development of the movement see Webster, 1964.

thought following in the wake of the African Church Movement, some began to challenge the hypothesis. Theological argument played a minor role in determining the missionaries' attitude. Rather it was their feeling of the superiority of European culture and their identification of those things good and moral as European and conversely those things evil and immoral as African.[10] They proposed to make Africa conform to the Victorian bourgeois society of England which appeared to them as the highest morality yet attained. Playing upon Africans' desire for the material benefits of Europe, they never failed to point out in long, dreary recitals of world history that monogamist peoples were the conquerors, the civilized, the inventors—in short, the master races. Polygamous peoples were the conquered, the savage, the imitators, in short 'the lesser breeds without the law'. The proud Yoruba people did not suffer this argument to go unchallenged.

Taking as criteria their emphasis upon an educated ministry, a literate laity, fine buildings and elaborate organization, the African churches can be grouped as follows: the African Church laying the most emphasis upon these things, the West African Episcopal the least, and the U.N.A. occupying the mid-point between the two.

The social position, economic status, ethnic composition and previous religious experience of the leadership of the African churches partially determined their policy towards African social customs in general and polygamy in particular. The African Church organization attracted those (often called Sierra Leonians because of their English names) whose parents had returned to Egbaland, cut their ties with Sierra Leone, and who identified themselves with Abeokuta rather than Freetown. The true Sierra Leonians remained in the mission churches. The African Church attracted some of the elite of traditional Yoruba society—those who continued to look to the chiefs as the source of authority

[10] The African churches through their Communion Council sued the C.M.S. for libel for a publication which described their doctrine on marriage as 'pernicious'. The courts upheld the C.M.S. In 1915 a Bishops' Encyclical advised that European-style weddings of couples having previously married by African rites be so arranged as 'to indicate a sense of shame'. Certain denominations in Nigeria practise this policy at the present time.

rather than the colonial administration. It attracted indigenous merchants who after 1900 challenged the dominant position of the Sierra Leonians in the commercial activities of Lagos. It became the home of a small group of radical intellectuals who used their talents to project the image of the Church. Furthermore, since the organization had come out of the C.M.S. and since it concentrated upon providing a spiritual home for dissident Anglicans, the strength of mission theories did not noticeably diminish as the Church grew older.

The second generation Egba Christians (with English names), born in polygamous homes whose fathers had remained catechumens in the mission churches rather than turn out their wives and children, plus the traditional elite whose position rested upon large family connexions influenced the African Church towards toleration of lay polygamy. The merchants favoured monogamy and the intellectuals divided in their allegiance.

The composition of the U.N.A. organization was similar to the African Church with three exceptions. First, the proportion of the groups was different—Egba Christian influence weaker and the traditional elite stronger. Second, while like the African Church, dissidents from the missions joined the U.N.A., the proportion of pagan converts increased and exerted more influence, as the church grew older. Third, the economic status of the membership was generally lower than in the African Church. Furthermore, unlike the African Church which broke from the Anglican over Church government the U.N.A. was established by nine men who aimed to adapt Christianity to African conditions. Consequently the U.N.A. was the first Church in Yorubaland to baptize polygamists.

The W.A.E. Organization worked at the opposite end of the Lagos social scale. The location of St. Stephen's cathedral in the poorest area of Lagos island indicated the social strata it attracted —servants, sixpence a day wage earners and petty hawkers— clerks being its most prosperous members. The Egba element was lacking, replaced by Ijebu and Native Lagosians. The membership was illiterate, 90 per cent being converts from paganism rather than second generation Christians.[11] The question of polygamy hardly arose. It was taken for granted.

The composition and background of the clergy was as important as the lay leadership. A comparison of the clergy of the three organizations indicates that their attitudes were determined by their previous theological training or lack of it, the economic circumstances forced upon them by their organization, and the society in which they lived, differing between Lagos and the interior or between various areas of Lagos itself.

Since the membership of the African Church was well-to-do and its resources ample, it paid its ministers equivalent to the missions. The membership—mostly 'old Anglicans'—expected and required its ministers to be professional and monogamous. The majority of the ministers had previously been clergymen in the mission churches. Trained as a professional class they expected to remain so.[12] As men in middle life they were unprepared to earn their living by other means. Monogamists, from monogamous parents, they looked askance at the polygamous family. Considering the middle-class society in which they moved it would have taken considerable aplomb to be openly polygamous.[13] United by background and practice, and wielding considerable authority in an episcopal church, the clergy offered vigorous leadership to the monogamist party in the organization.

In the U.N.A. the clergy like the membership were mixed, half previously ordained in the missions or mission catechists, and half drawn from the membership. Through lack of finances the

[11] In 1920 the W.A.E. Church claimed 4,000 members, less than 200 of which had been members of other churches. 'Our policy is to go among the heathen and find our own members.' Campbell to St. Arthur's Church, Accra, 13 March 1920, W.A.E. Minute Book 1903–39, *Campbell Papers*.

[12] In 1920 half the ministers in the African Church had been previously ordained in the missions, one out of six in the U.N.A., and none in the W.A.E. J. K. Coker called the clergy of the African Church 'old parrots of the Anglican Church' (Coker, 1935, p. 9).

[13] 'It is an open secret in this city (Abeokuta) that no one will give his daughter to a Bethelite.' (Nickname for African Churchmen) Moses Coker to J. K. Coker, 27 December 1904, *Coker Collection*; Bethelites found it difficult to get employment in the Egba government. See A. O. Ijaoye, 'Loss of originality in the Ministry', manuscript, *Oke Collection*.

organization paid inadequate stipends.[14] The clergy operated under economic stress, and sought to solve their problems through plantation agriculture or trade, both of which to be successful required a polygamous household.[15] Unlike the African Church, where the salaries of the clergy were drawn from a central fund, in the U.N.A. each congregation paid its own minister. Since Lagos parish stipends were more regular than in the interior, some of the Lagos pastors by strict economy were able to conform to the social pressures and remain monogamous. The clergy divided by marriage practice and their limited power in a congregational organization were unable to provide united leadership. After a protracted struggle (1895–1921) influenced by the changing character of the membership referred to above, the decision was taken to tolerate a polygamous clergy.

In the early years the W.A.E. Organization relied upon an honorary (unpaid) clergy drawn from the literate 10 per cent of the membership. Since they continued in their secular employment, and moved in a polygamous social system where a premium was placed upon wives, it was taken for granted that they would be polygamous. Later, when the organization engaged youths which it had trained for the ministry, a stipendary system was introduced. The Patriarch attempted to keep these youths monogamous but since the stipends were little more than annual bonuses the clergy sought other means of support. With the older clergy polygamous, and no demand for monogamy from the membership the Patriarch received little support for his efforts.

Prior to 1914 all the African churches had decided upon various degrees of toleration of polygamy among the laity. The degree of toleration increased as one moved from the African Church to the W.A.E. In the African Church polygamy was tolerated among the 'weaker' brethren, the ideal being monogamy,

[14] The African Church organizations and U.N.A. claimed approximately 10,000 adherents each. According to their respective central budgets adherents in the African Church were contributing 7*s*. each per annum, those in the U.N.A. 1*s*. *Report of the 29th Anniversary of the U.N.A.*, Lagos, 1920; the African Church Statistics for the Year 1921, unpublished manuscript Broad Street Archives.

[15] One churchman who rejected the whole argument of the connexion between economics and polygamy warned, 'man cannot depend upon economics to solve his moral problems' (Ojo-Cole, 1935, p. 14).

the clergy strictly forbidden a second wife. At the establishment of the organization in 1901, the Anglican policy was continued and the church licensed for European-style marriages. A year later upon pressure from the interior, the General Committee passed a resolution permitting the baptism and admittance to membership of polygamists but insisting upon a monogamous clergy. In the U.N.A. polygamy was permitted to both the clergy and laity. The question of lay polygamy arose at the second foundation meeting of the organization in 1891. No decision was taken for four years although the issue was raised repeatedly. In 1895 J. S. Vidal asked if the U.N.A. objected to the marriage of his daughter in Yoruba custom. The General Committee ruled that heathen-convert or Christian-born be allowed more than one wife.[16] In the W.A.E. the question never arose, polygamy being permitted to all. A formal pronouncement was not considered necessary.

During the period 1914–22 two schools of thought developed in the African Church Movement with regard to polygamy—one based on Lagos, which sought a gradual return to the mission societies' position, and one based at Agege which yearned to embed Christianity in a polygamous society. The Lagos school represented the urban class engaged in some aspect of modern commerce. Many were second or third generation monogamists, the offspring of Sierra Leonian and Egba Christians. Some were young indigenous Yorubas with the enthusiasm of the first generation convert who desired to use Christianity as an instrument of social change. The other school centred around a new agricultural class—the Agege Planters—who despised the urban life of Lagos, not because they had been unsuccessful competitors in it, but because they hated its hypocrisy and snobbishness, its horse-racing, lodge meetings, and Governor's balls, in short, its completely un-Yoruba nature. As wealthy and 'big men' they were expected to move among an elite guided in its social mores by those who had 'been to' Europe, who disdained to speak the

[16] J. K. Coker, 'Notes on the History of the African Communion 1918–1925', *National Archives, Ibadan*; U.N.A. Minutes of the General Committee (hereafter U.N.A. Minutes) 17 August 1891; 22 November 1895, Vol. I, 1891–1911, pp. 5–7 and 189–90.

Yoruba tongue except to their menials, and whose symbol of their religion was a top hat and stiff collar.[17] In the freedom of Agege they could apply European techniques to farming while at the same time firmly surround themselves with a Yoruba social setting. On their plantation kingdoms, the wives worked individual acreage selling in the local market and supplying the large family. The extended retinue helped to provide the labour for cash crop production. The plantation worshipped together, the planter as minister; disputes were settled, the planter as judge; traditional feasts were held, the planter as host. The plantation created a village unit, a number of families united by blood, economic, and social bonds, working, praying, and playing together.[18] It was a re-creation of the social unity so much desired, so often stressed in the pulpit, so regularly the burden of prayer. The Yoruba had looked to the Church to create this unity in the urban centres but the Church had failed because of denominationalism, economic competition, and the conflict between the old and new social classes. The planters felt they had solved the problem of combining western techniques and Christianity with social solidarity. They were anxious to spread their system founded on polygamy to all Yorubaland.

In the churches in Lagos, the Lagos school represented majority opinion in the African Church, minority opinion in the U.N.A., and the occasional adherent in the W.A.E. The Agege school on the other hand was strong in the W.A.E. and weak in the African Church. As these churches expanded into the hinterland, interior delegates made their presence felt in the governing bodies of each organization. Interior influence, on the whole, favoured a greater toleration of polygamy. Stresses arose in each organization as a result and developed in the most severe form in those organizations which expanded most rapidly and which tolerated polygamy the least. The African Church, which underwent precocious growth, was wracked with dissension while the W.A.E. remained quiescent.

[17] As an example of this Lagos snobbishness see *The Nigerian Pioneer*, 5 December 1919, p. 6.

[18] For a description of the Agege plantations see Webster, 1962 and 1963.

The Lagos school in the African Church led by Ade Olugbile and the Adeshigbin brothers, tolerated polygamy within the church. Much hinged around the word 'tolerate'. Polygamy was tolerated among the 'weaker' brethren. The church was not established to perpetuate the polygamous custom. It was expected to die out, killed by the exigencies of 'civilized' life. Even at the present time it was a fading custom, a luxury within the reach of only a few. The Church should place the highest ideal before its membership.[19]

An entire philosophy of development was implicit in this idea. The Yoruba would evolve towards European civilization in economic organization, social structure, and ideals. Since the spread of Christianity preceded this secular development, and since salvation was possible regardless of marriage custom, the proper role of the church was to remain flexible, tolerating polygamy until such time as the economic and social conditions of the Yoruba made it possible to attain the ideal—monogamy. The Lagos school could not tolerate a polygamous ministry. The role of the clergy was to be a living example of the ideal. The minister through his education and salaried position was expected to follow the European pattern. His fluency in English, the European dress of himself and his wife, and the way in which he ordered his home were the outward badge of the example he was expected to set.

The Lagos school represented a compromise between the mission position on one hand and Agege on the other. It was attacked by the missions as retrogressive and tolerating sin, and by Agege for being ashamed of polygamy, allotting to the Yoruba simply an imitative role in the process of development, and hankering for re-union with the mission churches.

The Agege school developed around the powerful figure of J. K. Coker supported by a majority of the planters at Agege. To them, the choice was not between polygamy and monogamy, but between polygamy and concubinage. Agege maintained that monogamy was only practised by ten per cent of the Christian

[19] M. S. Cole to J. K. Coker, 12 July 1913; J. K. Coker to Bishop Onatolu, n.d. *Coker Collection*; Macaulay, 1942.

men of Lagos. Lagos monogamy consisted of one legally married wife and one or more concubines outside the home officially unknown to the legal wife. Agege condemned concubinage as a degraded form of polygamy, a lower standard of morals than that held by their fathers and hypocrisy, a sin particularly singled out for condemnation in Christ's teaching.[20]

The men of Agege were disturbed by the interpretation Lagos put upon the word 'tolerate' which placed them in the position of weaker brothers. They believed that polygamy was the ideal state of family life and that the church, instead of introducing a foreign code, should uphold and reinforce the existing moral code of the Yoruba people. Because the church had failed to do this the moral restraints in the society were being loosened.

Agege did not feel that the toleration of polygamy had stunted the growth of the church. They gloried in the extension of the church in the interior, unlike the Lagos school which bemoaned its failure to dominate Lagos. Agege believed that the blindness of the mission society's policy on polygamy was a 'God given' opportunity for the African churches. It was not only the opportunity but the duty of the African Church to build across the street from every mission church in Yorubaland. It was the duty of the African Church to provide a spiritual home for the polygamous pagan, disillusioned with his old gods but refused admission by the missions.[21] Where the African

[20] The concern of all organizations about the concubinage system of Lagos is indicated by the wide range of comment. Anglicans—Address of Bishop Oluwole to the Synod, May 1911, *C.M.S.*, G3 A2/o, 1911, No. 121; Tugwell to Fox, 9 January 1903, *C.M.S.*, G3 A2/o, 1903, No. 28: The Methodists—Anwyl to Perkins, 29 June 1912, *W.M.M.S.* original Papers Lagos 1912: The U.N.A.—G. A. Oke, 'Foundation Stone Laying of Christ Church, Kano', *African Hope*, April 1922: 'Notes in H. S. A. Thomas's Address', *African Hope*, July 1921; *The Revised Constitution of the U.N.A.*, 1921, p. 2: The African Church organization —Mrs. A. E. Coates, 'Disadvantages of Foreign Marriage in Euler-Ajayi', 'General Report on the African Communion', 1913, *Oke Papers*; J. K. Coker, 'Review of Polygamy', undated (1913?) manuscript and J. K. Coker to Bishop Onatolu 24 December 1934, *Coker Collection*: West African Episcopal—J. G. Campbell, *Lagos Standard*, 15 March 1911; Campbell, *Observations on some Topics in Nigeria During the Administration of Lugard*, Lagos, 1918.

[21] Prior to 1920 the Baptist mission was considered an exception to the rule. First, it had not laid down as definite a policy as the others. Second, one Baptist organization (Araromi) was in communion with the African Church, and third,

Church failed in its duty the distraught pagan turned to Islam.[22]

Agege had no patience with that section of the Lagos movement who talked of keeping in step with the missions to prepare for eventual reunion ('a hankering after the onions of Egypt').[23] Agege worked instead for a union of all the organizations in the African Church movement. It was J. K. Coker and his supporters who initiated the African Communion in 1913 which provided for inter-communion with the U.N.A. and its polygamous ministry—an anathema to the Lagos school who regarded inter-communion as a move to introduce polygamy into the ministry of the African Church organization.

In 1907 the African Church organization split into two wings over issues of church government. The Agege school was strongest in Salem, while the Lagos school dominated Bethel organization. Through the influence of the clergy in both organizations the policy on polygamy laid down in 1902 had not been altered at the time of re-union in 1922.

In 1922 Salem and Bethel reunited. The two schools of thought were brought into close proximity and carefully balanced. J. S. Williams (previously of Bethel) a staunch protagonist of the Lagos school, was elevated to the primacy, while J. K. Coker was elected to the highest lay office in the church—president of the organization. Regardless of this delicate balancing the Lagos school predominated. Primate Williams refused co-operation with the African Communion. He won support for his policy in June 1925 when the general conference forbade polygamous U.N.A. clergy from officiating in the African Church organiza-

---

S. G. Pinnock was greatly respected and loved. Before 1920, Pinnock was missionary-in-charge in Abeokuta. He was replaced by B. L. Lockett, one of the leaders in the Baptist campaign to excommunicate polygamists. Lockett claimed that the Baptist churches in Abeokuta were 'thoroughly saturated with polygamist members', (Mission Meeting Minutes, 12–16 January 1921, *Roberson Collection*) and proceeded to use the 'big stick'. J. K. Coker warned him. 'Your declaration against polygamy makes it a necessity for the African Church to establish at Ijaiye to lead to Christ those who are being kept out on account of polygamy, without placing any burden on them not placed by Christ.' (Coker to Lockett, 23 July 1920, *Coker Collection*.)

[22] Coker, 'The African Church', n.d. Typescript, *Coker Collection*.

[23] Campbell, 1921.

tion.[24] When J. K. Coker lost his position and Ade Olugbile became president, the organization severed its connexion with the Communion.

After the death of Primate Williams and President Olugbile, 1933–34, the organization rejoined the Communion upon the urging of J. K. Coker. But its membership was half-hearted and short lived. Today it has again left the Communion and is seeking membership in the Christian Council—an organization of the mission churches of Nigeria.[25]

In the African Church organization the two schools of thought fought the battle of polygamy divorced from other issues. It was not injected into the split of 1907 or the re-union of 1922. In the U.N.A. the reverse was true. Polygamy was one of the underlying, but unacknowledged causes of a number of serious crises in the Church. It remained cloaked under disputes over a professional ministry, constitution revision, and the election of a primate. It has been pointed out that it took the U.N.A. four years (1891–95) to lay down a policy which tolerated polygamy among the laity. This decision was never challenged. The main struggle was over its policy towards the clergy which was fought out between the two schools of thought over the next twenty-five years. An official pronouncement was possible in 1921, thirty years after the founding.

Prior to 1899, the U.N.A. had been unable to secure an ordained clergyman. Lay elders especially designated, were responsible for the ministerial functions of the church. Ultimately this system was attacked by members of the Lagos school under the leadership of H. A. Caulcrick who cast doubts upon the validity of lay sacraments, and called for a professional ministry properly ordained and monogamous. In March 1895, the Caulcrick party forced the General Committee to a ten to eight decision in

[24] Minutes of the General Committee of the African Church (Bethel), 27 June 1918, Vol. III, pp. 65–68; Coker, 'Notes on the History of the African Communion 1918–1925', manuscript, *Coker Collection*.

[25] 'Report of the Commission to state the case of the African Church organization of their position with regard to the Communion', 27 February 1959, *Broad Street Archives*. The African Church application for membership was rejected by the Christian Council in 1962.

favour of a paid ministry.[26] The General Committee opened negotiations with the African Methodist Episcopal Church in Sierra Leone. The A.M.E. offered to provide an ordained minister upon two conditions—affiliation and expulsion of polygamous members.[27]

The Agege party led by D. A. Jones defended a polygamous ministry and used the threat of foreign domination since the A.M.E. was American controlled, to squash the negotiations with Sierra Leone. At the election for the General Committee in October 1896, Caulcrick's supporters who had been responsible for the negotiations were completely defeated.[28] The following year the membership and finances declined. In 1898, Caulcrick's party on a promise of remedying the sad state of affairs by means of a professional clergy, regained their seats in the General Committee. A compromise was reached. Foreign affiliation dropped. Three local candidates, one of which was D. A. Jones, were ordained by an American coloured missionary recommended by Blyden.[29] Jones was priested 1899 and appointed superintendent in May 1900. In 1903 Professor M. T. Euler-Ajayi made a public recantation of his views on polygamy quoted above and joined the U.N.A.[30] Both Jones and Euler-Ajayi proved capable men, the first as a missionary and the second as an able composer, writer, and organizer. Through their influence the issue was settled temporarily in favour of a polygamous clergy.

After 1900, G. A. Williams, editor of the *Lagos Standard* rose to prominence in the U.N.A. He had been one of the founders and connected with the General Committee as secretary, treasurer,

[26] 'Paper read by Caulcrick on a paid ministry', U.N.A. Minutes, 11 January 1895, Vol. 1, pp. 160–1; U.N.A. Minutes, 8 March 1895, pp. 166–7; Caulcrick, 1894.

[27] For the correspondence with Sierra Leone 1896–98 see U.N.A. Minutes Vol. 1, pp. 213–18, 260–1, 265, 290–3; D. A. Hughes, *Charge Delivered to the General Conference*, 6 September 1922.

[28] U.N.A. Minutes, 23 October 1896, Vol. 1, pp. 224–6.

[29] For the events surrounding the first ordination see U.N.A. Minutes, 1899, Vol. 1, pp. 330–2, 347–8; G. A. Oke, *A Short History of the U.N.A. 1891–1903*, Lagos, 1918, p. 8; Oke, 'Important Events in the History of the U.N.A. 1891–1915', Oke Papers.

[30] Oke, *Short History of the U.N.A. 1904–1924*, Lagos, 1936, pp. 1–2. For Euler-Ajayi's previous views see footnote 5 above.

and president until his death in 1919. During the fourteen years of his presidency he used his skill and diplomacy to preserve the unity of the organization. As a member of Caulcrick's party he had suffered defeat in the general election of 1896. He personally favoured a monogamous ministry but recognized the havoc which a militant advocacy would bring to the church. Instead he proposed a gradual reform by limiting ministers' wives and ordaining of only confirmed monogamists.[31] As an indication of the delicate balance of opinion in the general committee, a suggestion in 1918 that since the ministry was in fact polygamous, 1. Tim. 3:3–14 be substituted in the ordination service, created such a furore that Williams had the whole incident expunged from the minutes.[32]

From the inception of the U.N.A. the laity held unchallenged authority in the organization. During the presidency of Williams the clergy began to assert themselves. He recognized this development and cautiously encouraged it by delegating powers of the General Committee to the ministers' meeting. He did not believe however that a constitution which would legalize this devolution of power was desirable. He disapproved of a clerical body with independent authority derived from the constitution directly controlling ordinations, and indirectly the polygamy issue.[33]

Certain members of a young radical group of the Lagos school won seats in the General Committee. They supported the constitution because it would curb the autocratic power of the elders.

[31] H. A. Williams, 'The U.N.A. Church Defended', *Times of Nigeria*, 20 June 1921; for an instance of Williams taking action to limit a minister's wives see minutes of a Sub-Committee of the U.N.A., 12 September 1913, Vol. 11, p. 61–1.

[32] 1. Tim. 3:12, 'Let the deacons be the husbands of one wife . . .' See U.N.A. Minutes, 15 November 1918, Vol. 11, pp. 221–6.

[33] On 29 August 1898, powers were first delegated to the Minister's Meeting to nominate and recommend candidates for the Ministry. (G. A. Oke, 'Important events in the History of the U.N.A. 1891–1915'). In 1911 the General Committee overruled and took the case of G. T. A. Thompson into its own hands. Within a year it was necessary to revoke Thompson's licence. When the next case arose the Minister's Meeting refused to act until the General Committee apologized for its action on Thompson. U.N.A. Minutes, 23 September 1911 and 3 March 1916, Vol. 11, pp. 1–2 and 133–8.

They also desired to write a reform clause into it which would provide for monogamy as a condition of ordination. G. A. Williams used these divisions within the organization to delay the adoption of the constitution. It was drafted 1909, presented to the General Committee 1911, reviewed by a sub-committee 1914–16, and not signed until after Williams's death in 1919. Williams died in May and the constitution was signed in June 1919 by a General Committee under the control of the radicals, and supported by a clergy anxious to legalize their own powers. Almost immediately the radicals tabled a motion of revision.

R. A. Williams, leader of the radicals, succeeded to the presidency and T. B. Jacobs, another radical, was elected vice-president. They proposed three measures to reform the ministry: that candidates for ordination be and remain men of one wife, that ordained men be not allowed to add to their wives, and that these resolutions be written into the constitution. T. B. Jacobs informed the General Committee in July 1920 that he intended to bring a motion to limit ministers to one wife. The motion was tabled in the September meeting. After heated debate the motion was lost, the clergy voting against it.[34] The same month the parish committee of Christ Church, U.N.A., Ebute Metta recommended the ordination of a polygamist. The radical party attempted to hold up the ordination in November 1920 and again in February 1921. They failed. R. A. Williams and T. B. Jacobs both resigned.

With the radical party broken, the revision of the constitution was rapidly carried forward and came into effect in October 1921. In the foreword the U.N.A. set forth its attitude to marriage. Polygamy could not be proved a sin from the Bible. Neither polygamy nor monogamy were essential to salvation. The Church did not preach polygamy 'but tolerates it wherever that is the custom of the people'. Churches were not to be licensed for foreign marriages but where members had contracted these

[34] H. A. Williams, 'The U.N.A. Church Defended', *Times of Nigeria*, 20 June 1921; U.N.A. Minutes, 30 July 1920 and 17 September 1920, pp. 320–3 and 330–4.

marriages the Church would exercise full disciplinary powers to uphold the vows taken. It further stated that the U.N.A. abhorred the forcing of monogamy and detested concubinage as a 'degrading, sinful, and immoral habit'.[35] This was an exposition of the views of Agege with a sop given to the Lagos party through the use of the word 'tolerate' and the promise to uphold foreign marriage vows.

The failure of the radical party to elect their candidate to the primacy contributed to their defeat on the revised constitution. In 1918, prior to the final vote on the constitution, the office of primate became vacant through the death of D. A. Jones. The radical party candidate was G. A. Oke, monogamist and popular young minister, who as editor of the U.N.A. magazine, *African Hope*, exerted considerable influence in the General Committee. The majority candidate was David A. Hughes, an Agege planter and an older man. Hughes had more than one wife. The elevation of Hughes in June 1919 was a victory for the majority party, and assured the solid vote of the clergy against an anti-polygamy clause in the constitution.[36]

The elevation of the polygamist Hughes to the primacy, the resignation of the radicals from the General Committee, and the signing of the constitution in 1921, ended a quarter century of indecision in the U.N.A. By declaring for a polygamous ministry the organization affirmed its faith in the philosophy of the Agege school and alienated the other members of the African Communion, who felt that the U.N.A. position was theologically indefensible and socially retrogressive. One by one member churches severed their connexion with the Communion, leaving the U.N.A. isolated.

The W.A.E. organization attempted to put the Agege philosophy into practice by developing a form of marriage both African and Christian as well as polygamous, a form which combined the essential elements of traditional marriage with the

[35] *The Revised Constitution of the U.N.A. Church*, Lagos, 1921 foreword, pp. 1–2, Section 31 on Marriage, pp. 51–2 and Appendix 4, p. 60.

[36] U.N.A. Minutes, 28 April 1919 and 27 June 1919, Vol. 11, pp. 247–51 and 265–9.

blessing of the church. No concession was made to monogamy except that the church refused the elaborate ceremony for the second and additional wives.

Prior to 1909, the U.N.A. and W.A.E. organizations had introduced the Christian minister into the ceremony of the African wedding held in the home of the parents of the bride.[37] In 1909, the U.N.A. approached Patriarch J. G. Campbell of the W.A.E. to co-operate in improving African Christian marriage to make it 'more attractive and meet the religious scruples of the rising generation'. The result was that if the participants wished, the ceremony could be transferred to the church and performed before the congregation. The main features included an exhortation on African Christian marriage and the 'joining and blessing'. In the questions before the 'joining' the families of the bride and groom were asked if they had given and received the customary 'ano'. The ceremony recognized that when the 'ano' was given and received the couple were married by customary law. When in the 'joining' the minister said, 'we hereby join these two persons together in holy matrimony', the church was only adding its blessing to the union. In fashionable weddings the ceremony was accompanied by a best man, bridesmaids, flower girls, and page boys. The first such marriage recorded was solemnized by Campbell in St. Stephens, Lagos, on December 17, 1909.[38]

Campbell attempted unsuccessfully at the General Conference of the W.A.E. organization to make the African Christian form of marriage obligatory to all. The conference adopted a contrary resolution whereby the laity were at liberty to marry by European or African custom. At the ministers' meeting of 1914 he succeeded in carrying a resolution which made African Christian marriage compulsory for the clergy. A rider to the resolution demanded the immediate dismissal of any agent ordained or lay,

[37] The missions called this 'parlour marriage'. *Report of the Synod of the Diocese of Western Equatorial Africa*, May 1909, p. 89.

[38] G. A. Williams to J. G. Campbell, 22 June 1909, 'W.A.E. Minute Book 1903–39: *Order of service, Solemnisation of Matrimony, Nelson—Akinwanmi*, Jehovah Shallom, U.N.A. Lagos, 9 November 1944: 'Marriages in Christian Native Form 1909–1916', W.A.E. Minute Book.

who married according to European custom. Campbell attempted to regulate polygamy among the clergy by a number of measures, one of which forbade deacons and priests before seven years service from taking a second wife.[39] This was the philosophy of Agege put to practical demonstration. Polygamy was not simply tolerated but blessed by the Church. Foreign marriage was no longer a matter of option but forbidden.

By 1921 the African churches counted 100,000 adherents of the total Christian population of Southern Nigeria of 500,000.[40] The twin attractions of African leadership and toleration of polygamy had proved effective. But the internal wranglings between the Lagos and Agege philosophies prevented any hope that these 100,000 Christians would combine into one powerful unit. The intensity of the dispute blurred the image of the movement before the public and allowed the missions to paint their own picture of the African churches—corrupt, morally lax, retrogressive. Divided, the African churches could not compete with the major attraction of the missions—education. Individually they were unable to finance the grammar schools, teacher-training, theological, and agricultural colleges which would have made them the dominant force in Yoruba Christianity. Each organization fell back upon dissident clergymen and teachers from the missions, who could not free themselves from the organization, ceremonies, and theology of their training and experience.[41] A half century after the founding of the African churches, they were still being accused of mimicking the missions which fathered them.

The Agege school clearly saw these wider issues. It was prepared to cut the psychological mission strings, and proclaim a call to the race to combine patriotism with religion in support of

[39] 'Report of the Sixth Anniversary, 1909'. 'Order and Discipline within the Church' (prior to 1914); 'Minutes of the Ministers, Leaders and Preachers Meeting, Apr. 17, 1914; Minutes of the Tenth Annual Conference, Feb. 28, Mar. 1, 1918; Regulations to be observed in all churches', 8 September 1915; all from W.A.E. Minute Book.

[40] Talbot, *The Peoples of Southern Nigeria*, Vol. IV, pp. 120–3.

[41] 'I find truly that my brethren clergy cannot deviate from Anglicanism.' Aboyade-Cole (now Primate) to J. K. Coker, 2 April 1927. *Coker Collection.*

the African churches. Agege attempted the establishment of a grammar school to compete with mission institutions. It founded a theological college and a training farm, all conceived on a grand scale, and all of which failed when the African Communion collapsed.

After 1920 the mission churches, reacting to the success of the African Church movement, began to accept or tolerate a kind of concealed polygamy among the laity. The weapon of mass excommunication was less frequently used. Today there is every indication that many mission churches are tolerating as much polygamy as the African churches. Had the mission churches insisted upon a strict observance of the monogamy rule they would have been smaller and the African churches proportionately larger today.

The divergence between official mission policy and unofficial mission practice has inevitably led to the charge of hypocrisy. Since African churchmen insist that meaningful indigenization is dependent upon a more realistic attitude towards marriage custom, the monogamy–polygamy issue is vital to the entire role of the church in Africa. The acceptance of monogamy has been superficial except to a small stratum of the society. Yet it is this elite which holds influence and power in the mission churches. It is also this group which is most frequently charged with hypocrisy. The European-type economic and social environment of the elite has not resulted in monogamy, but in concubinage—an anathema to African churchmen who reject the theory that concubinage is an inevitable stage in the evolution of a polygamous society towards monogamy. Thus churchmen argue that under present mission policies, as African society continues to change in imitation of this elite, the problem will become more acute in the future. In any case, Christianity cannot afford to await the slow pace of this development. It must precede not follow it. Generations of Africans must not be excluded from Christendom and salvation awaiting the African industrial and social revolution.

REFERENCES

Bowen, T. J.
(1858) 'Should missionaries baptize polygamists?' *The Christian Index*, 16 June.
Campbell, J. G.
(1918) *Observations on Some Topics in Nigeria during the Administration of Lugard*. Lagos.
(1921) 'Something we ought to take note of', *Times of Nigeria*, 20 June 1921.
Caulcrick, H. A.
(1894) *Views of Some Native Christians ... on ... Polygamy*. Lagos.
Coker, J. K.
(1915) *Polygamy Defended*. Lagos.
(1935) 'Baptism', *African Church Chronicle*, April–June, Vol. 1. No. 4.
Euler-Ajayi, M. T.
(n.d.) *Polygamy*. (Lecture delivered June 1882). Published by Mojola Agbebi at Colwyn Bay, North Wales.
Gray, G. F. S.
(1958) *The Anglican Communion*. London.
Macaulay, Herbert
(1942) *The History of the Development of Missionary Work in Nigeria, with special reference to the U.N.A. Church*. Lagos.
Methodist Missionary Society Archives.
Ojo-Cole, Julius
(1935) 'Personal worship', *African Church Chronicle*, January–March, Vol. I, No. 3.
Oke, G. A.
(1918) *A Short History of the U.N.A. 1891–1903*. Lagos.
(1921) 'Notes on H. S. A. Thomas's address', *African Hope*, July.
(1922) 'Foundation stone laying of Christ Church, Kano', *African Hope*, April.
(1936) *Short History of the U.N.A. 1904–1924*. Lagos.
Report of the Synod of the Diocese of Western Equatorial Africa, May.
(1909)
Report of the 29th Anniversary of the U.N.A. Lagos.
(1920)
The Revised Constitution of the U.N.A. Church, Lagos.
(1921)
S.P.C.K.
(1929) *The Six Lambeth Conferences 1867–1920*. London.
Stock, Eugene
(1899–1916) *History of the Church Missionary Society*. London. 4 vols.
Sundkler, B. G.
(1961) *Bantu Prophets in South Africa*. London. Revised edition.
Talbot, P. A.
(1926) *The Peoples of Southern Nigeria*. London. 4 vols.
Webster, J. B.
(1962) 'Agege: plantations and the African Church 1901–1920', *Annual Conference of the Nigerian Institute of Social and Economic Research*, March 1962.
(1963) 'The Bible and the Plough', *Journal of the Historical Society of Nigeria*, December.
(1964) *The African Churches among the Yoruba*. Oxford.

Williams, H. A.
(1921) 'The U.N.A. Church Defended', *Times of Nigeria*, June 20.
Willington, John H.
(1890) 'A Bible class for polygamists', *The Wesleyan Methodist Missionary Notices.*

Résumé

ATTITUDES ET POLITIQUES DES ÉGLISES AFRICAINES YORUBA ENVERS LA POLYGAMIE

Les églises africaines (celles qualifiées d'églises éthiopiennes par Sundkler dans *Bantu Prophets*) sont les églises créées par les Yoruba révoltés par les méthodes missionnaires employées à la fin du XIXème siècle. Des branches francophones de ces églises existent chez les Yoruba du Dahomey et au sein d'un groupe affilié non-Yoruba établi dans l'ex-Cameroun Français.

La première partie de cette communication présente l'évolution de la pensée missionnaire chez les Anglicans, les Méthodistes et les Baptistes au Nigéria. Ces groupes missionnaires, après une certaine opposition, finirent par décider d'exclure de leurs églises les hommes mariés à plus d'une femme. Les Anglicans prirent cette décision en 1888 lorsqu'il devint évident qu'une grande partie de l'Afrique allait tomber sous le contrôle de l'Europe et que, par conséquent, les processus économiques et sociaux favorables à la monogamie allaient s'intensifier. Les Baptistes ne se décidèrent qu'après la fin de la première guerre mondiale étant donné le caractère 'congrégationnel' de leur église et également à cause de l'opposition manifestée par un de leurs missionnaires qui ne voulait pas sacrifier l'indépendance des congrégations locales, sacrifice nécessaire à la mise en application d'un tel édit officiel.

Les églises africaines se sont créées surtout par réaction de révolte contre l'arrogance culturelle des missionnaires arrivés après le partage de l'Afrique qui condamnaient l'ensemble des coutumes africaines, y compris la polygamie. Les églises africaines adoptèrent des doctrines différentes de celles des sociétés missionnaires dont elles étaient issues estimant qu'une indigénisation valable devait commencer par la tolérance de coutumes telles que la polygamie.

Au sein du mouvement des églises africaines deux écoles de pensée se développèrent: l'une urbaine et l'autre plutôt rurale. Dans notre communication, nous examinons les bases traditionnelles, sociales et économiques des deux groupes. Il n'est pas absolument exact de définir ces groupes comme étant l'un traditionnel et l'autre moderne car le groupe rural était dirigé par des gens formés en Europe qui appliquaient les techniques modernes de l'agriculture de plantation et qui gagnaient des sommes considérables ce faisant.

L'école urbaine considérait que la société Yoruba se trouvait dans une période transitoire entre une société traditionnelle et une société commerciale moderne. Les membres de ce groupe estimaient que pour ceux vivant dans le milieu social et économique moderne la monogamie était l'idéal à atteindre, alors que ceux qui vivaient dans le système traditionnel ne devraient pas se voir refuser le salut simplement parce que, du fait de pressions économiques et sociales, ils étaient forcés d'être polygames. L'école urbaine insistait bien pour dire que si la polygamie pouvait être tolérée il ne fallait pas forcément l'encourager. Ce groupe faisait remarquer également que l'exclusion des polygames de l'église encourageait les Yoruba à se tourner vers l'Islam.

L'école rurale voulait persuader les églises africaines à 'accepter' plutôt qu'à 'tolérer' des fidèles polygames. Ses membres étaient d'avis que le rôle du Christianisme était de modifier et non pas de changer de manière révolutionnaire la société Yoruba. Ils doutaient fort que la révolution industrielle à venir ne résulte dans la formation d'une société monogame en Afrique, et avançaient, à l'appui de cette théorie, le fait que les élites européanisées vivaient déjà dans un cadre socio-économique de style occidental. Ces élites avaient certes abandonné la polygamie mais l'avaient remplacée par un système de concubinage plutôt que par la monogamie. L'école rurale estimait que si la politique missionnaire n'était pas modifiée l'immoralité causée par le concubinage de l'élite urbaine s'étendrait à toute la société à mesure qu'un plus grand nombre de Yoruba serait mis en contact avec la nouvelle civilisation commerciale et industrielle.

Les deux groupes, rural et urbain, s'opposaient donc à la politique missionnaire officielle d'exclusion des polygames qui en pratique permettait quand-même à de nombreux polygames secrets d'adhérer à l'église—une différence entre la théorie et la pratique ouvrant la porte à des accusations d'hypocrisie. Les deux écoles étaient d'accord pour dire qu'il ne fallait pas que des générations entières d'Africains se voient refuser l'accès à l'église du fait du retard de la révolution industrielle et sociale.

XI. ETHIOPIANISM: PAST AND PRESENT

G. SHEPPERSON

. . . Ethiopia shall soon stretch out her hands unto God. Psalm 68, verse 31.
. . . behold, a man of Ethiopia. Acts of the Apostles, chapter 8, verse 27.

The history of Christianity, like the history of all great religions and social movements, is strewn with the wrecks of words, wrenched from their original meanings, widened or narrowed, and forced into a bewildering variety of vessels that churn their ways in seas of semantic confusion. The Church in Africa south of the Sahara has acquired and added to the many Christian verbal transmogrifications that came originally from the north. In its turn, it has produced its own eccentric ecclesiastical etymology, of which, perhaps the most striking example is the story of Ethiopianism.

This evocative expression in African Christianity is best approached chronologically. It is convenient to divide Ethiopianism into four periods: (1) from 1611 to 1871; (2) from 1872 to 1928; (3) from 1929 to 1963; (4) after 1963.

In 1611 the Authorized or King James Version of the Bible was first issued. Its translation from the Hebrew and Greek Scriptures frequently employed one of the sixteenth- and early seventeenth-century English words for a black man: Ethiopian. Indeed, the word 'Ethiopia' was given a much wider significance than modern Ethiopia and was often used for sub-Saharan Africa as a whole. In this way, as the Bible was read, openly or surreptitiously, to the slave populations of the British North American and Caribbean colonies, which were established in the seventeenth century, persons of African descent learned to recognize their lost country and heritage in the references to Ethiopia and Ethiopians. They began to cherish all Ethiopian references in the Bible which had a liberatory promise and which, when contrasted with the indignities of plantation bondage, showed the black man in a dignified and humane light. With the growth of the abolitionist movement and the development of independent Negro Churches in the New World in the last quarter of the eighteenth century, one of these references, the thirty-first verse of the sixty-eighth Psalm, became a standard slogan for Negro aspirations wherever the King James Version was understood. The spread of Christian missionary activity in West Africa in the nineteenth century, particularly in areas such as Sierra Leone and Liberia where Negro evangelists from the United States and the British West Indies were at work, extended the process. 'Ethiopia' had begun to stretch out her hands unto God in both the New World and the Old by the middle of the nineteenth century in the form of independent Churches, schools, and States: uprooted black men had begun to get ideas above the humble and humiliating stations in life to which white men had assigned them. The term 'Ethiopianism' was not, at this time, applied to this process; but the years in which it was first extensively employed, from the 1870s to the 1920s, drew heavily on these pre-1871 experiences of Negro liberation.

The period from 1872 to 1928 may be called the classical period of Ethiopianism because it was at this time that it exercised its greatest political influence and was most widely noticed in the European, American, and African press. The formation of independent African Churches, either by secession from established bodies or by relatively indigenous growth, appeared to threaten European domination in areas with substantial white settlement such as South and Central Africa or where colonialism, as a result of the Partition of Africa, was entrenching its arbitrary lines of territorial division. In 1872, in the words of a white South African writing at the time when the European fear of Ethiopianism was at its highest in his country, 'the beginning of that pernicious revolt against European guidance, now known as the Ethiopian movement, took place'.[1] It began with the renunciation of missionary control by a hundred and fifty-eight African members of the Hermon station of the Paris Evangelical Mission in Basutoland. The seceders eventually returned to the mission's fold but their example proved contagious. Six years

[1] Theal, 1908, p. 339.

later a separate Tembu Church was established by an African Wesleyan minister; and, in 1892, the first so-called 'Ethiopian' Church in South Africa was set up by another separatist Wesleyan in Pretoria. By this time the Ethiopian Church movement was in full flood in South Africa.

Its motives were, at first sight, complex: the stimulus of European ecclesiastical secession; reaction against over-strict disciplining of African converts by European missionaries; the desire of some African separatist ministers to increase their personal power and status by administering Church property and monies; the creation of tribal Churches in which due respect was paid to African custom; and a rejection of the colour bar in many European-controlled Churches. But European witnesses did not, in the main, notice the complexities of causation of these independent African Churches. They remarked only on the threat which they seemed to offer to European rule in Africa, particularly in the South and Central regions. This was emphasized when a branch of the African Methodist Episcopal Church was created in 1896 in Pretoria. This Church, founded in 1816, was one of the earliest independent American Negro Churches and many of its ministers had played notable parts in the anti-slavery and civil rights movements in the United States. When, therefore, James M. Dwane was sent from South Africa in 1897 to seek affiliation with the A.M.E. Church in America and when, the following year, one of its leading bishops, Henry M. Turner, a fiery and determined fighter for Negro rights who was well hated by whites in the Southern States of America, paid in return a five weeks' visit to South Africa, for many Europeans of that country it seemed that the writing was on the wall. That the African Methodist Episcopal Church in South Africa was intertribal and pan-African in its vision, added to the dangers which it seemed to offer to European control in Africa.

Europeans in South and Central Africa and their sympathizers abroad noted the proliferation, in numbers and doctrines, of independent African Churches. By the first decade of the twentieth century there were over seventy of them in South Africa alone; and when, in 1904, an American extreme fundamentalist Church, the Catholic Apostolic Church in Zion, baptized its first African converts in Johannesburg the spur was given to a bewildering accumulation of groups, which, unlike the adherents of such bodies as the 1892 Ethiopian Church and the 1896 A.M.E. Church, were not content merely to break away from a European parent Church and to make no basic changes in Christian doctrine, but seceded or set themselves up independently and elaborated complex, fundametalist doctrines of a pentecostal and apocalyptic nature. A generation later such Churches were to be categorized by academic analysts under such names as 'Zionist', 'Messianic', 'Prophetic', 'Aladura', 'Millenarian', 'Watch Tower', and many others. Before the late 1920s, however, the tendency of European observers was not to subdivide them into two basic streams of independent African Churches but, if they bothered at all to classify them, to lump them all together as 'Ethiopian'. Whether orthodox or unorthodox, they were all elements in 'Ethiopianism', a pan-African conspiracy, a threat to white supremacy in Africa which, to many witnesses, seemed part of a deeply-laid plan in which Negroes from the New World were heavily involved.

It may now seem curious that Europeans in South and Central Africa should have seen in this gallimaufry of independent African Churches between the 1870s and the 1920s any concerted danger to their rule. Many of the Churches were tribalistic and, hence, against any wider form of African nationalism. Some were other-wordly in their orientation and distrusted the political tactics of this world. Several were overtly respectable and conservative as the middle-class European Churches from which they seceded. Indeed, James M. Dwane, the Ethiopianist emissary to America in 1897, returned to the Anglican fold in 1900 as Provincial of a specially created Order of Ethiopia within the Anglican Church. The historian, therefore, looking back at the 'Ethiopianism' of this period, may not find it difficult to believe that, if independent African Churches and ministers played any seditious roles at this time, it is largely because scared Europeans, in spite of themselves, had put such ideas into their minds.

Some of this European fear can be understood by recalling the shock to the white man's confidence which was created by the defeat of the Italians at Adwa in 1896 by the Ethiopians proper. It was not difficult for Europeans, if not to confuse the victorious and nationalistic Ethiopians of Adwa with the 'Ethiopians' of the independent Churches in South Africa, at least to see in Menelik's victory over white men an example which the young African Churches, as vehicles of an incipient nationalism, might one day too easily follow.

Furthermore, between 1906 and 1927, there were at least seven occasions when members of the independent African Churches of South and Central Africa seemed a clear and present danger to the white man's order. The first was in 1906 at the time of the Bambata or last Zulu Rebellion. Current research suggests that the 'popular white belief that the Ethiopians had fomented the disturbances would appear to coincide with the theory so familiar in South African history of "agitator" caused rebellions.'[2] Nevertheless, some Ethiopians, if far from the centre of the Rebellion, were implicated in it.[3]

Three years later, what has been called its first wave of Ethiopianism, took place in Central Africa. It was also the first time that the Watch Tower movement threatened the *pax Europeana* in Africa. This American movement had been introduced into South Africa in 1907 by Joseph Booth,[4] a British missionary whose role—often unconscious and unwilling—in the development of Ethiopianism, from his arrival in Africa in 1892 until his deportation from Cape Town after the First World War was, in every sense, seminal. One of Booth's Malawi disciples, Elliott Kenan Kamwana, broke away from him and started in the Livingstonia area an African Watch Tower movement which employed to such effect all the potentially social revolutionary

[2] Marks, 1964, p. 7.

[3] An amusing, if symptomatic by-product of the South African Ethiopianist scare, was the discovery of a non-existent Native rising in 1907 in the Ila country of Rhodesia by G. Heaton Nicholls, a young district commissioner who later became a South African Senator and turned his experiences of Ethiopianist rumour-mongering into a novel, *Bayete!* (London, 1923), which should not be neglected by any student of Ethiopianism.

[4] Shepperson and Price, 1958, *passim.*

apocalyptic of this American creed that he was expelled from the Nyasaland Protectorate from 1909 until 1914.

The creation of the Union of 1910, the increasing alienation of Native land and the general decline of the educated African's status in South Africa led to the formation in 1912 of the South African Native National Congress. Members of Ethiopian Churches were associated with its formation, in particular the Rev. Henry Ngcayiya, who opened the proceedings of its first conference with prayer. Ngcayiya was later made member of a Congress deputation to the London Government to protest against the South African Native Land Act of 1913.

This Act declared that no Native might purchase or rent land except in certain scheduled areas. Its effect was to segregate increasing numbers of Africans into areas of worsening land. African protest—especially Zulu protest, for the Zulu felt the incidence of the Act very heavily—was bitter. 1913 thus became an important turning-point in the history of Ethiopianism: 'there was an effervescence of new and apocalyptic Messianic Separatist Churches in the fateful years when the Bantu population woke up to find what had happened to them in 1913.'[5] In fact, it was the parting of the ways for the movement: the pan-African vision of some of the leaders of the orthodox Ethiopian Churches was to be challenged by the tribalistic horizons of unorthodox leaders of 'Zionist'-style Churches who were intent on preserving the patrimony of their particular people from the rapacity of the white man. Before, however, this could spill over into civil disturbances in South Africa in 1921, the focus of militant Ethiopianism shifted to Central Africa.

This was in the form of John Chilembwe's rising against British rule in Malawi in 1915. Chilembwe was no messiah or prophet-style Ethiopianist leader. He represented the orthodox, respectable Baptist wing of Ethiopianism. Nevertheless, his movement attracted some followers of less orthodox independent African Churches, especially those who had been influenced by the Watch Tower prophecy that the world as they

[5] Sundkler, 1958, p. 7.

knew it would end in 1914 and who had seen in the outbreak of the First World War in that year striking confirmation of this. The Rising, like the Zulu Rebellion of 1906, led to renewed European fears of Ethiopianism and, because of Chilembwe's connexions with American Negroes and Joseph Booth, a resurgence of white worries about the seditious consequences of American sects, coloured or white, in Africa.

Although the term Ethiopianism was still used by Europeans as a convenient whipping-boy for their anxieties about African aspirations, in the years immediately after the First World War it was beginning to be replaced by 'Watch Tower' or 'Kitawala'. A variety of African Watch Tower movements in Tanganyika, Nyasaland, the Belgian Congo, and Northern and Southern Rhodesia rippled the surface of European complacency in Central Africa, especially the so-called Mwana Leza movement in 1925 in Northern Rhodesia.[6]

It was, however, a 'Zionist' episode in South Africa which, at the time, was much more disturbing. This was the clash between Enoch Mgijima's Israelites and the South African police at Bulhoek commonage in the Ciskei in 1921. After his expulsion from an American Negro body in South Africa, the Church of God and the Saints of Christ, Mgijima set up his own Church and moved its members, without permission, on to Crown land in a communal settlement. Resisting eviction by the police, 163 of his Israelites were killed and 129 wounded.[7]

The Mgijima massacre indicated that the fears of the authorities in the Union and other parts of European-dominated Africa of American-Negro-influenced Ethiopian conspiracies could not easily be set aside. An American Negro sea captain, Harry Dean, in a cryptic episode, was accused by the South African authorities of attempting to establish an Ethiopian empire and was deported from Cape Town.[8] From 1920 to 1927, too, Marcus Garvey's American Universal Negro Improvement Association, with its built-in Ethiopian Church and its Declaration of Rights of the

[6] Gann, 1964, pp. 231–6.

[7] Roux, 1949, p. 145.

[8] Dean and North, 1929: some of the veracity of this, at first sight, fantastic work has been confirmed by personal interviews in Chicago.

Negro Peoples of the World in 1920, was considered highly dangerous by the white police of Africa.

It was not, therefore, fortuitous that the International Missionary Conference at Le Zoute in Belgium in 1926 should have given special consideration to the problem of American Negroes and Africa. The Conference made guarded recommendations that the work of American Negro missionaries in Africa 'should not be impeded'.[9] That these had some effect was made clear in 1926 when an American Negro Baptist organization was allowed to recommence the Providence Industrial Mission in Nyasaland from which John Chilembwe had launched his Rising in 1915.

Indeed, by 1926, the year of the British General Strike and of complex labour problems, black and white, in South Africa, scares of Ethiopianist conspiracy were being replaced by fears of plots against white supremacy by the forces of the international labour movement. At first in South Africa, this was focused on a powerful African trade union, the Industrial and Commercial Workers Union. But it was later directed against the Communist elements in its midst. In fact, by 1926, secular rather than religious forces were coming to be seen as the main threat to the white man's order in South and Central Africa. Ethiopianism, while, for some years, it did not altogether lose its revolutionary overtones, came to be regarded more as a danger to Christian unity than to civil peace in Africa. As such, as the report published in 1928 of the General Missionary Conference on South Africa pointed out, the term 'Ethiopian Movement' was being replaced by the expression 'Separatist Churches'.[10] The second classical period of Ethiopianism had come to an end.

Before, however, one turns to a short discussion of its third and fourth periods, the two main neglected areas of this classical period must be briefly examined: first, regions of British South and Central Africa outside the Union and Nyasaland; and second, British West Africa.

The most neglected part of the first area is Basutoland—although the classical period began at Hermon in 1872 and Basuto

[9] Smith, 1926, pp. 122–4.

[10] Dexter Taylor, 1928, p. 74.

Ethiopians were active in the early politically-conscious separatist Church movement in the Rhodesias: for example, the Rev. Micah D. Maghatho who had left the Dutch Reformed Church to join the African Methodist Episcopal Church and established in 1906 a branch of it close to Bulawayo. His setting up of independent schools under African control led to accusations of 'the Ethiopian movement confusing political propaganda with religious teaching'[11] by the Chief Native Commissioner in Southern Rhodesia. Another African from Basutoland, Willie Mokalapa, who had gone to Barotseland for Coillard's Paris Evangelical Mission but had quickly broken away from it, was active in the Ethiopian movement which lasted from about 1900 to 1906 in Lewanika's country. Lewanika had invited Ethiopians like Mokalapa to Barotseland because he was not satisfied with the progress Lozi pupils were making at orthodox missionary schools in learning English and the skills necessary to the modernization of his realm. Mokalapa did not live up to his expectations but the Ethiopianist spirit in Barotseland succeeded in creating by the end of 1906 the Barotse National School.[12] That it was a school for sons of the Lozi royal family and indunas (chiefs) indicates why Lewanika toyed with Ethiopianism: not for any pan-African or wider African nationalist promise which, in an elementary way, informed some of the Ethiopianist spirit in South Africa, but for the strengthening of the Lozi State against the incursions of the British South Africa Company. This is an early example of Ethiopianism as an agency of 'tribalism', an aspect of it which was to become pronounced after the late 1920s.

Another early instance of this 'tribalistic' element in Ethiopianism was the part played by the African Methodist Episcopal Church and other South African Ethiopianist forces in 'the great Ndebele movement for the establishment of a National Home, either by grant or purchase, which was led by Lobengula's eldest son, Nyamanda, in the period immediately after the First World War'.[13]

It is possible that a parallel process was at work in some parts

[11] Ranger, 1964, p. 58. [12] Ranger, n.d. [13] Ranger, 1964, p. 60.

of Bechuanaland before about 1916. London Missionary Society workers at the Phuduhutswana chiefdom in 1909, reported African prophets preaching that 'God was going to destroy all white people and the blacks were to have everything, and far more, than they could desire'.[14] It seems, however, unlikely that this sentiment was part of the inter-tribal, modern African nationalistic tendency in classical Ethiopianism. An L.M.S. missionary, commenting on the spread of Ethiopianism in the area in 1914, reported that the chief was 'at the head of the movement which was from his point of view a political rather than religious one'.[15]

West African witnesses of Ethiopianism in South and Central Africa noticed particularly its political importance. A Yoruba writer in 1908, defending the Ethiopian movement called it 'a struggle between those who recognize the claim to equal participation in social and political rights with others and those who for themselves and their order assert a certain fictitious superiority of race, and claim for it as a consequence of causes, however accidental, exclusive and special privileges'.[16] It did not, however, need the persecution of Ethiopian Churchmen by South African whites to trigger off kindred movements in British West Africa. The term 'Ethiopian' as a symbol of African pride in indigenous culture and achievement was used by West African writers and speakers well before the classical period of Ethiopianism opened in 1872. An example of this may be found in the words of James Africanus Beale Horton, Sierra Leone pioneer of the spirit of modern African nationalism, who wrote in 1868 in his book, *West African Countries and Peoples*, that 'Origen, Tertullian, Augustin, Clemens Alexandrinus, and Cyril who were fathers and writers of the Primitive Church, were tawny African bishops of Apostolic renown. Many eminent writers and historians agree that these ancient Ethiopians were Negroes.'[17]

This was the spirit which informed the writings and sermons of the Yoruba Baptist minister, Mojola Agbebi, whose role in the development of the African Church movement in Nigeria, is

[14] Pauw, 1960, p. 47.
[15] Ibid., p. 50.
[16] Omoniyi, 1908, p. 4.
[17] Horton, 1868, p. 66.

highly important.[18] His attitude towards European-dominated Christianity in West Africa from which he had broken away was trenchantly revealed in one of his sermons in 1902, when he criticized its alliance with Imperialism.[19] The remedy, Agbebi told his congregation, was the exploration of Africa's own religious heritage:

> . . . remember that it was 'God who in times past suffered all nations to walk in their own ways'. Conduct yourselves, therefore, in accordance with that idea. Do not be alarmed at the hideousness or grotesqueness of some forms of heathenism. Somewhere beyond the ugly exterior there lies a fine interior.[20]

Agbebi's spirit was nurtured in local conditions in Southern Nigeria—the narrow-minded restrictions of much white missionary activity, its frequent racialism and association with the growth of Imperialism in West Africa—but it was fed by his connexions with Ethiopianist agents beyond his own country, such as Joseph Booth and a number of American Negroes. The career of a man such as Mojola Agbebi demonstrates that there was something of an informal Ethiopianist International at the turn of the twentieth century and for its first decade and a half.

It is interesting, however, to note that, while the African Church Movement of Southern Nigeria often used the expressions of Ethiopianism in its publications and discourses, in its first generation, it does not appear to have called any of its major Churches 'Ethiopian'. It was not until 1921 in Nigeria that 'the Ethiopian Church was born out of the discontent engendered by a rigid adherence to foreign forms within many of the African churches'.[21] The tendency thereafter was to increase the use of African symbolism and music within the independent African Churches. It is curious, therefore, to notice that the term 'Ethiopian Church', which, in the third period of Ethiopianism (1929–63) as it has been designated above, came to stand in South Africa and elsewhere for the more orthodox type of independent African Churches in which 'church organization and Bible interpretation

[18] Webster, 1964, pp. 94–100, 75–76, 189–90, etc. Since this paper was written, an important article has appeared which supplies a valuable new perspective for the study of Ethiopianism in West Africa: see Ayandele, 1963.

[19] Agbebi, 1902, p. 10. [20] Ibid., p. 11.

[21] Webster, op. cit., p. 93; see also p. 131.

S

are largely copied from the patterns of the Protestant Mission Churches from which they have seceded'[22] was applied to exactly the opposite process in the early 1920s in Nigeria.

In the Gold Coast, in the early twentieth century, although independent African Churches were being created, it has been claimed that 'they were not so significant . . . as in other parts of Africa'.[23] Certainly, none of them seem to have called themselves specifically 'Ethiopian'. Perhaps this was due to the influence of the 'one significant breakaway movement',[24] the Gold Coast African Methodist secession in 1898 which affiliated itself with the powerful American Negro Church, the African Methodist Episcopal Zion Church. Nevertheless, the writings of some of these early Ghanaian secessionists, especially the A.M.E.Z. minister, S. R. B. Attoh Ahuma, showed the authentic Ethiopian historical spirit in their exploration of the African past. In particular, the concept of Ethiopianism was given something of a new ideological dimension in 1911 by the early Ghanaian nationalist, J. E. Casely Hayford, in a novel-like volume entitled *Ethiopia Unbound.* Using 'Ethiopia' in the Ethiopianist manner as a synonym for black Africa, Hayford, in spite of his friendly connexions with Negro intellectuals in America, cried out that it was not so much Afro-Americans that Africa needed as 'Africans or Ethiopians'.[25] Africa's redemption was to be its own work. Christian missions had been agents of the European partition of Africa—' "We shall go to the Ethiopians," the white man seemed to say, "and shall teach them our religion, and that will make them ours, body and soul—lands, goods, and all." ' Africans must look to their own resources, see Africa as 'the cradle of the world's system and philosophies, and the nursing mother of its religions', Hayford proclaimed, and strive to cast off the bonds that foreigners had twisted around Ethiopia.

When the third period of Ethiopianism (1929–63) opened, the political importance of the independent African Churches was by no means lost. Although, as has been noticed, 'Watch Tower'—

[22] Sundkler, 1961, p. 54. [23] Kimble, 1963, p. 164. [24] Ibid., p. 163.

[25] This and the following two quotations are from Hayford, 1911, pp. 4, 158, 194–7.

particularly its involvement in the Northern Rhodesian Copperbelt disturbances of 1935—was tending to replace 'Ethiopianism' as the term for independent African religio-political 'conspiracy', the original word was by no means lost in the original, conspiratorial sense. A bizarre book published in London in 1936, Daniel Thwaite's *The Seething African Pot, A Study of Black Nationalism, 1882–1925*, mixed both of the terms together and was probably responsible for the confusion of the two words in the chapter on new religious sects in Africa in Mr. Jomo Kenyatta's book, *Facing Mount Kenya* of 1938: 'The most popular and the one which conforms with African secret societies is Ethiopianism, which has a strong hold in South Africa, and which is well known by the name of the "Watch-Tower Movement" '.[26]

Such semantic confusion was to become a leading feature of the 1929–63 period. Against a mounting background of sectarian complexity, the Rev. Allen Lea, writing in 1928, had indicated laconically the emergence of this confusion when he noted that the expression 'Separatist Churches' was replacing 'the Ethiopian Movement' and commented that it 'is not possible to classify non-European-controlled Churches into Separatist and Ethiopian'.[27] But as the interest of students of social sciences in religio-political phenomena among the indigenous inhabitants of Africa and elsewhere increased, attempts at classification were made. The publication of Bengt G. S. Sundkler's important *Bantu Prophets in South Africa* in 1948 provided a terminology ('Ethiopian' for the orthodox, imitating independent African Churches and 'Zionist' for the unorthodox, initiatory independent African Churches) which was widely adopted, thereby destroying much of the generic nature of the term, 'Ethiopianism', as it had been widely employed by white men and Africans alike in the classical period, particularly from 1892 to 1915, when the first South African specifically-styled Ethiopian Church was founded and the two great crises, the Bambata and Chilembwe Rebellions of 1906 and 1915 respectively spurred bewildered Europeans to adopt it as a convenient general expression for the explanation of

[26] Kenyatta, 1938, p. 269: cf. also p. 275.

[27] Dexter Taylor, op. cit., p. 74.

a process with which they were completely out of sympathy and which they were incapable of understanding in its full complexity. In the revised version, however, of his *Bantu Prophets* in 1961, Sundkler added to his Ethiopian–Zionist dichotomy a third type which he called 'Messianic'. In addition, the independent Churches of Africa by this time were frequently described by a cluster of terms, wrenched from their original Christian contexts, which had often arisen in studies made in American and Pacific environments: millennial, millenarian, apocalyptic, eschatological, Cargo Cult, pentecostal, prophetic, nativistic, revitalization, to name the major ones. It seemed that the opportunity had been lost to construct a terminology that would be more than superficially relevant to the historical contexts of Ethiopianism.[28]

In 1963, however, a World Council of Churches report on African independent Church movements, which was drawn up by African and European ministers, suggested a helpful terminology which, although not ideal, deserves to be widely adopted as a means of finding one's bearings across the troubled seas of Ethiopianism.[29] The publication of this important report clearly brings to an end its third period.

In the fourth, post-1963 period, it is clear that the struggle for terminological clarification will have to be continued—particularly when it is observed that a valuable study of the Third World which was published in 1964 replaced indiscriminately 'Ethiopianism' by 'Zionism' as a generic term for 'the phase of primitive proto-nationalism in independent churches and cults' in Africa.[30] Three further tendencies should also become important. The first is a movement away from an indiscriminate association of independent Church movements with proto-nationalism and anti-colonialism.[31] Important though this political function undoubtedly has been and is, the challenge to the African governments of Zambia and Malawi of the Lumpa

[28] Cf. Shepperson, 1963, p. 86.

[29] Hayward, 1963, pp. 8, 13, 70–71.

[30] Worsley, 1964, pp. 86–88.

[31] But this will not necessarily mean that scholars, especially African scholars, will not find important links between Ethiopian-style movements and African nationalism: see here Ogot, 1963, pp. 256–8. But compare Baëta, 1962, pp. 86–88.

Church and the African Jehovah's Witnesses should serve to show that independent African Churches do not play a uniformly forward role in the advancement of African nationalism—indeed, today's seditious Ethiopian may be tomorrow's upholder of the white man's regime, as the career of John L. Dube in South Africa indicated. The second tendency may be the exploration of 'the very significant question of why Africans, who have felt it necessary to make such large modifications in the transmitted systems of secular government, have been largely content to follow the transmitted forms of ecclesiastical office and rule':[32] that is, a shifting of emphasis in the study of Christianity in Africa from separatist unorthodoxy to non-separatist orthodoxy. And the third tendency ought to be an increase in the study of the independent Churches from the theological viewpoint—not only the observer's but also their own. Even in the classical period of Ethiopianism when literacy was little advanced in Africa, the leaders of these Churches were often highly literate and they have left a by no means insubstantial body of writing. Studied comparatively, it might illuminate the manifold facets of Ethiopianism so that this too readily envisaged rough diamond of African Christianity would be given at least its rightful place in the history of the Church and of human endeavour.

REFERENCES

Agbebi, Mojola
(1902) Inaugural sermon delivered at the celebration of the first anniversary of the 'African Church', Lagos, West Africa, 21 December 1902.

Ayandele, E. A.
(1963) 'An assessment of James Johnson and his place in Nigerian history, 1874–1917. Part I, 1874–1890', *Journal of the Historical Society of Nigeria*, II, 4, pp. 489–90.

Baëta, C. G.
(1962) *Prophetism in Ghana*. London.

Dean, Harry and North, Sterling
(1929) *Umbala*. London.

Dexter Taylor, J.
(1928) *Christianity and the Natives of South Africa*. Lovedale.

Gann, L. H.
(1964) *A History of Northern Rhodesia*. London.

[32] Oliver, 1964, p. 15.

Hayford, J. E. Casely
(1911) *Ethiopia Unbound*. London.
Hayward, Victor E. W. (ed.)
(1963) *African Independent Church Movements*. London.
Heaton Nicholls, G.
(1923) *Bayete!* London.
Horton, James Africanus Beale
(1868) *West African Countries and Peoples*. London.
Kenyatta, Jomo
(1938) *Facing Mount Kenya*. London.
Kimble, David
(1963) *A Political History of Ghana*. Oxford.
Marks, Shula
(1964) 'Christian African participation in the 1906 Zulu Rebellion'. Mimeographed paper presented to the Conference of the Society for African Church History, London, September 1964.
Ogot, Bethwell A.
(1963) 'British administration in the Central Nyanza District of Kenya, 1900–1960', *Journal of African History*, IV, 2.
Oliver, Roland
(1964) *African History and the Outside World*. London.
Omoniyi, Bandele
(1908) *A Defence of the Ethiopian Movement*. Edinburgh.
Pauw, B. A.
(1960) *Religion in a Tswana Chiefdom*. London.
Ranger, Terence
(1964) 'The early history of independency in Rhodesia', *Religion in Africa*. Edinburgh, Centre of African Studies (mimeographed).
(n.d.) 'Ethiopianism in Barotseland, 1903–1905'. (Unpublished paper.)
Roux, Edward
(1949) *Time Longer Than Rope*. London.
Shepperson, George
(1963) 'Church and sect in Central Africa', *Rhodes Livingstone Journal* (Manchester), No. 33.
Shepperson, George, and Price, Thomas
(1958) *Independent African: John Chilembwe*. Edinburgh.
Smith, Edwin W.
(1926) *The Christian Mission in Africa*. London.
Sundkler, B. G. M.
(1958) *The Concept of Christianity in the African Independent Churches*. University of Natal Institute of Social Research (mimeographed).
(1961) *Bantu Prophets in South Africa*. London.
Theal, George McCall
(1908) *History of South Africa*. London.
Thwaite, Daniel
(1936) *The Seething African Pot: A Study of Black Nationalism, 1882–1925*. London.
Webster, James Bertin
(1964) *The African Churches among the Yoruba, 1888–1922*. London.
Worsley, Peter
(1964) *The Third World*. London.

Résumé

L'ÉTHIOPISME—HISTORIQUE ET SITUATION ACTUELLE

Cette communication a pour objetif de faire l'historique de l'expression 'Éthiopisme' qui, depuis 1892 environ, a été utilisée quelquefois comme terme générique pour les mouvements des églises africaines indépendantes et quelquefois pour décrire uniquement l'un de ces mouvements: celui des églises indépendantes africaines qui s'étant séparées d'une église métropolitaine en ont gardé la plupart des doctrines et formes d'organisation. L'Éthiopisme, dans l'acception générique du terme, a souvent des associations anti-européennes, anti-coloniales et proto-nationalistes; alors que, dans son deuxième sens, sans être dépourvu totalement d'associations d'idées politiques, il soit nettement plus respectable. Cette communication a pour but de servir de guide pour dissiper des confusions sémantiques auxquelles ces deux sens donnés au mot Éthiopisme et d'autres encore, ont donné lieu en classant ce phénomène selon 4 périodes différentes:

(1) *1611–1871.* Période préliminaire pendant laquelle les associations libératoires de l''Éthiopie' et des 'Éthiopiens' (expressions utilisées dans la version du King James de la Bible pour l'Afrique et les hommes noirs) furent explorées par les écoles, églises et états noirs indépendants en Amérique du Nord, dans les Caraïbes et dans les zones d'Afrique tombées sous l'influence européenne. Le Psaume 68, verset 31 devint une sorte de slogan pour un mouvement officieux en vue de la libération africaine qui fut en partie organisé par les églises séparatistes.

(2) *1872–1928.* Période classique de l'Éthiopisme. Des mouvements sécessionistes africains des églises blanches de l'Afrique Centrale et septentrionale (souvent qualifiées spécifiquement d'églises Ethiopiques selon la tradition d'avant 1871) semblaient à beaucoup d'Européens, très mal renseignés sur les complexités sociologiques de ces mouvements, constituer une menace pour le contrôle européen surtout au moment de la rébellion des Zoulous en 1906, des émeutes de Chilembwe en

1915 et du massacre de Mgijima en 1921. Avec le recul possible maintenant, il est apparu que beaucoup de ces mouvements Africains en fournissant des possibilités 'respectables' de progrès pour les Africains ou en soulignant le tribalisme n'étaient pas en fait l'avant-garde du nationalisme africain que les européens effrayés pensaient qu'ils étaient.

A cette époque les confusions dans la terminologie se multiplièrent à cause de l'attribution des termes de 'Watch Tower' et plus souvent de 'sioniste' aux mouvements des églises indépendantes de caractère apocalyptique ou 'pentecostal'. De plus, quoique la défaite des Italiens par les vrais Éthiopiens à Adwa en 1896 fut une source de fierté pour les Éthiopiens politico-religieux vivant dans une Afrique dominée par les Blancs, elle ne fit qu'ajouter à la confusion terminologique en suggérant, d'une manière ou d'une autre que le territoire de ce qui s'appelle aujourd'hui l'Éthiopie avait quelque chose à voir avec l'Éthiopisme alors qu'en fait il ne s'était aucunement trouvé associé aux origines de ce mouvement.

En 1928, le développement des mouvements syndicalistes internationaux (surtout en Afrique du Sud) fit apparaître que c'était des forces séculières telles que les syndicats et les partis politiques africains plutôt que les mouvements des églises indépendantes qui constituaient les menaces les plus graves à la suprématie blanche.

La communication appelle l'attention sur deux zones d'étude de l'Éthiopisme dans sa période classique qui ont été relativement négligées:

(i) le Basutoland, le Barotseland, le Béchuanaland et les Rhodésies; et

(ii) certaines régions de l'Afrique Occidentale Britannique.

Elle indique le rôle important qu'a joué le tribalisme pour les mouvements des églises indépendantes dans le premier groupe et suggère celui de l'historiographie africaniste pour le second.

(3) *1929–1963*. On fait remarquer la prolifération des aspects politiques et proto-nationalistes de l'Éthiopisme dans la zone des

mines de cuivre de la Rhodésie du Nord dans les années 1930 et dans les débuts du nationalisme au Kénya. Les tendances essentielles de cette période, cependant, furent un déclin de l'importance de l'Éthiopisme comme adjuvant au nationalisme africain moderne et une augmentation de la confusion dans les termes résultant en partie de l'application aux mouvements des églises indépendantes d'une terminologie empruntée aux études faites en Amérique et dans le Pacifique.

La publication, en 1963, d'un important rapport sur les mouvements des églises indépendantes africaines (Victor E. W. Hayward, rédacteur, *African Independent Church Movements*, Edinburgh House Press: London 1963) après une conférence du Conseil Mondial des Églises sur ce sujet qui eut lieu à Mindolo, Rhodésie du Nord en 1963, suggéra une terminologie qui, sans être idéale, est très utile à l'étude de l'Éthiopisme et mérite d'être adoptée de manière généralisée.

(4) *Après 1963*. La communication, en conclusion, indique quatre tendances qui peuvent apparaître dans l'étude de l'Éthiopisme, que le terme soit utilisé dans son ancien sens générique ou dans son sens moderne plus limité: (1) Continuation des efforts tendant à dissiper la confusion de termes. (2) Reconnaissance du fait quoique les mouvements des églises africaines indépendantes aient souvent eu et continuent à avoir une importance dans la lutte nationaliste contre le colonialisme ce fait n'a pas un caractère uniforme. (3) Conscience du fait que l'étude du christianisme non-séparatiste et orthodoxe en Afrique a peut-être beaucoup l'enseignements à apporter sur les contacts des sociétés africaines avec la culture européenne qui risquent d'être cachés si on accorde trop d'importance à l'étude des églises africaines indépendantes; le rôle prépondérant dans l'étude du christianisme en Afrique peut ne plus être accordé seulement aux mouvements séparatistes et non-orthodoxes. (4) Nécessité d'étudier les mouvements des églises africaines indépendantes d'un point de vue théologique—non pas seulement du point de vue de l'observateur mais de celui de ces églises mêmes. Même au cours de la période classique de l'Éthiopisme, lorsque l'analphabétisme était encore très répandu en Afrique, les dirigeants de ces églises étaient souvent

des personnes très éduquées qui ont laissé pas mal d'écrits. Une étude comparative de ces documents pourra aider à remettre l'Éthiopisme en Afrique, sous toutes ses formes, ou dans le contexte qui lui appartient au sein de l'histoire de l'Église et de l'effort humain.

XII. CHURCH GROWTH AND INDEPENDENCY AS ORGANIC PHENOMENA: AN ANALYSIS OF TWO HUNDRED AFRICAN TRIBES[1]

D. B. BARRETT

This paper gives some results of research done using a large-scale comparative model of the history of religion in sub-Saharan Africa, based on a sample of 211 of the 742 tribes to the south of the 15th parallel north.[2]

THE COMPARATIVE AND CROSS-CULTURAL METHODS

The greater part of the total religious investigation done in Africa to date may perhaps be described as of the 'microscopic' variety—descriptions and analyses in considerable depth of a single tribe or region or period or institution.

In contrast to this approach, the 'macroscopic' or cross-cultural method seeks the insights that can be obtained by examination of comparable phenomena across a large number of units, whether tribes, congregations, denominations, or nations. The method is postulated on the idea that one's impressionistic judgements concerning a large number of social units are often found to be in error when the actual data are examined. Empirical relationships between institutions, whose existence has been masked by the fact that the relationship does not hold under all circumstances, can then be obtained and their significance interpreted. This method assumes that there is something organic beneath the phenomena, which the analysis can uncover.

Inevitably, this broad approach is subject to the criticism of over-simplification. For example, a division of all tribes into two

[1] Full details of the tribes studied, the methodology employed, and the results obtained, together with case studies, maps, and historical background, are given in Barrett, 1967.

[2] The ethnographic classification used in this model is that proposed by Murdock, 1959. From an index of 6,000 names used for African tribes, he classifies 853 as tribes, lists all alternate tribes and sub-tribes and delineates their approximate territory on a map of the whole continent.

categories, those possessing the ancestral cult, and those lacking it, ignores the great variations that exist in the practice of this institution.[3]

Similarly, the vast range and diversity of factors involved in the growth of both mission and independent churches might appear to preclude large-scale comparison. This is particularly true of the phenomenon of independency, by which is meant here the rise of independent church movements (separatism). When examined, they appear to be a vast number of apparently disparate regional manifestations. Even when some analysts claim to see a connexion between several such movements, others may vigorously deny it. For instance, Bishop Matthew Ajuoga of the Church of Christ in Africa (an ex-Anglican body in Kenya claiming 60,000 adherents), objects to his church being classed with the Orthodox separatist movements among the Ganda and Kikuyu, on the grounds that the latter are under a new foreign influence, that of Constantinople, and are therefore a quite different phenomenon.

This paper, however, assumes that there are numerous common background factors at work which can be revealed by this broader method. We deal here only with the phenomenon of independency, and we investigate only the one problem: to what extent, if at all, are separatist movements fundamentally similar in origin, wherein does this similarity lie, and what overall explanation does this suggest? The attempt is made, therefore, to get beneath the more immediate local and regional causes to uncover something of the common basic socio-religious climate out of which independency has emerged.

THE PHENOMENON OF INDEPENDENCY

Independent church movements, usually formed by secession from a parent mission body or historical church, have been reported from at least 250 distinct tribes in 33 sub-Saharan nations. A very considerable literature exists, numbering at least 1,500 books, articles, notes and essays in twenty languages

[3] Fortes (1965) both examines these variations and illustrates the value of the comparative approach, in this case for some dozen tribes.

published to date. The literature, which formed the point of departure for this study, deals with movements in 50 different tribes; the data on the other 200 tribes were obtained through field work and other inquiries. Movements were observed, for instance, in countries only recently involved—Chad, the Central African Republic, and Upper Volta.

The nature of the study and of the resulting model required a somewhat precise definition of what constituted the presence of independency in a tribe. The phenomenon has such diffuse edges that it was necessary to choose a narrower definition than could be employed in a purely historical study. Independency was therefore defined as the formation and existence within a tribe of any organized religious movement, even as small as a single organized congregation, which claims the title Christian in that it acknowledges the lordship of Christ, and which has either been founded as a new kind of religious entity under African initiative and leadership outside the mission churches, or which has separated by secession from a mission, historical church or an existing independent church; with the further criterion that it was initiated from within its own tribal ranks on its own tribal territory, rural or urban, and under its own tribal leadership, or that the tribe concerned had contributed significantly within its own territory to a similar movement originating in another tribe. In other words, we are to examine what might be called the 'spontaneous generation' of independency.[4]

Employing this strict definition, it was found that no movements had been reported from two distinct geographical groupings: the first (Senegal, Gambia, Guinea, Portuguese Guinea, Mali, Niger, Sierra Leone,[5] and Liberia) has in common a strong Muslim influence, and the second (Somalia, Ethiopia, French Somaliland, Sudan, Rwanda, and Burundi) appears to have in common Hamitic and Sudanic feudal elements also present in a corridor of tribes resistant to independency stretching from Rwanda up to the Sudan.

[4] See Appendix, Table I, p. 285, for full data.

[5] The definition excludes both the early schisms of 1819 onwards (Fyfe, 1962) and the current spread of bodies from Nigeria in Sierra Leone, along with all other imported sects such as Jehovah's Witnesses.

THE METHODOLOGY OF THE ANALYSIS

It was necessary to choose a representative sample of tribes from which generalizations to the whole of sub-Saharan Africa could be made with confidence. The difficulties involved in ethnographic sampling have been fully discussed by Murdock in relation to the formation of the Human Relations Area Files at New Haven.[6] His proposed Africa sample consists of 131 tribes south of the 15th parallel north. He further increases the value of the sample by giving for each tribe comparable values of thirty standard cultural variables, such as social stratification, political system, and the presence of polygamy. This was chosen as our basic listing and named Sample A. It is the sample to be used when making generalizations for the continent about traditional society.

Since the impact of colonial rule, however, the social unit within which people have lived is not the tribe, but the tribe-within-the-nation—that part of a tribe which exists in a nation, cut off from its other part or parts by the arbitrary drawing of a colonial frontier through its territory. We may give this entity the name of tribal unit. The Fang, for example, may be said to consist of the three tribal units Fang-1 (in Gabon), Fang-2 (in Cameroun), and Fang-3 (in Spanish Guinea). It was found that 21 per cent of all tribes in Sample A had been seriously or significantly divided in this way. Sample A was therefore extended by treating these split tribes as in each case two (or three, or four) tribal units; the result was a sample of 164 tribal units, to be named Sample B, from which generalizations to the continent in the colonial era will be made.

The sample was further extended by the inclusion of all tribes known to have separatist or other kinds of religious movement. This resulted in a listing of 262 tribal units, known as Sample C. It is not, of course, representative like the earlier two, but it is legitimate to use this sample for analysis of the kind of tribes in which independency occurs.

The construction now began of the model of the history of religion in sub-Saharan Africa. Three time-phases were de-

[6] Murdock, 1957.

lineated: the traditional period, before and up to the time of European impact on the tribe; the colonial and missionary period, from impact up to the present; and the contemporary period, defined as the religious situation resulting from the interaction of the two earlier periods, and covering the present state of the historical churches and religious movements, but also including all known movements since colonial impact. For each tribe, data was now collected from the vast corpus of literature available on African ethnography, traditional religion, the colonial phase, missions, and the current social, political, and economic situations in the various nations. For each tribe, approximately one hundred variables were measured, providing a detailed socio-religious profile which could then be compared, by inspection or statistically, with all other profiles. In order to add the time dimension to the model, the date (year) of eight important events in the life of the tribe was recorded, covering the arrival of colonial rule, missions, and, *inter alia*, the publication of the scriptures in the tribe's language. Full information in this latter respect—the publication dates for all portions, New Testaments and Bibles—was obtained for the whole sample from the files of the American Bible Society.

The model, now in the form of a 262 × 100 data matrix, was then subjected to a number of analytic questions. Hypotheses were developed and tested against the model. A computer program of statistical testing revealed that certain traditional and colonial-missionary variables were significantly correlated with such variables as the growth of the Protestant or Catholic churches, or with the presence of independency. These significant variables were then combined to form indexes of church growth and of propensity to independency for each of the tribes in the sample.

THE BACKGROUND CORRELATES OF INDEPENDENCY

In the literature, several observers have attempted explanations of the rise of independency in terms of the kind of nation in which it has occurred. At first sight, national variables do seem predominant: South Africa's apartheid, Kenya's white settlers, the

Congo's economic crises, seem to offer sufficient explanation. However, such factors were found in the present analysis to be insufficient cross-nationally. There were always other nations who did not fit any simple theory. Portuguese Angola, for example, has had a relatively oppressive colonial rule and has continuously increased its white settlers from 9,000 in 1900, to 80,000 in 1950, and to 220,000 in 1961, and yet has been virtually free of independency; while Nigeria, with a liberal colonial regime and no white settlers, initiated separatism as long ago as 1888.

It was found empirically that, of the twenty-two national variables included in the model, only six were significantly correlated with independency. Movements tended to occur in nations that were of high literacy, with a high average *per capita* income, with (despite the case of Angola) a high ratio of white to black population, with a large number of mission bodies at work, with a high ratio of Protestant ordained missionaries to population, and with a low percentage of Muslims among the populace. These results, although interesting, do not have enough explanatory power on which to build any theory. It is necessary, therefore, to penetrate deeper by moving on to consider the tribal correlates.

Because tribe-within-the-nation is more precise than nation as a working unit, numerous important relationships now stand revealed. In fact, of the thirty tribal variables investigated, eighteen correlated significantly with the presence of independency. Separatism tends to occur in tribes that are over 115,000 in population, of Bantu race, with a complex political system, which practise general polygyny, and which have the ancestral cult and the worship of the earth goddess; further, it is more likely if white settlers have occupied tribal land; if scripture portions have been translated, followed by the New Testament and the complete Bible; if an adjacent tribe has independency; and so on.

What this means can best be illustrated by taking two examples.[7] Let us begin with the question of polygamy. Dr. E. G.

[7] These relationships are set out in table form in the Appendix, Tables II and III, pp. 285, 286.

Parrinder[8] and others have written that polygamy has only rarely been the cause of separatism, and this is certainly true at the conscious level. What, however, are we to make of the following facts? General polygyny, with an incidence of over 20 per cent, is the traditional norm in 34 per cent of African tribes; 44 per cent restrict polygyny to the sororal or non-sororal varieties; whereas for 22 per cent, polygyny is limited and infrequent or even (in the case of 7 per cent) absent entirely.[9] When this variable is cross-tabulated against the presence of independency, we find that the phenomenon occurs in 30 per cent of the tribes with general polygyny, in 24 per cent where polygyny is restricted, and in only 6 per cent of tribes with limited or no polygyny. Whatever the conscious motivation may be, therefore, it appears that separatism has roots in polygyny. The only two exceptions in the sample to this generalization are the Nandi (Kenya) and the Nama (South-West Africa), who have limited polygamy, but have had separatist movements.

A widespread religious institution is that of the ancestral cult, the relationship of a living family to its recently-departed members who still frequent the family land. According to the literature, the cult is present in some form and is important for 70 per cent of all tribes; for 29 per cent, the literature states, usually with emphasis, that it does not exist. Thus while the ancestor-cult is the 'dominant cult' of the Tlhaping and is 'the core of Mossi religious behaviour', there is 'no cult of the dead' among the Nuer, 'no trace' of it among the Turkana, and for the Lele there is 'no cult of the dead, and their names are not recalled in ritual'. Our finding in the present analysis is that independency has occurred in 37 per cent of all tribes having the ancestor-cult, and in only 9 per cent of tribes without it. In Sample B, there are only three exceptions to this generalization that movements arise in tribes with an ancestor-cult: the Suk (Kenya), the Baya (that part in the Central African Republic) and, again, the Nama, have no cult but have had secessions.

Another example concerns the translation of the complete Bible into the tribal language. By 1964, some 23 per cent of all

[8] Parrinder, 1952.

[9] These figures are taken from Sample A.

tribes have their own version published. Among these, independency has occurred in 64 per cent of the cases; but it has occurred in only 10 per cent of tribes without their own complete Bible.

A whole set of similar empirical findings about other variables could be given. They are taken from Sample B, which previously had been tested in various ways in order to determine its reliability in representing the structure of sub-Saharan Africa in the colonial era, and had been found reliable. The results therefore indicate that we have found basic tribal correlates of independency applicable to the universe of 742 tribes.

A SCALE OF RELIGIOUS STRAIN

Some order should now be brought into this unwieldy mass of empirical findings. It was decided to regard all the correlating variables as the major socio-religious common background factors out of which the phenomenon had emerged. These were then phrased as dichotomous questions and combined into an index or scale, along which every tribal unit could be located, thereby providing a single measure in place of the previous multiplicity. The position of a tribal unit on this scale is the sum total of affirmative answers to the eighteen questions now to be set forth.[10]

Scale of Religious Strain for a Tribal Unit

A. *In traditional culture*

1. Is this a Bantu tribe?
2. Is it over 115,000 in population?
3. Is polygyny general or common, and not limited?

B. *In traditional religion*

4. Is the ancestor-cult important?
5. Is there an earth goddess?

[10] The arbitrary numbers in nine of the questions were chosen because each broke the sample into two roughly equal groups, of which it could then be stated that the group for which the answer to the question was affirmative was more prone to independency than the group with a negative answer.

C. *In the colonial period*

6. Did colonial rule arrive more than 100 years ago?
7. Have white settlers occupied tribal land?
8. Is the national average income over $70 (£25) per year?

D. *In the missionary period*

9. Did the missions arrive more than 60 years ago?
10. Have scripture portions been published in the tribal language?
11. Has the New Testament been published?
12. Has the Bible been published?
13. Was the New Testament published more than 60 years ago?
14. Do the ordained Protestant missionaries in the nation number more than 22 per million population?

E. *In the current period*

15. Are Muslims in the nation less than 50 per cent?
16. Are Protestants in the tribe 20 per cent or over?
17. Are Catholics in the tribe 20 per cent or over?
18. Is there independency in any adjoining tribe?

This scale is a measure of propensity to independency. It appears to be measuring some kind of socio-religious pressure to separatism: hence we may call it the scale of religious strain.

When position on this scale is cross-tabulated against independency, the result is striking. No movements have occurred in tribes with 5 or less of the 18 factors; and every one of the 28 tribal units in Sample C which has 13 or more factors has already initiated movements. Further, the scale not only predicts the presence of independency: it also predicts the intensity with which a tribal unit participates. The 232 tribal units which the analysis places on the scale may be divided into four groups corresponding to four types of tribes at different stages of involvement with independency. Names may be given to the stages as follows:

A. *Dormancy* (84 tribal units, all having 5 factors or less on the scale); these are mostly smaller tribes with so far little or no involvement with settlers, missions, or scriptures. In several, however, such as the Tiv (Nigeria), the religious situation is so markedly similar to that of countless other tribes elsewhere before independency began that the theory we are soon to evolve indicates that separatism is dormant and, in some cases, imminent.

B. *Marginal separatism* (45 tribal units, with 6 or 7 factors): 11 cases have secessions which on examination prove to be marginal ones involving a handful of congregations. In this category are the Suk (Kenya), the Banda (Central African Republic), and the Sara and Ngama (Chad). The Yakö (Nigeria) likewise have two small separatist groups.

C. *Pressure* (75 tribal units, with 8 to 12 factors): in this group the odds are even on independency; 37 cases are involved in it. The intensity of involvement increases as we move up the scale. At the lower end (8 factors) is the Ngumba-1 tribal unit (Cameroun), a small forest tribe which around 1935 broke with the American Presbyterian Mission on being denied services and scriptures in their own language, and formed l'Église Protestante Africaine. At the upper end (12 factors) the socio-religious pressure to secede has become so great that tribes with large-scale involvement are appearing: the Ibo and Ibibio (Nigeria) and the Luo (Kenya).

D. *Inevitable independency* (28 tribal units, with 13 to 17 factors): the adjective is chosen to illustrate the massive sociological conditioning to which this group is subject, for all cases have initiated movements, almost all on a very big scale, and several for half a century or more. One tribe stands in isolation at the top of the scale with 17 factors—the Zulu (South Africa), whose first secession occurred in 1890 and who today have the phenomenal number of over two thousand independent church bodies.[11]

It may be noted in passing that this strain may also produce other reactions than independency—such as political movements,

[11] The missing factor is No. 17: Catholics number only 5·5 per cent in South Africa.

syncretisms and so on. For an example we may take the non-separatist East African Revival: all tribes that have responded most to it are found to be high on the scale (Ruanda 11, Ganda 13, Luo 12, Kikuyu 14, Kamba 16, etc.), while adjoining tribes who have resisted Revival are found to be low on the scale (Maasai 7).

The Interpretation of the Scale

We must now inquire what fundamental cause, at work across the continent, lies underneath the eighteen socio-religious determinants. Whatever it is, it must presumably be due to their interaction and the consequent production of religious strain.

We must first examine the traditional factors. What is it, for example, about the institutions of polygamy and the ancestor-cult that might possibly cause religious strain? The answer immediately comes to mind: it is these two against which the missions have, over the years, mounted their strongest assaults, and before which they have met with their greatest resistance. Both institutions have been heavily involved in one way or another with independency; for the former we may follow the complicated pattern among the Yoruba, traced for us by J. B. Webster in his paper in the present volume; while for the latter we need only remember the reassertion of the ancestral cult among the Zulu Zionist churches or in the Church of the Ancestors among the Nyanja (Malawi), or in Dini ya Misambwa (The Religion of the Ancestral Spirits) in Kenya.

Another traditional religious institution, particularly in West Africa, is the worship of the earth goddess with attendant fertility rituals. Naturally this has also come under missionary attack; and it too appears to have resulted in schisms which, in themselves, appear somewhat quaint. One thinks here of the R.O.F. (Reformed Ogboni Fraternity), a religious secret society maintaining the cult of the earth mother, alias Eve, and which was begun by a Yoruba Anglican priest, Ogunbixi.

These traditional factors all have in common the family, its institutions, its land and its productivity. Now all these in fact are so closely interwoven that to attack one is unwittingly to attack the whole complex. It is therefore not surprising that African society should have experienced the missionary assault on one or more of these institutions as an assault on the whole of society, centring on its basic unit, the family. A somewhat similar explanation can be made for the appropriation of ancestral land by white settlers. The family was being undermined, inexplicably, by the colonial-missionary attitude and actions.[12]

There is still missing one ingredient essential for independency, however. So far, there had been no hint of inconsistency in the attitude of the missions on the issues involved. Their tenets, apparently, gave them no alternative but to denounce the traditional way of life. At this point, an event of fundamental importance in the religious life of the tribe took place: the Holy Scriptures were translated and published in the tribe's own language. They provided an independent standard of reference for African Christians, who now began to detect discrepancies between missions and scriptures on the points at issue. The slender biblical basis for monogamy was noted, together with the polygamous practice of the Patriarchs, the vital importance of family and land, the long lists of respected ancestors, the Old Testament emphasis on fertility and sexuality. These, set forth in black and white, had a profound impact. Africans now began to criticize mission teaching on these points and to defend their traditional institutions as biblical.

This crucial role of vernacular scriptures can be abundantly illustrated. The Luo is one of many tribes which have attained independency soon after a scripture publication. On the other hand, absence of translation imparts a marked resistance. From the Ivory Coast to Cameroun, only two large southern tribes have been resistant to independency: the Fon of Dahomey (800,000) and the Edo or Bini of Benin City (400,000). Both also are the only large tribes with no vernacular New Testament or Bible yet, despite a long history of missionary contact (in the case of the Bini, five centuries).

The remaining factors in the scale of religious strain can be

[12] For a detailed account of this missionary assault on one society, the Duala, see the paper by R. Bureau in this volume.

shown to support this interpretation, as can be seen from the final section of this paper when the generalized theory is set forth in its most concise form. Here it will suffice to say that propensity to independency increases as more of the scriptures become published; that their increasing circulation presupposes a relatively high average income; and that the whole process of religious strain must clearly increase when the factors have all been present for a considerable length of time.

THE DYNAMICS OF THE MOVEMENT

The development of the entire movement over the last hundred years was now studied. It was found that the scale of religious strain, which has been shown to be capable of predicting to some degree the present incidence of independency, gave a remarkably good account of the history of the phenomenon too. Twelve of the 18 factors on the scale are functions of time. By examining what these factors were a century ago in South Africa, for example, we find that in 1864 the Zulu had a total of 11 factors, and the Tembu and Sotho (that part of this large tribe in Basutoland) stood at 12 factors each; all at the top of the third category that has earlier been named Pressure, where the socio-religious pressure to secede becomes appreciable. These peoples were, in fact, on the brink at that time. The first secession south of the Equator was a minor one in Basutoland in 1872, six years before the Sotho Bible was published. Soon afterwards, in 1882, came the much bigger National Tembu Church, in a tribe which had had its own Bible for twenty-three years. By that time, the Zulu had added 3 more factors (the New Testament in 1865, the Bible in 1883, and adjacency to the Tembu) and in 1890 formed their first secession, the Zulu Mbiyana Church. Similar analyses can be made in West, East, and Central Africa.

The whole movement, in fact, appears to have been spreading from tribe to adjacent tribe in an extraordinarily regular manner over the last hundred years. The pattern may be examined in tabular form in the Appendix (Table I). In brief, independency may be seen to have spread by means of three mechanisms: (1) epicenters are formed in unrelated areas on average every five years; (2) adjacent tribes become involved, forming long chains; and (3) the chains begin to link up into large clusters.

Examples of this current expansion are legion. The Luo now have 9 separatist bodies, including from the Church of Rome (Maria Legio, 1963) and the Anglican Church (Church of Christ in Africa, 1957). The latter now claims members in 56 new tribes, and is part of the East African United Churches—a body of 40 independent churches formed partly of bodies refused admission to the Christian Council of Kenya. Similarly, in Rhodesia, scores of new secessions were reported in 1964.

What this implies for the future is continued expansion at an increasing tempo. Every tribe on the continent is moving slowly, a factor at a time, up the scale. Since the 742 tribes have added an aggregate total of some 2,000 factors to their scores in the last hundred years, we can expect several new tribes each year to produce secessions.

VERIFICATION OF THE THEORY

This paper will close with a tentative theory derived from the analysis. It has only been possible here to give a fraction of the evidence from which it has been deduced: illustrations could be given from most of the 262 tribal units studied and from the 250 involved tribes. A full test of the theory was, however, made in the case of Luo independency in Kenya, with which the author has been personally acquainted. Interviews with Bishop Ajuoga provided striking empirical verification at points where the cross-cultural evidence was somewhat weak.

A GENERALIZED THEORY OF THE RISE OF INDEPENDENCY IN SUB-SAHARAN AFRICA

The Background Factors

(1) The bases of African society have for centuries been a complex of institutions centering on the family and the home. With variations from tribe to tribe, the family land is the inalienable preserve of the family ancestors, who are feared and respected in the ancestral cult. In many societies, the fertility of

land, animals, and polygamous marriage depends on the cult of the earth mother.

(2) Christian missions early enjoyed remarkable response. Preoccupied with their task of church-building, they had little time for any encounter in depth with indigenous beliefs and systems of thought. The initial attitude of courtesy towards traditional society gave way around the period 1880–1914 to the disparaging of institutions unacceptable to Western ideas of morality and religion.[13] A subconscious alarm at this assault on, apparently, the basic unit of the family, spread across the continent.

(3) The religious strain generated by this assault varied greatly from tribe to tribe. There is no single indispensable factor nor unique set of conditions by which the strain has arisen. Rather, it has been the product of the interaction of several of a total of eighteen socio-religious factors representing traditional, colonial, and missionary conditions in the tribe concerned.

(4) With the publication of the Scriptures, society began to detect a serious discrepancy between missions and biblical religion in connexion with the one or two traditional institutions under attack. Missions had inadvertently overstepped their biblical authority, and had been vocal where the Bible was silent. Gradually the Scriptures became an independent standard of reference to legitimate this grievance.

Reaction to Mission

(5) The onset of independency in a tribe occurs when the level of religious strain lies between certain limits. Below 6 factors, it does not occur. Between 6 and 7 factors, marginal separatism—a handful of congregations—may occur. From 8 to 12 factors, the probability of secession becomes increasingly stronger. Beyond 12 factors, all tribes appear to have large-scale involvement. The higher a tribe's position on the scale, the greater is the intensity

[13] This shift in attitude is well illustrated in the present volume by the contrast between the early policy of the North German Mission (E. Grau's paper) and the cases cited by F. B. Welbourn (p. 187) and E. B. Idowu (pp. 430–1).

of the involvement. Independency, which was tribal at origin, now takes on a multitribal or universal character.

(6) The immediate occasion and cause of the actual flashpoint (the secession when it occurs) is, relatively, of smaller importance, since any one of a number of situations would have produced it once the level of religious strain were high enough. These local, regional, and personal factors, together with the strain, constitute the total 'explanation' of independency.

(7) The spread of the movement takes place from tribe to adjacent tribe, either by spontaneous generation with migrants, labourers, or traders as unwitting agents, or occasionally by direct external stimulation. Long chains of adjoining involved tribes come into being, new epicenters are formed every five years or so, and the chains link up in huge elongated clusters.

(8) The future of independency would seem to be one of continued steady expansion into new tribes and regions. The eighteen background causative factors are largely unaltered by the coming to power of Africans in Church and State. Dialogue between independent and historical churches, and with traditional religion, has not yet become sufficiently penetrating to alter the situation appreciably. Meanwhile, two vast clusters of involved tribes, physically adjoining each other in long chains, are in process of formation, one stretching from the Ivory Coast to Northern Angola, the other from South-West Africa up to Kenya.

Independency is clearly playing an increasing part in the expansion of Christianity in Africa.

SUMMARY

This study shows that, despite the disparate nature of the multiform manifestations of independency in Africa, the phenomena begin to be seen as one single organic movement when subjected to large-scale comparative analysis. Similar treatment of the growth of the Protestant and Catholic churches may be expected to yield similar insights.

APPENDIX

Table I

The Spread of Independency by Chains, 1858–1965

Chain[1]	*Tribal units*[2]	*Date of first secession in tribe*[3] *(epicentric tribe first)*
1. Ghana	10	1858 Fanti, 1903 Ga, 1911 Ewe, 1921 Ashanti, Akyem, Adangme, Akposo, 1954 Buem, 1965 Popo
2. South Africa	11	1872 Sotho, 1882 Tembu, 1885 Tlhaping, 1890 Zulu, 1904 Swazi, 1910 Xosa
3. Nigeria	17	1888 Yoruba, 1891 Ibo and Ijaw, 1893 Egba, 1895 Ijebu, 1899 Gun, Ife, Isoko, Ekiti, Igbira, Ibibio, 1950 Edo, Itsekiri
4. Central Africa	11	1908 Tumbuka, 1915 Nyanja, 1925 Nyakyusa, 1925 Lala, 1954 Bemba, Bisa
5. Ivory Coast	10	1913 Adjukru, Ebrie, Avikam, 1915 Assini, Agni, Attie, Abe, Ari, Alagya, Dida
6. Uganda	2	1914 Ganda, 1935 Lango
7. S. Rhodesia	5	1915 Zezuru, Ndebele, Korekore, Tawana, Manyika
8. Lower Congo	10	1921 Kongo, 1930 Teke, Yombe, Sundi, Kunyi, Yaka, 1953 Vili
9. Central Kenya	2	1922 Kikuyu, Kamba
10. Cameroun	4	1930 Duala, 1935 Ngumba, Fang
11. Western Kenya	4	1930 Luo, 1930 Wanga, 1960 Nandi, Suk
12. South-West Africa	2	1946 Nama, 1955 Herero
13. Chad	4	1951 Sara, Ngama, 1960 Banda, Baya
14. South Congo	3	1958 Luba, Lulua, Tetela
15. Upper Volta	1	1959 Mossi
16. Tanganyika	2	1960 Gogo, Nyamwezi

Notes:

1. The chain name here may include tribes in adjacent nations.
2. The total is that of all tribal units within the chain.
3. Where no date is given, the exact year is not known.

Note further that this table is not exhaustive: it lists 79 of the 250 tribes known to be involved in independency.

Table II

Independency and Polygamy: 157 Tribal Units

Polygamy	*Independency*	
	Present	*Absent*
General polygyny	16 (30%)	38 (70%)
Less common polygyny	17 (24%)	53 (76%)
Limited polygyny	2 (6%)	31 (94%)

Table III

Independency and Ancestor-cult: 111 Tribal Units

Ancestor-cult	Independency	
	Present	Absent
Present	29 (37%)	50 (63%)
Absent or unimportant	3 (9%)	29 (91%)

REFERENCES

Barrett, D. B.
(1967) *Schism and Renewal in Africa: an Analysis of Six Thousand Contemporary Religious Movements*. Nairobi, Kenya.

Fortes, M.
(1965) 'Some Reflections on Ancestor Worship in Africa', in Fortes and Dieterlen (eds.) *African Systems of Thought*. London.

Fyfe, C.
(1962) *History of Sierra Leone*. Oxford.

Murdock, G. P
(1957) 'World Ethnographic Sample', *American Anthropologist*, LIX, pp. 664–87.
(1959) *Africa: its Peoples and their Culture History*. New York.

Parrinder, E. G.
(1952) *Religion in an African City*. London.

Résumé

LE DÉVELOPPEMENT DES MISSIONS ET DES ÉGLISES SÉPARATISTES CONSIDERÉ COMME PHÉNOMÈNE ORGANIQUE: ANALYSE PORTANT SUR 200 TRIBUS AFRICAINES

L'essentiel des recherches religieuses en Afrique a consisté jusqu'à présent en études détaillées portant sur un domaine limité, sur une tribu, une région ou encore sur un seul aspect de la religion. La présente communication fournit certains des résultats obtenus après une analyse d'un genre différent et beaucoup plus vaste puisqu'il s'agit d'une étude faite au moyen d'un modèle à grande échelle et comparatif de l'histoire des religions en Afrique sub-saharienne ayant utilisé un échantillon de 211 des 742 tribus vivant au sud du 15ème parallèle-nord.

Avec cette méthode, il est possible de démontrer qu'un phénomène tel que les efforts missionnaires chrétiens ou le développement des églises indépendantes (séparatistes) présente certains traits communs d'où il est possible de tirer des théories générales. On peut alors expliquer pourquoi ces phénomènes ont eu un développement très accusé dans certaines régions et chez certaines populations et moins rapide dans d'autres.

Cette étude traite uniquement du problème du développement du séparatisme religieuse dans les 250 tribus et les 33 pays où elle a été signalée jusqu'à présent. Nous mettons en évidence, en nous fondant sur un échantillon représentatif du continent dans son ensemble, 18 variantes socio-religieuses, nationales et tribales que l'on peut mettre en corrélation avec la présence du phénomène de séparatisme. A partir de cela, nous les avons groupées sous forme d'indice permettant de mesurer les tendances religieuses de chaque tribu du continent à n'importe quel moment au cours des dernières 150 années.

On voit alors que le séparatisme se produit lorsque cette tendance religieuse atteint certaines limites mesurables. Au dessous d'un certain seuil on ne trouve pas et ceci à aucun moment, de tribu ayant eu l'initiative d'un mouvement indépendant; au-dessus d'un certain plafond toutes les tribus subissent le phénomène. Dans toutes les tribus du continent la tendance augmente graduellement et par conséquent il est de plus en plus probable qu'à l'avenir on y observera le même phénomène. On a pu suivre des mouvements réguliers de dispersion géographique et d'évolution graduelle depuis les débuts du mouvement il y a 100 ans.

L'interprétation de cet indice forme la base d'une théorie généralisée de séparatisme qui explique le développement de mouvements séparatistes apparemment disparates dans toutes les régions du continent. Quoiqu'ils n'aient aucun lieu conscient et que souvent même ils nient vigoureusement l'existence de toute ressemblance de base entre leurs expressions d'indépendance et d'autres, ces mouvements, en fait, ont tous émergé à partir d'un fonds socio-religieux commun caractérisé par une réaction à l'encontre des efforts missionnaires. Dans chaque tribu, une ou deux institutions traditionnelles essentielles à l'existence de la famille—d'habitude soit la polygamie, soit le culte des ancêtres ou de la fertilité ou de la terre elle-même—ont fait l'objet d'un assaut de la part des missionnaires dirigé apparemment contre la famille. Quoique ceci ait causé une inquiétude certaine, cela n'a pas en soi produit de réaction.

L'étincelle ne s'est réellement produite que lors de la publication dans les langues vernaculaires de certaines parties des Écritures. Ces textes semblaient indiquer au sujet du ou des problèmes en cause, des variations entre la position missionnaire et la position de la Bible et devinrent ainsi une sorte de norme de référence indépendante permettant de justifier une certaine désaffection à l'égard des missions. Lorsque la tendance ainsi produite a atteint un certain niveau, tout était prêt pour l'émergence du phenomène séparatiste.

Par conséquent, on peut considérer le séparatisme comme étant une entité organique unique dont l'évolution a suivi certains modèles bien définis de par le passé et continuera à le faire pendant un avenir indéfini.

XIII. SOME TRADITIONAL AFRICAN RELIGIONS AND CHRISTIANITY

R. LAROCHE, W.F.

Christianity comes not to destroy but rather to transform the institutions of the peoples to whom it brings the message of Christ. Among many African peoples religion and culture are one and the same. Can Africans then abandon their pagan cults and embrace the Christian religion without having to renounce their culture and their traditional institutions? Sociologists teach that the culture of a people tends to form an integral and organic whole: one cannot suppress particular elements in it without damaging it as a whole. Must an African who becomes Christian give up being himself? Must he abandon the institutions among which he has grown up and so become a stranger among his own brethren? Conversion to Christianity does not lead to this, although it requires the African to abandon certain beliefs and practices incompatible with this religion.

In this study we shall first give a brief description of the principal beliefs and practices which characterize traditional religions among the Bantu of the Congo (Leopoldville), Rwanda, Burundi, Uganda, Tanzania, and Kenya. We shall see that in these religions, alongside elements of error incompatible with Christian doctrine, there are elements of truth which can be preserved and incorporated in the Christian religion. In this way the pagan who becomes Christian does not have to turn his back upon his whole religious past to embrace a new religion entirely foreign to him.

We do not pretend to discuss every part of the area defined here, because beliefs and customs vary from one tribe to another. Nevertheless we believe that what we say is applicable to the greater number of tribes under consideration.

TRADITIONAL RELIGIONS

Religion and its Elements

Taken in a broad sense, religion may refer to a person's fundamental principles, what he actually lives or dies for; today atheism, secular humanism and hedonism, for instance, are sometimes conceived under the heading of religion. Here we are concerned with religion in its strict sense.

In its strict and true sense the word religion connotes the idea of relation, that is, the relation of the creature to the Divinity. Subjectively religion is a virtue which determines man to give God the worship and honour which are His due. Objectively, as a religious system, it is the sum of beliefs and practices relating to the Divine Being, supreme and personal, upon Whom man recognizes his dependence and with Whom he must remain in relation. Thus religion is a sum total, doctrinal, ritual, and moral, considered in itself and taken as a whole. It can be incorporated into a society which we call the Church, or on the other hand be presented as a simple system of beliefs and practices independent of all social organization properly so called.

The sentiment of religion in man implies belief in the existence of one or more superior beings upon whom he feels himself to be dependent; from this follows the necessity to pay worship to the divinity or to those superior beings and to submit to a moral code. The human soul feels linked with one or more of these invisible and powerful superior beings. It knows its destiny to be in their hands, and thus feels the need to honour them, to present them with offerings and to invoke their aid.

These are the fundamentals of all religions: a religious sentiment born of awe, reverence, and at the same time confidence in and submission towards a divine being or beings; a body of doctrine, of more or less defined beliefs; a system of law and practical rules which are not simply precepts imposed by society or the individual conscience but which emanate from the sovereign being or beings; and finally a system of formal worship, a number of rites by which man, either individually or in a group, maintains favourable relations with the superior being or beings. In the traditional African religions these fundamental elements are to be found in part, but joined together with numerous beliefs and practices which are vain or erroneous.

Belief in God and the Worship Due to Him

Among the beings of the invisible world whom they worship, Africans recognize the existence of a superior being who is more powerful than other spirits, and give him a name and other attributes: it is this being whom we call God. He is not simply the first among the spirits and *manes* of the ancestors: He is a Being apart, the Creator and Law-Giver of the universe, the Supreme Master of life. He is good by nature, just, all-powerful, and omniscient. He is invisible to man and has neither beginning nor end.

In times past some ethnologists and missionaries thought that certain African tribes did not worship God. Today it is generally agreed that one can hardly find a tribe which has no cult of the Supreme Being, which is explicit and practised with greater or lesser frequency according to the tribe. It appears that certain formulae of prayer can be used to invoke the ancestors equally with the Supreme Being, or that prayers addressed to ancestors can be intermingled with invocations of God. The worship of God is not always conducted as a separate function but often integrated into the activities of daily life.

Worship of Ancestors and Other Spirits

Africans believe in the existence of the soul as distinct from its envelope, the body, although their ideas do not correspond in all respects to reality. They believe in survival after death, the survival of the spirit, of this essential part of the human being which constitutes his individual personality and which survives the destruction of the body. Thus they regard funeral ceremonies and mourning as of great importance. The rituals are long and complicated, and based upon filial piety and the desire to give the dead man the honours due to his rank, so that his spirit may be content in the next world.

It is believed that the *manes* of the dead are endowed with great power whose exercise is generally limited to the affairs of members of the family and their friends. The dead are thus still part of the family and the clan, and interested in all that takes place. Their power is exercised for good and evil. The attitude to the ancestors is not universally the same. In certain tribes those who have been piously buried according to the prescribed rites, especially near relations, are really loved and venerated, and one need not fear them as long as one does not forget them. Elsewhere the ancestors are feared and it is believed that they are quick to take vengeance if they do not receive the attentions they desire or if the customs are not well and truly observed.

The cult of the ancestors includes different practices, hymns, invocations, dances, libations, food-offerings, sacrifices of living animals, faithful observance of ancestral customs and precepts, amulets and talismans worn in their honour, veneration of small images which represent certain spirits, and the use of other fetishes believed to be inhabited or influenced by the *manes* of the ancestors.

This cult is an integral part of daily life and is something natural in African eyes. They see nothing supernatural in their relations with the dead. They think that the deceased ancestors in a small way play the part of providence towards the living. This cult contains elements of love, veneration, and gratitude to the dead, but equally includes numerous practices based upon fear or self-interest. Indeed, belief in the extraordinary power of the dead and the part they play among the living to a great extent explains attachment to the traditional religion.

The cult of spirits and of heroes of old is almost the same as that of the ancestors, except that here it is a case of invisible beings who are even more powerful and whose influence extends to an entire tribe or country or even beyond. Such a personage was the hero Lyangombe, of human origin, who is venerated in Tanzania, in Congo (Leopoldville), in Rwanda, and Burundi.

Occult Causes and Forces

There is a general conviction that natural objects and elements have secret properties which man can utilize to his own profit and of which it is possible to neutralize the evil effects. Among the knowledgeable are diviners, magicians, healers, sorcerers, and casters of lots: such persons can make these forces active for good or evil. From this it follows that there is a quantity of remedies, talismans, amulets, and prophylactics of all kinds. But for the African it is not a question of an appeal to supernatural forces but simply the use of natural properties and influences, as it were impersonal forces which proceed from natural objects and elements. In addition there are personal occult forces, the spirits of nature and those of the ancestors with whom each family maintains a constant relation.

It is generally believed that the action of these occult forces can be observed: every misfortune is attributed to an occult cause which is hidden under the apparent natural explanation. The real cause of accidents, of physical misfortunes, of illnesses is the action of some malevolent spirit or ancestor, or the result of the malice of the living. For these reasons there is frequent recourse to diviners and magicians, to the wearing of amulets and talismans, and to the use of magic recipes and remedies.

Morals

A distinction is made between good and evil and every tribe has moral precepts to which all must submit. Nevertheless, even if one admits that Africans may be influenced by certain vestiges of revelation, it cannot be anything else for them other than an imperfect knowledge of natural law. The moral precepts which have the force of laws consist of customs, ancestral traditions, and *tabus* which, if broken, result in sanctions either of the civil authority or the invisible world.

What is the nature of the moral obligation imposed on the conscience by these moral rules? How is the author of these precepts conceived? If they are broken, who is it that is offended? Is it the Supreme Being? One could conclude that Africans have no notion of morally good and morally evil because it seems that they observe *tabus* for the reason that the ancestors have ordained it thus, or because it is a custom. Thus the force of the moral law would derive, not from God, but from the ancestral customs;

and the violation of these customs and *tabus* would be to offend, not the Supreme Being, but the spirits and *manes* of the ancestors.

Nevertheless it does seem that at least certain among them realize that disregard of moral obligations is an offence against the Supreme Being. Given the knowledge that the African has of the existence of this Being and the attributes he predicates of Him, he does realize that certain forbidden actions, more or less numerous according to the judgement of different persons, are offences against the Creator and not only against the ancestors, society, and one's neighbour.

The Force of Custom

Custom, what one has received from one's ancestors, what one has always believed and done to preserve one's own vitality and that of the clan, and whose breach will bring about known evil consequences, prescribes that in such and such a circumstance one must follow a certain practice, offer a particular sacrifice, or perform a certain action—or abstain from it. It is not discussed. The why and wherefore are not sought. One simply obeys. Customs include the rules of politeness, the duties of justice, the services required of each man by the common good, family and social relations, sacred *tabus* and moral laws, totems, medical recipes, magic practices and divination, scientific knowledge, and the rites and ceremonies of the cult. They are thus an inheritance transmitted as a whole by the ancestors and the distinctive characteristics of each tribe. Certain customs are no more than exterior practices, not apparently motivated by any corresponding idea; others are connected with the cult of the ancestors and spirits, and are accompanied by religious ceremonies.

Custom exercises a considerable influence on the life of an African. He follows custom out of a family spirit, out of religious sentiment, and often also out of fear. For any unfaithfulness can bring down upon him and his family the malevolence of the dead and all sorts of evils. The customs correspond to needs born of his mentality and of his conception of nature, of humanity, and of the invisible world. The cult of the ancestors acts as a vigilant guardian of the customs of which one of the most important precepts is that nothing must be omitted from the traditions. Thus the temptation to neglect custom is rare.

Religion Impregnates the Whole Life of the African

It is believed that the things and beings of this world are in constant relation with the invisible world and that men are in a state of complete dependence upon superior powers. The African is convinced that in the activities and in the events of life he must conform to the order of things as established by the invisible world. These superior powers are principally the *manes* of the dead and spirits, and also more or less the Creator, who, according to fairly widespread belief, occupies Himself very little with the government of the world. Hence his daily relationship is maintained with the *manes* and with the spirits by invocations, offerings, and sacrifices.

It seems thus correct to say that Africans, in their traditional manner of life, tend to be instinctively religious, in their own way and according to their own ideas. Religion is one with their life, a life lived religiously, a life which absorbs the whole man, which is identified with them, with their thoughts and actions. The religious element, whether pure or deformed, is a single body with individual, family, social and political life, with the necessities of existence, with laws and bans, with beliefs and ancestral customs. Religion is mingled with the festivals, the days of mourning, with work and all the various incidents of life. In Africa no distinction is made between the religious and secular in life, or between spiritual and material, at least in practice. The world of the African is a single whole and it is constantly animated in every way by religion, its rites, offerings, sacrifices, and invocations. It is difficult to distinguish it from medicine, science, superstition, and magic, and from law and custom. Thus religion is not merely a religious system with a creed, a moral code and a liturgy: rather it is an institution in which one has one's whole life.

In the practice of the religion of the ancestors the African finds a certain confidence and tranquillity of spirit, for he believes himself to live in the midst of familiar beings, albeit invisible, who can hear him and undertake his defence. The numerous rites and *tabus* to which he has to submit can seem to us an intolerable burden. In his eyes this is otherwise: the talismans and amulets he wears, the *tabus* that restrict his liberty, the customs to which he must conform, the signs that must be observed, the offerings and evidences of veneration that he must present to the *manes* and to the spirits, all are part of the cloak with which he covers himself to overcome his fears and to ensure his vitality. The practices that appear to us like magic, like a recourse to occult forces, are for him the normal relation with the invisible beings who make up part of his world. He makes no distinction between natural and supernatural. If he perceives one, it is extremely vague.

FROM TRADITIONAL RELIGION TO CHRISTIANITY

The Rule of Conduct for the Church

From earliest times the Catholic Church has given her missionaries as a rule of conduct that they should respect the culture and personality of those to whom the Gospel is preached. In the encyclical *Summi Pontificatus* Pius XII reminds us that the Church, in carrying out her evangelical mission, sets out to respect the customs and traditions of peoples in the greatest possible measure. While the religion she preaches is one in its doctrine and in its hierarchy, he emphasizes that the Church belongs to all times and to all civilizations, and that she contains within herself enough wealth and comprehension to satisfy the legitimate aspirations of all peoples, to lead all to God by the same means of salvation: 'The Catholic Church does not disdain the doctrines and institutions of pagan peoples, but purifies them from all error and impurity; she perfects them and crowns them with Christian wisdom.'

It is the Church's duty to translate divine revelation into every language, to bring it within range of all cultures, so that every disciple of Christ can gain contact with his Redeemer in a manner suitable to his own mentality and feelings. Every single one must be able to think and live in Christ, in Christianity, in terms of his own soul. If the content of revelation is immutable and meant for all men, there are many different ways of presenting it, adapting it, and making it live.

Nevertheless this adaptation cannot be a religious syncretism in virtue of which one would accept beliefs opposed to the objective content of the Christian religion or introduce into the cult rites which are still inspired by an erroneous or superstitious cult. Nor may adaptation lead to the mutilation of the truth; the Church desires to present to her neophytes the whole truth, the complete Christian message, but in a manner most in keeping with their mentality and lawful aspirations.

Good Elements in the Traditional Religion

Admittedly, we must not emphasize too much the similarities between pagan cults and Christianity, for that would lead the pagans to believe that already they are very close to the truth and that their traditional religions differ from Christianity only on secondary points.

None the less, while preserving objectivity, there is room for the discovery in traditional beliefs and practices of many points of contact with Christian doctrine which can lead up to the teaching and practice of the Christian religion. Relieved of the mythological and erroneous accretions which deform them, these elements of truth can open the door to the true faith.

The traditional religion has nourished in the souls of Africans a religious feeling of eminent quality. In these souls it has preserved a belief in the Supreme Being, Creator, and Lord of the Universe, and a feeling of dependence upon Him, together with a realization of the limits of human nature. Equally there can be found a distinction between the visible and the invisible world; the belief in the existence of the human soul, as distinct from the body and surviving it after death; a belief in a world beyond which there live the spirits and 'disincarnate' souls; a moral sense which suffices to distinguish between good and evil and a sentiment of liberty, responsibility, duty, and justice; the obligation of obedience to moral precepts, and some notion of sin, not merely as an infraction of the will of superior beings but as an offence against God; a well organized ritual, with prayers, offerings, sacrifices, and rites as an expression of submission, gratitude, and supplication; the belief that supernatural power can be communicated to objects by rites and formulae.

At one with culture, religion is indissolubly linked to the whole of life whose personal and communal activities it animates. The celebration of ritual ceremonies takes place in common and for the common good. The spirit of solidarity plays a principal part in this and the existence of the individual cannot be conceived outside the framework of his integration in society. There is the practice of submission to established authority which has the right of unquestioned final decision.

Elements of Feebleness and Error

Religion acts as a unifying factor in African culture. It is like a soul that keeps the whole body healthy. The cult of the ancestors has made a profound impression on that culture and its components.

In its manifestation in African religion the cult of the dead and of spirits is not acceptable. Above all it is a religious cult, addressed to invisible beings who are believed to be very powerful, and often given to anger, using their extraordinary power both to do good or to do harm to human beings. Such a cult is unacceptable because it credits created beings with power which in fact they do not possess, and because it presupposes that these invisible beings have an ability to intervene at will in human life which is outside the divine control. The cult which Christians have for the angels and saints, on the contrary, depends upon God, for it is founded upon their union in charity with God: they can intercede for the living, but their activity depends immediately upon the divine will.

Even if one believes that God Himself governs the world and makes use of the *manes* and spirits as intermediaries between Him and men, the fact remains that in this coexistence of the cult of the Supreme Being and that of the ancestors and spirits, God—without being altogether forgotten—is relegated to the background; others are more frequently honoured and worshipped. Even if it is believed that these superhuman beings derive their power from

God fundamentally, the fact is that they are not honoured as a consequence of their dependence upon God. In practice they are invoked and honoured as autonomous powers which exercise their will in a free and arbitrary manner, thus usurping—at least in part—the honours due to God.

The souls of the departed, once separated from the body, have accomplished their earthly destiny, and normally must remain in the place God assigns to them according to their deserts. They are wholly dissociated from the living and have no means of remaining in a habitual relationship with them. Deprived of the body, the departed soul is also deprived of its natural means of knowledge, that is to say the senses. It is no longer possible for it to know by its own means what takes place in the world of the living. According to the divinely established order the soul must be united to the body to have the power to act upon exterior things. Once deprived of its natural instrument, the body, it cannot reach out to material places and objects: all action in the sensible world is impossible for it. Christians affectionately remember their dead ones and remain in union with them through prayer; and Christian doctrine teaches that one may ask a deceased person to obtain a favour from God. And if our Christian hagiography is based on historical accuracy, there have been quite a few instances where the deceased and the devil have manifested themselves to people on earth. These, however, remain exceptional and always suppose a special permission of God.

The exaggerated confidence that has been placed in the occult forces of nature and frequent recourse to the intervention of the *manes* and spirits create a mentality which is wholly opposed to the Christian spirit. It allows the belief that it is not God but rather intermediate invisible beings and the occult forces of nature which control man's destiny.

The traditional religious conceptions have an anthropocentric character rather than being centred upon the Creator. The spirits and the ancestors, the energies inherent in nature, whether beneficent or malevolent, and even God Himself, are thought of in terms of whether they can do good or harm to human beings.

It follows logically that only a false explanation of the origin of evil can be given if one attributes it to the ill-will of spirits, or of the *manes*, or of men who maliciously release occult and malevolent forces. If we find among some Christians a similar conception of God and of religion, based on personal interest, it is because they have not yet understood their religion.

From Religions to Religion

Christianity does not come to create a new people in Africa. It comes rather to put into touch with the divine message a people already created by God. It comes to apply to them divine revelation and the divine redemption, to the people itself and to all that is good, rational, and truly human in its culture and institutions. As with the individual soul, so with the history of peoples, there are elements which prepare the way to religion: these are the traditional religions. None the less, a people which accepts Christianity must undergo certain changes in its beliefs, practices, and attitudes; changes which will be more or less profound according to the people concerned.

If the Church has always respected the personality and culture of different peoples, it must be admitted that missionaries have not always been faithful to this golden rule. On the other hand, it was difficult for them to bring in an abstract Christianity, wholly disengaged from western culture, because the Christian religion has always been incarnate within a culture, first Hebrew, then Greek, then Roman, and finally western. One must not be astonished by the number of Africans who have come to identify the Christian religion with western civilization and who have hesitated to show themselves in favour of 'the white man's religion' because they feared that in becoming Christians they must at the same time accept a foreign culture wholly incompatible with their own traditions.

It is inevitable that evangelization, even in its purest form, must produce a shock to the culture to which it brings the doctrine of Christ. In becoming Christian, every culture undergoes a transformation, a conversion. It must accept new elements and purge itself, and correct and even abandon certain traditional institutions. This is true in particular of a closed society which opens itself to a new religion. On the other hand culture is not a static entity but rather something which is identified with the human community which is itself in a state of continuous development. Thus the integration and adaptation of the Gospel message to the culture of a people, while not able to ignore the institutions of the past, must take account of the dynamism of evolution which is at work in every culture at every moment in its history. In Africa today very many peoples are in a state of evolution and formation; we have only to consider the tendency of certain African communities to emancipate themselves from the tribal system and the progressive introduction of modern techniques and new economic structures which are bringing about radical changes in the traditional way of life. In the same way there is a change in the relation of the individual to the community. Formerly the community was paramount, the family group or clan being, so to speak, the person. Today more and more importance is attached to the individual, with the consequence of certain inevitable psychological, social, and cultural changes. Even religious, moral, and legal values do not escape this evolutionary process. But these changes do not prevent African cultural groups from preserving and affirming their own personalities.

Christianity has already obtained a great number of conversions of a wholehearted and lasting nature; there still remains the task of Christianizing African society and culture. Ordinarily the conversion of society lags behind individual conversion. Africans have welcomed the Gospel message but have not yet said goodbye to beliefs and practices which for centuries have been part of their philosophy of their present existence and of the life beyond the grave. What do they expect from their religion? For them religion is not distinct from culture and is indissolubly linked to the whole of life and its activities. A comparison of the acceptance of a religion with all the power and promises the Christian religion represents, with a knowledge of how limited a use is made of it, of how it inspires only one side of life, is greatly disillusioning. How can such a religion satisfy the religious sentiment which is so highly developed among Africans and their need to have constant recourse to the supranatural and invisible world?

The new religion cannot be a sort of copy of the cult it comes to replace. It is not necessary to substitute for each of the practices of the cult of the ancestors some corresponding Christian rite or festival. The Christian religion contains enough riches to satisfy all the religious needs of Africans, but its supernatural values must be brought within their range in such a way that they can grasp them, understand them, and live them.

To satisfy African needs Christianity must not only integrate all the good elements to be found in the African mentality but equally find means to unite Christian and daily life in such a way that the first inspires the second. The African wants to live his religion with conviction and interior experience. He has always understood that religion is not just a well-constructed system of truths demanding belief and precepts demanding practice. He knows rather that it is a cultural institution in which one lives and through which one dwells in a constant relation with the Divinity and the supranatural world even if there are in the background what are plainly religious ideas and convictions. This concept of religion is fundamentally correct. It deserves to be enriched and cultivated by Christianity in Africa.

REFERENCES

Arnoux, Alex., P. B.
(1948) *Les Pères blancs aux sources du Nil.* Libr. Missionnaire, Paris.
Baumann, H. and Westermann, D.
(1948) *Les Peuples et les civilisations de l'Afrique.* Trad. franç. par L. Homburger. Payot, Paris.
Bourgeois, R.
(1956) *Banyarwanda et Barundi.* Académie Royale des Sciences Coloniales, Bruxelles. Tome III, 'Religion et magie'.
Delafosse, M.
(1941) *Les Noirs de l'Afrique.* Payot, Paris.
Denis, L., S.J.
(1951) 'Préambules de la foi, apologétique et mentalité bantoue', *Revue du Clergé Africain*, Mayidi, Congo (Léopoldville), 6, 241.
(1953) 'Fétichisme, magie et christianisme', *Revue du Clergé Africain*, 8, 104.

Deschamps, H.
(1954) *Les Religions de l'Afrique Noire.* Presses Universitaires de France, Paris.
Gluckman, Max
(1955) *Custom and Conflict in Africa.* Basil Blackwell, Oxford.
Huntingford, G. W. B. and Bell, C. R. V.
(1950) *East African Background.* Longmans, London.
Kaigh, F.
(1947) *Witchcraft and Magic of Africa.* R. Lesley, London.
Kenyatta, Jomo
(1953) *Facing Mount Kenya.* Secker & Warburg, London.
LaRoche, R., W.F.
(1957) *La Divination.* The Catholic University of America Press, Washington, D.C., Ilème Partie, pp. 209–338.
Lufuluabo, F. M., O.F.M.
(1963) 'Pour une christianisation en profondeur de l'âme bantoue', *Revue du Clergé Africain*, 18.
MacMillan, W. M.
(1949) *Africa Emergent.* R. and R. Clark, Edinburgh.
Malinowski, B.
(1948) *Magic, Science and Religion.* The Free Press, Glencoe, Illinois.
North American Assembly on African Affairs, Wittenberg College, Springfield.
(1952) Report, *Africa is Here.* 'Wholeness in African life: a challenge to the Christian Church', p. 85 seq.
Parrinder, E. G.
(1954) *African Traditional Religion.* Hutchinson's University Library, London.
Robert, J. M., P.B.
(1949) *Croyances et coutumes magico-religieuses des Wafipa paiens.* The Tanganyika Mission Press, Kipalapala.
Roelens, V., Mgr.
(1920) *Instructions aux missionnaires Pères Blancs du Haut-Congo* (Beaudoinville, Afrique Belge), Ière partiè, 87.
Seumois, X., P.B.
(1965) 'Adaptation de la catéchèse moderne à l'Afrique d'aujourd'hui', *Revue du Clergé Africain*, 20.
Tempels, P., O.F.M.
(1949) *La Philosophie bantoue.* Trad. de A Rubbens, Presses Alpha, Paris.
Van Bulck, G., S.J.
(1955) 'Existence et portée du monothéisme africain', *Formation religieuse en Afrique Noire*, (Compte rendu de la Semaine d'Études de Lèopoldville, 22–27 août, 1955). Ed. Lumen Vitae Bruxelles, 20 seq.
Van Caeneghem, P. R., Rev.
(1956) *La Notion de Dieu chez les BaLuba du Kasai.* Académie Royale des Sciences Coloniales, Bruxelles.
van Kets, Raf, O.P.
(1965) 'The dialogue between the Church and contemporary cultures', *Concilium* (Anvers), 1, p. 78.
Van Wing, J., S.J.
(1920) 'L'Être Suprême des Bakongo', *Recherches de Science Religieuses*, 10, 170.
(1938) *Études Bakongo.* Tome II, 'Religion et magie'. Bruxelles.

Welbourn, F. B.
(1965) 'Initiation rites, African and Christian', *African Ecclesiastical Review*, 7, p. 58. (Uganda.)
Westermann, D.
(1949) *The African Today and Tomorrow*. Oxford University Press, London.

Résume

CERTAINES RELIGIONS TRADITIONNELLES AFRICAINES ET LE CHRISTIANISME

Le christianisme ne vient pas détruire mais plutôt transformer et enrichir les institutions des peuples auxquels il apporte le message du Christ. En devenant chrétien, l'Africain n'a pas à embrasser une culture étrangère même s'il doit abandonner certaines de ses croyances et pratiques traditionnelles incompatibles avec la religion chrétienne.

Cette étude, limitée au milieu Bantou du Congo-Léopoldville, Rwanda, Burundi, Uganda, Tanzania et Kenya, veut montrer qu'il y a dans les cultes traditionnels africains de bons éléments qui peuvent conduire au christianisme et être incorporés dans la doctrine chrétienne.

RELIGIONS TRADITIONNELLES

La Religion et ses éléments

Au sens strict, le mot religion signifie l'idée de relation, relation de la créature avec la Divinité. Toute religion est composée des éléments suivants: un sentiment religieux fait de crainte, de révérence, de confiance et de soumission envers l'Être ou les êtres supérieurs; un corps de doctrine, de croyances; un ensemble de lois et de règles pratiques; enfin un culte, un certain nombre de rites. Or les religions africaines contiennent quelque chose de ces éléments.

Croyance en Dieu—Culte qui lui est rendu

Les Africains reconnaissent l'existence d'un Esprit supérieur, Être à part, Créateur et Ordonnateur de l'univers et Maître suprême de la vie; il est bon, juste, tout-puissant, éternel. On rend vraiment un culte à l'Être suprême, individuellement et en société.

Culte des ancêtres et des esprits

Les âmes, ou mânes, des défunts sont supposées être douées d'une grande puissance qu'elles exercent à l'endroit de leurs descendants. Les défunts, quoique invisibles, font encore partie de la famille et veulent être honorés. Sinon, ils se vengeront. Le culte des ancêtres comprend de nombreuses pratiques, comme les chants, invocations, dances, libations, offrandes de nourriture, sacrifices, l'observation des coutumes, le port d'amulettes et de talismans.

Ce culte est inspiré par la piété filiale, la gratitude, mais souvent aussi par la crainte et l'intérêt. On n'y voit rien de préternaturel, mais une relation normale avec le monde invisible.

Le culte des esprits est sensiblement le même.

Causes et forces occultes

Forces impersonnelles: les propriétés secrètes qu'ont les choses de la nature. Forces personnelles: les mânes des défunts et les esprits. On croit voir l'action de ces forces occultes partout et on leur attribue tout ce qui arrive de fâcheux.

La morale

On fait la distinction entre le bien et le mal. Les prescriptions morales ont pour la plupart leur origine dans les coutumes et traditions ancestrales; mais au moins un certain nombre sont perçues comme émanant de l'Être suprême et on a l'idée, plus ou moins précise, qu'on peut l'offenser.

Force de la coutume

Les coutumes sont ce qu'on a reçu des ancêtres. Il n'est pas question d'y déroger, car on croit que les ancêtres veillent à ce que les vivants les observent.

La religion imprègne toute la vie de l'Africain

La religion est mêlée à toute la vie, elle en inspire et contrôle toutes les activités; elle peut à peine se distinguer de la médecine, de la science, des croyances et coutumes ancestrales, de la superstition et de la magie. La religion est une institution dont on vit. Elle est souvent à base de crainte et d'utilité. Elle tient les vivants en constante relation avec le monde invisible.

DES RELIGIONS TRADITIONNELLES AU CHRISTIANISME

Règle de conduite de l'Église

L'Église catholique respecte les usages et traditions des peuples; elle les corrige s'il y a lieu, les oriente vers la vérité. Elle s'efforce d'adapter les pratiques de la religion chrétienne à toutes les cultures et civilisations. Mais elle n'admet aucun élément d'erreur dans le culte et la doctrine chrétiennes.

Bons éléments dans la religion traditionnelle

La croyance à lÊtre suprême, à l'âme et sa survie; la distinction entre le bien et le mal moral; liberté et responsabilité des individus; sens du devoir et de la justice; culte bien organisé; croyance à une force supra-naturelle communiquée à des objets. Esprit de solidarité. Influence de la religion tant dans le domaine religieux que séculier de la vie quotidienne. Importance attribuée aux célébrations en commun. Respect de l'autorité.

Eléments de faiblesse et d'erreur

Tel qu'il apparaît dans les religions traditionnelles, le culte des ancêtres est inacceptable, car il attribue aux ancêtres et aux esprits une importante partie du culte dû à Dieu seul qui est, non pas totalement délaissé, mais relégué à l'arrière-plan. Les ancêtres sont invoqués, pratiquement, comme des puissances autonomes, agissant indépendemment de Dieu.

On accorde une confiance exagérée aux forces occultes qui semblent contrôler le destin des hommes.

La religion a un caractère anthropocentrique au lieu d'être centrée sur Dieu.

Des religions à la Religion

Le christianisme vient appliquer le message évangélique à un peuple déjà créé par Dieu, à lui et à tout ce qu'il a de bon, de rationnel et de vraiment humain dans ses institutions.

Il était difficile aux missionnaires de présenter en Afrique un christianisme à l'état pur car il a toujours été incorporé à une culture déterminée; rien d'étonnant à ce qu'on ait été porté à croire que la religion chrétienne est la 'religion des Blancs'.

Toute évangélisation produit nécessairement un choc sur la culture à laquelle elle apporte la doctrine du Christ; en devenant chrétienne, une culture doit subir une transformation, une conversion.

L'adaptation du message évangélique à la culture d'un peuple doit tenir compte des institutions du passé mais aussi des changements qui se produisent dans cette culture à chaque moment de son histoire. Plusieurs peuples africains sont actuellement en état d'évolution et de formation, ce qui entraîne inévitablement des changements psychologiques, sociaux, moraux, culturels.

Le christianisme a déjà obtenu un grand nombre de conversions individuelles en Afrique, sincères et durables; il reste à christianiser la société.

La nouvelle religion ne doit pas être une sorte de copie du culte qu'elle vient remplacer. Dans l'adaptation, il faudra tenir compte du sentiment religieux très développé en Afrique, de la place importante que la religion occupe dans la vie et ses activités quotidiennes et aussi de l'habitude de recourir aux rites cultuels et de vivre en relation avec le monde supérieur. Pour l'Africain, la religion est une institution culturelle dont on vit, qui tient en relation constante avec la Divinité et le monde supérieur. Cette conception de la religion est fondamentalement correcte et mérite d'être reprise et enrichie par le christianisme en Afrique.

XIV. CHRISTIANISME ET CULTURE AFRICAINE: APPORT AFRICAIN À LA THÉOLOGIE

V. MULAGO

Le sujet que nous avons choisi pour ce Séminaire International Africain sur l'Influence du Christianisme en Afrique Tropicale: Le Christianisme et la Culture Africaine, l'Apport Africain à la Théologie, est un sujet controversé et délicat.

Nous voudrions éviter les deux extrêmes qui consistent, ou dans un refus catégorique et a priori de toute Théologie autre que la Théologie traditionnelle, c'est-à-dire occidentale, que l'on baptise trop facilement Théologie universelle ou mondiale, ou dans une africanisation superficielle, basée sur une sorte de romantisme de 'l'âme africaine', de 'l'âme bantu'.

D'une part, nous revendiquons le droit de pouvoir nous exprimer, même théologiquement, en Africains, mais, d'autre part, nous voulons que ce langage ait toute la richesse et toute la profondeur de notre africanité. Et cela, non pas dans un souci de conserver, coûte que coûte, notre passé ancestral, mais afin d'être des chrétiens authentiques, fidèles à nos origines et à l'Église. La vraie adaptation est une fidélité à la loi de l'Incarnation de l'Homme-Dieu.

C'est pourquoi, nous diviserons cet exposé en deux parties:

1. Les bases ou fondements de l'apport africain à la Théologie dans les croyances traditionnelles.
2. Quelques jalons d'une africanisation en Théologie.

BASES DE L'APPORT AFRICAIN

Les fondements de l'apport africain à la Théologie nous semblent pouvoir se ramener à deux:

—La croyance en un Être Suprême.
—Le sentiment inné de la participation.

Croyance en un Être Suprême

Nous n'allons pas reprendre le travail accompli par les chercheurs pour prouver la croyance des Bantu et des autres Africains en Dieu,[1] mais nous nous contenterons ici de dégager, parmi les attributs de l'Être Suprême, ceux qui soulignent des conceptions que l'on pourrait appeler 'pré-chrétiennes'.

1. *Dieu est la source première de toute vie et de tout moyen vital.* Il est la plénitude même de l'être. 'Par dessus toute force est Dieu, Esprit et Créateur, le *mwine bukomo bwandi.* Celui qui a la force, la puissance par lui-même. Il donne l'existence, la subsistence et l'accroissement aux autres forces. Vis-à-vis des autres forces, il est "Celui qui accroît la force".'[2]

Dieu est le participable imparticipé, le Principe non-principié de tout être et de toute vie. En langage classique, on dira que Dieu est la cause efficiente première de l'être.

Expliquons-nous.

Il faut nettement distinguer la causalité résultant de la communication—participation de vie et la causalité efficiente basée sur la communication-participation de moyens vitaux. Pour ce qui est de la communication-participation vitale, l'homme, le *ntu* humain, a pour cause immédiate transmetteur de vie, dans la ligne verticale, ses parents, ses père et mère. Les parents euxmêmes ont reçu leur *ntu* de leurs ascendants, jusqu'à l'ancêtre fondateur du clan, qui, lui, a reçu sa vie directement de la Vie increée, du *Bonheur par essence* (= Imana des Banyarwanda et des Burundi), du *Principium et Finis* de toute vie et de tout être (= Nyamuzinda des Bashi).

Dans la ligne horizontale, tous ceux qui communient à la vie émanée d'une même source, immédiatement ou médiatement, pleinement ou partiellement, deviennent *intercauses* et exercent, les uns sur les autres, une causalité censée réelle, suivant un

[1] Cf. entre autres: Colle, 1925, pp. 37–42; 1937, pp. 170–4; Kagame, 1956, pp. 315–57; Lufuluabo, 1961, pp. 426–34; Parrinder, 1961; Pauwels, 1958; Smith, 1961; Tempels, 1949; Theuws, 1955, 1958; Thomas, 1959a, pp. 681–771; 1959b, pp. 5–21; 1960, pp. 74–90; Van Wing, 1959, pp. 281–344; Zuure, 1926, pp. 733–76; 1929; Van Den Bosch, 1928, pp. 987–99; Van Caeneghem, 1956.

[2] Tempels, 1949, p. 42.

certain ordre hiérarchique. C'est le cas des membres d'une même famille, d'un même clan, des familles et des clans alliés.

Pour ce qui concerne la communication-participation de moyens existentiels, il ne s'agit plus d'une causalité productrice de vie, mais d'une causalité efficiente productrice de moyens vitaux. Ces moyens sont toutes les opérations, tous les objets qui mettent en contact avec le monde invisible; ce sont aussi tous les moyens naturels et 'supra-naturels' de conservation et de renforcement de la vie.

Tous ces moyens ne puisent leur efficacité, en fin de compte, que dans l'Efficient premier, la Source première de toute vie et de tout être. Sur ce point, les Bantu sont catégoriques.[3]

2. *Transcendance de Dieu.* Pour bien saisir la transcendance de Dieu chez les Bantu, il faut souligner le fait que l'Être Suprême, 'principe non-principié', n'est pas inclu dans les catégories des êtres ou *ntu.* 'Ces derniers sont conçus comme a priori principiés; si leur "cause ultime" était également *ntu*, il deviendrait un "être" (ou *ntu*) contradictoire, parce qu'il serait à la fois un "être", alors qu'il serait considéré comme "non-principié".'[4] En langue bantu, *l'être* se traduit par *ntu.* Ce *ntu* comprend quatre catégories.[5] L'être principié, en effet, peut être considéré comme:

(a) *Muntu:* être personnifié, être-qui-a-l'intelligence: *substance* chez Aristote et les scolastiques. Il ne faut pas confondre la catégorie *muntu* avec le même mot signifiant homme grammaticalement.

(b) *Ci(ki)ntu:* être qui n'a pas d'intelligence, être non personnifié: *substance* en philosophie scolastique. Ainsi, à la catégorie scolastique *substance* correspondent deux catégories bantu.

(c) *Ku(bu)ntu:* façon, manière d'être. Cette catégorie correspond à sept catégories aristoléliciennes: la *quantité*, la *qualité*, la *relation*, l'*action*, la *passion*, la *situation*, l'*habitus*.

On peut traduire le terme *Ku(bu)ntu* par *modalité.*[6]

[3] A ce propos, on lira avantageusement les considérations de Kagame sur la cause efficiente, l'origine de son observation et le passage de la cause efficiente à la 'cause première' (1956, pp. 315–18).

[4] Kagame, op. cit., p. 319.

[5] Cf. Kagame, op. cit., pp. 99–120; Jahn, 1961, pp. 105–33.

[6] Jahn, op. cit., p. 110.

(d) *Hantu:* sert à désigner à la fois la *localisation spatiale* et la *localisation temporelle* (*ubi*, *quando*).

Cependant, ce serait mal rendre la notion du *ntu* que de la traduire simplement par être,[7] le *ntu* et l'être n'étant pas coextensifs. Les catégories du *ntu* ne contiennent que les êtres participés, principiés, créés. L'Être imparticipé, non-principié, n'est pas *ntu*, bien qu'il soit la source, le *père* des hommes et de tous les êtres.[8]

3. *Dieu est Créateur de toutes choses.* C'est là une vérité admise par tous et qui ne doit pas nous retenir longtemps. Légendes et contes parlent de l'Être Suprême comme d'un Créateur, et le terme employé est très souvent technique, réservé à certaines actions artisanales ou artistiques.

'L'Esprit existe, disent les Baluba du Katanga, le Créateur qui créa les montagnes et les vallées'.[9] 'O, Esprit, Père-Créateur, le prient-ils, Dieu qui crées par Toi-même, qui as créé la Terre et les animaux qui y vivent. . . .'[10]

Dieu est donc reconnu comme Créateur, 'mais en outre, il crée par lui-même; personne d'autre n'intervient; il crée comme et quand il veut, il n'a de compte à rendre à personne'.[11]

C'est pourquoi, comme dit une sentence des Baluba du Kasaï:

> Toute chose appartient à Dieu,
> C'est Celui d'en-haut qui l'a créée.

Et les Bakongo, dans de nombreuses devinettes, expliquent que toutes les choses dont les hommes ignorent la nature et le but sont 'des choses de Nzambi' (Dieu).

4. *Providence divine.* Ce Dieu, Créateur des hommes et de toutes choses, continue à s'occuper de ses créatures. Les Bakongo reconnaissent que, dans tous les évènements, c'est Dieu qui joue le rôle principal, les hommes n'ayant qu'un rôle secondaire: 'C'est Dieu qui prépare le pain de manioc, nous autres hommes, nous ne préparons que les condiments.'

[7] Erreur commise par Jahn, op. cit., pp. 110–12.
[8] Cf. Kagame, op. cit., p. 110.
[9] Theuws, 1955, p. 113.
[10] Ibid., p. 92.
[11] Lufuluabo, 1961 (tiré à part, p. 21).

Dieu s'intéresse à la vie de l'homme et à la marche générale du monde.

Il sait tout, 'même ce qui est caché dans les galeries d'une termitière'.

'Il connaît le jour et la nuit.' Il est le seul Maître de la terre, et malgré les maléfices et les sortilèges, c'est Lui qui décide du cours des évènements.[12] C'est Dieu, *Imana*, qui donne la fécondité aux mères et aux champs, nous disent les Rwandais: c'est Lui qui engendre, Lui qui cultive, qui fait grandir hommes et bêtes, qui fait germer le grain, pousser les plantes et les arbres. C'est Lui qui, par la bouche des devins, ses ministres, parle aux hommes, leur fait connaître ce qui est caché à et augure.

Les Barundi ont toute une série de proverbes relatifs à la Providence de Dieu:[13]

Les Baluba du Kasaï expriment l'intervention mystérieuse de la divine Providence par la charmante image de Dieu cuisinant les aliments de l'homme:

> Là ou Dieu s'occupe à faire la cuisine,
> On n'y voit pas de fumée;
> Cependant soudain vous voyez le plat de manioc
> Et l'écuelle de viande sous les yeux.

5. *Dieu est Père*. Nous pourrions nous étendre longtemps sur les attributs de Dieu chez les Bantu. Soulignons plutôt celui qui les résume tous.

Ce Dieu, unique, immatériel, tout-puissant, source de toute vie et de tous moyens vitaux, au-dessus de tous les êtres, Créateur de toutes choses et dont la providence couvre toutes ses créatures, les Bantu aiment à le considérer surtout comme Père.

'Les relations de Dieu à l'homme sont d'ordre strictement personnel. Il me connaît, il m'entend, il me comprend, il s'occupe de moi et de ma vie personnelle.'[14]

L'attitude filiale des Baluba du Katanga vis-à-vis de Dieu se retrouve dans toutes leurs prières à Dieu. 'Le ton et le style sont

[12] Theuws, o.c., p. 32.
[13] Cf. Rodegem, 1961. Faisons remarquer que ces proverbes sont les mêmes chez les Banyarwanda, quelquefois avec de légères variantes.
[14] Theuws, 1950, p. 30.

tout autres dans les invocations adressées aux esprits tutélaires, surtout aux esprits de la chasse, qui sont importés . . . donc finalement des étrangers'.[15]

Dieu n'est pas seulement le Père des hommes, mais également le Père de toutes choses. Les Bashi l'appellent '*Ishe w'abantu n'ebintu*': Père des hommes et des choses. Et les Baluba du Katanga adressent à Dieu cette belle prière qui révèle à quel point l'idée de paternité est fondamentale chez les Bantu:[16]

O Kaleba (Dieu) qui distribues les dons aux hommes,
donne-moi aussi que je puisse manger de la viande . . .
Kaleba, Père des hommes,
Père des choses,
Père des insectes . . .
Aujourd'hui, je Te supplie,
J'espère en Toi pour obtenir ce que je Te demande.
O Esprit . . .
qui as créé la terre et les animaux qui y vivent.

C'est Dieu qui est réellement le vrai 'Genitor', puisque, nous disent les Banyarwanda: 'N'engendre vraiment que Dieu, et les hommes ne font qu'éduquer.'[17]

Ainsi, la paternité de Dieu est l'attribut numéro un de la Théodicée bantu, et, sans être d'accord avec sa terminologie, on peut conclure avec E. Possoz:[18]

Parmi toutes les lois naturelles, l'homme primitif s'est tenu à la paternité. Parmi toutes les lois humaines, il s'en est tenu là. L'ethnologie aura trouvé son premier principe lorsqu'elle aura admis, sans plus revenir en arrière, que la paternité, (ou la maternité, au besoin) fut aussi le principe de base de la pensée primitive en société, du droit primitif et sa philosophie et d'une conception du monde, visible et invisible. . . . Pourquoi chercher ailleurs les causes? On avait conscience de la paternité d'un Père de toutes choses, créateur du monde entier, visible et invisible. . . .
Tout droit humain sort de la même cause paternelle. . . .

Nous croyons donc que, chez les Bantu, dire que Dieu est Père, c'est tout dire. Cette paternité divine se communique aux hommes par la création, qui est une participation à la vie de Dieu et à sa paternité; elle est la synthèse des attributs de Dieu.

[15] Theuws, 1958, p. 30.
[16] Ibid., p. 29. Cf. Lufuluabo, 1964, p. 20.
[17] Kagame, 1956, p. 351.
[18] 1962, p. 99.

Ces affirmations s'appuient sur un texte de Saint Paul aux Romains:

En effet, la colère de Dieu se révèle du haut du ciel contre toute impiété et toute injustice des hommes, qui tiennent la vérité captive dans l'injustice; car ce qu'on peut connaître de Dieu est pour eux manifeste; Dieu, en effet, le leur a manifeste. Ce qu'il a d'invisible depuis la création du monde se laisse voir à l'intelligence à travers ses oeuvres, son eternelle puissance et sa divinité en sorte qu'ils sont inexcusables.[19]

Sentiment inné de la participation

Le deuxième fondement de l'apport africain à la Théologie est le sentiment de la participation à la même vie et aux mêmes moyens existentiels. C'est cette communion qui explique la solidarité bantu et qui est le centre et la synthèse des coutumes et des traditions de nos peuples.

Les Africains croient fermement qu'il y a communion vitale ou lien de vie qui rend solidaires les membres d'une même famille, d'un même clan. Le fait de naître dans une famille, un clan, une tribu nous plonge dans un courant vital spécifique, nous y 'incorpore', nous façonne à la manière de cette communauté, modifie 'ontiquement' tout notre être et l'oriente à vivre et à se comporter à la façon de cette communauté. Ainsi, la famille, le clan, la tribu est un tout dont chaque membre n'est qu'une partie. Le même sang, la même vie participée par tous et reçue du premier ancêtre, fondateur du clan, circule dans toutes les veines. C'est à la sauvegarde, au maintien, à l'accroissement, à la pérennité de ce trésor commun qu'il faut travailler de toutes ses énergies: retrancher impitoyablement tout ce qui s'y oppose, favoriser coûte que coûte tout ce qui l'aide: voilà le dernier mot des coutumes et des institutions, de la sagesse et de la philosophie des Bantu.

La vie peut être considérée sous une double forme:

(*a*) Comme communauté de *sang*: c'est l'élément principal et primordial:

[19] Rom 1: 18–20.

(*b*) Comme communauté de *propiété*: c'est l'élément concomitant et qui rend possible la vie.[20]

Chez les Bantu, pas plus qu'ailleurs, la communauté n'est pas l'effet d'une alliance.

'La communauté ne se fait pas, elle est donnée. Elle ne procède pas de sentiments, mais elle repose sur l'inconscient. Elle n'a pas besoin de résulter d'une conviction, car elle se comprend d'elle-même. On ne s'y affilie pas, on lui appartient.'[21]

Ce qui différencie la communauté de l'alliance, c'est que la première est 'essentiellement unique; la vie qui en elle s'élève à la puissance est une et indivise';[22] alors que l'alliance est essentiellement un choix, et constitue un autre ordre, essentiellement différent.

Les Bantu le savent si bien que, dans leurs alliances, ils font presque toujours intervenir un élément communautaire pour leur donner plus de solidité: c'est la raison du pacte du sang qui s'efforce de faire entrer l'autre dans sa propre famille et inversement.

Tout considéré, on pourrait résumer comme suit la participation vitale bantu:

1. La Participable imparticipé, le principe non-principié: source de toute vie et de tout moyen vital.

2. Voulant communiquer sa vie à d'autres êtres, Dieu créa le premier ou les premiers ancêtres du clan ou des clans primitifs. Le mode de la production n'est pas exprimé, mais on s'accorde à dire que l'ancêtre fondateur tomba du ciel (*Kigwa:* le Tombé) et fonda le clan.[23] Les ancêtres ont reçu la mission de prolonger et de perpétuer la vie dans leurs descendants, avec l'intervention positive de Dieu, qui continue son oeuvre créatrice par le don de nouvelle naissance.

Après Dieu viennent les premiers pères des hommes, les fondateurs des divers clans. Ces archipatriarches, les premiers à qui Dieu communiqua sa force vitale, ainsi que le pouvoir d'exercer sur toute leur descendance leur influence d'énergie vitale, constituent le chaînon le plus élevé reliant les humains à Dieu. Ils occupent dans la conception nègre un rang si élevé

[20] Cf. Van der Leeuw, 1948, p. 240.
[21] Ibid., p. 238.
[22] Ibid., p. 248.
[23] Cf. Tegnaeus, 1950.

qu'ils ne sont plus considérés comme de simples trépassés[24]. . . . Ce sont les premiers renforçateurs de vie après Dieu, et pour chaque clan ils sont comme l'image, la personnification de Dieu.[25]

3. A côté des âmes désincarnées des ancêtres, même supérieurs à elles, il existe les esprits des anciens héros, qui ont également reçu de Dieu la mission de renforcer et d'influencer la vie humaine. Leur culte, avec celui des ancêtres révèle, dans toute sa force, la conception de l'union vitale.

4. Dans le monde présent, la plénitude de vie consiste pour l'homme en sa plus ou moins grande ressemblance avec la vie de Dieu, des ancêtres et d'autres esprits supérieurs. Cette ressemblance, cette participation vitale est, en même temps, la base du rang social. Le rang social est en connexion avec le rang vital dont il dépend, et qui, à son tour, émane de l'influence vitale des ascendants défunts sur la génération vivante.

Le premier ancêtre se prolonge dans ses successeurs. Dans le cadre familial, le père de famille est le prolongement de ses ancêtres; dans le cadre clanique, le 'patriarche' ou le chef de clan; dans le cadre tribal et national, le roi avec sa mère: c'est le médiateur et le canal universel de la vie et des moyens vitaux. Le roi reçoit son investiture des représentants des premiers fondateurs des clans et des premiers occupants du sol. Il devient ainsi le représentant, non seulement de ses propres ancêtres, mais de tous les ancêtres. Le roi n'est rien par lui-même; tout ce qu'il est, il l'est par une puissance supérieure qui l'habite, et sa 'puissance n'étant pas une capacité personnelle, on attend d'elle toute espèce de salut qui se puisse concevoir. Cette puissance doit surabonder'.[26]

5. Sont dits *un*, au sens propre, tous ceux qui, vivants ou morts, descendent du même ancêtre éponyme, tous ceux en qui circule la même vie, le même sang, en lignée paternelle chez les peuples à droit patriarcal, et en lignée maternelle chez ceux qui sont régis par le droit matriarcal; donc les membres de la même famille, du même clan.

6. Par le mariage, chacune des parties contractantes, ainsi que

[24] Tempels, op. cit., p. 42.
[25] Ibid., p. 103.
[26] Van der Leeuw, op. cit., p. 109.

tous les 'siens', est introduite dans la famille de l'autre partie. Le mariage est un trait d'union entre familles, qui deviennent, de ce fait, *co-familles*. Ceux que le mariage unit ainsi deviennent *un*.

7. Sont encore assimilés aux membres de la famille les frères de sang.[27] Cette union, comme la précédente, entraîne dans son courant tous les *un* des deux contractants. Le fait de *s'entre-boire* produit, pour ceux qui s'y soumettent, les mêmes effets que la communion à la même vie.

8. L'enracinement au même sol, l'usage des mêmes moyens vitaux, le fait d'être sujets de la même autorité, produisent un effet similaire à celui de l'union vitale: effet non purement juridique, politique et social, mais qui affecte l'être même, le *ntu* et le modifie intrinsèquement.[28]

Ainsi, toute la société: famille, clan, tribu, nation, peut être considérée au point de vue de l'union vitale et de la participation. C'est même la mesure de la participation vitale qui est la norme de la hiérarchie des êtres et du rang social. Le *Muntu* ne compte à ses propres yeux et aux yeux de la société que dans la mesure où il participe à la vie et en est transmetteur. La logique est ferme à ce point de vue: qui a donné la vie ou un moyen vital à un autre lui devient supérieur.

QUELQUES JALONS D'UNE AFRICANISATION EN THÉOLOGIE

Ces dernières années, on a fort discuté sur le problème de l'adaptation de la Théologie et on s'est demandé si, en Afrique, la Théologie doit être africaine.

Nous ne voulons pas reprendre la discussion, mais démontrer que l'adaptation théologique en Afrique n'est pas seulement souhaitable, mais aussi possible, et même nécessaire si l'on veut permettre aux Africains d'essayer de saisir et d'exprimer le

[27] Tegnaeus, 1952; Hazoumé, 1937.

[28] Par exemple le fait de manger au même plat n'est pas chose indifférente; le fait d'habiter l'un à côté de l'autre influence nécessairement la vie du voisin en bien ou en mal.

L'extension de l'union vitale aux moyens existentiels, à l'enracinement au même sol, à la soumission à une même autorité ouvre des perspectives infinies à la communauté bantu. C'est dans la mentalité bantu elle-même que sont contenus les principes qui combattront l'esprit 'clanique' (au sens péjoratif) et le 'tribalisme'.

donné révélé et ses conséquences. Du fait même que des chrétiens africains, ayant leur mentalité et leur culture propres, et tenant de la foi certitude et lumière, s'efforcent par un travail rationnel, de comprendre et d'exprimer les mystères révélés et leurs conséquences, ils font de la théologie africaine. Ici, comme dans tout autre domaine, l'adage 'quidquid recipitur, ad modum recipientis recipitur' est d'application, en y ajoutant toutefois que le 'modus' du théologien est un 'modus' divino-humain. Supprimer l'un des deux aspects de ce 'modus', c'est du coup même supprimer la théologie. Mais il faut compléter l'adage '. . . et quidquid exprimitur, ad modum exprimentis exprimitur'.

Pour les Catholiques, les directives du Siège apostolique sur le respect des cultures des peuples à évangéliser et leur place dans l'Église sont explicites. Le travail théologique n'est pas exclu du mouvement d'incarnation que l'Église ne cesse de réaliser en tous temps et sous tous les espaces, afin de rester fidèle à la mission reçue de son Époux, le Verbe Incarné, dont elle est le prolongement et le rayonnement. En Afrique, l'Église sera africaine, et la Théologie elle-même devra y être africaine du moment qu'elle est la fruit du travail des théologiens africains.

Cette Théologie africaine pourra bien se greffer sur les deux réalités que nous venons d'exposer comme base de son africanisation: la croyance en Dieu, Père-Créateur, et le sentiment inné de la partipation vitale.

1. La conception que les Bantu se font de Dieu pourra être exploitée comme base d'un traité 'Deo Uno et Trino'. Ce Dieu, source de toute vie, est en même temps la source de toute communauté, de toute participation dans la communion. Source de toute vie et de tous moyens vitaux, il est Père, il possède la nature divine, la Vie divine originellement, et communique sa Vie depuis toute l'éternité. Le terme de cette fécondité, c'est la deuxième Personne divine, le Fils. Le Fils possède totalement la Vie divine, comme le Père mais, puisqu'il la possède par communication, il se distingue du Père qui en est le principe. Et depuis toute l'éternité, le Père et le Fils s'aiment et sont tendus l'un vers l'autre. Cet amour s'exprime dans une troisième personne, le Saint-Esprit, qui est comme le regard mutuel du Père

vers le Fils et du Fils vers le Père, un mouvement de va-et-vient, un courant vital entre les deux premières Personnes. Comme la paternité et la filiation, la spiration, ou procession du Saint-Esprit, est éternelle en Dieu.

En Dieu existe donc une famille, une communauté basée sur une communion-participation (univoque) à une même Nature, à une même Essence, à une même Vie. C'est l'unité la plus parfaite, dont toutes les autres ne sont que des rayonnements et des imitations.

Chez les Bantu, Dieu sera présenté comme la Vie par excellence et par essence, Vie féconde et Amour communicatif dans une communauté de Trois.

2. *Dieu créa l'homme à son image.* La création sera présentée comme une communication de la Vie de Dieu et de son Amour à l'homme. 'Dieu dit: "Faisons l'homme à notre image, à notre ressemblance! . . ." Dieu créa donc l'homme à son image, à l'image de Dieu il le créa.'[29] Et pour montrer que la Vie de l'homme est bien une participation à la Vie du Créateur, la Bible précise: 'Alors Yahvé Dieu modela l'homme avec la glaise du sol, il insuffla dans ses narines une haleine de vie et l'homme devint un être (une âme) vivant (e).'[30]

Mais Dieu n'est pas un solitaire. Sa créature ne le sera pas non plus.

> Yahvé Dieu dit: 'Il n'est pas bon que l'homme soit seul; je veux lui faire une aide qui soit semblable à lui' . . . Alors Yahvé Dieu fit tomber un profond sommeil sur l'homme et celui-ci s'endormit. Il prit une de ses côtes et referma la chair à sa place. Puis, de la côte qu'il avait tirée de l'homme, Yahvé Dieu façonna une femme et l'amena à l'homme. Alors celui-ci s'écria: 'Cette fois, celle-ci est l'os de mes os et la chair de ma chair! Celle-ci sera appelée "femme", car elle fut tirée de l'homme, celle-ci! C'est pourquoi, l'homme quittera son père et sa mére et s'attachera à sa femme, et ils deviendront une seule chair'.[31]

L'homme, par sa création, participe à la Vie de Dieu et à son unité. Mais Dieu a voulu que l'homme participe aussi à son mystère trinitaire. Adam et Eve forment, dès le commencement la première famille, la première communauté humaine. Et le

[29] Gen. 1: 26–27. [30] Gen. 2: 7 [31] Gen. 2: 18–24.

Seigneur Dieu bénit ce premier couple et lui donna le don de la fécondité: 'Soyez féconds et multipliez-vous, remplissez la terre et soumettez-la.'[32]

Ainsi l'homme est rendu participant de la fécondité divine; il devient coopérateur de Dieu dans le prolongement de la création. C'est de ce premier couple que sont issus tous les hommes et toutes les familles humaines.

Dieu, qui a créé les hommes par amour, pour qu'un jour ils le contemplent et vivent éternellement près de Lui, les a fait prendre part à sa Vie intime. Ce don que nous ne méritons pas, nous l'appelons 'Vie de la grâce' ou 'grâce sanctifiante', qui n'est autre chose qu'une communication de la Vie trinitaire: il nous fait participer à ce qui constitue substantiellement les Trois Personnes.[33] En participant ainsi à la Vie de Dieu, notre âme acquiert quelque parenté avec Dieu.[34] Par la vie de la grâce les premiers hommes étaient les enfants de Dieu et les héritiers du ciel, et ressemblaient à Dieu d'une façon extraordinaire.[35] Adam et Eve devaient transmettre à leurs descendants, non seulement la vie humaine (naturelle), mais aussi la Vie divine, la Vie de la grâce. Mais ils péchèrent gravement contre Dieu, et perdirent ainsi, pour eux-mêmes et pour tous leurs enfants, le privilège d'être enfants de Dieu, en perdant la vie de la grâce sanctifiante.

Nous croyons que les Bantu seront très sensibles à une telle présentation vitale de la création et de la grâce.

3. *La Vie manifestée dans le Verbe Incarné.*[36] Dieu qui ne se laisse jaimais vaincre en miséricorde va réintégrer l'homme dans sa dignité primitive d'enfant de Dieu et de participant de la Nature divine. A cet effet, la deuxième Personne prend notre nature, s'en sert pour nous re-communiquer la nature et la vie divines, faisant de nous ses frères; car Lui, sanctificateur, et nous, sanctifiés, nous avons tous un même Père.[37] 'Puis donc que les enfants avaient en commun le sang et la chair, lui aussi y

[32] Gen. 1: 28.
[33] Cf. Crouzel, 1956, p. 166.
[34] Ibid., p. 147. Cf. 2 Peter 1: 1–4; Eph. 2–19.
[35] Cf. *Catéchisme biblique*, Paris, 1958, p. 50.
[36] Cf. Jn. 1: 1–16; 1 Jn. 1: 1–3.
[37] Hb. 2: 11–13, 17.

participa pareillement.'[38] C'est pourquoi il va, comme nous, naître d'une femme,[39] mère vierge, qui l'enfantera d'une manière merveilleuse[40] 'couverte' qu'elle sera 'de l'ombre de la puissance du Très-Haut', de l'Esprit-Saint qui viendra sur elle.[41] Nous avons, par conséquent, un grand prêtre de notre race, Dieu et Homme à la fois: 'Tenons ferme la profession de foi. Car nous n'avons pas un grand prêtre impuissant à compatir à nos faiblesses, lui qui a été éprouvé en tout, d'une manière semblable, à l'exception du péché. Avançons donc avec assurance vers le trône de la grâce afin d'obtenir miséricorde et de trouver grâce, pour une aide opportune.'[42]

Ainsi, Dieu, qui avait parlé jadis aux hommes par les prophètes, nous parle désormais en son Fils,[43] qui est la manifestation parfaite de sa Vie et de son Amour sur terre. En le voyant, Homme comme nous et égal à Lui dans la divinité, le Père trouve en Lui ses complaisances. Sa mort sur la croix est le moment culminant de son acte de réparation et de rédemption. C'est de la croix que la Vie divine est déversée en torrent intarissable sur l'humanité jusqu'à la fin du monde, croix représentée par le Sacrifice eucharistique, notre Pâque à nous, les disciples et les frères du Christ, fondateur de notre famille, de notre 'clan' d'enfanta de Dieu.

4. *L'Église, communauté des 'associés-en vie surnaturelle'.* Comme un homme, un *muntu*, se prolonge dans sa famille, comme l'ancêtre fondateur continue à vivre dans son clan, ainsi et d'une manière plus vraie—puisqu'il vit réellement en chacun de ses fidèles et dans toute l'Église—et transcendante—puisqu'il est Dieu—le Christ se prolonge dans son Corps mystique, qui est le lieu de la présence et de la communication de la Vie divine.

Qu'il nous suffise d'écouter le témoignage de Saint Augustin: 'Tout homme est un seul homme dans le Christ, et l'unité des chrétiens, c'est un seul homme.'[44] Et cet homme, qui est-il? Il est tous les hommes, et tous les hommes sont lui—.[45] Cet homme

[38] Hb. 2: 14.
[39] 'Dieu envoya son Fils, né d'une femme' (Gal. 4:4).
[40] Cf. Lc. 1:26–38; 2: 1–20.
[41] Lc. 1: 35.
[42] Hb. 4: 14–16.
[43] Hb. 1: 1–2.
[44] *In Ps. 29, enarr. 2;* ML 36, 219.
[45] *In Ps. 127*; ML 37, 1686.

unique qui est tous les hommes, et auquel sont identifiés tous les hommes, c'est le Christ total, tête et corps, le Christ mystique. 'La tête, c'est l'homme qui est né de la Vierge Marie. . . . Le corps de cette tête, c'est l'Église.'[46]

La conclusion est que nous ne sommes pas seulement du Christ, mais que nous sommes le Christ, parce que, d'une certaine façon, le Christ total, c'est la tête et le corps.[47] C'est parce que nous sommes le Christ que sa sanctification devient notre sanctification, son sacrifice, notre sacrifice, ses mérites, nos mérites: '*Quia et ipsi sunt ego*': 'parce qu'eux aussi sont moi'.[48]

Tous ceux qui participent à la Vie divine, dont le Christ est l'unique transfuseur, ne font plus qu'un seul homme, parce que le même Christ, un et indivisible, est le principe unificateur de tous ses membres: 'un unique homme'—*unus homo*. Il s'agit de la Vie divine qui s'épanche jusqu'à nous dans l'unité du Christ médiateur, et de l'Incarnation qui se prolonge, par la grâce et la divinisation des fidèles, dans l'Église tout entière. . . . Il n'y a, dans le christianisme, que le Christ, tout en tous; il n'y a donc, dans la doctrine chrétienne, qu'une doctrine, mais complète, du Christ complet, Dieu et homme, tête et membres: toute la vie de l'Église vient de l'Incarnation, qui va 'jusqu'au bout d'elle-même',[49] en s'efforçant de faire de l'humanité 'un seul homme répandu par toute la terre et se développant au cours des siècles'.[50]

Pour faire saisir aux Bantu ce qu'est l'Église, il faudrait recourir à des comparaisons avec le principe de solidarité des communautés africaines. Ce qui unit les membres d'une communauté bantu, c'est d'abord le sang, c'est-à-dire l'unité de sang, l'unité de vie. C'est ensuite la communauté de propriété, de moyens vitaux. Cette comparaison faciliterait l'intelligence de la communion des saints et des devoirs qui en découlent pour chaque membre de la grande famille des chrétiens. Au sang correspond, dans l'Église, la Vie divine, une et indivise dans tous les fidèles du Christ. A la communauté de propriété correspond la

[46] *Cf. In Ps. 90, sermo 2*; ML 37, 1159–60.
[47] *In Ps. 26, enarr. 2* ML 36, 200.
[48] *In Ioannem, 108*; ML 35, 1916 (cf. Jn. 17: 19).
[49] Mersch, 1951, Tome II, pp. 135–6.
[50] *In Ps. 118, sermo 16*; ML 37, 1547.

communion des biens surnaturels et des mérites dans l'Église, en vertu de laquelle chaque chrétien agit au profit ou au désavantage de toute l'Église, selon qu'il pose un acte bon ou mauvais. Chaque baptisé porte sur ses épaules tout le poids de l'Église et il est responsable du bien ou du mal qui s'y tait. Chacun doit, comme partie, pourvoir au progrès du tout, afin de réaliser la vie de l'humanité dans le Christ.

5. *Symbolisme bantu et sacramentalisme chrétien.* Pour entrer en contact les uns avec les autres et resserrer l'union, les Bantu se servent du symbole, qui a comme rôle de capter ce qu'il y a de sacré et de divin dans la créature, et veut annuler les limites des choses pour les unifier et en faire un tout. Il veut supprimer les distances de temps et d'espaces pour que l'homme forme *un* avec son semblable et avec le monde, et pour que tout le créé soit mis au service de l'homme.

Cette aspiration de l'âme bantu à transformer les choses en récipients de puissance et de sacré, à réduire le monde à l'unité, nous la trouvons réalisée d'une façon éminente et sublime dans l'Église. Le symbolisme y atteint son point culminant dans le sacrement, 'c'est-à-dire l'union du surnaturel avec l'élément naturel et corporel'.[51]

Les sacrements ne sont pas quelque chose d'accidentel à la religion chrétienne; c'est sa source même et le moyen de son parachèvement. Les sacrements de l'Église sont des moyens de nous mettre et de nous maintenir en contact avec le Christ; ils sont le prolongement et l'expansion de sa sainte Humanité d'où découlent pour nous la Vie et la Vérité. Ils nous mettent en contact les uns avec les autres et consomment notre union réciproque, nous transformant à l'image du Fils de Dieu et réalisant ainsi une unité de plénitude de tous les disciples du Christ.

Par les sacrements les Bantu réaliseront leur aspiration à l'union vitale avec Dieu, avec le monde invisible et avec leurs frères dans la foi. L'homme ne pourrait aspirer à un moyen d'accroissement plus grand de son être. Les sacrements font fusionner notre vie avec celle du Christ, font couler en nous les

[51] Scheeben, 1947, p. 570.

énergies divines. Ils réalisent ainsi ce que les Bantu essaient de produire par leurs symboles et le dépassent merveilleusement et divinement. C'est Dieu Lui-même qui daigne entrer en contact avec nous, pour que nous devenions *un* avec Lui et avec tous ses enfants.

CONCLUSION

Nous aurions encore beaucoup de choses à dire sur les approches théologiques de la culture africaine. Ainsi les commandements de Dieu et les préceptes de l'Église peuvent être étudiés comme étant la constitution et les moyens de sauvegarder notre vie d'enfants de Dieu et de l'Eglise; le péché comme l'ennemi de notre vie divine et l'handicap de l'interaction vitale dans la communauté ecclésiale; la liturgie et le culte comme une initiation et des moyens de renforcer notre vie surnaturelle, de la vivre en communauté et de l'extérioriser; l'apostolat et l'Action catholique comme l'exercice de la paternité spirituelle des baptisés les uns vis-à-vis des autres, comme l'épanouissement de notre fécondité spirituelle, etc. Nous n'avons touché que les points les plus importants et qui nous semblent constituer la clé de voûte d'un éventuel édifice théologique bantu.

Nous avons positivement répondu à la question controversée de la possibilité d'une Théologie africaine. Non seulement elle est possible et souhaitable, mais nécessaire, et cela, non dans un avenir plus ou moins proche, mais aujourd'hui, pour les Africains d'aujourd'hui. Du fait que l'Église s'adresse à des hommes concrets, son message doit s'exprimer dans un langage adapté, et son visage doit être reconnaissable par ces hommes. Le Christ ne demande pas à l'Africain de se dépouiller de sa personnalité pour être son disciple. Mais, au contraire, l'Africain, devenu disciple du Royaume, est appelé à apporter son 'africanité' dans ce Royaume, pour l'enrichir et contribuer à sa beauté variée.

Saint Jean, dans sa vision de la Jérusalem messianique, constituant l'univers nouveau, se réjouit de l'apport des nations à la richesse de l'Église:

Les nations marcheront à sa lumière, et les rois de la terre viendront lui porter leurs trésors. Ses portes resteront ouvertes le jour—car il n'y aura pas de nuit—et l'on viendra lui porter les trésors et le faste des nations.[52]

Cependant, les trésors et le faste que les nations apporteront au Corps mystique du Christ ne sont rien en comparaison de l'ineffable don qu'elles en recevront:

Ce qui était dès le commencement,
ce que nous avons entendu,
ce que nous avons vu de nos yeux,
ce que nous avons contemplé,
ce que nos mains ont touché du Verbe de vie;
—car la vie s'est manifestée:

Nous l'avons vue, nous en rendons témoignage et nous vous annonçons cette Vie éternelle, qui était auprès du Père et qui nous est apparue;—ce que nous avons vu et entendu, nous vous l'annonçons, afin que vous aussi soyez en communion avec nous. Quant à notre communion, elle est avec le Père et avec son Fils Jésus Christ.[53]

REFERENCES

Colle, P.
(1925) 'La notion de Dieu chez les Bashi', *Congo*, 1925, pp. 37–42.
(1937) *Essai de Monographie des Bashi* (polyc.). Bukavu.
Crouzel, H.
(1956) *Théologie de l'image de Dieu chez Origène*. Paris.
Hazoumé, P.
(1937) *Le pacte de sang au Dahomey*. Paris.
Jahn, J.
(1961) *Muntu: l'homme africain et la culture néo-africaine*.
Kagame, A.
(1956) *La Philosophie bantu-rwandaise de l'Être*. Bruxelles.
Lufuluabo, F. M.
(1961) 'Vers une théodicée bantou', *Église Vivante*, pp. 426–34.
(1964) *Orientation préchrétienne de la Conception bantoue*. Léopoldville.
Mersch, E.
(1951) *Le Corps mystique du Christ*.
Parrinder, G.
(1961) *West African Religion*. London.
Pauwels, M.
(1958) *Imana et le culte des Mânes au Rwanda*. Bruxelles.
Possoz, E.
(1962) 'La Magie des primitifs', *Présence Africaine*, No. 40.
Rodegem, F. M.
(1961) *Sagesse Kirundi*. Tervueren.

[52] Apoc. 21: 24–26.

[53] 1 Jn. 1: 1–3.

Scheeben
(1947) *Les Mystères du christianisme.*
Smith, E. W.
(1961) *African Ideas of God.* London.
Tegnaeus, H.
(1950) *Le Héros civilisateur.* Upsala.
(1952) *Blood-Brothers.* Stockholm.
Tempels, Pl.
(1949) *La Philosophie bantoue. Présence Africaine*, Paris.
Theuws, Th.
(1955) *Textes luba.* Elisabethville (CEPSI).
(1958) 'Croyance et culte chez les Baluba', *Présence Africaine*, 18–19.
Thomas, L. V.
(1959a) *Les Diola.* IFAN-Dakar, Vol. II, pp. 681–771.
(1959b) 'Animisme et christianisme', *Présence Africaine*, No. 26, pp. 5–21.
(1960) 'Les Diola de Basse-Casamance', *Afrique-Documents*, No. 51, pp. 74–90.
Van Caeneghem
(1956) *La Notion de Dieu chez les Baluba du Kasai.* Bruxelles.
Van Den Bosch
(1928) 'Quelques notes sur le nom et la notion de l'Être Suprême et d'un dieu-vengeur chez les Balendu', *Anthropos*, No. 28, pp. 987–99.
Van Der Leeuw, G.
(1948) *La Religion dans son essence et ses manifestations.* Paris.
Van Wing, J.
(1959) *Études Bakongo.* Bruges.
Zuure, B.
(1926) 'Immana, le Dieu des Barundi', *Anthropos*, No. 21, pp. 733–76.
(1929) *Croyances et pratiques des Barundi.* Bruxelles.

Summary

THE AFRICAN CONTRIBUTION TO THEOLOGY

In discussing the African contribution to theology two pitfalls must be avoided—the refusal to adopt any theology except Western theology, and the superficial 'africanization' which is too often based on a romanticizing of the 'African' or 'Bantu' soul. The claim of Africans to express themselves theologically must aim at preserving not only their ancestral past but at being authentic Christians, faithful to their origins and to the Church.

This paper is divided into two parts: (1) Bases or foundations of the African contribution to theology in traditional beliefs, and (2) some suggestions for the Africanization of theology.

The foundations of the African contribution to theology

consist of belief in a Supreme Being, and the innate feeling of participation. God is regarded as 'the first source of life and of any means of life', as transcending all categories of being (*ntu*) and as the Creator of all things. He takes care of His creatures and is concerned with the life of man and with the functioning of the world. God is the Father of man and of all things and this fatherhood is His most important attribute according to Bantu theology. The relationship between man and God is therefore a personal one, necessitating on the part of man a filial attitude which is characteristic of the tone and style of prayers addressed to the Supreme Being.

The second basis of the African contribution to theology—the feeling of participating in a common life—explains Bantu solidarity and the belief in the vital communion existing between the members of a family, clan, or tribe. Each member of such an entity must strive towards the safety and preservation of the whole. God as the source of life communicated it to the first ancestors of the clan or clans, whose duty it is to perpetuate life in their descendants. The ancestors and the dead constitute the invisible element of the community, and in the present world the complete achievement of man lies in his resemblance to the life of God and of the ancestors. All those who participate in this common life are said to be *ntu*.

An African theology may very well spring from these two elements—belief in God, the Father-Creator, and the feeling of participation. The Bantu concept of the Supreme Being could be used as the basis for a treatise on 'the Mystery of God'. The Creation will be presented as a communication of the Life of God and of His love for man. Since a divine person 'lived among us' God speaks to us through His Son, who is the manifestation of divine life. When God became Incarnate, a new mankind was created and all those who belonged to this new family or clan constitute the Church of Christ. From these bases a treatise on 'God Incarnate' and His extension, 'the Church', can be developed. The desire of the Bantu for contact with each other and union through symbols is achieved in the sacraments of the Church which make it possible for us to merge our lives with that of Christ. God's commandments and the precepts of the Church can be studied as the constitution and means of safeguarding our life as children of God and of the Church. Sin is the enemy of our divine life and the handicap to vital interaction in the church community. Liturgy and worship are an initiation and a means to strengthen our spiritual life and to live it communally. Missionary efforts and 'Catholic Action' may be regarded as the training and achievement of our spiritual fecundity. These are some of the most important points which could be the basis for an African theology.

Saint John, in his vision of the messianic Jerusalem, rejoices in the contribution of nations to the wealth of the Church (Apoc. 21: 24–26). However, the treasures and splendour that the nations might bring to the Mystical Body of Christ are nothing to be compared to the ineffable gift they will receive from Him: a communion with the disciples of the Word of Life, which really means a communion with the Father and His Son Jesus Christ.

XV. THE WAYS AND MEANS OF COMMUNICATING THE GOSPEL

JOHN MBITI

INTRODUCTORY

The speed of change in modern Africa is so great that nobody can keep up with all of it. A hundred years ago when Christianity began to spread in tropical Africa, human life was almost static, following, as it did, the rhythm of the seasons and the cycle of nature from birth to death. Pioneer missionaries and early converts communicated the Gospel to our forefathers in ways that seemed to suit their times and ideas, but conditions have radically altered now, and this Gospel, which remains basically the same for all time, has to accommodate itself to our new situation. The success of this will depend to a great extent on how the Gospel is communicated to the hearers of today.

We live in a heterogeneous society, ranging from illiterate peasants in rural communities to highly qualified professionals doing business in the skyscraper offices of our fast-growing cities. As on the day of Pentecost, the Gospel should be presented in such a way that each person will hear it in his 'own language'. We must now search for ways and means of communicating the Gospel to make it intelligible to its hearers, and to bring out its true depth effectively.

TEACHING

There is too much preaching and too little teaching in our churches all over the continent. In traditional Africa there was plenty of teaching and no preaching. Why have we allowed this principle to become practically reversed in communicating the Gospel? Preaching alone will not deepen the Faith in Africa, and what the majority of Christians require is a clearer picture of Biblical knowledge, the life and mission of the Church in the world. Our Lord preached to the crowds, and *taught* them, especially those who followed Him, in order to make the people understand what He came to accomplish.

The Scriptures. Owing to the many languages in Africa, we do not yet have the Bible, or even the New Testament, translated into the language that everyone can understand. Furthermore, illiteracy is still a grave problem with which we must continue to reckon.[1] The written revelation of God is thus hidden from many, and it is the duty of the Church to convey the teaching of the Bible to everyone and, in particular, to the believers. Bible Societies, with the help and co-operation of missionary groups and local churches, are undoubtedly giving this issue its proper priority, but the Scriptures should not be allowed to become dusty ornaments as in parts of the older Christendom. The Bible is the living word of God through which His Spirit is speaking in human history. Our teaching must therefore be based on the sacred Scriptures, and we must ask ourselves constantly what their relevance is to our changing historical environment. What was relevant to Europe in the Reformation period need not necessarily be relevant to the Africa of today; neither can we be satisfied simply with a mechanical and literal interpretation and/or teaching of the Bible.[2]

The reading of the Bible should be encouraged in all Christian circles. Where and when possible, there could be Bible-reading contests on a 'local, national, or even continental basis'.

The Pulpit. The Sunday worship is the only occasion when most Christians have an opportunity to hear the Church's teaching, and our pastors and catechists do well to 'redeem the time' and use it more for teaching than for bombarding their congregations with countless moral injunctions. The Pastoral Epistles lay great emphasis on the idea of teaching the believers, and we cannot expect our converts to become mature in the Faith if they are not taught the things that pertain to it.

The Catechism. This by its very definition presumes teaching, and Church history bears witness to its impact (e.g. the Cate-

[1] See this problem as discussed by Weber, 1957.

[2] For further discussion on the use of the Bible in evangelization see Chirgwin, 1954.

chismal school of Alexandria especially during the time of Clement and Origen, Martin Luther's Kleiner Katechismus, and many others). Churches in Africa rightly give catechumenal instructions to baptismal and/or confirmation candidates. Except for the Roman Catholic the majority of the catechisms are not comprehensive enough, and should be expanded to cover a wider range of Christian doctrine and matters of concern. These instructions should certainly be continued beyond the immediate time of baptism or confirmation, partly because the believers (and adherents) need this further teaching, and partly in order to eradicate the wrong idea that Christian knowledge ends with baptism or confirmation. See the Appendix (p. 342) for a suggested Catechism.

Christian Literature. More and more people are becoming literate in Africa, but the supply of reading material is still very inadequate. The Church has this golden opportunity to feed the hungry minds, most of which she has herself taught to read and write. This important means of communicating the Gospel requires no further emphasis. The need is great, for books and pamphlets could certainly cover items like commentaries, devotions, doctrine, apologetics, discussion of problems arising out of the contact between Christianity and traditional society, etc.

Use of African Languages. For most people in tropical Africa, an African language is still the mother tongue, and forms the psychological background for their thinking and understanding. Great emphasis should be given to the use of African languages in communicating the Gospel, and in making Christian concepts assimilated in the life of the Church. Obviously there are many biblical concepts which are foreign to the vocabulary of African languages, but an attempt should be made to convey these concepts in a language understood by the hearers. This is no mean task, and calls for much research and experimentation. The Gospel has to sink into the thinking process, the attitude, and the vocabulary of the people, if it is to make its lasting impact upon the life of the whole person and the whole community. Key words of Christian vocabulary can be produced in booklets, and explained from the pulpit and during catechism instructions.

African Theology. So far the Church in tropical Africa, except in Ethiopia, depends entirely on imported theology from Europe and America. Christian theology is basically the same in all places and at all times, since it deals with the eternal truth of the knowledge of God as revealed to man through different avenues and most clearly through the Incarnation. But there are methods and modes of conveying this truth which are appropriate in certain areas and at certain times, without necessarily being equally adequate elsewhere. Africa has its own way of looking at and interpreting the world, and the time is now ripe to bring Christian theology into the picture. This would be accomplished through the development of an 'African' theology whose scope must be sufficiently wide to comprehend the depths of the Christian Faith and to interpret it to the people in terms of their understanding and needs. It may be of value to find out whether we can use the tribal setting as a means of discovering a fresh approach to Christian theology. In any case, a theology suitable for the Church here must necessarily include: (*a*) traditional (both Western and Eastern) Christian theology; (*b*) biblical theology; and (*c*) the theology of African religious concepts and practices, and, where possible, their theological encounter with Islam. It remains to be seen whether an approach along these lines will become fruitful or perhaps end up in a cul-de-sac. The Church in Africa cannot, however, afford to remain without a theology when she is confronted with so many theological challenges today.[3] But we cannot artificially create an 'African theology' or even plan it; it must evolve spontaneously as the Church teaches and lives her Faith and in response to the extremely complex situation in Africa. It may well happen that there will be not one but several types of African theology, which, if it is of value, must be another expression of the theology of the Universal Church.

[3] As a beginning, an attempt should be made to build up a bibliography of theological works by Africans, either already published, in process of publication, or in the form of dissertations.

AUDIO-VISUAL AIDS

This is an area of great potentialities, and the Church is undoubtedly aware of it. But more use of these aids should be made, particularly for the sake of the illiterates.

Stories and Drama. Folk stories are popular in every group of African societies. Story telling is perhaps the most widely used method of communicating tribal or national wisdom, ideas, historical events, morals, etc. Almost everyone knows and can narrate several stories. Some of them even circulate beyond tribal boundaries. Many portions of the Bible are, or can be, told in story form. This makes it very easy for biblical knowledge to be conveyed to the people since they are psychologically prepared to assimilate teaching through stories. Christians should be encouraged to tell biblical stories in addition to the folk stories of their particular communities. This would mean that children and young people from a Christian environment would grow up with a sound knowledge of the narratives pertaining to the Faith, and would find Christianity more relevant to their tribal background. Non-Christian homes would undoubtedly be reached as well, since stories circulate widely over large areas.

Many biblical stories readily lend themselves to dramatization. Sunday schools, catechism classes, and other Christian groups can dramatize them without difficulty or expensive costumes. The African is often said to be a born actor; and through acting these biblical narratives, the life of ancient Israelites could begin to shine through our tribal setting in a way which people would understand more readily than when they simply hear it proclaimed from the pulpit.

Both story telling and drama from biblical episodes would readily appeal to our illiterate population. The method would also help to widen people's vocabulary of Christian ideas, and make biblical teaching relevant to African backgrounds. In this connexion it would also be useful to teach the meaning of the names used in some of the narratives, since many biblical names have meanings and African people often use names which convey particular meanings and ideas.

Modern African literature and drama will undoubtedly continue to exercise an increasing influence upon people, especially in urban areas. They can become weapons of evangelization while retaining their primary function as works of art.

Traditional Rites. This field has been almost completely neglected, and often despised, in the process of evangelizing tropical Africa. There are tribal 'rites of passage' connected with the life of the individual and which are focal moments in community life as well. Often such rites are performed at critical points like birth, initiation, marriage, and death. These are points when the community is most susceptible to any influence. Christians could certainly 'baptize' many of these traditional rites, and give them a Christian content and blessing. (After all, a good number of the Christian rites were originally borrowed from either Hebrew or pagan sources.) For example, tribal rites of naming children could be brought into the Church and used as occasions for baptizing and naming children of Christian parents. Likewise the rites performed to protect expectant mothers could be adopted and used in the Church to thank God for child-bearing and to pray for expectant mothers and childless couples.

Hymns and Music. Africans are extremely fond of singing. Music is one method of communication, and can serve many purposes. Each of the denominations working in Africa has brought and translated its own hymns which have become popular and widespread among the congregations. There are undoubtedly great hymns of Christendom which belong to, and enrich, the universal Church. But a good many of the hymns used in tropical Africa are of second-rate quality and often slanted according to denominational allegiance. The fact that nearly all these hymns are translations, and are sung to imported tunes, makes their teaching appear foreign. As in the case of traditional rites, there are many African tunes which could and should be 'baptized' into Christian usage. People would sing them feeling that the tunes 'belong to us'; but new words with a Christian content would obviously have to be supplied to replace old ones. In this way part of Christian knowledge would become linked with the musical life of the people. While accepting and using some of the great hymns of the Church, it is necessary for the Church here to respond by creating more hymns and music which arise spontaneously and in a way which is both suited and meaningful to local needs and expressions. Africa must sing unto the Lord, not only through the ear, but from the heart, articulating and not merely repeating her response to the Faith.

African musical instruments must also be brought into Church worship. Already this is being done in some countries, but in others there is still the widespread attitude that these instruments are either 'inferior' or 'devilish'. Only the rhythmic beat of the drum can fully awaken the emotions of the African people: the piano or organ is too weak for that. The Gospel must reach the whole person, and music is one of the alleys that penetrate into the whole person of Africa. So let the Gospel be conveyed through music and hymns produced on the local soil, speaking a language that is familiar and meaningful.[4] It might be of value also to explore the possibilities of using a certain amount of dancing where this is likely to prove an effective witness of the Church—after all, dancing before the Lord has a religious value in the Bible (2 Sam. 6:14; Ps. 149:3, 150:4).

Portions of the Scriptures can also be chanted, as in many churches in Ghana. There are musicians capable of doing this, and these biblical lyrics should prove interesting and useful in other parts of Africa.

Church Architecture. This is, for historical reasons, imported from overseas, and almost everywhere one finds church buildings patterned after true or corrupt copies of western architecture. If worship is to become fully meaningful, then the architecture of the churches should be determined by the congregation and not vice versa. Naturally there is need for research and experimentation in this vast field, but it is high time the Church began to take this issue seriously. Would, for example, a round or oval church building be more conducive to worship than a rectangular or square one for an African congregation since traditional houses and villages are generally built in a round shape? This would, among other things, bring the altar and the pulpit closer to the

[4] Cf. Rattenbury, 1941, and Hildebrandt, 1951. See: Weman, 1960.

middle of the worshippers and cultivate a more practical sense of oneness and community fellowship. Or again, what is the place of the open space, with trees and grass as part of the church building? Surely Africa can still afford such open spaces as part of the physical environment for a worshipping congregation—we are not yet as crowded as Belgium or Holland! Could not this become one way of expressing, in the African scene, the cosmic meaning of the Cross?[5]

While taking into serious consideration the local needs, one must not, however, lose sight of the Church's function of being both local and universal. Perhaps in rural areas the local aspect will become predominant, but in urban areas the universal will receive more attention. In both cases account should be taken of the liturgical movement so that we do not erect churches which are liturgically out of date even before they are completed.

Art and Sculpture. This has inexhaustible potentialities and should be exploited. By the use of art and sculpture, biblical stories and ideas can be portrayed in tangible and pictorial figures which take into account the local culture and interpretation that people give to Christian teaching. Already there are outstanding artists in Africa who have depicted religious themes through African eyes and as seen against a background familiar to the people of this continent. Pictures made showing, for example, 'the Prodigal Son', 'Angels', sheep eating by the 'still waters', etc., as conceived and interpreted by African artists using local colour, would be a great step forward in presenting the Gospel in a 'language' capable of being understood by the people here. This would also eradicate the wrong impression that Christianity is simply a Western religion and that the Bible is a European book. This method would certainly show that Christianity is not so foreign and remote; and would open up a creative way of interpreting biblical teaching in a context with which the people are familiar.

Radio and Television. These two media are becoming increasingly powerful in Africa. Their influence is exceptionally great.

[5] Cf. Hammond, 1960. What he discusses is in the context of European churches, but his challenging remarks can also be applied to African churches.

Ownership of a radio set is a badge of social status, and our societies are rapidly becoming 'transistorized' as in Europe and America. Already the Christians are using the radio, and own some powerful radio stations in Ethiopia and Liberia. No doubt our Church leaders are aware of the potentialities, dangers, and responsibilities of these modern media of communication.

'INDIGENIZATION'

It is not enough simply to proclaim the Gospel. Christianity must become 'native' in tropical Africa just as it is 'native' in Europe and America. It must therefore deepen its roots in the context of our corporate community life, the soil where the Gospel is being planted. By her very nature, the Church is a corporate Body; and although Africa is fast moving in the direction of 'individualistic' life of the technological man, we can still capture the strength of communal life and perhaps incorporate it into the Church. While there is still this deep sense of communal life, then it is necessary to use it in the process of evangelization.

Kinship is the architectural skeleton of corporate life. The Gospel should be addressed not simply to the individual but to the whole corporate group of which he is a member. In miniature the person is the family, the household, the clan, and the tribe or nation. That is the social structure and the mental climate of his existence. Alone he cannot be 'saved'; and the Christian Faith becomes fully meaningful to him only within the context of his group solidarity. If we want him 'saved', then he must be allowed to bring with him into the Body of Christ, all his many relatives. African traditional religions are not departmentalized areas of life: they are incorporated into the whole life of the people. If the ultimate goal of preaching and accepting the Gospel is to transpose allegiance from tribal religions to the Lord Jesus Christ, then the process of transposition should be entire and not partial, radical and not casual. We should therefore aim at a 'mass innoculation' with the Gospel, and thereby reach the individual as well. The reverse order is the method so far followed by evangelizing societies in our countries. But so long as the individual is severed from the mass, from his kinsmen and relatives, from his community group to which he belongs by blood and culture, he will be frustrated and torn between loyalties. One will be the loyalty to a 'pagan' or non-Christian community with all its demands, and the other will be the loyalty to the Church. More often than not he will yield to the former. This is the basic conflict in the lives of the innumerable casualties who withdraw from Christian gatherings and eventually from Church life altogether. All this does not mean that we minimize the challenge and demands of the Gospel: viz., 'Follow Me, and leave the dead to bury their own dead' (Matt. 8:22 par.); or, 'If any one comes to Me and does not hate his own father and mother . . . and even his own life, he cannot be my disciple' (Lk. 14:26). The centre of allegiance and obedience must unquestionably be Christ, and then the other things may follow later.

This problem demands two fundamental approaches: (i) more attention should be given to kinship ties and household structure of African people, in presenting the Gospel to them; (ii) their keen sense of community and kinship relationship should be grafted into the new and eschatological community of the Body of Christ, with Him as the Head. If this transfer is accomplished, the individual will see the Christian Faith in terms of a corporate existence in which tribal solidarity is superseded and intensified by the solidarity in Christ which has a deeper cohesion, a wider membership and fuller experience of communion.

The Christian Faith should therefore be strongly rooted in the family. Already we see the rapid disintegration of the traditional family life but the home is still the base. Evangelization of the home and the household should take first priority, to which 'personal evangelism' can be added later. This task involves visiting homes, proclaiming the Gospel to the whole household, and founding Christian families. Where possible, the household and relatives should be baptized on the same occasion. In this way, several households would all become incorporated into the household of God.[6] Indigenization must include every aspect of

[6] See the All Africa Churches Conference 'Report of the Christian Home and Family Life Seminar', Mindolo, (1963).

the Church's life—personnel, ideas, and institutions, as well as such items as symbolism, architecture, music, etc. Any one of these aspects is not enough, only a thoroughgoing and comprehensive indigenization can be revolutionary enough to make a lasting and fruitful impact. But artificial attempts to indigenize may not only fail but could wreck the work already established.

THE CHURCH HERSELF

The Church as the Body of Christ is herself the living channel, par excellence, of communicating the Gospel. Not only does she teach and proclaim the Gospel, but she is the embodiment of that Gospel; and her voice goes forth not only in audible words but in her very existence and life. As she makes her numerical expansion and spiritual growth, there the Gospel is being proclaimed and communicated. She cannot be severed from her message, and neither can that message become meaningful except within the embrace of the Church.

Worship and the Sacraments. It is at worship that the Church's proclamation of the Gospel is most laudible. At the Sacraments of Baptism and the Eucharist this worship comes to a climax, and becomes so intense that the dichotomy between earthly and heavenly realities is momentarily removed. All the ways and means which we have mentioned above put the hearer in a position to hear and understand the Christian message. But it is only in the Church, through worship and the Sacraments, that this objective truth becomes a real personal experience for the hearer. It is here that the Giver and the recipient of Redemption meet in an intimate rendezvous. The relationship is so intimate that it is expressed in terms like 'the Body of Christ', 'the Bridegroom and the Bride', being 'in Christ', etc. So the Church may and should employ these methods to communicate the Gospel and sow it in people's hearts, but she is the only 'place' where men can come and find the Lord of their lives and ultimately the Reality of their gropings.

The Sacraments portray the Gospel in tangible ways which can reach the person through all the senses of human perception. They are Christocentric in their institution and practice. They epitomize the whole Gospel from the Incarnation to the Parousia. They proclaim what has already happened historically and eschatologically, and anticipate what will happen at the End. Christian life is empty and meaningless without the Sacraments which are the channels of God's grace.

Baptism identifies the believer with the Redeemer: it is the Sacrament of Birth. It proclaims the death and the Resurrection of Jesus Christ our Lord. Through Baptism a person becomes mystically united with the Lord and is born again. He undergoes the process of regeneration, and is transferred from the kingdom of darkness to the Kingdom of God. He dies and rises with Christ in newness of life, and is given the badge of divine ownership. Now he becomes a member of the Messianic community, and shares in all the privileges of that community.

The Eucharist nourishes the person who has been born anew through Baptism. It brings the individual and the community into the most intimate communion with the Lord. The community partakes of the Body and Blood of the Lord, and thus shares in all the divine mysteries. The Eucharist spans the whole period from the Death of Christ to His Parousia, bringing into the present the whole Gospel in its past and future dimensions.

As water, bread, and wine are used at these Sacraments, the Gospel is proclaimed in a form which people can hear, see, touch, taste, and smell. Everyone can therefore catch some glimpses of the Gospel when it is portrayed through the Sacraments. The Church can ask or find no better opportunity than this, when the whole Gospel could be expounded, radiating from the theme of the Sacraments. The curriculum for catechumen instruction could be formed on the basis of the Sacraments.

Many churches in Africa strongly emphasize Baptism and either minimize or ignore the Eucharist. Baptism is received as a mark of identification with the missionary culture, or simply as a purification rite not unlike some of the tribal rites. Its sacramental value is thus lost or completely unknown. The Eucharist tends to be associated with magico-superstitious ideas, and some churches either do not have it or only very occasionally. These debased views and practices of the Sacraments make it practically impossible for the Gospel to shine through them. Our churches and leaders should certainly be given a better knowledge of the meaning and value of the Sacraments. The celebration of the Sacraments should also be made more dramatic. For example at Baptism, the drum could be played solemnly to create and convey the sense of 'dying with Christ' as the candidates approach the water and are immersed (or sprinkled or marked with the sign of the Cross). Then with an outburst of rhythmic joy, the idea of 'rising with Christ' can be dramatized as they come out of the water (or after being baptized). At the Eucharist, the idea of fellowship, praise, thanksgiving, renewal, etc., can likewise be dramatized through the use of music and the actual physical setting.

These two Sacraments also epitomize the eschatological tension of the Gospel in which the Church is called to live. They point to the fact that already Christians have been incorporated into the eschatological Man, Jesus Christ, and that they have already died and risen with Him. They partake of the Messianic banquet, and live in the End-period. But paradoxically, Christians are waiting for the End, for the Parousia, for the final establishment of God's reign in the universe. They have only 'tasted the powers of the Age to Come' (Heb. 6:4 f.), but have not finally taken full possession of it; they have eschatologically 'come to Mount Zion and to the city of the living God . . .' (Heb. 12:22) but they are still pilgrims, seeking 'the city which is to come' (Heb. 13:14). This Gospel tension must accompany both the proclamation and profession of the Faith, and it is most fully realized in and through the Sacraments.

We must therefore seek to make the Church the centre of existence from which African peoples may derive the fulfilment of their life's aspiration whether in time of need or in time of feasting, and where they may experience a communal life which has a vaster scope and meaning than tribal life without Christ could ever provide. If they can discover this in the Church, they will learn to look to Jesus Christ as the Founder, the Sustainer, and the Finisher of a new and better humanity. The Church will become for them a community in which their corporate aspirations are not destroyed but fulfilled and intensified, in which tribal foundations are not simply shaken and replaced with a vacuum but are made more secure in Christ. The God who made man and provides him with children, life, and rain, will now become man's light, and man will have fellowship with his Creator.

In this way, through the preaching and teaching of the Gospel, Jesus Christ will so confront the peoples of Africa, that in Him and through Him they will find access to God Whom they already acknowledge in their traditional ideas, to be the Creator of all things. Jesus Christ will be known, among other things, as the One Who strengthens kinship between man and man, and the One Who established kinship between man and God. In this manner, this eternal Gospel of the Incarnation will begin to accommodate itself in the African environment, making its challenges felt and its promises realized.

REFERENCES

All Africa Churches Conference
(1963) 'Report of the Christian Home and Family Life Seminar'. Mindolo.
Chirgwin, A. M.
(1954) *The Bible in World Evangelism.*
Hammond, P.
(1960) *Literature and Architecture.*
Hildebrandt, F.
(1951) *From Luther to Wesley.*
Rattenbury, J. E.
(1941) *The Evangelical Doctrine of Charles Wesley's Hymns.*
Weber, Hans Ruedi
(1957) *The Communication of the Gospel to Illiterates.*
Weman, H.
(1960) *African Music and the Church in Africa.*

APPENDIX

Proposed Catechism for Use in Africa

Note: This skeleton covers the main substance of Christianity which could be introduced in an average African community, in the form of a catechism. It is intended to cover a period of one and a half to two years. Scriptural references are left out in the skeleton, as these would have to be supplied when the catechism is worked out in full. It is hoped that the instructor would draw parallels and/or contrasts from African life and ideas, in order to make the Christian Message clear and more readily retained through the method of 'association'. The aim of each lesson should be: to broaden the learner's vocabulary of Christian ideas, to increase his knowledge of Christian truth, and to deepen his experience of the Faith. Where and when possible, direct teaching should be supplemented by some of the methods and means we have suggested in the essay, e.g. drama, booklets, arts, traditional rites, etc. The last section is optional and may be given only to the more capable catechumens, or for post-baptism and post-confirmation instruction. It is in the teaching of the catechism, that, among other things, a theology may begin to evolve.

I: INTRODUCTION AND BACKGROUND

Early Jewish People:
- Creation of all things. First man and woman
- Patriarchs
- Jewish tribal life:
  - Livestock and wandering
  - Marriage and family life
  - Wars with one another and other tribes
  - Trade and farming
  - Death and the departed
  - Folk-stories
- Settlement in Egypt (Africa)

II: GOD AND HUMAN LIFE

God in the life of Jewish people:
- Revelation
- Covenant 'Promised Land'
- Exodus and the birth of the Jewish nation
- The law—Moses, Decalogue, marriage, foods, etc.
- Rulers—elders, judges, kings, theocracy
- Prophets and prophecy
- God in their history—as 'the Chosen People'
  - Levitical priesthood

Worship and sacrifice (Temple(s))
Keeping God's Commandments
Scriptures—Old Testament (Old Covenant)
New Testament (New Covenant).

III: GOD AMONG MEN (INCARNATION)—JESUS CHRIST

New Covenant
Birth and genealogy of Jesus
Life of Jesus
Ministry—Healing, visiting people
Teaching—Fatherhood of God
Kingdom of God
Revealing God among men
Death and resurrection
Meaning of His Ministry
Gospel
Salvation
Sacraments—Baptism, Eucharist
New Creation and its destiny
The disciples—Apostles
The Gospels
New Testament (New Covenant)

IV: THE PEOPLE OF GOD—THE CHURCH

Names: Disciples, Saints, Followers of Jesus, the Faithful, Redeemed Community, Brethren, People of God, etc.
Early Church life—communal, fellowship, mutual help, 'Agape', brotherhood, opposition from outsiders, worship, use of O.T., household Church life, etc.
The Holy Spirit—Person of the Trinity
'Proceeding'
In O.T. times
In the life of Jesus Christ
In the Church—God's people
Expansion of the Early Church:
Apostles—Peter, John, Paul, Silas, etc.
Other Christians—Virgin Mary, Luke, Mark, etc.

'Missionary' work, rapid expansion
Persecution and martyrdom
'The Acts of the Apostles'
Epistles and the Revelation
Spread of Christianity
in Palestine, Asia Minor, and Asia
in Africa and Europe
Church Fathers:
African Church Fathers and their influence in Christendom
(Islam: beginning of Islam, Prophet Muhammed
Spread in Africa
Christianity wiped out in many parts of Africa
Christianity in Egypt, Ethiopia, and the Sudan
Islam in Africa today.)
Universal Church:
Orthodox
Roman Catholic
'Protestant' and others
Denominations
Church Unity and the Ecumenical Movement
Church Militant and Church Triumphant
Missionary work, especially in Africa
Coming of Christianity to Africa
Missionaries and early converts
Local and national Church
Church in Africa today
Problems of the Church in Africa
All-Africa Conference of Churches
Our Youth and the Church

V: THE LIFE OF GOD'S PEOPLE

Practical aspects of Christian life:
Faith
Prayer and the Lord's Prayer
Worship—Fellowship, Praise, Adoration, Meditation, etc.
Sacraments—birth, nourishment, growth
Temptation, Sin, Confession

- The Bible and how to use it
- Creed(s), Apostles' Creed
- Christian hymns
- Christian Family life—sex, courtship, marriage, children, parents, relatives, etc.
- Propagating the Faith—Evangelism
- Suffering and the problem of Evil—sickness, accidents, death etc.
- Personal Growth in Faith, Love, Purity, etc.
- Christian Ethics—love, justice, truthfulness, joy, kindness, visiting sick, forgiveness, mercy, etc.
- Church Calendar—Feasts, Christmas, Easter, Saints' days, etc.
- Christian Stewardship—material (money, crops, cattle, etc.) time, tithing, and free-offering, etc.
- Gratitude—to God, to people
- Fasting
- Sunday and Christian gatherings for worship.
- Local Church—body of local believers, new solidarity centred upon Christ.

Ordained Ministry—Deacon, Pastor, Priest, Bishop
Church support for Ministers
Place and work of the Laity
Youth in the Church
Christians in the world—tribal environment, urban life, non-Christians, 'detribalization', national life, and citizenship, etc.
The State and Authority.
Biographical sketch of Christian men and women—to see 'Faith at work'.
Christian Vocabulary—Amen, Church, Gospel, etc.
  Names—Jesus, Jehovah, Mary, Abraham, etc.

VI: FURTHER DOCTRINAL TEACHING

Eschatology
Christology
God—Father, Son, Holy Spirit
  Holy Trinity
  Revelation

Man—Creation of, sin, evil

New Man in Christ—salvation, atonement, sacrifice, redemption, and sanctification.

Church—according to the New Testament (Body, Temple, etc.)
local, national, universal, Triumphant
Sacraments, Communion of Saints
The ordained ministry and the laity
Mission of the Church in the world

The Scriptures

Angels and demons

Death and the Christian hope

Destiny of all things in Christ.

Résumé

COMMENT COMMUNIQUER L'ÉVANGILE

L'Afrique est en train de subir une évolution rapide et ce changement exige que l'on trouve de nouveau moyens de communiquer l'Évangile afin d'atteindre chacun dans sa situation particulière.

ENSEIGNEMENT

Les Écritures devraient former la base de notre enseignement. Puisque beaucoup de nos frères sont encore analphabètes, il faut voir comment on peut les atteindre par des moyens qui leur seront accessibles. La chaire doit être utilisée plus pour l'enseignement de la Foi chrétienne que simplement pour des sermons donnant des conseils moraux. Le culte du dimanche est pour beaucoup de chrétiens la seule occasion où ils peuvent être instruits et nos prédicateurs devraient mettre ces quelques moments à profit dans toute la mesure du possible.

Les catéchismes utilisés dans nos églises ne sont pas suffisamment complets, sauf celui de l'église catholique. Il faudrait qu'ils soient plus importants et aient plus d'envergure. Quand cela sera possible, l'instruction religieuse devrait continuer après le Baptême ou la Confirmation.

A mesure que le nombre d'alphabétisés augmente, le besoin en livres se fait de plus en plus sentir. Le domaine de littérature chrétienne est vaste et l'Évangile pourrait être transmis par l'intermédiaire de livres de dévotions, de commentaires, de biographies et de livres traitant des problèmes actuels auxquels nous nous heurtons.

Les langues africaines sont encore les langues maternelles de la plupart des habitants de l'Afrique Tropicale et l'on devrait essayer de les utiliser pour communiquer les concepts chrétiens et bibliques. Par exemple, des mots-clés pourraient être choisis et expliqués dans des classes de catéchisme, dans les sermons et dans des livres simples.

Jusqu'à présent l'église en Afrique tropicale, sauf dans le cas de l'église éthiopienne, dépend d'une théologie importée. Cet état de choses présente certains avantages très limités mais ne peut suffire à tous moments. L'Afrique a sa propre façon de considérer et d'interpréter le monde et il faudrait tenir compte de ce fait en élaborant une théologie chrétienne. L'Église ne peut se permettre de ne pas avoir sa théologie indigène alors qu'elle se heurte à tant de problèmes théologiques. Cette théologie devrait faire une synthèse de la théologie de l'ancien Christianisme, de la théologie biblique et de la théologie des religions africaines.

MOYENS AUDIO-VISUELS

Les contes folkloriques sont un moyen traditionnel de communication. Beaucoup de parties de la Bible se prêtent très bien au conte et ceci devrait évidemment plaire aux Africains. On peut aussi monter des pièces à partir des contes ce qui constitue une étape plus avancée de la communication et qui permet d'adapter les histoires de la Bible au contexte africain. Ces deux méthodes devraient s'avérer tout particulièrement utiles pour les analphabètes.

Beaucoup de rites de passages pourraient être baptisés et mis en rapport avec l'instruction chrétienne.

Nous recommandons également beaucoup l'utilisation des chants et instruments de musique traditionnels. Certains passages des Écritures pourraient être mis en musique et chantés par des choristes ou par les fidèles comme c'est déjà le cas au Ghana.

L'architecture de nos églises constitute également un moyen de communication. Cette architecture devrait être déterminée par les fidèles et non pas vice-versa. L'autel devait être le point central, au milieu des fidèles. Dans notre contexte africain nous devrions essayer de trouver des moyens d'exprimer notre conception de la réalisation cosmique de la Croix et ceci pourrait se faire,—c'est un moyen parmi beaucoup d'autres,—par l'incorporation du ciel, des arbres et de l'herbe dans l'architecture de nos églises.

L'art et la sculpture peuvent également servir à représenter les idées et histoires de la Bible en utilisant des locaux auxquels les fidèles sont habitués. Ceci permettrait aussi de lutter contre l'opinion prétendant que le christianisme est une religion étrangère.

L'Église utilise la radio et la télévision et a déjà des stations de radiodiffusion en Éthiopie et au Liberia.

AFRICANISATION

Le Christianisme devrait devenir indigène à l'Afrique. La personne tout entière doit arriver au salut non pas comme individu mais dans l'ensemble de sa communauté. Nous devrions avoir pour but une inoculation massive de l'Évangile ce qui, entre autres, ferait disparaître les tensions causées par une double allégeance. Par double allégeance nous entendons, d'une part, celle à la communauté non-chrétienne avec toutes ses exigences et de l'autre, celle à l'Église. Ceci ne diminue pas le défi de l'Évangile.

Il faudrait qu'une attention plus approfondie soit portée aux systèmes de parenté et aux structures familiales. Le sens africain des rapports avec la famille et la communauté devrait se greffer sur la vie de la communauté eschatologique du Corps du Christ. La Foi Chrétienne devrait prendre racine au sein de la famille si nous voulons qu'elle ait une influence durable sur nos sociétés.

L'ÉGLISE ELLE-MÊME

L'Église est la voie vivante de la communication de l'Évangile qu'elle représente. Ceci est tout particulièrement clair dans le culte dont la célébration des sacraments du Baptême et de l'Eucharistie sont les moments saillants. Dans l'Église les faits objectifs de l'Évangile deviennent l'expérience personnelle de ceux qui vivent 'dans le Christ'. Les sacrements résument l'Évangile de manière mystique et tangible de l'Incarnation à la Parousie. La vie chrétienne reste vide sans sacrements; cependant, en Afrique on a tendence à accorder trop d'importance au Baptême qui constitue la marque d'identification avec la 'culture missionnaire'. L'Eucharistie est souvent associée à des craintes magiques. Les services de ces deux sacraments devraient être mieux et plus clairement expliqués.

Les sacrements résument également la tension eschatologique de l'Évangile dans laquelle l'Église est appelée à vivre: les chrétiens ont été incorporés au Christ, sont morts et ressucités avec lui. Mais, paradoxalement, ils attendent la Fin, la Parousie la manifestation complète du Règne de Dieu.

L'Église devrait devenir le centre de l'existence de ses fidèles et ainsi remplir le vide de la vie tribale sans le Christ. C'est ainsi que l'Évangile éternel pourrait s'acclimater à l'Afrique.

PART THREE

TRENDS AND PROSPECTS IN AFRICAN CHRISTIANITY

INTRODUCTORY REVIEW

(a) *African Christianity and Modern Problems*

Dr. Reardon sharpened a question posed by Professor Idowu's paper on the problem of the churches in Africa as follows: Christianity came in with European colonialism; how are we to prevent its going out with European colonialism? While Professor Idowu did not suggest that Christianity had not come to stay in Africa, he did point out that the Church is still a dependent one, looking to missionaries from outside for manpower and material resources, dependent in its theology, its liturgy, and its church discipline, in fact in its whole expression of the Christian life. It should not be forgotten that historically the Church once before came to tropical Africa along with European civilization and, when that influence was removed, simply disintegrated. We should consider how far the Church in Africa today possessed assets which it did not have when the Portuguese evangelization of the fifteenth and sixteenth centuries came to an end, and how far it displayed some of the same weaknesses of that earlier period.

There appeared to be some similarities between the two situations. The training and availability of African clergy had not kept pace with the rapid expansion of the Church. Taking the Catholic Church, the existing ratio between priests and members is 1 : 10,000; with the best present efforts a ratio of 1 : 9,000 might conceivably be achieved in ten years' time. Considering that the normal ratio is about 1 : 1,000, this state of affairs showed up the utter inadequacy of the supply of African clergy for the needs of the Church. If foreign clergy were withdrawn now, there would be a sort of 'South American' situation, with a vast Catholic community cut off from the sacraments and any effective Christian teaching.

On the Protestant side, the 'missions' had developed into the 'churches' along different lines in different places. However, had not much of this remained a sort of legal fiction so long as the African churches could not in fact provide for their own needs in personnel and funds?

Everywhere today pastoral care and instruction were woefully inadequate, an uncomfortable reminder of the earlier Portuguese situation when Christian teaching was limited to the tiny minority who were prepared to learn Latin and be taught in Portuguese. One factor which contributed to the Portuguese failure was that missionary work appeared to be closely linked with the slave trade. Fortunately the nineteenth-century missionary effort could be linked rather with the anti-slavery movement and in addition most past and contemporary leaders of African nationalism had been products of mission schools, paralleling the provision of leadership by the free churches in the movements for political, social, and economic emancipation of the working classes in England. However, their Christian background was generally only grudgingly recognized (if at all) by African nationalists with their global criticism of the Church as a 'European' affair.

On the positive side intense language study had been done by missionary agencies and Scripture translations made into many vernaculars. A start, however feeble, had indeed been made towards attaining the goal of self-supporting and self-propagating African Churches, which had not been the case in the past. It was doubtless necessary, in the face of such scanty resources, for Catholics and Protestants seriously to consider joining forces where such co-operation raised no problems of conscience, as for example in Bible translation work or in scientific or humanitarian institutions, i.e. hospitals, welfare clinics, social research centres, etc. The Church would survive in Africa only if it could achieve a fundamental change in the way of life of the peoples.

Discussing Mr. Long's paper, Professor Shepperson summed up the situation in these words: 'The complex story of Watch Tower in Africa mirrors, in religious terms, much of the secular politics and philosophies of socialism and social change from the 1870s onwards.' He developed this theme as follows:

Within two years of the introduction of the doctrines of the Watch Tower Bible and Tract Society into Central Africa in the first decade of the present century, the movement had begun to split into those African groups who were content to follow the leadership of American and European agents and those who broke away from these and set up their own Watch Tower bodies which sometimes followed the original doctrines and which, in other instances, elaborated these into relatively new and more Africanist forms.

In whatever form of association with the parent American body, the Watch Tower movement has had its greatest effect in Zambia, Malawi, the Congo, and in the border regions of the neighbouring territories of Central and East Africa.

The proliferation of independent African religious groups—of which Africanist Watch Tower is a leading but by no means the only feature—by Malawi migrants (usually Tonga) is an important element in the Central-East-South African labour cycle. This cycle and other migratory labour forces in Africa need to be studied carefully with respect to the kind of Christian and other religious bodies which they establish in the areas to which they remove themselves. It would probably be found that they set up, in the case of Christianity, groups which were, in the main, allied with 'orthodox', European or American-led missions. It would be a mistake to suppose that labour migrants are great proliferators of independent, 'heretical' Africanist churches and groups. Nevertheless, in the case of Watch Tower, it must never be forgotten that the movement, Euro-American or Africanist in leadership, originated and developed in the course of a long and complex labour cycle, having Malawi as its centre, in the first sixty years of the present century.

Few writers on Watch Tower, of whatever variety, in Africa and in other so-called underdeveloped countries, comment on what has been and probably still is one of its greatest attractions for its adherents: its provision of an historical philosophy. For peoples whose sense of history was, through no fault of their own other than the sheer accident of birth, limited in chronological and geographical extent, Christianity as a historical religion in its very essence, provided a philosophy of history. Few Christian groups, however, in their initial contacts with Africans, articulated this historical philosophy as clearly as did the followers of Pastor Charles Taze Russell and, later, of Judge Rutherford, Russell's successor in 1917 as President of the Watch Tower Bible and Tract Society. Their systematic expositions of this historical philosophy, based on Russell's original *Studies in the Scriptures*, reached out through book, pamphlet, leaflet, gramophone record, cinema film, and last, but not least, the human voice, bringing a view of universal history to many whose horizons had been originally restricted to a cluster of villages and to a relatively narrow circle of kinsmen. Whether Watch Tower will continue to supply this function today is doubtful. New, secular versions of historical philosophy—some, incidentally, as intrinsically millenarian as anything of Russell's—vie for African allegiance. But, in the past, Watch Tower, with its dramatic unrolling of the centuries, according to a pre-arranged divine pattern, has undoubtedly filled a social and spiritual need—if one may dare to separate those adjectives—of the highest order.

Furthermore, Watch Tower allegiances, particularly those closely connected with the parent American body, like Mr. Long's Serenje Lala, have given Africans a feeling not only of being linked to a long and well-ordered past but also of being part of an extensive and well-arranged present which, through the intricate and widespread organization of Jehovah's Witnesses, starting at Columbia Heights in Brooklyn, U.S.A., and reaching out, through its complex system of the pastorhood of all believers, elaborate documentation, report and check at every stage, down to the smallest villages, must give its adherents a feeling of belonging to an enormous body of universal proportions. It would be interesting to learn whether this impression has increased during the post-war period when the Witnesses have started holding large rallies for their followers in Central Africa.

To-day, 'orthodox' followers of Jehovah's Witnesses and, perhaps also, 'unorthodox' Africanist Watch Tower groups are not considered anti-colonial. From the late 1930s, Central African colonial governments began to regard them with less suspicion and, in some areas, it would seem, started positively to encourage them as safety-valves. And, of course, in an age of independent African governments, these groups can hardly be called agents of imperialism—except, however, when they refuse to salute the flag or to consider politics as anything but the agency of Satan. However, I must note that the Tanzanian Government has declared the Watch Tower Bible and Tract Society unlawful on the grounds that, to quote from the official statement, 'the activities of the Society in the United Republic have been incompatible with the maintenance of peace, order and good government'. Nevertheless, up until at least the mid-1930s, if not later, Watch Tower groups, willingly, often played an anti-imperialist role. Something of their role in the fight against colonialism can be seen in this quotation from a Rhodesian police report of 1923. An African Watch Tower preacher was reported as saying, 'In America, the home of my church, the natives are equal to the white men and that is why the English people in Rhodesia do not want the American type of religion in this country. If the American Churches are allowed to open here—that is the Church of the Watch Tower—all the natives will leave the other churches and join the Church of the Watch Tower.'[1] This primitive Watch Tower fantasy, in an age of mass communications informing Africans of the civil rights struggle in the United States and at a time when America does not appear to Africans as a uniformly liberatory force, gives this statement a curiously old-fashioned air. But it was this kind of belief, in addition to its built-in 'anti-governments of this world' attitude, that gave to Watch Tower its anti-imperialist associations.

[1] National Archives, Salisbury, Rhodesia: N.3/5/8, Administrator's Report, 17 July 1923, Salisbury, 'Native preacher—Kunga'.

The change today indicates that, for Watch Tower, as for other Christian bodies in Africa, a chronological approach is necessary. This would appear to be true for their social composition as well as for their political and ideological attitudes. Mr. Long's Jehovah's Witnesses group in the 1960s, whose members own 'the only two diesel-engine grinding mills and four of the six motor vehicles in Nchimishi' are, at least at first sight, very different beings from the hundred and twenty-odd Watch Tower men who were tried at Kasama in Zambia for various offences in 1919. Mr. L. H. Gann, the official historian of Northern Rhodesia, has said of them that 'they appealed to a rural proletariat in an isolated part of Northern Rhodesia where there were few opportunities for economic advancement and much distress'.[2] The social composition of the African Watch Tower adherents associated with the Copper Belt disturbances of 1935 was, again, probably—and here I must stress the word 'probably'—of a different nature: at least, the African Watch Tower followers on the Copper Belt at that time were, presumably, not making an appeal to a rural proletariat. Again, the complexity of social composition in Central African Watch Tower groups is illustrated by a report from the Livingstone Criminal Investigation Department for 1934 in which it was noted that the local Watch Tower sect had split into two groups, one of which consisted of domestic servants, and the other of unemployed.[3]

The student of Watch Tower and similar forces in Africa, whether a practising Christian or not, must pay as much attention to the Bible as the groups he is observing do. Here it is interesting to note that Mr. Long quotes from a 1958 Watch Tower pamphlet in which there is a quotation from Micah (IV, 5): 'Nation shall not lift up sword against nation, neither shall they learn war any more'. This suggests a pacifist, quietist attitude amongst certain contemporary Witness groups in Zambia. In the mid-1930s, it was different; local groups chose different passages from Micah, ones which seemed to the Administration to ring with sedition: Micah (III, 11, Rev. Version), 'The heads thereof judge for reward, and the priests thereof teach for hire'; (VII, 3), 'Their hands are upon that which is evil . . .; the prince asketh, and the judge is ready for a reward; and the great man he uttereth the mischief of his soul.'[4]

To mention the ransacking of the Bible by the various African and other Watch Tower groups is to imply the importance which the acquisition of the skill of reading has for them. Mr. Long stresses the emphasis which the contemporary Witnesses place on literacy classes in rural African society. This can be seen at the beginning of the movement in Malawi and Zambia in the first two decades of this century. Watch Tower literature was relatively cheap and plentiful and, partly for this reason, the movement spread amongst Africans avid for reading material which could not be readily supplied by many other missions. In emphasising this point, however, one

[2] Gann, *History of Northern Rhodesia* (London, 1964), p. 169.

[3] Ibid., p. 304.

[4] Ibid., p. 305.

must indicate that this early Watch Tower literature was in English, not in the vernaculars. Such Watch Tower translations probably did not appear to any great extent until the late 1920s and early 1930s. Thus, for the first two decades of the movement, perhaps, another function of its literature was that it helped to provide training in English for Africans from missions in which the emphasis was on the vernaculars rather than on the language of the ruling Power. If this assumption is correct, it might be said that, for all the reservations I have made earlier about changing social composition of African Watch Tower groups at different periods and in different places, there has always been an element in them of what Mr. Long, following the vocabulary of his Serenje Lala, calls the *basambashi*, or what we might call generally the 'smart', the idea that it was—perhaps is?—smart to be a Watch Tower man.

Except by making the boundaries of the already over-elastic term unduly inclusive, I doubt whether any Watch Tower group, even the most anti-imperialist, has contributed much to pan-Africanism either in practice or theory: theirs is a view which, in practice, by the very nature of their assumptions about God and man, is of little use to the practical pan-Africanist because of the Witnesses' distrust of all worldly governments. Africanist Watch Tower, on the other hand, while it has often been, in practice, highly critical of European rule and thus, implicitly, anti-imperialist, and, thereby, on the road to pan-Africanism, has usually been so attached to local and particular causes and discontents that the wider implications of its criticisms of foreign Powers are lost.

(b) *Adjustment to New Tasks*

Fr. Bell considered that the discussions at the Seminar had thrown up two points which seemed to constitute a dilemma or contradiction. It had been suggested on the one hand, that Christianity made progress best in situations of social upheaval and change and, on the other, that it should try to integrate itself with the traditional pattern of life if it sought to be fully effective. This problem was particularly acute for the foreign missionary faced with the large-scale break-up of traditional culture in a process of rapid social change. 'Should he adopt his apostolic action so as to contribute to the acceleration of this change or should he try to slow down the process so that the good human values in the traditional way of life were not lost in the shuffle? Or should he strive to adopt a completely neutral view, merely preaching the Gospel and leaving to the Africans the task of integrating it into a new way of life?'

Other pertinent questions within this area are those of the relations of the Churches with the new independent governments and of the place of these specifically African problems within the context of the world-wide situation confronting Christianity. Here it was noted that nationalists blamed Christian missionaries as much for having allegedly destroyed African culture as for having impeded modern advance by trying to preserve elements of this culture, as for example, by the use of the vernaculars and of African symbolism in religious rites. The basic fact of the situation appears to be that Christianity is engaged with forms of living not completely in accord with itself. In the process of the change the people's traditional identity is inevitably altered if not completely lost, and those who have initiated such changes have no real control over the new identity which the people come to construct for themselves.

Three distinct levels of this change can be distinguished: the first is exterior, a surface phenomenon; the second is one of social evolution, which represents change at a deeper level; the third is found in thought patterns, and this takes place at the deepest levels, where religious attitudes also belong. There is a time-lag in this three-level process, the surface changes being much more rapid than the deep-level ones, so that the Church tends inevitably to be somewhat behind the times in adapting itself. Christianity has come not to destroy but to fulfil and to redeem, but the fact remains that not everything in traditional society can be fulfilled or redeemed in the Christian sense. And, at the same time, a constant effort is required on the part of the Church to make itself relevant to the real needs of the modern situation.

In the new independent states of Africa, the Churches must first of all strive for a full understanding of what government and people are struggling to attain. The Churches must identify themselves as far as possible without compromising their own principles, with the national social, economic, and even political aims, adapting their action to the new situation and co-operating in the national effort to the fullest practicable extent. The Churches have always been in the vanguard of African development and indeed possess a splendid record in endeavours for the general advancement of the people. The legitimate aspirations and demands of the new nations deserve their fullest support.

There was considerable evidence at the seminar to the effect that Christian agencies were already making positive and imaginative response to this challenge. For example, realizing that one of the urgent needs for nation-building is personnel trained in the socio-economic fields, men and women who can join technical competence to a deep commitment to serve Christ and the common good of their societies, the White Fathers have undertaken several projects to provide the necessary preparation. They have Social Training Centres located in Mwanza, Tanzania; in Bukavu, Congo; and in Bobo-dioulasso, Upper Volta. The two-year course offered in these centres is built around studies in Social Ethics and includes economics, sociology, trade unionism, credit unions, co-operatives, book-keeping, public speaking, and logic. The Tanzanian Centre also has a school of journalism. The Fathers of the Jesuit African Mission have established a Centre INADES (Institut Africain pour le Developpement Économique et Social) at Abidjan, Ivory Coast, from which a staff of qualified resident tutors conduct correspondence courses for French-speaking Africans in social and economic studies.

At a Roman Catholic Pan-African Catechetical conference held at Katigondo in August 1964 it was decided to set up an All-Africa Catechetical Institute composed of two sections: one for the training of Catechetical specialists and the other for continuing research into the problem of adapting catechetical methods and liturgical practice to African modes of thought and ritual. This institute which will be situated in Rwanda and, at the request of the African Bishops, will be under the direction of the White Fathers, will carry out systematic collection and classification of all published material pertaining to catechetical and liturgical adaptation.

On the Protestant side the most significant effort in this context is the Ecumenical Institute at Mindolo near Kitwe, Zambia, which has schools for writers and artists and conducts residential courses of varying duration for farmers and smallholders, community developers, home-makers, and those engaged in various industrial, commercial, and social activities. The courses are intensely practical and are geared to forging links between the Church and the African world.

A joint enterprise by Roman Catholics and Protestants, with the financial support of the Ford Foundation, namely, the Institute of Social Studies ('Feres Project') at the Hague, Holland, also deserves mention in this connexion. It is undertaking detailed and authoritative field and documentary studies of all aspects of Christian activity in specified (including African) countries in turn, with a view to securing comprehensive, unified, and dependable statistics and other information.

XVI. MARIAGE ET FAMILLE DANS LES GROUPES CHRISTIANISÉS OU EN VOIE DE CHRISTIANISATION DE DAKAR

V. MARTIN

Dans cette communication, nous nous proposons:

1. de présenter rapidement la communauté catholique africaine de Dakar;
2. d'insister sur les situations matrimoniales rencontrées.

Ce travail repose sur un recensement que nous avons exécuté en 1961 près des catholiques de l'agglomération dakaroise. Il apparaîtra donc surtout comme descriptif et statistique. En effet nous avions alors comme objectif de situer la minorité catholique dans le contexte dakarois et de relever les situations particulières aux diverses ethnies.

I. LA CHRÉTIENTÉ DE DAKAR

1. *Les populations de Dakar*

Commençons ici par situer notre population dans l'ensemble urbain de Dakar. Au recensement administratif de 1961, Dakar accusait 370.000 habitants, gros accroissement par rapport au chiffre de 1955 (230.000).

Mettons d'abord à part les 40 000 non africains, pour la plupart européens et libano-syriens. Nous obtenons pour la population africaine la répartition suivante:

—Oulofs et Lébous	60%
—Toucouleurs, Peuls, Saracolés	20%
—Sérères	7%
—Mandingues	7%
—Diolas	4%
—Maures et autres	2%

Il reste difficile de préciser dans quelle mesure ces populations sont réellement fixées à Dakar. Disons seulement que la population flottante se situe entre 10 et 15% de l'ensemble recensé.

2. *Les Chrétiens dans la cité*

Au prémier abord, il pourrait sembler que règne là une certaine uniformité, celle provenant de la prépondérance de l'Islam.

En effet, on ne peut qu'être frappé par la densité des lieux de prière musulmans. Il n'est aucun quartier qui ne possède une mosquée même modeste. Rien que dans l'agglomération, il y en aurait près de 80.

L'Islam s'affirme d'abord en face des religions traditionnelles, du moins sur le plan de la statistique, aucun animiste n'osant se déclarer tel à l'occasion d'un recensement. Le même phénomène, il est vrai joue en faveur du christianisme, et nous-mêmes, n'avons pû nous dispenser d'inscrire 1.500 adultes, non baptisés et non catéchumènes, se disant malgré tout chrétiens.

Au recensement de 1955, les Musulmans formaient 81% de la population dakaroise, 92% des africains. Ces proportions sont à peu près les mêmes aujourd'hui si on se réfère au sondage de 1961.

Quels sont en regard les effectifs chrétiens?

Nous pouvons retenir le chiffre de 53.000 catholiques. Il convient d'y ajouter quelques centaines (400 en 1955) de protestants. Les catholiques, à l'intérieur de la cité, représentent donc 14% de la population totale. Les africains, au nombre de 24.000 constituent 7% de leur propre population.

Par 'africains', nous entendons tous les originaires du continent africain et des îles adjacentes. Ainsi les natifs de l'Archipel du Cap-Vert et leurs enfants, qu'ils soient restés ou non de nationalité portugaise sont ici comptés comme africains.

Les 'non africains' comprennent en premier lieu les européens, surtout français et quelques 2.000 Libanais. Rappelons que le recensement administratif donne le chiffre de 38.000 non africains (en excluant les Cap-Verdiens et les Métis). La différence avec le chiffre des catholiques—29.000—est imputable tant à la part de l'Islam chez les Libanais (7.000) qu'à la présence d'autres confessions ou opinions chez les européens.

En 1955, le chiffre total des chrétiens était de 38.000 dont 23 000 non africains. L'équilibre numérique, tend à s'établir entre les deux communautés. Malgré une forte augmentation de leurs effectifs, les Européens constituent aujourd'hui 55% du total des chrétiens contre 60% en 1955.

Cette population chrétienne vit à l'état de dispersion au milieu de la masse musulmane: 20% seulement des catholiques africains habitent des quartiers à dominante chrétienne, le plus souvent en raison du caractère européen de ceux-ci. Il est cependant peu de quartier où les catholiques ne soient présents, ne serait-ce qu'en infime minorité. Ainsi un tiers d'entre eux vit dans des secteurs où leur proportion n'atteint qu'un très faible pourcentage.

Cette dispersion correspond à ce qu'on peut observer dans la carte ethnique de Dakar. Dans la masse ouolof complètement islamisée, les autres groupes, qu'ils soient ou non eux-mêmes islamisés, ne peuvent s'insérer que dans des proportions assez minces et d'une façon sporadique. Notons seulement des concentrations plus fortes pour les groupe sérère et mandjaque, constitués de travailleurs saisonniers, qui se contentent d'habitat très modeste, dans des secteur dits 'irréguliers'.

3. *Les groupes ethniques christianisés ou en cours de christianisation*

Parmi les nombreux groupements qui composent le panorama ethnique de Dakar, nous n'aurons à en retenir ici que quelques uns. En effet, la chrétienté du Sénégal, tardivement implantée sur le continent, s'est heurtée rapidement à l'influence musulmane et a dû limiter ses efforts aux régions restées animistes, ellesmêmes déjà minoritaires.

Ainsi, le catholicisme dakarois, outre l'élément européen, a été formé par trois apports: l'héritage de Gorée-Dakar, la double immigration en provenance des îles du Cap-Vert et des pays du Sud, enfin, l'implantation progressive des Sénégalais d'origine rurale.

Pour faciliter l'exploitation du recensement, nous avons distingué six groupes principaux. Nous en donnons ici une rapide nomenclature.

1. *Les originaires et metis:* Ce groupe rassemble tous les Catholi-

ques sénégalais issus d'un milieu social extracoutumier: ressortissants des anciennes communes (Gorée, Dakar, St-Louis, Rufisque) et métis ne se reconnaissant aucune appartenance ethnique particulière.

2. *Les Cap-Verdiens:* Nous avons recensé 4.500 catholiques dans ce groupe, qui pourrait également englober quelques 200 personnes d'une autre religion: protestants, adventistes, témoins de Jéovah, spirites.

Nous pouvons diviser cette population en quatre sous-groupes suivant les pays d'origine: les plus nombreux, parce que plus anciennement implantés à Dakar, restent les Praia-Maio (50%). Viennent ensuite les St-Vincent et St-Antoine (1/3), les Brava et Fogo (13%), les autres îles (St-Nicolas, Sal, Boa-Vista) ne fournissent qu'un faible contingent.

3. *Les Sérères:* Sur les 20.000 Sérères pouvant habiter Dakar nous en avons recensé 3.700. On peut donc escompter que 20% de ce groupe résidant ou passant à Dakar, sont christianisés.

4. *Les Diolas:* Les différentes fractions diolas de Dakar ont donné le chiffre de 3.000 catholiques soit à peu près la moitié de leur colonie dakaroise.

5. *Les Mandjaques:* Cette appellation renferme les Mandjaques proprement dits (3.600), les Mankagnes (500), les Papels et Balantes (250) tous groupes originaires de Guinée Portugaise mais dont beaucoup, surtout les Mankagnes, ont déjà séjourné en Casamance. Bien que de fond animiste, ces groupes se déclarant 'christaô', nous les avons enregistrés comme tel.

6. *Les autres africains:* Cette catégorie englobe tous les ressortissants des autres Etats africains et en premier lieu les Dahoméens et Togolais (1.800). L'ensemble du groupe se chiffre à 2.500 individus, un certain nombre a été recensé dans les camps de l'armée de la Communauté, mais la plupart sont des fonctionnaires et employés de commerce.

4. *Répartition générale des groupes*

Nous constatons pour les six groupes, l'ordre d'importance suivant:

1. Cap-Verdiens,	4 492–22%	5. Originaires et métis	2 521–12,5%
2. Mandjaques	4 287–21%	6. Les 'autres'	2 523–12,5%
3. Sérères	3 721–18%		
4. Diolas	2 888–14%		

On remarque d'abord la prépondérance des apports originairement étrangers au Sénégal. En effet, Cap-Verdiens, Mandjaques et autres totalisent 55% de l'effectif.

Les populations du Sénégal intérieur—Sérères et Diolas—forment un tiers.

Quant aux anciennes chrétientés locales, elles ne sont représentées que dans la proportion de 6%.

Un regroupement plus large des ethnies pourrait s'opérer en fonction des milieux qu'elles représentent, du moins approximativement. Nous aurions alors à distinguer deux milieux:

(*a*) un milieu extra-coutumier composé des Originaires, Métis, Cap-Verdiens et autres.

(*b*) un milieu traditionnel formé de Sérères, Diolas et Mandjaques.

Numériquement, ces deux milieux s'équilibrent à peu près à Dakar.

Il serait intéressant de suivre, sur une période assez longue l'évolution des effectifs de ces divers groupes. Ici encore, nous n'avons comme référence assez sûre que le recensement de 1955, date il est vrai encore bien rapprochée. Nous avions alors cette répartition:

1. Cap-Verdiens	24%	4. Originaires	15%
2. Autres	20%	5. Sérères	13%
3. Mandjaques	15%	6. Diolas	13%

Les modifications récentes avantagent donc Mandjaques et Sérères, au détriment des 'autres' passés du 2ème rang en 1955 en queue de liste, leur immigration étant stoppée.

Mandjaques et Sérères ont augmenté de 100% au cours des six dernières années, les Diolas de 60%, les Cap-Verdiens de 32%, les Originaires et Métis de 20%. Par contre le chiffre des Dahoméens a diminué de 10%.

Cependant, pour juger de l'évolution sur une période importante, nous pouvons recourir aux registres de baptêmes. C'est ce que nous avons essayé de faire en attribuant à chaque numéro d'acte, l'ethnie de l'intéressé.

Une première tranche par groupe détaillé a été étudiée de 1936 à 1960.

Nous obtenons les proportions suivantes pour les groupes traditionnels:

Pour l'avant-guerre	36%
de 1940 à 1950	44%
après 1950	56%

Ce dernier résultat confirmant notre calcul sur les effectifs actuels, la méthode utilisée semble donc également valable pour les périodes antécédentes. Avant guerre, la chrétienté africaine était donc encore, pour près des deux tiers composée des Cap-Verdiens (48%) Métis et Originaires. D'autres part, l'élément européen, ne représentant alors qu'un tiers des effectifs globaux, le groupe extra-coutumier s'imposait également numériquement sur le plan de l'ensemble.

C'est tout de suite après guerre que s'amorce la montée des effectifs de baptêmes. Toutes les ethnies y participent, à partir de 1954. Sérères et Mandjaques accentuent leur progression, rattrapant les effectifs Cap-Verdiens. Notons qu'au cours de cette même période, la croissance de baptêmes des Diolas est beaucoup plus lente. Quant aux Européens, on note une diminution à partir de 1955.

Signalons enfin que depuis 1936, le chiffre total annuel des baptêmes a presque quadruplé. Quant à celui des Sérères, Diolas, Mandjaques, il a plus que quintuplé.

Cette progression dénote l'importance du problème de l'émigration comme le montre cette enquête sur les dates d'installation à Dakar.

5. *Dates d'installation à Dakar*

L'enquête a porté sur 6.800 recensés soit 70% des domiciliés nés de Dakar. Le mouvement d'installation à Dakar n'a vraiment démarré qu'après la dernière guerre mondiale. En effet les 4/5 de nos immigrants ne sont à Dakar que depuis 1945.

On observe la progression suivante:

Avant 1920	1%
1920 à 1929	4%
1930 à 1949	15%
1950 à 1960	71,5%
Total =	100

Chez les Métis et originaires le mouvement vers Dakar a été progressif mais il a atteint son plein au moment du transfert de la capitale depuis Saint-Louis (1958): 57% des immigrés sont alors devenus dakarois.

L'immigration Cap-Verdienne est très ancienne et a été continue: 28% sont arrivés avant 1940 surtout dans les années 1930–34. Cependant 40% ne sont à Dakar que depuis 1955.

Chez les autres groupes, l'immigration n'a été importante qu'à partir de 1950, concernant de 75 à 80% de ces populations.

Jusqu'en 1934 les Cap-Verdiens l'ont emporté dans le courant migratoire suivis de loin par les Mandjaques 11%. Sitôt après guerre, les Cap-Verdiens n'ont plus formé que le tiers, puis le quart progressivement supplantés par les Mandjaques et les apports sérères et diolas.

Dans l'émigration, il y a participation diverse des sexes. Les femmes sont en général plus nombreuses 90 pour 100 hommes, sauf chez les Sérères, les Mandjaques et les 'Autres', en raison de l'importance des migrations cap-verdiennes et diolas. Notons cependant que le déséquilibre des sexes était autrefoie plus accusé, sauf pour les Diolas, où se maintient aujourd'hui une majorité féminine importante (60 hommes pour 100 femmes).

Par contre, chez les Cap-Verdiens, tendance à une augmentation des effectifs masculins.

Parmi les nouveaux immigrants on en trouve peu de plus de 30 ans (16%), sauf chez les Cap-Verdiens (25%). L'âge à l'immigration se situe entre 20 et 30 ans (42%), légèrement avancé chez les Diolas et les Mandjaques.

Qu'en est-il de cette progression des migrations à tendance définitive?

Ecartons les catégories 'Autres' et les Originaires et Métis, dont les mouvements ont été occasionnés par des appels particuliers et transitoires (besoins de l'Administration). Nous obtenons la progression suivante:

Base 100 en 1945, situation en 1960:

Mandjaques	de 100 à 500
Diolas	de 100 à 370
Sérères	de 100 à 320
Cap-Verdiens	de 100 à 220

Afin de mieux situer cette progression dans le contexte général, nous nous permettons de renvoyer le lecteur à ce que nous écrivions en 1960 (*Recensement démographique de Dakar* (1955) p. 49).

Si on ne tient compte que des immigrants, la moitié de ceux-ci se serait installée dans les cinq dernières années. Cette proportion peut paraître exorbitante; mais il est sûr que, depuis 1958 en particulier, la ruée vers Dakar n'a cessé d'augmenter comme en témoigne l'extension des quartiers irréguliers.

Pour 100 immigrants annuels dans les années 1940 à 1949, on en compterait 170 entre 1950 et 1954, 224 en 1955, 290 en 1957, 455 en 1958, 720 en 1959.

Ces chiffres ne concernent que la population reconnue comme résidant à Dakar. Quant à la population saisonnière ou flottante, elle atteint comme pour l'ensemble 15% des recensés avec des différences notables par groupes et sexes (ainsi 35% des Sérères et 25% des Diolas). Forte prépondérance féminine chez les Sérères et Diolas, grosse majorité masculine chez les Mandjaques et autres.

Tous ces saisonniers arrivant à l'âge du mariage, ce phénomène comme nous le verrons, crée parfois de graves perturbations dans lessituations matrimoniales.

6. *La pratique religieuse. Le baptême*

Nous n'avons fait encore aucune enquête spéciale sur la pratique religieuse, nous réservant cette opération pour une étude ultérieure qui doit porter sur les attitudes et comportements religieux. Nous nous en tiendrons donc ici aux actes religieux essentiels, attitude en face du baptême et du mariage catholique.

(*a*) *Les catéchumènes.* Sur l'effectif catholique que nous avons annoncé, 2.300 ayant plus de 7 ans ne sont pas baptisés, soit 11,5%. Cependant 1 non baptisé sur 3 fréquente le catéchuménat. Le taux d'assiduité à l'enseignement catéchuménal est le suivant pour les ethnies en cours de christianisation.

Sérères	hommes	74%	des non baptisés.
Sérères	femmes	65%	„ „
Diolas	femmes	45%	„ „
Diolas	hommes	37%	„ „
Mandjaques	hommes	29%	„ „
Mandjaques	femmes	23%	„ „

Il nous reste donc une certaine population religieusement marginale: population non baptisée et non inscrite au catéchuménat, vivant dans une situation indécise par rapport à l'animisme traditionnel, sans vouloir opter d'une façon définitive pour le christianisme. Dans ce cas plus d'un tiers des Mandjaques, 8% des Diolas, 3% des Sérères.

(*b*) *Les baptêmes d'enfants.* Des enquêtes récentes ont été consacrées aux délais constatés dans l'administration du baptême des enfants. Entre la naissance et le baptême, s'observe en effet un certain temps dont la durée est très variable suivant les régions et les milieux. D'une façon générale les délais tendent à s'allonger. La régression de la mortalité infantile a favorisé indirectement crette tendance, la crainte de perdre le nouveau-né n'intervenant plus aujourd'hui aussi vivement qu'autrefois: d'autre part la discipline ecclésiastique s'est adaptée à cette évolution. L'obligation canonique (Can. 770) du 'quamprimum', n'intervenant 'au plus tôt', toujours en vigueur connait suivant les diocèses de multiples interprétations.

Quoiqu'il en soit de cette diversité, il semble que le dégré d'empressement apporté par les parents à faire baptiser leurs enfants soit assez révélateur, de leur comportement religieux.

Aussi ces mêmes enquêtes permettent-elles d'établir des corrélations entre fidélité au baptême à la pratique religieuse générale.

Dans le cas de la communauté catholique de Dakar, nous éviterons cependant de tirer dès maintenant des conclusions concernant le degré d'imprégnation chrétienne.

Nous sommes en effet en face de groupements d'âge religieux divers, aux origines multiples, d'habitudes religieuses parfois différentes. Aussi nous nous contentons de présenter une situation.

Cette étude sur les délais de baptêmes a été faite à partir des registres des paroisses. Elle ne concerne donc que les seuls baptisés à Dakar. D'autre part nous nous sommes limité à quelques périodes seulement: 1934–38; 1946–50; 1956–60. Pour les différenciations ethniques, nous nous sommes basé sur les noms de famille et la connaissance que nous en avions à la suite du recensement.

La comparaison entre les trois périodes retenues manifeste pour l'ensemble une amélioration de l'empressement au baptême au cours de ces dernières années.

En particulier, les huit premiers jours qui ne connaissaient jusqu'en 1950 qu'une fréquentation de 5 et 6% atteignent en 1956, 12%. De même les baptêmes tardifs après le 4ème mois sont tombés de 32% en 1938 à 25% en 1960.

Cependant le relèvement ne se constate que pour quelques groupes: européen, sérère et diola. Ailleurs, il y a stabilisation et même régression chez les 'autres' et les Libanais.

Le classement peut se faire d'abord en tenant compte de certaines échéances, les mêmes pour tous les groupes. Aussi dans nos tableaux avons-nous retenu la semaine pour le premier mois, la quinzaine pour le 2ème mois, ensuite une division mensuelle.

Nous obtenons l'ordre suivant pour l'empressement au baptême dans les années 1956–60.

1. Sérères
2. Diolas
3. Européens
4. Dahoméens et autres
5. Mandjaques
6. Métis
7. Cap-Verdiens
8. Libanais

A l'observance des premiers huit jours sont fidèles 38% des Sérères, 11% des Européens et Diolas, 5 à 7% des autres groupes à l'exclusion des Libanais (2%).

A la fin du premier mois sont baptisés les trois quarts des Sérères, la moitié des Diolas, le tiers des européens, Mandjaques et autres, le quart des métis, 19% des Cap-Verdiens et seulement 9% de Libanais.

Chez les Européens, Mandjaques et 'autres', un deuxième tiers est baptisé au cours des 2ème et 3ème mois.

Chez les Métis et surtout les Cap-Verdiens, les délais s'allongent démusurément, à tel point qu'en fin d'année il en reste encore de 11 à 16% à baptiser.

Les Libanais sont les moins empressés avec un tiers de l'effectif dans les trois premiers mois, un autre tiers du 4ème au 7ème mois.

Dans ce dernier groupe, le baptême, occasion d'une grande fête, exige la conjonction d'un certain nombre de conditions, dont le rassemblement d'une famille très dispersée, si bien que de délai en délai plusieurs frères et soeurs peuvent être présentés ensemble au baptême. De là, le nombre de baptême de plus d'un an: 17%.

Peut-on d'après ces chiffres interpréter la diversité des comportements en face du baptême? Il y a d'une part la rigidité des échéances que le clergé a mission de rappeler mais il y a aussi une certaine appréciation des délais par les familles elles-mêmes. Or celle-ci comme nous allons le voir, varie d'un groupe à l'autre.

En effet, le comptage par délais très rapprochés—le jour ou la semaine—manifeste l'existence de certains seuils ou paliers plus fréquentés. Pour simplifier nous pouvons retenir cinq catégories de délais.

Premier délai: Il s'arrête aux dixième jour chez les Sérères au vingt-deuxième chez les Diolas et les Mandjaques, couvre tout le premier mois chez les Européens, Dahoméens, Métis et Cap-Verdiens. Il peut être reculé à la fin du deuxième mois pour les Libanais. Cette catégorie comprend tous ceux qui ont le souci de répondre à l'esprit de la discipline de l'Eglise.

Deuxième délai: Il correspond à la fin du premier mois chez les

Sérères, à la fin du deuxième mois chez les autres groupes. Pour les Libanais on peut reporter la limite à la fin du troisième mois. C'est la catégorie des observants assez tièdes.

Troisième délai: La pratique des deuxième et troisième mois chez les Sérères, des troisième et quatrième mois chez les autres groupes, du cinquième mois chez les Libanais constitue une catégorie que l'on peut taxer de négligente.

Quatrième délai: Pour tous les groupes, la fin de la première année marque un quatrième seuil.

Cinquième délai: Au-delà de la premère année.

A la première catégorie appartiennent 31% du total, 50% des Sérères, 37% des 'Autres', 18 et 19% des Libanais et Cap-Verdiens.

A la deuxième catégorie 21% du total (entre 13% Cap-Verdiens et 28% Diolas).

A la troisième catégorie 20% (entre 23% Mandjaques et 10% Libanais).

A la quatrième catégorie 18% (entre 41% Libanais et 9%).

A la cinquième catégorie 10% (entre 4% Sérères et 17% Libanais).

(*c*) *Les baptêmes d'adultes:* De 1930 à 1960 environ 3.500 baptêmes ont été conférés à des adultes dans les paroisses de Dakar. Dans ce nombres le groupe mandjaque figure pour 2.000 dont 800 entre 1956 et 1960. Au cours de ces dernières années près des trois quarts des baptisés adultes appartiennent donc à cette ethnie. Viennent ensuite les Diolas, pour la plupart de la région d'Oussouye. Les Sérères, bien que trés nombreux au catéchuménat, sont normalement baptisés dans leur pays d'origine.

Dans ces effectifs la part des femmes qui n'était au total que de 19% avant 1939 arrive depuis à 29%. Bien que constituant la moitié des baptêmes sérères, les trois quarts des baptêmes diolas, l'élément féminin chez les Mandjaques ne représente encore que 20% (1956–60).

A partir de la trentaine, on compte assez peu de baptêmes: 13%. Les plus gros effectifs (40 à 45%) se rencontrent entre 20 à 30 ans. Notons également que l'âge au baptême devient plus précoce. Avant la guerre, 30% seulement des baptisés adultes ayant moins de 20 ans contre 48% depuis la guerre.

Toutes ces remarques manifestent qu'il s'agit là d'une population surtout saisonnière. Cette mobilité explique le chiffre assez faible des baptisés adultes trouvés au recensement: 1900. En particulier sur les 2.000 Mandjaques baptisés de 1930 à 1960, 540 seulement ont été recensés.

(*d*) *Menages et situations de baptême des parents et enfants*—Plusieurs cas ont été envisagés.

(a) *Les parents sont catholiques:* 2.851 ménages soit 79,5%. Dans le cas de mariage religieux, il est très rare (1%) que des enfants restent non baptisés. Dans les unions irrégulières, et les ménages des seuls hommes ou femmes, 6% ne sont pas baptisés. Au total dans 4% de ces ménages, des enfants de plus de 1 an ne sont pas baptisés.

(b) *L'un des conjoints est catholique, l'autre musulman:* Nous n'avons ici enquêté que sur 139 ménages. Dans 60% de ceux-ci les enfants sont baptisés.

(c) *L'un des conjoints est catholique, l'autre païen:* 269 familles. Dans 90% des cas les enfants sont baptisés.

(d) *Les chefs de famille sont païens:* Sur 266 familles de la catégorie, 143, soit 54%, font baptiser leurs enfants.

II. LES SITUATIONS MATRIMONIALES

Tant du point de vue sociologique que pastoral, l'étude des situations matrimoniales revêt une importance particulière. Bien que nous nous proposions ici surtout une description démographique, les connexions et comparaisons que nous serons appelé à établir devront, souhaitons-le, un peu mieux situer les problèmes. Dans ce domaine, plus que dans tout autre, nous ne pouvons avancer qu'avec précaution. En effet, le maniement d'un questionnaire s'avère ici parfois délicat et l'interprétation des réponses, difficile. Outre les renseignements, somme toute assez neutres, concernant l'état-civil, il nous a fallu de plus juger des diverses situations par rapport à la discipline de l'Église. De là, les distinctions que nous avons établies à propos des personnes unies par un lien conjugal.

1. D'abord le mariage religieux, seul reconnu comme légitime par le Droit Canon.
2. L'union devant le seul État-Civil
3. L'union consensuelle ou concubinage
4. Le mariage coutumier (pour les non baptisés).

Normalement nous aurions dû référer les états de veuvage, de séparation ou de célibat à ces différentes sortes d'unions. Les renseignements exacts ayant été difficile à obtenir, nous avons simplifié ces données.

Pour le veuvage, nous nous en tenons aux déclarations des intéressés sans précision sur leur état antérieur. Quant au divorce, nous l'entendons au sens très restrictif de rupture actuelle du seul lien religieux. Il s'agit donc des divorcés non remariés, reconnus par l'Église comme 'séparés'. Les divorcés, remariés à la suite d'un premier mariage religieux, sauf comptages particuliers, rentrent dans les catégories 'mariés à l'état-civil' ou 'union consensuelle'. Notons aussi que surtout dans le cas des personnes âgées vivant seules, il a pu y avoir confusion entre célibat, veuvage et séparation d'un lien consensuel.

Enfin, bien que notre recensement ait porté sur l'ensemble de la population baptisée, nous n'avons pu prospecté dans son ensemble la fraction de catholiques passés à l'Islam pour des raisons de convenance matrimoniale. Cependant cette dernière étude est en cours pour diverses chrétientés rurales, à partir des registres de baptêmes.

1. *L'ensemble de la population*

Avant d'aborder la situation de la seule population catholique, faisons quelques observations concernant l'ensemble de la population dakaroise.

Très forte nuptialité, mais grande instabilité conjugale, telles sont les conclusions qui se dégagent des enquêtes antécédentes. Bien que se mariant tard, vers 27 ou 28 ans, très peu d'hommes restent tout eleur vie célibataires. Au delà de la cinquantaine, la proportion des célibataires varie entre 4% et 6%. (France 1956, 12%.)

Quant aux femmes, elles sont très tôt mariées. La moitié des 15–19 ans le sont déjà et entre 25 et 30 ans on ne compte plus que 6% de célibataires. (France 14%.) Par contre, nombreuses veuves à partir de la quarantaine, ainsi que 10% de divorcées.

La mobilité conjugale peut se calculer d'après le nombre de mariages contractés. Chez les hommes, on constate (sondage 1955) que pour 100 mariés de tous âges, il y a eu 175 mariages. Le nombre de leurs épouses étant de 121, ils seraient donc veufs ou séparés d'une cinquantaine de femmes.

Mais il est vraisemblable qu'il s'agit plutôt de divorcés, les chances de survie d'un homme à son épouse étant assez faibles. Côté femmes, 100 mariées de tous âges ont contracté en tout 147 mariages.

Cette instabilité semble inégalement grave suivant les ethnies.

Moindre chez les Peuls et Sérères, elle est particulièrement forte chez les Lébous et Ouolofs. On peut d'autre part, la mettre en relation avec le degré de polygamie.

Arrivons-en la nature du lien conjugal. Le mariage à l'état-civil est encore très rare en 1955 et ne concerne que 6% des mariés. La polygamie affecte 15% des hommes mariés. Faible chez les Maures (4%) les Diolas (5%) elle touche 19% des Ouolofs et 26% des Lébous. Au total, 30% des femmes mariées le sont à des polygames.

Suivant les groupes socio-professionnels il semble que la polygamie augmente avec le niveau social:

— fonctionnaires, petits patrons, commerçants	17,5%
— Ouvriers	11%
— Manoeuvres, boys	8,5%

Mais c'est évidemment en fonction de l'âge que croît la polygamie:

moins de 24 ans	2,5%	40–49 ans	19,5%
moins de 25–29 ans	3,5%	50–59 ans	25,5%
moins de 30–39 ans	10,5%	40–69 et plus	29%

D'après le sondage 1960, la polygamie serait aujourd'hui en accroissement

18% chez les 30–39 ans
33% chez les 40–49 ans
40% au-delà.

Qu'en est-il exactement? Dans l'état actuel d'exploitation de ce recensement, nous ne saurions nous prononcer.

2. *Comparaisons entre époques*

Le tableau suivant met en regard les pourcentages trouvés tant en 1955 pour les deux communautés qu'en 1961 pour la communauté chrétienne.

Situations	*Hommes*			*Femmes*		
	1955		1961	1955		1961
	Mus.	*Chrét.*	*Chrétiens*	*Mus.*	*Chrét.*	*Chrétiens*
Célibataires	44	52	50,5	20	35	39
Mariés	53	45	48,0	—	—	—
Mariées 1ères épouses	—	—	—	55	52	53
Mariées Autres épouses	—	—	—	11	—	—
Veufs (ves)	1	1,5	1,0	8	9	7
Divorcés (es)	2	1,5	0,5	6	4	1
Ensemble	100	100	100	100	100	100

(Toute population de + 14 ans, résidants et non résidants)

On remarquera une grande stabilité des taux, sauf pour les divorcés qui ont été entendus différemment.

Proportion légèrement plus forte de musulmans hommes mariés, en raison de facilités de remariage qui prolonge leur vie conjugale. Du côté féminin, même pourcentage d'épouses de premier rang. La polygamie chez les musulmans, si elle diminue le nombre de célibataires provoque un relèvement des taux de veuvage et de divorce.

Suivant les groupes d'âge, cet autre tableau résume la situation:

Groupes d'ages	*Pourcentages de Maries*				
	Hommes		*Femmes*		
	1955	1961	1955 (M + C)		1961
	Mus. + Chrét.	*Cath.*	*1ères épouses*	*Autres épouses*	*Chrét.*
14 à 19 ans	—	—	43	5	13,0
20 à 24 ans	11	11,5	68	11	49,5
25 à 34 ans	55	60,5	73	12	71,5
35 à 44 ans	83	84,5	67	13	66,0
45 à 54 ans	88	83,0	55	11	48,0
55 à 64 ans	87	84,0	37	7	30,0
65 et +	84	60,0	18	3	14,0

Nous pouvons remarquer ici le décalage des sexes dans l'âge au mariage. Ce n'est que vers la trentaine qu'apparait un pourcentage élevé chez les hommes et qui se maintiendra. A partir de ce même âge la proportion des femmes mariées ne cesse de diminuer.

Entre les deux communautés religieuses, peu d'écarts du côté masculin. Par contre comportement différent du côté féminin. Taux de nuptialité très supérieur à tous les âges de chez les musulmanes. Notons seulement qu'entre 25 et 45 ans la proportion des épouses de premier rang est la même.

Groupes d'ages	*Hommes*					*Femmes*				
	Cél.	*Mar.*	*Veuve*	*Div.*	*Total*	*Cél.*	*Mar.*	*Veuve*	*Div.*	*Total*
14–19	100,0	—	—	—	100	87,0	13,0	—	—	100
20–24	88,5	11,5	—	—	100	50,5	49,5	—	—	100
25–34	39,5	60,5	—	—	100	26,0	71,5	1,5	1,0	100
35–44	14,5	85,4	0,5	0,5	100	24,5	66,0	7,0	2,5	100
45–54	13,5	83,0	2,5	1,0	100	25,5	48,0	25,5	1,0	100
55–64	8,0	84,0	6,5	1,5	100	21,0	30,0	48,5	0,5	100
65–et +	5,0	60,0	32,5	2,5	100	24,5	14,0	61,0	0,5	100

Pour la seule population catholique (tableau suivant) en effet, on peut remarquer que beaucoup de femmes restent célibataires: à partir de 25 ans, un quart pour chaque groupe d'âges. Comme nous le notions tout à l'heure, il se peut qu'aient été comptées parmi les célibataires, des femmes ayant auparavent vécu en union consensuelle. Quoiqu'il en soit, cette incertitude dans les déclarations fait elle-même problème.

3. *Célibat et mariage. Groupes ethniques*

Hommes—Pour l'ensemble des chrétiens hommes, la moitié a été classée parmi les célibataires. Taux plus forts 55% et 56% chez les Diolas et Mandjaques. Taux plus faible chez les Cap-Verdiens (35%), les Sérères (37%) et les Métis (43%). Chez les 20–24 ans, seuls les Cap-Verdiens présentent un taux important de mariés 24%; il n'est ailleurs que de 10%.

Chez les plus de 35 ans, il ne reste plus que 13% de célibataires, mais seulement 8% chez les Sérères.

Femmes—Là aussi gros écarts entre un taux de 57% pour les Diolas et 30% pour les 'autres' en faveur du célibat. Taux pour l'ensemble: 39%.

Le mariage précoce touche surtout Mandjaques et 'Autres' où près du quart des 14–19 ans est marié. Au-delà de 35 ans, mis à part les Sérères et 'Autres' (13 et 14%) les taux de célibat sont encore importants. Ce tableau résume la situation.

Ethnies—pourcentages de celibataires par ages

Ages	*Mét. et Orig*	*C.V.*	*Sér*	*Dio*	*Mj*	*Aut*	*Total*	*Mét. et Orig*	*C.V.*	*Sér*	*Dio*	*Mj*	*Aut*	*Tota*
14–19 an	100	100	100	100	100	100	100	99	89	90	94	71	76	87
20–24 an	88	76	90	92	91	90	88	68	56	48	64	35	28	50
25–34 an	41	35	29	44	46	39	39	41	31	17	38	20	16	28
35–et +	10	13	8	17	18	13	13	20	24	13	27	—	14	25
Tous âges	43	35	37	55	56	50	50	41	35	50	57	37	30	39

4. *L'âge au mariage*

Les registres de mariages comportent la date de naissance des intéressés, il est donc facile de se livrer à des études sur l'âge au mariage.

Nous l'avons fait pour la période 1947–57 en distinguant, d'une part les Métis et Cap-Verdiens, d'autre part les Africains autochtones.

L'enquête a porté sur 780 mariés. Nous obtenons les taux

suivants en précisant qu'il s'agit des seules unions religieu ses (mariages ou remariages).

Groupe d'ages	*Hommes*		*Femmes*	
	Métis Cap-Verdiens	*Africain Autochtone*	*Métis Cap-Verdiens*	*Africaine Autochtone*
15 à 20 ans	—	—	8,0	14,0
20 à 24 ans	16,5	7,5	46,5	35,5
25 à 29 ans	26,5	27,5	17	24,0
30 à 34 ans	16,0	27,0	7,5	13,0
35 à 39 ans	11,5	19,5	4,0	5,5
40 à 44 ans	10,0	8,5	7,0	2,5
45 à 49 ans	8,5	4,0	5,5	2,5
50 à 54 ans	5,0	3,0	4,5	3,0
55 à et plus	6,0	9,0		
	100,0	100,0	100,0	100,0

Du côté masculin, le mariage, bien que plus précoce chez les métis et Cap-verdiens où 16% se marient de 20 à 24 ans, est retardé pour un grand nombre (41% après 35 ans).

Les deux tiers des africains sont mariés avant 35 ans.

Du côté féminin, une moitié se marie avant 25 ans, avec une avance chez l'africaine (14% avant 20 ans).

Chez les métisses également beaucoup de mariages retardés. L'âge moyen au mariage est cependant le même pour tous les groupes. Chez les hommes il est de 34 ans, chez les femmes de 27 ans. Si on ne calcule que sur les mariés de moins de 40 ans, il se ramène à 29 ans pour les hommes 24 ans pour les femmes.

Il y aurait donc une différence moyenne de 7 ans entre les conjoints. Pour un tiers des ménages étudiés, l'écart va de 0 à 4 ans, pour un autre tiers de 5 à 9 ans. Enfin pour 10% des ménages l'écart s'élève à plus de 15 ans.

Constatons aussi que dans quelques cas, la femme est plus âgée que son mari: 18% des couples métis, 10% des couples africains.

5. *Les catégories d'unions*

Mettons de suite à part le mariage coutumier. Nous avons appelé ainsi les unions des non baptisés, mais nous ne saurions affirmer qu'il s'agisse vraiment du mariage sanctionné par la coutume. Il se peut que ce ne soit là bien souvent qu'une union temporaire et de rencontre.

Nous nous expliquons.

Sur les 560 mariés de cette catégorie, 460 soit 80% appartiennent à l'ethnie mandjaque. Or précisément, dans le même groupe, chez les baptisés apparait également un pourcentage excessif de situations irrégulières (65,5). Sans préjuger des raisons profondes qui font hésiter les Mandjaques à s'engager dans le mariage indissoluble, on peut supposer que pour une part intervient l'absence d'une sanction apportée par le contrat coutumier.

3.200 recensés sont engagés dans un mariage religieux soit 61% des baptisés. Proportion légèrement supérieure du côté masculin —63%—un certain nombre d'épouses n'accompagnant pas leur mari dans les migrations (et donc n'étant pas recensées).

En mariage uniquement civil, nous avons compté 520 personnes, 9% des mariés. Ici les femmes l'emportent légèrement (9,5%). Rappelons que la discipline du diocèse exige pour le mariage religieux l'union civile préalable pour les populations relevant effectivement de l'État-civil: Européens, Métis français, Cap-Verdiens. Elle le conseille vivement pour les ressortissants sénégalais, sans l'exiger cependant.

L'union consensuelle est pratiquée par environ 1 550 baptisés.

Comme nous le verrons à propos de chaque groupe ethnique, certaines de ces unions revêtant un caractère stable pourraient à la riguer passer pour des mariages coutumiers (et officialisés par la parenté).

Repartition des mariés suivant les catégories d'unions

Categories	*Effectifs*			*Repartition en %*					
	H	*F*	*Ens.*	*H*	*F*	*Ens.*	*H*	*F*	*Ens.*
Baptisés									
Mariage Religieux	1 673	1 533	3 206	57,0	53,0	55,0	63,0	59,0	61,0
Union Civile	245	276	521	8,5	9,5	9,0	9,0	10,5	10,0
Union Consensuelle	748	798	1 546	25,5	27,5	26,5	28,0	30,5	29,0
Total	2 666	2 607	5 273	—	—	—	100	100	100
Non Baptisés									
Mariage Coutumier	274	285	559	9,0	10,0	9,5			
Ensemble	2 940	2 892	5 832	100	100	100			
(Indéterminé)	(12)	(66)	(78)						

6. *Ethnies et mariages religieux*

A ne prendre que la population baptisés vivant conjugalement nous obtenons cette répartition:

— Mariés à l'Église:	Hommes	63,5	Femmes	64,5
— Union Civile:	Hommes	9,0	Femmes	11,0
— Union Consensuelle:	Hommes	27,5	Femme	24,5
		100,0		100,0

Un tiers de la population chrétienne mariée se trouve donc du point de vue canonique en situation irrégulière. Cette proportion se ramène à 18% et 16% si on tient compte de toute la population baptisée de plus de 14 ans.

Nous donnons ici l'ordre dans lequel se présentent les groupes ethniques par rapport au mariage religieux (baptisés mariés seulement).

	Ensemble	*Hommes*	*Femmes*
1. Sérères Thiès	94,5%	97%	91%
Sérères Sine	89,0%	92%	86%
Originaires	87,0%	88%	86%
2. Métis	70%	63%	73%
Diolas Fogny	67,5%	73%	62%
3. Togolais-Dahoméens	60,0%	58%	63%
Voltaïques-Ivoiriens	59,5%	55%	66%
Cap-Verdiens de Païa	55,5%	59%	58%
4. Autres Diolas	44,5%	54%	41%
Autres Cap-Verdiens	38,5%	41%	37%
Mandjaques	34,5%	36%	33%

Ainsi voit-on se dégager quatre paliers d'observance, chacun rassemblant des populations très diverses.

Dans une première série tous les Sérères; mais on s'aperçoit que les vieilles missions de la Petite Côte et du Sine connaissent un certain fléchissement, qui les rapproche des anciennes populations de Gorée, Dakar, Rufisque, avec lesquelles elles entretiennent depuis longtemps des relations Dans ces groupes les hommes sont plus observants que les femmes, certaines étant unies à des étrangers parfois musulmans.

Une deuxième série manifeste une grosse disparité de taux par sexes, à l'avantage des femmes chez les Métis et des hommes chez les Diolas Fogny.

La troisième série concerne les groupes du Sud ainsi que les Cap-Verdiens de Praïa. Relevons pour les femmes du Sud des taux supérieurs de régularité.

La quatrième série manifeste des taux allant de 54% chez les hommes Diolas d'Oussouye à 34% chez les Mandjaques. A cette catégorie appartiennent aussi les Portugais de St-Vincent, St-Antoine, Brava, Fogo et St-Nicolas.

Par catégories socio-professionnelles, on constate que le mariage religieux est mieux observé dans les classes plus aisées. Ainsi, chez les cadres et employés, 75% des hommes et 79% des femmes sont unis à l'Eglise, alors que ces taux ne sont que de 60% et 58% chez les ouvriers et domestiques.

Cette différence se retrouve dans tous les groupes ethniques, sauf les Sérères.

	Métis	*Cap-Verdiens*	*Sérères*	*Diolas*
Cadres et Employés	81%	66%	88%	78%
Ouvriers et domestiques	61%	40%	86%	55%

7. *Les mariages purement civils*

Les mariés au seul Etat-Civil constituent, nous l'avons vu, 9% et 11% de notre population avec les variantes suivantes:

'Autres' Hommes	18%	Diolas Hommes	10%
'Autres' Femmes	15%	Mandjaques Hommes	9%
Cap-Verdiennes	14%	Mandjaques Femmes	9%
Cap-Verdiens	12%	Métis Hommes	7%
Diolas Femmes	17%	Sérères Femmes	4%
Métisses	10%	Sérères Hommes	1%

Il se peut que la catégorie 'Autres' ait été ici un peu gonflée, beaucoup de militaires appartenant à ce groupe n'ont en réalité qu'une situation matrimoniale enregistrée par l'armée.

Parmi les Cap-Verdiens, on relève chez les Praïa peu d'unions civiles (6,5%). Par contre chez les Brava—Fogo, il y a 20% d'unions civiles et chez les St-Vincent—St-Antoine, 25%.

8. *Les unions libres*

D'un point de vue purement légal, est considérée comme union libre, toute union non sactionnée par un lien de nature religieuse, ou civile. En réalité, la persistance de régimes coutumiers locaux attribuant des pouvoirs aux organisations familiales ou tribales intermédiaires, devrait rentrer en ligne de compte. Il ne s'agirait plus toujours d'union purement consensuelle entre individus mais de contrat devant un tiers reconnu par la coutume. Il nous a été pratiquement impossible de faire cette distinction qui relève d'une étude sociologique spéciale, particulièrement interessante dans des milieux en cours d'évolution.

Nous nous bornerons donc aux chiffres suivants qui nous livrent les taux d'union libre par ethnies:

Pourcentages en unions libres sur le total de baptisés mariés

	Ensemble	*Hommes*	*Femmes*
Mandjaques	57,0	55	58
Cap-Verdiens	38,5	37	40
Diolas	28,5	20	34
Autres	23,0	25	21
Métis et Originaires	12,5	18	8
Sérères	7,5	6	9
Ensemble	29,0	28	30

9. *Âges et taux de mariages religieux*

Si on prend les différents groupes d'âges on s'aperçoit d'une diversité de taux dans l'observance du mariage religieux. L'irrégularité diminue régulièrement mais lentement avec l'âge.

	Hommes	*Femmes*
15 à 24 ans	52%	37,5%
25–34 ans	39%	37,0%
35–44 ans	35,5%	33,5%
45–54 ans	31%	27%
54 et plus	24%	25%
Tous âges	36%	35%

Par ethnies on, notera cependant, quelques exceptions. Chez les Cap-Verdiens de 35 à 44 ans, il y a accroissement de l'irrégularité, mais ceci est dû aux apports plus récents de l'immigration. Chez les femmes sérères s'observent des taux assez variables.

Du côté masculin, la vie matrimoniale commence facilement

par l'union libre, sauf chez les Sérères où on ne compte que peu d'irrégularité. Pour les autres groupes on ne trouve de faibles pourcentages que vers la cinquantaine pour les Métis (10,5) et les Diolas (16,5), vers la soixantaine pour les autres (12%). A ce dernier âges, Cap-Verdiens et Mandjaques comptent encore plus d'un tiers d'irrégularité.

Du côté féminin, les taux diminuent lentement jusqu'à la cinquantaine, bien qu'à cet âge 42% des Cap-Verdiennes soient encore en situation irrégulière.

L'analyse précédente nous montre que malgré son extension, l'irrigularité doit être jugée différemment suivant les groupes. Précoce chez les Cap-Verdiens, Diolas, Mandjaques et autres, elle semble durer plus longtemps chez les premiers et se résorber plus vite ailleurs.

Nous ne saurions dire non plus dans quelle mesure et sous quelles influences, ces unions se dissolvent ou se transforment en unions légales. Il reste toute une enquête à faire sur les comportements matrimoniaux. Disons simplement que sur la foi des chiffres, l'union consensuelle parait davantage chez certains (Cap-Verdiens) comme un succédané du mariage par crainte peut-être de l'engagement définitif, chez d'autres comme un début d'une union que l'on fera par la suite sanctionner.

10. *Ethnies et choix du conjoint*

A propos des seuls chefs de ménages, un relevé a été fait concernant l'ethnie de leur épouse.

Au total dans 75% des ménages de conjoints on trouve le même groupe, avec cette diversité suivant les ethnies.

Pourcentages de mariés dans le même groupe

	Hommes	*Femmes*	*Ensemble*
— Sérères	88,5	80	84
— Mandjaques	77,5	90,5	83,5
— Cap-Verdiens	97	71,5	82
— Diolas	79,5	54,5	64,5
— Autres	48,5	95	64
— Métis et Originaires	52,5	57	54,5

Un premier groupe où l'exogamie est plus rare est constitué par les Sérères, Mandjaques et Cap-Verdiens hommes. Dans un deuxième groupe nous trouvons, les Diolas et 'Autres' mais avec de gros décalages suivant les sexes.

Enfin les Métis et Originaires, hommes ou femmes, s'unissent plus volontiers à d'autres ethnies.

Disons surtout qu'un choix hors ethnie s'impose du côté masculin aux 'Autres' et aux Mandjaques en raison d'un déficit féminin chez eux.

De même, le surplus des femmes chez les Diolas, Cap-Verdiens et Métis invite celles-ci à accepter un mari hors de leur groupe. Quant aux Sérères l'équilibre des sexes favorise les mariages au sein du groupe. Voyons ce qu'il en est pour chaque groupe:

Les Originaires et les Métis: La moitié environ des hommes (52%) et un peu plus de la moitié des femmes (57%) fondent un foyer à l'intérieur de leur propre groupe. Le reste, pour les hommes, se trouve uni le plus souvent avec des Cap-Verdiennes (36%): pour les femmes avec toutes les autres ethnies, mais de préférence avec celles du Sud (20%).

Suivant l'âge, l'exogamie ne cesse de reculer dans les générations plus jeunes. C'est ainsi que 36% des Originaires de moins de quarante ans et 25% des métis du même groupe d'âge la pratiquent alors que chez leurs aînés—les plus de cinquante ans—les taux étaient respectivement de 63% et de 57%.

Dans ces groupes l'exogamie semble plus fréquante dans les classes sociales inférieures (61% des ouvriers, 46% des cadres).

Les Cap-Verdiens: Presque tous les hommes (97%) se marient dans leur propre groupe. L'effectif des femmes mariées étant ici bien supérieur à celui des hommes (135 femmes pour 100 hommes), les Cap-Verdiennes outre le contingent uni à des congénères (72%) se rencontrent au foyer des Antillais (10%), des Dahoméens et Togolais (9%), des autres Africains (5%) et des Européens (4%).

La part des mariées hors du groupe est cependant moindre dans les îles de Brava et de Fogo. Relevons aussi que les Praïa sont pour 20% d'entre elles mariées à des africains alors que cette proportion n'est que de 6% pour les Brava-Fogo et 8% pour les St-Vincent—St-Antoine.

Une préférence est également donnée aux unions entre personnes de même île. Ainsi 68% des hommes ont épousé des femmes de chez eux (Praïa, 72%; St-Vincent, 70%; Brava-Fogo, 60%). Mais alors que les hommes de Praïa se trouvent des épouses dans les autres îles, il est plus rare que ceux des autres îles s'en cherchent chez les Praïa.

Notons que l'exogamie est chez la Portugaise facteur de promotion sociale. Alors que dans les ménages entièrement Cap-Verdiens on ne trouve que 8% d'épouses de cadres moyens, ce taux est de 37% chez les autres.

Les Sérères: Chez les Sérères 89% des hommes et 80% des femmes sont mariés dans leur groupe. Les unions exogamiques se rencontrent surtout chez les hommes de plus de 50 ans avec des femmes de Dakar, Gorée, Casamance.

Là aussi un surplus de femmes mariables favorise des unions avec des hommes du Sud (10%), des Mandjaques, Diolas ou Originaires. Pour ces femmes également, l'exogamie favorise l'ascension sociale.

Les Diolas: La répartition des sexes au mariage manifeste un très fort déséquilibre: 146 femmes pour 100 hommes. Cependant dans 20% des cas, le choix d'une compagne se dirige soit vers une métisse, soit vers une Sérère, soit vers une Mandjaque.

Quant aux femmes seulement un peu plus de la moitié (54%) est unie à des congénères. Les originaires d'Oussouye se portent plus volontiers vers les Mandjaques (26%) qui sont venus à la ville pour la vente du vin de palme; celles de Bignona s'allient de préférence avec des Dahoméens et Togolais (13%).

Notons cependant une nette remontée de l'endogamie chez les plus jeunes (84% des moins de 40 ans contre 68% des plus de 50 ans).

Les Mandjaques: Ici domine l'élément masculin avec 86 femmes pour 100 hommes; aussi une très forte proportion de femmes (90%) est-elle mariée dans la même ethnie, sauf quelques isolées avec les Diolas (3%) et les autres (3%).

Chez les hommes, l'exogamie (22%) est surtout le fait des générations plus âgées, unions contractées à l'époque où les femmes n'émigraient pas encore.

Signalons la forte proportion d'unions avec les Diolas de la région de Cabrousse et Oussouye, (15%) à l'occasion de migrations en vue de la récolte et de la vente du vin de palme.

Les Dahoméens, Togolais, Ivoiriens, Voltaïques: Population à forte dominante masculine (51 femmes pour 100 hommes). Presque toutes les femmes de ce groupe ayant émigré avec leur mari, ou étant venues le rejoindre, peu d'exogamie parmi elles (4%).

Par contre ce déficit féminin invite les hommes à porter leur choix vers des Cap-Verdiennes (17%), des Métisses (10%), des Sérères (10%), des Diolas (10%), et Mandjaques (4,2%).

En résumé on peut constater que l'exogamie est davantage pratiqué par les groupes urbanisés originaires et Métis. Son importance chez les Diolas et les Africains du Sud est dûe en grande partie au déséquilibre des sexes dans ces groupes.

Très élevé autrefois ce déséquilibre tend aujourd'hui à se réduire, le mouvement migratoire attirant de plus en plus l'élément féminin, d'où la place plus grande de l'endogamie chez les jeunes générations: 78% chez moins de 40 ans, 69% chez les plus de 40 ans.

Soulignons également l'attrait de promotion sociale que peut revêtir pour la femme l'union exogamique. Alors que dans les ménages de même ethnie, 14% des épouses sont unies à des employés ou cadres, ce taux s'élève à 38% dans les autres ménages. Ceci se vérifie surtout dans les Cap-Verdiennes, Sérères et Mandjaques.

11. *Ménages et situations matrimoniales*

Mis à part les ménages en union coutumière, la proportion des couples mariés à l'Eglise est au total de 58%. Des taux supérieurs se rencontrent chez les Sérères (87%), les Métis et Originaires (72%) les Diolas (67%). Ont des taux inférieurs, les Dahoméens —(52%), les Cap-Verdiens (47%), les Mandjaques (35,5%). Cet ordre correspond aux données individuelles relevées précédemment.

La corrélation—ménage religieux, choix du conjoint—manifeste que le mariage religieux est plus fréquent dans les unions pratiquées entre personnes de mêmes ethnies: 61,5% contre 55%.

On constate en effet davantage de situations irrégulières dans les groupes suivants, lorsque leurs ressortissants ont un conjoint d'une ethnie différente: hommes et femmes métis, Originaires, Sérères, Femmes diolas, hommes Dahoméens Par contre la mixité joue à l'avantage du mariage religieux chez les hommes Diolas, les hommes et femmes Mandjaques.

Chez les Cap-Verdiens, les mariages hors groupe changent peu la proportion générale. Mais à l'intérieur du groupe, le pointage par île d'origine manifeste un même phénomène. Ainsi les chefs de famille originaires de Praïa ayant une épouse de chez eux, présentent un taux de mariage religieux de 65% et ceux mariés à l'extérieur 43%. Même réflexion pour les Brava où les taux passent de 52% à 30%.

12. *Mariages et religions*

Dans leur presque totalité—92%—les chrétiens s'unissent entre eux. Le reste fournit un effectif d'environ 400 personnes dont près de 300 unis à des païens. Disons de suite que si le chiffre de 39 hommes unis à des musulmanes nous semble correspondre approximativement à la réalité, celui de 88 femmes dans des foyers de musulmans nous paraît très inférieur. Nous n'avons pu en effet recenser les cas d'apostasie ou d'irrégularité entraîné par ce genre d'union.

(a) *Les unions avec une partie musulmane.* Il s'agit de 31 mariages religieux, 41 unions civiles, 55 unions libres. Peu de mariages religieux mixtes, la discipline ecclésiastique en vigueur au Sénégal s'y opposant. Dans 20 cas sur 31, la dispense a été consentie au profit de femmes, dont 10 originaires.

En union civile on relève de même la présence de 21 originaires, soit la moitié des cas recensés.

Dans l'union libre nous relevons surtout la présence de femmes Cap-Verdiennes, Originaires et Diolas.

Au total le seul pourcentage important de mariés avec des musulmans se rencontrerait chez les Originaires, 7,7% du groupe. Depuis toujours en effet à Dakar, ce groupe est en contact très étroit avec l'Islam, les deux communautés entretenant ici des liens de parenté.

Viennent ensuite les Diolas—3%—ethnie où se rencontre également un grand voisinage de religions.

(b) *Les unions avec une partie païenne:* La moitié des cas relevés concerne des hommes et l'ethnie mandjaque. Il s'agit également dans 90% des cas, d'unions consensuelles. Le catéchuménat mandjaque, fertile en baptêmes de jeunes hommes, conduit en effet rarement à la formation d'un couple chrétien; 18% des mandjaques sont unis à des païennes.

Signalons également que le même problème se pose mais en moindre proportion, pour les Diolas de Sud-Casamance (4,5%).

13. *Divorces et séparations*

Nous n'avons enregistré que peu de cas de séparations ou de divorces, une centaine. Ceci provient du fait que nous avons considéré comme unions libres de nombreux cas de remariages. Disons en passant que le recensement de 1955 accusait 200 divorces chez les chrétiens, ce qui nous donnerait un taux de 2,5% personnes en situation de divorce. En ne tenant compte que des personnes mariées, il serait de 5%. Il nous semble que ce sont ces derniers taux qu'il faudrait retenir.

14. *Les femmes célibataires ou veuves avec leurs enfants*

Notre recensement devrait normalement faire apparaître l'importance de certaines situations particulières, tel le cas des filles mères.

En réalité nous nous heurtons à la difficulté déjà signalée. Comment au cours d'une enquête rapide, distinguer entre les états de célibat, de veuvage, de séparation? Comment surtout juger entre les unions passagères et les unions plus stables, même si elles restent consensuelles? Disons d'abord que sur le total des femmes recensées 8,5% sont des célibataires ou veuves ayant avec elles un ou plusieurs de leurs enfants (moins de 14 ans). Ce taux varie peu quelque soit le groupe d'âge. Si on se base sur les 15–29 ans, où n'interviennent que peu le veuvage et la séparation, la proportion des filles mères pourrait donc être d'environ 8% avec les variations suivantes:

Cap-Verdiennes	15,5
Métis	8,5
Diolas	8
Mandjaques	5
Sérères	4
Autres	3,5

Si on calcule sur le total des seules célibataires de 15–29 ans on trouverait un taux de 12,5% de filles mères: 25% chez les Cap-Verdiennes, 9 à 11% chez les autres groupes sauf chez les Sérères, 6%.

15. *Émigration et éloignement prolongé des conjoints*

Le recensement nous a permis de relever un certain nombre de cas où les conjoints se trouvaient éloignés l'un de l'autre du fait de leur travail. Bien que cette situation ne modifie pas l'état juridique, sa fréquence mérite cependant d'être signalée.

Au total 300 mariés ont été recensés sans leur conjoint.

Du côté masculin, sur les 200 dans ce cas (6,5% des mariés) on relève environ 120 Sérères, soit 21% des hommes de l'île de Fadiouth, tous mariés religieusement. Pour les autres groupes signalons quelques cap-verdiens (6%) et Diolas (4%).

Du côté féminin, la proportion se situe entre 2% et 5% suivant les ethnies.

Il y aurait toute une étude à faire sur les conditions dans lesquelles émigre la totalité ou seulement une partie de la famille. Sur ce point encore, nous espérons que l'enquête rurale en cours nous fournira quelques éclaircissements.

Summary

CHRISTIANITY IN DAKAR: SOME REMARKS ON THE MARITAL SITUATIONS FOUND AMONG THE BAPTIZED POPULATION

In Dakar, a city of 370,000, a great ethnic variety may be found. The European population still amounts to 40,000. The main

African groups may be listed as follows: Wolofs and Lebous, 60 per cent; Toucouleurs, Peuls (Fulanis), and Sarakoles, 20 per cent; Sereres 7 per cent; Mandingoes 7 per cent; Diolas 4 per cent; Moors 2 per cent. The fluctuating population varies between 10 per cent and 15 per cent.

From the religious point of view, there is a strong Moslem majority: 80 per cent. Almost all the Christians are Catholics. Among them 24,000 are Africans amounting to 7 per cent of the total African population. The Christian African population lives scattered among the Moslem masses: only 20 per cent of African Catholics live in predominantly catholic districts. Although they may be found everywhere in the city, one third of them lives in districts where they amount only to a very small percentage of the whole population. With the exception of the European element which is extremely unstable, the Dakar catholic population has a threefold origin: the natives of Gorée–Dakar–St. Louis, the immigrants coming from either the Cape Verde Islands or the Southern countries (especially Dahomey) and finally the recent Senegalese immigrants coming from the rural areas (Sereres, Mandingoes, Mandjaques).

In spite of very marked cultural and linguistic differences which maintain barriers among the various groups, it is possible to distinguish two main social environments: the westernized group including persons of mixed blood, natives of the old Senegalese 'communes' and ports of call, Cape-Verdians and Dahomean immigrants; the traditional group recruited in the more recent missions of the Casamance and Serere regions. Until 1946 the latter group was a minority (36 per cent) but amounts now to a little more than half the total Christian African population.

At the socio-professional level, the following classification is found:

common labourers and unskilled workers	43
workers and white collar workers	50
executives	3
undetermined	4
total	100

It can be said, on the whole, that there is a correlation between the traditional environments and the less favoured groups on the professional level.

From the purely religious point of view, we have studied so far only the behaviour concerning marriage practices. Among the Christian population three types of union may be distinguished:

1. Religious marriage, the only type to be recognized as legitimate by the Church.
2. Civil marriage.
3. Consensual union or 'concubinage'.

61 per cent of the married population were married in Church
10 per cent of the married population were married by law
29 per cent of the married population live in consensual unions.

One-third of the married Christian population is therefore in an irregular situation as far as (canon) law is concerned.

According to the various ethnic groups, we can observe three levels of observance: the first category includes the Sereres and 'natives' where 92 per cent and 87 per cent respectively have contracted religious marriages; the Diolas (67 per cent of them married in church), the Dahomeans, Togolese, and Praia Cape-Verdians (60 per cent belong to the second category); in the third category we can list the Cape-Verdians from the other islands (38 per cent married in church) and the Mandjaques (34·5 per cent).

If we consider the various age-groups, we find that the percentages of religious marriages vary according to the age-groups concerned. The irregularity rates decrease regularly but slowly with the increasing ages.

	Men	*Women*
15–24 years	52%	37·5%
25–34 years	39%	37%
35–44 years	35·5%	35·5%
45–54 years	31%	27%
54 and above	24%	25%
all ages	36%	35%

However, some exceptions may be noted according to the various ethnic groups. Among Cape-Verdians of the 35–44 age-group there is an increase in the irregularity rates, but this is due to the more recent immigrants. Some rather variable rates may be observed among Serere women. Among the men, marital life often starts with a 'free union', except among the Sereres where irregularities are rare. For the other groups, only small percentages of irregularities are found around the age of fifty for the Mixed Bloods (10·5 per cent) and Diolas (16·5 per cent), and around the age of sixty for the others (12 per cent). At that latter age, more than one-third of irregularities is still found among the Cape-Verdians and Mandjaques. On the women's side, the rates slowly decrease until about the age of fifty, although even at that age 42 per cent of Cape-Verde women are still in an irregular situation.

The analysis above shows that despite their extension, irregular marriages have to be judged differently in the various population groups. While they occur early in life among the Cape-Verdians, Diolas, Mandjaques, and others, it would appear that they last longer among the first groups mentioned than among the rest where they disappear more rapidly. We cannot at present say to what extent and under which influences these unions are dissolved and transformed into legal ones. Basing ourselves on the figures available, we can only say that to some groups (Cape-Verdians) the consensual union appears to be a sort of pseudo-marriage perhaps contracted because of the fear of a permanent commitment while for some other groups it is considered to be the beginning of a union which will become legalized later on in life.

For heads of families only, an inquiry was made in order to determine the ethnic group of the wife. For the total sample, it was found that in 75 per cent of the cases both husband and wife belonged to the same group, and the following differences were observed in the various ethnic groups considered: the first group where exogamy occurs most rarely is that of the Serere, Mandjaque and Cape-Verdian men. A second group is formed by the Diolas and 'others' but there, there are wide discrepancies according to sex. Finally, Mixed Bloods and 'natives', both men and women, contract marriages outside their groups more willingly. It should be pointed out that for 'others' and Mandjaques the choice of a marriage partner outside the group is due mainly to a deficit in the number of the women in each group. The correlation between a religious husband and the choice of a partner shows that religious marriages occur more frequently when both partners belong to the same ethnic group: 61·5 per cent as opposed to 55 per cent. There are more irregular situations in the following groups when their members have spouses of different ethnic groups: men and women of mixed blood, Diola women, Dahomean men. On the other hand 'mixed' marriages are more often religious unions in the case of Diola men and Mandjaque men and women.

Among Cape-Verdians, exogamous marriages seem to have little influence on the overall distribution. But within the group a classification according to the island of origin shows a similar phenomenon. Thus heads of families, natives of Praia and married to a woman of the same island, show a religious marriage rate of 65 per cent while those married to women from other islands have a rate of 43 per cent. The same applies to natives of Brava where the respective rates are 52 per cent and 30 per cent.

Practically the whole of the Christian community intermarries (92 per cent). The rest amounts to about 400 people of whom about 300 are married to pagans. We must point out however that while the figure of thirty-nine men married to Moslem women seems to be a close approximation of the facts, that of eighty-eight women in Moslem households seems to be much too low. For we were unable to list the cases of apostasy or of irregularity determined by that type of union.

We recorded only very few cases of separations or divorces, only about thirty on the whole. This is due to the fact that many cases of re-marriage were recorded as 'free unions'. We may mention, in passing, that the 1955 census showed 200 divorces among Christians which would give a percentage rate of 2·5 per cent of divorced. If we take into account the marrieds only, we have a percentage of 5 per cent. We feel that the latter figure is probably the more correct one.

XVII. RELIGION AND SOCIO-ECONOMIC ACTION AMONG THE SERENJE-LALA OF ZAMBIA[1]

NORMAN LONG

This paper sets out to explore, within the context of a contemporary rural African community, the relationship between religion and socio-economic action. In it, I describe the religious ethic of a congregation of Jehovah's Witnesses among the Serenje-Lala of Zambia (formerly Northern Rhodesia) and discuss the position that Jehovah's Witnesses occupy in the changing social and economic structure of the community as a whole.

The church congregation chosen for study is one of eleven congregations of Jehovah's Witnesses in Chibale Chiefdom, Serenje District, and lies in the north-western sector of the chiefdom. It serves an area of approximately eighteen by ten miles which roughly corresponds with the administrative Parish of Kapepa.[2] The total resident adult population for Kapepa Parish, when I made a census in March–April 1963, was 497, of whom 91 were practising Jehovah's Witnesses, 10 were practising Presbyterians (United Church of Central Africa), 4 were Roman Catholics, and the rest had no church affiliation. Jehovah's Witnesses were the only group holding regular weekly religious meetings.

ORGANIZATIONAL ASPECTS

Jehovah's Witnesses in Zambia form part of a wider international, American-based organization which, in 1963, served 181 countries. The main headquarters of the movement is in Brooklyn, New York, where there is a printing press and a large administra-

[1] The material for this paper was collected in 1963–64 during my tenure as Commonwealth Scholar and Research Affiliate of the Rhodes–Livingstone Institute.

[2] The identity of the parish is concealed under a pseudonym.

tive staff to maintain contact with branch offices throughout the world.[3] The branch office for Zambia is in Kitwe, and it is here that the publications of the Watch Tower Bible and Tract Society are distributed throughout the country, that big assemblies are planned and records are kept concerning the over-all running of the organization. In 1963 there were some 28,300 active Jehovah's Witnesses in Zambia, and the main publications were available in four languages, English, Bemba, Nyanja, and Lozi.[4]

Each church congregation is under local leadership, though attempts are made to prevent the local unit from becoming too autonomous. First, there is a hierarchy of officials whose job it is to supervise the running of a number of local congregations and make reports to the branch office.[5] Secondly, the branch office distributes booklets dealing with various organizational matters and requires congregation leaders to submit monthly reports to the office and encourages them to write for advice when problems arise. The Society has its own printed forms for

[3] Three legal corporations act as co-ordinating bodies for the work of Jehovah's Witnesses, the Watch Tower Bible and Tract Society of Pennsylvania, the Watch Tower Bible and Tract Society of Brooklyn, and the International Bible Students' Association, whose headquarters is in London. Some confusion has resulted in Central Africa from the use of 'Watch Tower' to cover both the African Watch Tower movement and Jehovah's Witnesses of the Watch Tower Bible and Tract Society. African Watch Tower groups, originally inspired by the doctrines of Jehovah's Witnesses, have no official link with the Watch Tower Bible and Tract Society, though they do make use of the literature printed by the Society. They had a strong following in Northern and Southern Rhodesia, Nyasaland, and the Congo before and during the Second World War, and small congregations of them still exist in some parts. In contrast, Jehovah's Witnesses first established a permanent headquarters in Lusaka in the mid-1930s but their main phase of expansion came immediately following the last war. For further discussion of the distinction between the two movements, see Professor G. Shepperson's contribution in Thrupp (1961: 227–47). Jehovah's Witnesses in Serenje District date back to the late 1930s. To my knowledge, there are no congregations of African Watch Tower in the district at the present time. A fairly extensive bibliography of published material on Jehovah's Witnesses and African Watch Tower in Central Africa is found in Kaufman (1964).

[4] The figures are taken from Jehovah's Witnesses' *Year Book for 1964*.

[5] Above the congregation level, there are two main kinds of full-time workers, the Circuit Servant, who has about 15 to 20 congregations in his charge and is generally a locally-trained African speaking the vernacular of the region he is working in, and the District Servant, who supervises the work of several Circuit Servants. District Servants are mostly European missionaries.

all reports and for the ordering of books and pamphlets, and a constant stream of literature goes out to all congregations.

From among the members of a congregation seven are appointed for special duties. Of these, the Congregation Overseer, his assistant, and the Servant of Bible Studies, are the more important and together they make up the *Three Committee* which meets regularly to discuss the affairs of the congregation.

Church meetings take place both during the week and at the weekends. A mid-week Bible study and literacy class is normally held on Wednesdays, and on Saturdays and Sundays a series of meetings take place which focus on the reading and discussion of various Watch Tower Bible and Tract Society publications. After these meetings, Witnesses disperse for house-to-house preaching. They are expected to fulfil a minimum of ten hours per month, and each member must submit to one of the congregation officials a weekly report of his preaching activities.

From what has been said about the making of reports, the use of official literature, and the appointment of leaders, and I have only mentioned these briefly in passing, it is clear that the local congregation is part of a highly bureaucratized religious organization. Promotion comes only to those who have a good preaching record, judged by the number of hours put in and by the number of converts made, and who are well-versed in Watch Tower publications and doctrine. Thus, within the bureaucracy, emphasis is placed on individual achievement and self-discipline as pre-requisites for advancement in the hierarchy.[6]

DOCTRINE AND ETHIC

The doctrines of Jehovah's Witnesses centre on the belief that we are now living in the 'time of the End', after which God will inaugurate 'a new heaven and a new earth'. This last phase before God's New Kingdom is characterized by a mounting lawlessness on earth which will culminate in the battle of Armageddon, the final struggle that will take place between the powers of Evil and the powers of Good. Satan and his protaganists will be

[6] For more details on church organization, see Watch Tower Bible and Tract Society (1955).

crushed and God will emerge as victor. Only those who have been faithful to Jehovah God will survive the onslaught and inherit the new paradise on earth. Christ will remain in heaven along with 144,000 specially-chosen companions but will rule earth from heaven. Theocratic government will replace all forms of secular government and God will appoint 'princes' to be Christ's agents on earth from among the survivors of Armageddon. According to Jehovah's Witnesses, Bible chronology indicates that Christ's rule started to become effective on earth from 1914 when He was enthroned in heaven, but it cannot be totally effective until after the battle of Armageddon when the faithful will, with God's help, rebuild the earth.

> Everyone who lives through Armageddon will have a part in this good work. Paradise will be earth-wide. The whole world will be made into a garden. This will be happy work. Every person will be making something good and useful. No one will be working for another man. Each man will enjoy the results of his own labour, and the work of his own hands. Isaiah 65:21:22 gives a picture of what it will be like: 'They shall build houses and inhabit them; and they shall plant vineyards, and eat the fruit of them. They shall not build and another inhabit; they shall not plant and another eat; for as the days of the tree are long and fruitful shall be the days of my people, and my chosen ones shall long enjoy the work of their hands.' . . . The cleansed earth, ruled by Christ under the direction of the Great Gardener, Jehovah God, will be a place of even greater plenty than that ancient promised land was. (Watch Tower Bible and Tract Society, 1958:221.)

All manner of evil will be removed from the face of the earth. There will be no death, no sickness, and no hunger. 'Nation shall not lift up sword against nation, neither shall they learn war any more.' (Micah 4:3).

Jehovah's Witnesses see themselves as the 'chosen people' who have been set the task of warning others about the coming destruction. They describe themselves as God's theocratic organization on earth, 'the New World Society', and believe that salvation can come only to those who accept the faith. All other Christian bodies are Satan-influenced and their adherents will not enter the New Kingdom. Baptism is a milestone on the way to salvation, but salvation itself can only be attained through continued good works. All Jehovah's Witnesses therefore should go out preaching, study the Bible thoroughly and be attentive to the needs of their families. And this leads to an examination of the practical ethic as expressed by Witnesses in Kapepa Parish.

Before a person can be baptized he has to undergo a period of biblical instruction, but baptism is by no means the end of Bible education. Official publications all lay stress on the fact that being a Jehovah's Witness is a *process* and not a *state*. One must progress spiritually. One must become mature in the knowledge of the Bible and must acquire the ability to teach others, and of course to do this one must be able to read the Scriptures. Hence the importance of holding literacy classes in African rural areas. Moreover, spiritual advancement means also that each individual must pay attention to his own 'personal organization':

> He must have organization about everything he does, including his personal appearance, his living quarters and all his actions, in order that the high standard of God's ministry may not be found fault with (II Corinthians, Ch. 6, v. 3). (Watch Tower Bible and Tract Society, 1955:261.)

A Witness should therefore keep a record of his preaching activities and devise a schedule for such work and for his own Bible study. Also, as one man explained:

> a disciple of Christ should appear clean and decent because then he will preach a clean Gospel and the message will be received well by all. He will appear dignified. . . . In Old Testament days, the people did not shave because they had no razor blades, but in these days we do have such things and should make use of them, for dirtiness is associated with evil and cleanliness with God.

In a discussion with another Witness about the well-groomed appearance of many of the members he said, 'We are looked upon as *basambashi*.' The word *basambashi* is used generally by both Witnesses and non-Witnesses to describe someone who has a reasonably high standard of living. He dresses well, eats well, and possesses plenty of furniture and other items of property, and is said to 'govern himself'. Successful farmers and storekeepers are given as examples. Thus the concept is mostly used to refer to those persons who have achieved high economic status in the community by making use of the new opportunities open to them in a money economy.

The importance that Jehovah's Witnesses as a group attach to the concept of *basambashi* is illustrated in the following texts. When talking of acquiring skills, one Witness emphasized that:

> Every man should make use of the opportunities available for obtaining skills, like the Development Area Training Centre. There are various reasons why particular individuals attend courses but my reason was that I thought I should train for something that would give me a good living, for I did not complete my education properly. The Bible teaches, even from the very early history, that each individual should have his own special work. The prophets had work for the body and work for God. Jesus and his disciples had their own special skills as well as work for God. Today every Christian must have a job so as to help himself. Everyone should have work for himself in order to reach the level of *basambashi* and follow the ways of God. If a person attains this balanced life then he will have a life of abundance in the New World. A person who neglects the teachings of the Bible and who makes no effort to advance will have nothing in the New World.

On another occasion, it was argued before the congregation that it had been God's original intention to make men into eternal *basambashi* but that Adam chose to reject God's law:

> Thus it was our disobedience that brought death and suffering, they were not part of God's design. It is now up to us to attain the level of *basambashi* in this world, for being Jehovah's Witnesses we are already part of the New World Society. At the end of the world we shall be rewarded even more.

As Isaiah taught that the world would be rebuilt by God's chosen people, so the Witnesses of Kapepa Parish believe that by acquiring skills and improving their own standards of living, both materially and spiritually, they are preparing themselves for the new life and the tasks ahead. Wealth in itself is not considered evil but 'a man should not try to hide his wealth from God or from other men for Jehovah knows all'. Wise investment is encouraged: 'Do not squander your money away on beer and cigarettes.' 'Keep your family well-clothed and well-fed.' By 'family' Jehovah's Witnesses generally mean elementary family and some say that the traditional Lala matrilineal system of descent and inheritance is not God-ordained for the Bible makes no mention of it. One Witness farmer explained that he had decided to leave his property to his eldest son and not to his sister's son, as custom demands, because 'my son is of my blood and not my nephew'. Also husband, wife, and children should eat together and not separately as is customary among pagans and they should sit together as a family when attending religious meetings.

At a National Assembly of Jehovah's Witnesses in Kitwe in May 1963, which was attended by about 24,000 people, a short play was enacted to show the difference that conversion brings to family life. The play highlights several of the points raised earlier and indicates that some aspects of the ethic are not confined to congregations in Chibale but are probably general for Witnesses throughout Zambia. The performance of such plays is a regular feature of assemblies and I have recorded the same characterization of conversion at several assemblies held in Serenje District.

The first scene presented a picture of the 'typical' pagan household. The husband, wife, and children are dressed in rags; they live in a dirty house with little furniture. They eat from dirty plates, the husband by himself and the wife and children from the same dish. The wife never sweeps the floor and there is no table cloth on the table. They have no beds and have to sleep on the floor. The children are badly behaved and the parents show no interest in them. The children wear beads round their waists as a protection against sickness. Two Jehovah's Witnesses visit the household. They are both smartly dressed, the man wearing a suit and the woman a well-tailored costume. They receive a cold reception and are soon interrupted by some friends of the husband who bring him beer. Finally, however, they do get some response from the wife who buys *The Watchtower* magazine and so they leave to preach elsewhere.

A few days later, the same Witnesses look into their diary and see that they have planned a return visit to the household. This time they are pleasantly surprised to find the house looking cleaner and to get more of a welcome. Both husband and wife are interested to hear what they have to say concerning the coming Kingdom of God. It transpires that after they left last time the wife persuaded the husband to start teaching her to read, using the magazine as a guide, and as a result both of them had been enthralled with what they had read. Before leaving, the preachers arrange for the couple to attend meetings and for them to receive private Bible study lessons.

Scene three portrayed the same family transformed. They are now converted to the faith and regularly attend literacy classes. (The audience claps loudly when the wife makes her first attempt to read.) The husband has stopped drinking beer and smoking cigarettes. Instead he has invested his money in good furniture. They now have a new table and chairs, a table cloth, and beds, pots, and pans. A vase of flowers stands on the table and the whole family sits down together to eat. They now use knives and forks. The husband is dressed in a grey suit and his wife and children have new clothing and wear shoes. The children no longer have beads around their waists. The house is sparkling and the children well-disciplined. When a friend comes to disturb the husband to go out drinking with him he refuses and gets on with his Bible studies. The family has now become part of the New World Society.

The ethic of Jehovah's Witnesses commends a certain style of life. The characteristics associated with this are the wearing of good clothing, and the buying of good furniture and household equipment. Thus every man in Kapepa congregation should aim at becoming *basambashi* and should try to gain some special skills so that he has some local means of earning cash with which to purchase these various items of property. In addition, importance is attached to becoming literate, for only by being literate can one satisfactorily perform one's religious roles. Jehovah's Witnesses, however, do not see their secular style of life as separate from their religious ways. To them it is rather an extension of their religious approach: to be a member of the New World Society means spiritual advancement and promise of a new life, but it also implies a certain practical orientation towards life in this world.

As part of this New World Society, Witnesses contrast themselves with those of the Old World who have failed to respond to the message of the New Kingdom. They see themselves apart from the old way of things, and preach a form of millenarianism. Yet at the same time they hold a this-worldly oriented ethic which focuses on individual achievement and self-discipline, the rationale for this being that they are preparing themselves for the great day when Jehovah's Kingdom is established on earth.

An individual is held responsible for all his actions and the rules and objectives set out in the various publications of the Watch Tower Bible and Tract Society serve to guide him. The ethic itself has ascetic elements. There is a ban on polygyny, and smoking and drinking and too much dancing are strongly disapproved of. Time and money are valued and should not be wasted; they should be spent improving oneself spiritually, socially, and economically. Throughout there is an emphasis on individualism and industriousness, and church organization and discipline work to uphold the values of the group.

CHANGING SOCIAL AND ECONOMIC STRUCTURE AND SOCIAL CHARACTERISTICS OF JEHOVAH'S WITNESSES

Important agricultural changes have occurred in Kapepa Parish in recent years. Traditionally the Lala have practised a form of ash cultivation known as the *Citeme*, or 'small circle' *Citemene*, system, growing finger millet as the staple crop. But, with the introduction of a Peasant Farming Scheme in 1948 by the Agricultural Department, there has been a move away from traditional methods. Under the scheme individuals can acquire cattle and farm implements on a Government loan and can receive instruction in crop rotation, animal husbandry, and ploughing. Thus, though a majority in Kapepa continue to rely on traditional methods, there is now an increasing tendency for those who possess plough and oxen, or who have access to them, to cultivate millet this way rather than by *Citeme*.

In 1958, Turkish tobacco was introduced as an experimental crop and the soils were found to be particularly favourable. By 1963 there were 44 growers in Kapepa (out of a total of 214 male cultivators) each with an acre or less of tobacco and receiving an average annual income from the crop of about £35, and the more successful growers between £70 and £100. Most Peasant Farmers also produce a small surplus of maize, beans, groundnuts, and vegetables which are transported to Broken Hill and the

Copperbelt towns for sale. The net result of all this, together with the regular influx of cash from town in the form of remittances and investments made by retired labour migrants, has been an over-all increase in prosperity, manifest in the growing number of brick settlements and stores, the existence of two diesel-engine grinding mills and several cars and lorries. And this in turn has led to greater economic differentiation within the community.

Connected with these changes has been a change in settlement patterns. Prior to about 1950 the basic residential unit was the village which had a core of matrilineally-related men and women. But, with the growth of new forms of production and of wealth, the village has tended to fragment into smaller settlements based on the elementary family, or on a small group of uterine siblings and their immediate descendants.[7] In March–April 1963, I counted eleven registered villages as against 49 other settlements, comprising Peasant Farms, stores and 'individual settlements'.[8] Just under half (or 47·7 per cent) of the *de facto* population were residing in settlements other than recognized villages. Of these 49 smaller settlements, 31 consisted of a

[7] The proliferation of smaller settlements cannot, however, be regarded simply as a reflection of changing economic conditions. Another major feature was a change in administrative policy which was implemented in Serenje District in 1950. This was the introduction of the parish system of local government. The idea was to establish a parish framework within the existing Native Authority structure, so that, within each chieftaincy, adjacent villages would be grouped together to form small administrative units, 'parishes'. Under the system, it was visualized that some persons would be given permission to set up their own independent settlements, so long as they agreed to comply with certain building and agricultural standards. There seems little doubt that the implementation of the parish system in Serenje, as in other parts of Zambia, has also contributed to the breakdown of the village into smaller units. For a general statement of the aims of the parish system, see Hailey (1950: 158–9). Turner (1957:41) and Harries-Jones (1963:57–58) discuss its introduction in the Mwinilunga and Kasama Districts respectively.

[8] The Peasant Farm and what I have called the 'individual settlements' are distinct in that the Peasant Farm is a group practising semi-commercial, plough agriculture, whereas the individual settlement is a group mostly engaged in non-plough, subsistence cultivation. Moreover, the terms 'Peasant Farm' and 'Peasant Farmer', when used in this paper, refer only to those units or persons registered with the Agricultural Department and do not include a small number of cases where some improved techniques are used but not under the aegis of the Agricultural Department.

single elementary or polygynous family, with, in some cases, an additional dependant or two. Relating type of structure to settlement type it was found that 16 out of the 24 Peasant Farms and all eight stores were of this simple structure. Thus it appears that large matrilineal descent groups are somewhat incompatible with cash-crop farming and the accumulation of wealth above subsistence needs and are giving way to smaller 'family' units.[9]

Within this setting Jehovah's Witnesses differ significantly from the rest of the population in terms of a number of social characteristics.[10]

Comparing the residence patterns for Witnesses and non-Witnesses one finds that of the 91 Witnesses 74·7 per cent live outside the village in small settlements, as against only 40·2 per cent of non-Witnesses. Moreover, of these Witnesses a majority live at Peasant Farms and stores which, for the most part, are based on a single elementary family. (cf. Tables I and II Appendix.)

Further comparisons can be made of the occupations, skills, and type of agriculture practised by the 214 men in the parish, of whom 47 are Jehovah's Witnesses. 51 per cent of the Witnesses follow occupations from which they derive some regular cash income. Of these, 12 are Peasant Farmers, 4 are storekeepers, while the remaining 8 grow tobacco for sale and at the same time practise subsistence cultivation. Of the 167 non-Witnesses, only 19·2 per cent fall into the cash-income categories. (cf. Table III Appendix.) Again there is a marked difference between the two groups with regard to skills practised. Considering bricklaying, carpentry, sawing, tailoring, metalwork, driving, and shoe-repairing as skills, then 57·5 per cent of the Witnesses are skilled and only 21·6 per cent of non-Witnesses. (cf. Table IV Appendix.)

[9] See Schneider and Gough (1961: 631 f.) for further discussion of this point, using data from a wide range of different matrilineal societies. Another aspect of social change in Kapepa which I do not examine here is the emergence of new criteria for evaluating status—wealth, education, and leadership in non-tribal associations (e.g. Church or political party).

[10] The data presented below relate only to those correlations found to be statistically significant. Witnesses and non-Witnesses were also compared with respect to the age and sex structure of the two groups but here the distributions were not significantly different.

Proportionately more Witnesses practise some form of plough cultivation and more grow tobacco. 46·8 per cent of the Witnesses use plough methods exclusively and 21·3 per cent cultivate by a combination of plough and *Citeme*. In contrast, only 17·8 per cent of non-Witnesses use the plough and 9·6 per cent a combination of plough and *Citeme*. (cf. Table V Appendix.) As for tobacco growing, 18 out of a total of 44 growers are Jehovah's Witnesses.

The pattern that emerges, then, is that a substantial number of Witnesses are utilizing the new economic opportunities made available in Kapepa Parish through the introduction of new farming techniques and cash-cropping, and have moved out of their villages to set up independent settlements and become farmers or storekeepers. Indeed, several of them have achieved high economic status within the local community. Some measure of their economic success is gauged by considering the ownership of various items of property in the area. Individual Jehovah's Witnesses own the only two diesel-engine grinding mills and four of the six motor vehicles. Also proportionately more of them possess cattle and farming implements and other items, such as radios, Western-type furniture, sewing machines, and brick houses. (cf. Tables VI and VII Appendix.)

Comparing now the characteristics of the members of the congregation with the style of life expounded in their religious ethic, one cannot fail to notice the close correspondence that exists between them. Witnesses tend to live in small settlements based on the elementary family, which is consistent with the importance that the ethic places on the elementary family as a fundamental Christian grouping. Proportionately more of them fall into the cash-income categories, are skilled and are of higher economic status; and the ideological counterpart of this is the value that is attached to capital investment, to the acquisition of skills and to the attainment of a *basambashi* standard of living. Witnesses may also be distinguished from the rest of the population by their smart dress. Most of the men, for example, wear jackets and ties and carry briefcases when they attend religious meetings or when out preaching. Here, too, they receive backing from the ethic which holds that one should pay particular attention to one's personal appearance when propagating the 'good news'. Similarly, the higher figure for literacy among Witnesses (cf. Table VIII Appendix) ties in with the stress placed on gaining first-hand knowledge of the Scriptures and the publications of the Society.

It seems reasonable to suggest therefore that the ethic serves to legitimize and provide religious sanctions for the mode of life and achievements of Jehovah's Witnesses in Kapepa Parish; but it may also have been a major factor motivating individual Witnesses towards a fuller exploitation of the new economic opportunities open to them. Relating conversion histories to economic mobility, for instance, one finds that of 18 Witnesses of higher economic status (12 Peasant Farmers, 4 storekeepers and 2 diesel-engine mill owners) 13 had already joined the church before they established their farms or businesses and had been in the movement for at least five years prior to this. Further discussion of this point, however, would require careful weighting of a whole range of factors and some assessment of the individuals concerned according to their level of religious commitment, and is too complex a problem to embark on here.

CONCLUSION

It has not been within the scope of this paper to relate these findings to a wider body of theory on the sociology of religion but in order to clarify the argument it is necessary to discuss briefly the relationship of religious ethic to dogma.

In the foregoing account I have isolated only those aspects of doctrine which seemed to me to be important for understanding the ethic. My main interest has been the believers' orientation towards practical affairs of everyday living, and this is what I mean by 'religious ethic'. Obviously, however, the link between doctrine and ethic is an intimate one in that, what Weber calls, 'the annunciation and promise' of a religion and its evaluation of the life-situation determine to some extent the *kind* of ethic that can evolve.[11] But social and cultural factors too can play their

[11] See Weber's essays on religion in Gerth and Mills (1948: 267–362) and Weber (1930).

part. Thus the ethic of a particular religion or denomination may vary according to the social and economic circumstances of the group of believers, though the doctrine remains essentially the same. This, I think, would clearly emerge from a comparative study of Jehovah's Witnesses found in different areas of Zambia. For example, in the economically less-developed places in Serenje District, one finds in their ethic an emphasis on the *imminence* of the Millenium and on the *rewards* that the faithful will receive in the New Kingdom, rather than on the need to *prepare oneself* for the new life by engaging in certain new forms of socio-economic action, as described for Kapepa Parish.

The general point I am making here is that one can view doctrine as providing a whole series of possible courses of legitimate action which carry church approval. Thus, within the doctrinal framework, different groups of adherents may select out for elaboration, or special emphasis, different aspects of dogma and thereby present somewhat different religious ethics. Each form the ethic takes, however, will bear some relation to the felt needs (spiritual, social, and economic, etc.) of the particular group of believers, who operate within a specific social setting. In this paper I have examined one such religious orientation and one set of socio-economic circumstances. It requires further comparative and historical research on the ethic and social composition of Jehovah's Witnesses in Central Africa and elsewhere to fit this study into a wider perspective.

APPENDIX

Table I

Residence Patterns for Adult Witnesses and Non-Witnesses

Type of settlement	*Witnesses*	*Non-Witnesses*	*Totals*
Village	23 (25·3)	243 (59·9)	266 (53·6)
Individual settlement	24 (26·4)	82 (20·2)	106 (21·3)
Peasant Farm	35 (38·5)	74 (18·2)	109 (21·9)
Store	9 (9·8)	7 (1·7)	16 (3·2)
TOTALS	91 (100·0)	406 (100·0)	497 (100·0)

Percentages shown in brackets

Table II

Structure of 49 smaller settlements according to Settlement Types

Type of structure	*Farm*	*Store*	*Individual settlement*	*Total*
Based on elementary family	12 (9)	8 (4)	5	25 (13)
Based on polygynous family	4	—	2	6
Based on uterine or classificatory sibling group	6 (3)	—	10 (2)	16 (5)
Based on 4–5 gen. matrilineal descent group	2	—	—	2
TOTALS	24 (12)	8 (4)	17 (2)	49 (18)

Settlements owned by Jehovah's Witnesses shown in brackets.

Table III

Primary Occupations of Male Witnesses and Male Non-Witnesses

Occupation	*Witnesses*	*Non-Witnesses*	*Totals*
Subsistence cultivator	23 (48·9)	135 (80·8)	158 (75·8)
Subsistence cultivator growing tobacco	8 (17·0)	13 (7·8)	21 (9·8)
Peasant Farmer	3 (6·4)	2 (1·2)	5 (2·4)
Peasant Farmer growing tobacco	9 (19·2)	11 (6·6)	20 (9·3)
Storekeeper	3 (6·4)	2 (1·2)	5 (2·4)
Storekeeper growing tobacco	1 (2·1)	2 (1·2)	3 (1·4)
Government employee	— —	2* (1·2)	2 (0·9)
TOTALS	47 (100·0)	167 (100·0)	214 (100·0)

Percentages in brackets.
* both = Court messengers.

Table IV

Proportion of Male Witnesses and Male Non-Witnesses skilled

Whether skilled or not	*Witnesses*	*Non-Witnesses*	*Totals*
Non-skilled	20 (42·5)	131 (78·4)	151 (70·6)
Skilled	27 (57·5)	36 (21·6)	63 (29·4)
TOTALS	47 (100·0)	167 (100·0)	214 (100·0)

Percentages in brackets.

Table V

Type of Agriculture practised by Male Witnesses and Male Non-Witnesses

Type of agriculture	*Witnesses*	*Non-Witnesses*	*Totals*
Citeme only	15 (31·9)	121 (72·5)	136 (70·6)
Plough only	22 (46·8)	30 (17·8)	52 (24·3)
Plough and *Citeme*	10 (21·3)	16 (9·7)	26 (12·1)
TOTALS	47 (100·0)	167 (100·0)	214 (100·0)

Percentages in brackets.

Tables VI and VII compare male Witnesses and male non-Witnesses with respect to economic status and are based on the analysis of the ownership of major property items. To place individuals into the three economic status categories, I have used a type of Guttman Scale Analysis. For more details, see Guttman (1954). The data have been processed under two separate clusters of five property items each. Table VI gives the results for the first cluster, made up of: (1) grinding mill, (2) farm implements other than plough, (3) four or more cattle, (4) plough, and (5) bicycle.

Table VI

Economic status of Male Witnesses and Male Non-Witnesses: First Cluster of Property Items

Economic categories	*Witnesses*	*Non-Witnesses*	*Totals*
I (High)	10 (21·3)	12 (7·2)	22 (10·3)
II (Medium)	22 (46·8)	64 (38·3)	86 (40·2)
III (Low)	15 (31·9)	91 (54·5)	106 (49·5)
TOTALS	47 (100·0)	167 (100·0)	214 (100·0)

Percentages in brackets.

Category I = (1) Those possessing all five items.
(2) Those possessing all but grinding mill.
(3) Those possessing cattle, plough, and bike only.
Category II = (1) Those possessing plough and bike only.
(2) Those possessing bike only.
Category III = Those possessing none of five items.

Table VII gives the results for the second cluster of property items, comprising: (1) motor vehicle, (2) radio, (3) 'Western-type' furniture, (4) sewing machine, and (5) brick house.

Table VII

Economic status of Male Witnesses and Male non-Witnesses: Second Cluster of Property Items

Economic categories	*Witnesses*	*Non-Witnesses*	*Totals*
I (High)	10 (21·5)	6 (3·6)	16 (7·5)
II (Medium)	18 (38·3)	71 (42·5)	89 (41·6)
III (Low)	19 (40·4)	90 (53·9)	109 (50·9)
TOTALS	47 (100·0)	107 (100·0)	214 (100·0)

Percentages in brackets.

Category I = (1) Those possessing all five items.
(2) Those possessing all but motor vehicle.
(3) Those possessing furniture, sewing machine, and brick house only.
Category II = (1) Those possessing sewing machine and brick house only.
(2) Those possessing brick house only.
Category III = Those possessing none of five items.

Both tables show a marked difference between Witnesses and Non-Witnesses. In Table VI 68·1 per cent of Witnesses fall into the top two categories and only 45·5 per cent of Non-Witnesses. In Table VII 59·6 per cent of Witnesses are placed in the top two categories and only 46·1 per cent of Non-Witnesses.

Table VIII

Literacy and Level of Education of Adult Witnesses and Non-Witnesses

Education/ Literacy	*Males*		*Females*		*Total*
	Witnesses	*Non-Witnesses*	*Witnesses*	*Non-Witnesses*	
Illiterate	6 (12·8)	82 (49·0)	30 (68·2)	211 (88·3)	293 (72·0)
Literate no formal education	10 (21·2)	14 (8·1)	9 (20·5)	4 (1·7)	18 (4·4)
1–4 years schooling	17 (36·2)	40 (24·5)	3 (6·5)	16 (6·7)	56 (13·8)
5–8 years schooling	14 (29·8)	31 (18·4)	2 (4·5)	8 (4·5)	39 (9·6)
TOTALS	47 (100·0)	167 (100·0)	44 (100·0)	239 (100·0)	406 (100·0)

Percentages in brackets.

REFERENCES

Gerth, H. H. and Wright Mills, C.
(1948) *From Max Weber*, Routledge & Kegan Paul.
Guttman, L.
(1954) 'The Israel and Alpha Technique for Scale Analysis' in Riley, M. W., Riley, J. W., and Toby, I. (Eds.): *Sociological Studies in Scale Analysis*, New York, Rutgers University Press.
Hailey, Lord
(1950) *Native Administration in the British African Territories*, Part II, London H.M.S.O.
Harries-Jones, Peter
(1963) 'Kasaka: A Case Study in Succession and Dynamics of a Bemba Village', *Rhodes-Livingstone Journal*, No. 33, June.
Kaufman, Robert
(1964) *Millénarisme et Acculturation*, Institut de Sociologie de l'Université Libre de Bruxelles.
Schneider, D. M. and Gough, K. (Eds.)
(1961) *Matrilineal Kinship*, University of California Press.
Thrupp, Sylvia L. (Ed.)
(1961) 'Millennial Dreams in Action', *Comparative Studies in Society and History, Supplement II*, The Hague.
Turner, V. W.
(1957) *Schism and Continuity in an African Society*, Manchester University Press.
Watch Tower Bible and Tract Society
(1955) *Qualified to be Ministers.*
(1958) *From Paradise Lost to Paradise Regained.*
(1963) *1964 Yearbook of Jehovah's Witnesses.*
Weber, Max
(1930) *The Protestant Ethic and the Spirit of Capitalism*, Translated by Talcott Parsons. George Allen and Unwin, London.

Résumé

RELIGION ET ACTION SOCIO-ÉCONOMIQUE CHEZ LES SERENJE-LALA DE ZAMBIE

Cette communication a pour but de décrire la morale religieuse d'un groupe de Témoins de Jéhovah parmi les Serenje-Lala de Zambie (ex-Rhodésie du Nord) et présente la position occupée par les Témoins de Jéhovah dans la structure sociale et économique en cours d'évolution de la communauté dans son ensemble.

Les Témoins de Jéhovah en Zambie se rattachent à une organisation de caractère international dont le siège est aux États-Unis et qui, en 1963, couvrait 181 pays. Pour la Zambie, le siège régional se trouve à Kitwe et c'est à partir de cette localité que les publications de la 'Watch Tower Bible and Tract Society' sont distribuées dans tout le pays. C'est là également que sont organisées les grandes assemblées et que l'on conserve les archives concernant l'ensemble des activités de l'organisation. En 1963, le nombre de Témoins de Jéhovah actifs s'élevait à 28.303 pour toute la Zambie.

Les doctrines des Témoins de Jéhovah sont fondées sur la croyance que nous vivons actuellement à 'l'époque de la Fin', et qu'après cette époque Dieu inaugurera un nouveau Paradis et une nouvelle Terre. Cette dernière phase avant l'avènement du Nouveau Royaume de Dieu est caractérisée par une augmentation de dérèglement des moeurs sur terre qui aura pour point culminant la bataille de l'Armageddon, combat final entre les forces du Mal et les forces du Bien. Dieu sortira vainqueur de cette épreuve et ses Fidèles hériteront du Nouveau Paradis Terrestre. Les Témoins de Jéhovah se considèrent comme le 'Peuple Élu' qui a pour mission d'avertir le reste du monde de la destruction qui l'attend. Ils se décrivent comme étant une organisation théocratique de Dieu sur terre, 'La Société du Monde Nouveau', et croient que seuls ceux qui acceptent la foi peuvent être sauvés. Tous les Témoins de Jéhovah se doivent donc d'approfondir leur connaissance des Écritures afin de pouvoir prêcher la 'Bonne Nouvelle' du Royaume à venir et donner des preuves directement choisies dans les Écritures afin d'interpréter dans ce sens les évènements mondiaux. Les diverses publications de la 'Watch Tower Bible and Tract Society' leur servent de guide.

Lorsqu'arrivera le nouveau Paradis, les Témoins de Jéhovah seront appelés à aider à la reconstruction de la terre: 'Ils construiront des maisons et les habiteront; ils planteront des vignobles et en mangeront les fruits; ils ne construiront pas pour qu'un autre habite ces lieux; ils ne planteront pas pour qu'un autre mange les fruits . . . et ils profiteront longtemps du travail de leurs mains.' (Isaïe, 65:21, 22.)

La morale pratique exprimée par les Témoins de Jéhovah du groupe étudié ressort de cette position doctrinale de base. Le progrès spirituel devrait s'accompagner de certaines modifications dans la vie de tous les jours. Par exemple, les Témoins doivent s'attacher à leur 'organisation personnelle', ceci comprenant leur apparence personnelle, leurs conditions de vie et tous leurs actes, 'afin que l'on ne puisse critiquer le ministère de Dieu' (II Cor. 6:3). Chaque individu doit noter son programme de prédications et établir un plan d'étude de la Bible. Lorsqu'il va prêcher, il doit également se présenter proprement et décemment vêtu. Les Témoins doivent également tenter de devenir *basambashi*. Le mot *basambashi* est utilisé pour décrire quelqu'un dont le niveau de vie est relativement élevé. Une telle personne s'habille bien, mange bien et possède beaucoup de meubles et autres biens et l'on dit d'elle 'qu'elle se gouverne'. Les fermiers et commerçants qui ont bien réussi sont cités en exemple.

La morale donc, recommande un certain 'style de vie'. Les caractéristiques en sont de bien s'habiller, et d'acheter de bons meubles et des produits de qualité pour la maison. En outre chaque membre du groupe devrait essayer d'acquérir certaines qualifications spéciales lui permettant de gagner de l'argent grâce auquel il pourra améliorer son propre niveau de vie et se préparer à vivre dans le Nouveau Royaume. De plus, on attache de l'importance à l'alphabétisation, car seul le lettré peut remplir son rôle religieux de façon satisfaisante.

Néanmoins, les Témoins de Jéhovah ne considèrent pas que leur style de vie séculier soit quelque chose de séparé de leurs pratiques religieuses. Pour eux, c'est plutôt une extension de leur conception de la religion. Le fait de faire partie de la Société du Monde Nouveau promet une vie nouvelle mais implique également une certaine orientation à donner à la vie dans le monde actuel.

Parmi les autres caractéristiques de leur morale on peut noter l'importance attachée à la famille élémentaire constituant un groupement Chrétien de base ainsi que l'importance des investissements judicieux ('Ne gaspillez pas votre argent à acheter de la bière et des cigarettes'), et la nécessité d'en finir avec les 'mœurs du Vieux Monde'.

Si on examine maintenant la structure économique et sociale de la communauté, on voit que des changements importants ont eu lieu au cours des derniers 15 ans. En 1948 les agriculteurs ont commencé à utiliser la charrue et 1958 a vu l'introduction du tabac Turc comme récolte industrielle. Le résultat en a été une augmentation généralisée de la prospérité de la région et une plus grande différenciation économique. On a vu proliférer également de petits centres fondés sur la famille élémentaire ou sur un groupe de parents utérins et de leur descendance immédiate. Par conséquent, le village composé d'un noyau d'hommes et femmes apparentés matrilinéairement n'est plus le seul groupement résidentiel significatif dans la région.

Si on compare les Témoins de Jéhovah au reste de la population, on s'aperçoit qu'ils ont tendance à vivre dans des communautés plus petites et basées sur la famille élémentaire; il y en a relativement beaucoup qui ont des occupations leur fournissant un revenu régulier en argent (par exemple, ils sont agriculteurs ou commerçants) et la majorité d'entre eux pratique l'agriculture utilisant la charrue. Le nombre d'alphabètes est relativement élevé parmi eux; beaucoup d'hommes sont maçons ou charpentiers qualifiés, et beaucoup d'entre eux ont un statut économique relativement plus élevé que celui du reste de la population. Il y a donc une corrélation étroite entre le mode de vie de la majorité du groupe et sa morale religieuse. Par conséquent, je crois qu'on peut dire que la morale fournit une sanction religieuse du mode de vie, et des réalisations des membres du groupe. Elle a peut-être constitué également un facteur important amenant des Témoins individuels à exploiter plus pleinement les nouvelles possibilités économiques disponibles.

En conclusion, nous estimons qu'il est nécessaire de faire une distinction analytique entre la doctrine et la morale car la morale d'une religion donnée peut varier selon les circonstances sociales et économiques particulières dans lesquelles se trouvent les croyances quoique la doctrine elle-même reste essentiellement semblable. On pourrait facilement illustrer cette thèse en comparant les Témoins de Jéhovah dans les diverses régions de la Zambie.

XVIII. THE PREDICAMENT OF THE CHURCH IN AFRICA

E. BOLAJI IDOWU

INTRODUCTORY

This is not an easy paper to write. The first reason, which should be obvious, is the size of Africa. It must be remembered constantly that Africa is a vast continent, with almost innumerable languages and a variety of complex cultures. Secondly, opinion is divided among Africans as to what position should be taken in one's attitude to Christianity in Africa. One position is that of the extreme nationalist who can now see no good at all in what the Church has been doing in Africa and therefore condemns the Church and her work. Another position is that of the loyal children of the Church who feel only gratitude and who regard anything that savours of criticism as disloyalty. They feel it their duty to be jealous guardians of her reputation and consider any suggestion of reform as an attack upon her. There is yet another position—that of those who claim that they also are true children of the Church but realize that their house needs to be put in order; they are aware that one of the gifts of God to man is the possibility of detachment for the purpose of self-criticism and that this is designed for a salutary end. If the walls of a building are cracking ominously, the best remedy is not to keep patching them up here and there; it is to examine the foundation carefully and effect necessary repairs.

Which of these positions this paper takes will be obvious.

THE COMING OF CHRISTIANITY

It is not certain when Christianity first came to Africa. Edwin Smith is right in saying in a work written in 1926[1] that '. . . from almost the earliest period of her history the Church has never been absent from Africa. Christian communities existed in Africa

[1] Smith, 1926, p. 8 ff.

long before they were found in the British Isles and Northern Europe . . .' As early as 1491, Portuguese priests had landed in Angola. In 1751, an Anglican Clergyman, the Rev. Thomas Thompson, had visited the Gold Coast. By the beginning of the nineteenth century, several missions had visited various parts of Africa, 'all branches of the Church in Europe vied in holy rivalry to spread the Christian faith'. In various places in Africa there are signs of ancient Christian civilizations, or civilizations which had something of Christianity in them, which have perished, whose history is now unknown, but traces of which could be seen in some of the local customs, practices, or indigenous rituals.

The Church came into Africa when she was ready for something new. In general, she was a land torn by the ravages of the slave-trade and by inter-racial feuds, a land where diseases were gaining mastery and enervating or destroying human lives. Africa was seeking new or different ways of life. The traditional cults in their conservative forms were out-worn and, as practised, appeared to have served their original purpose. Africa was yearning for something that she could not define and contact with the outside world began to give a direction and a shape to her yearning. She was discovering a new notion of being and power, seeking to free herself from oppression, and to make herself great in a new way. Islamic powers from Egypt, the Sudan, and Siam, had already made a deep impression on various parts of the continent. European traders, explorers, and investigators had begun to arrive.

The Buganda Kings, for example, had been in touch with Islam through Zanzibar, and had been fascinated by a new kind of power which they connected with Islamic religion. They had therefore asked to be taught the truths of that religion for pragmatic reasons. Mutesa I, a great opportunist, had made friends with the Sultan of Zanzibar, sending him gifts and receiving in exchange guns, powder, and spirits. He had submitted himself to Islamic instruction and for a period professed to be a Muslim. Then Stanley visited him and, from that moment, his allegiance began first to waver and then changed, because he felt that the white man would be a stronger ally against Egyptian aggression and a better source of a technological mastery which promised untold power.[2]

Another illustration is that of Ṣodẹkẹ, the King of Abeokuta in Yorubaland. He was eagerly awaiting the arrival of Thomas Birch Freeman. When Freeman arrived he clasped him in his arms and exclaimed, 'My people told me that their friends in England would not neglect them. But I feared you would not venture so far. Now, I see you and my heart rejoices. I hope the English will never leave us!' The sequel to this was an historic meeting summoned by the great king to his courtyard—there were present the traditional priests, the leaders of the Muslims, and Freeman and the ex-slave Christians. The priest of the traditional religion and the Muslim leaders were ordered to explain their religious beliefs. Freeman was then asked to speak. The King summed up by saying, 'This white man's religion is true, and both you and I will follow it!'[3]

THE NUCLEI OF THE CHURCH

The Church aimed at making converts throughout Africa. 'Whosoever will, may come' was, as usual, the keynote of her Gospel call. But, by and large, the nuclei of the Church particularly in East, Central, and West Africa were liberated slaves. Dom Henrique, a slave trader, intended the capture of slaves on the African coast 'to promote the conversion of African territories into Christian dependencies of Portugal'. The first governor of the Dutch settlers at the Cape, Van Riebeeck, 'gave instructions that "to stimulate the slaves to attention while at school and to induce them to learn the Christian prayers, they should be promised a glass of brandy and two inches of tobacco".'[4] According to Roland Oliver, 'The problem of freed slaves did much to attract missions to East Africa, and even more to interest the British Government in missionary enterprise. The C.M.S. had been running since 1855 a Christian village at Nasik for slaves. . . . Similarly, it was the work of the French Congregation of the

[2] Oliver, 1952, p. 1 ff.
[3] Deaville Walker, 1942, pp. 24–32.
[4] Smith, 1926, p. 8.

Holy Ghost among the ex-slaves of Réunion which prompted Bishop Maupoint to visit Zanzibar and to establish a permanent mission there in 1863.'[5] Freetown was a slave settlement; so was Liberia. And although Freetown was founded before the Missions, there is no doubt about its Christian motive. Both Freetown and Liberia early became foci of missionary activities. In Nigeria, the call for missionaries was from the ex-slaves who had found their way back home from Sierra Leone, and they constituted the nucleus upon which the Church was built. One could multiply these instances. The important point to be stressed here is that these ex-slaves were the first genuine converts and they were the solid foundation which made for the establishment of the Church in Africa. The significance of this we shall see presently.

HOW CONVERTS WERE MADE

The question of the motives of missionary activities in Africa is now being raised afresh. There are those who would argue that the basic motive of European missions in Africa was one of ultimate 'conquest' and domination. The extreme nationalists as well as certain historians would maintain that the missions used the Bible and the Gospel message only as means of softening up Africans and thus preparing the ground for exploitation and imperialism. Christianity, they would say, is no more than an engine of colonial policy. It seems that the correct evaluation is that motives were rarely unmixed, inasmuch as with the best intentions of evangelism went the notion that Africans needed to be re-made, given a new and 'superior' culture, and delivered from all that Europeans considered to be the thraldom of their native environment.[6] With this went the determination to bring Africa not only under European influence especially by way of commerce, but also under European imperialism, *for her own benefit*. Dom Henrique, whom we have already mentioned, aimed at bringing 'African territories into Christian dependencies of Portugal to be administered by a military order'.[7]

But whatever may have got mixed up with missionary motives, there is no doubt that they were initially based upon genuine

[5] Oliver, 1952, p. 18. [6] Deaville Walker, 1942, p. 14 ff. [7] Smith, 1926, p. 8.

obedience to the Christian commitment to preach the Gospel to all the nations as well as upon 'humanitarian' feelings.

David Livingstone wrote:

> Is that a sacrifice which brings its own blest reward in healthful activity, the consciousness of doing good, peace of mind. . . . Say rather it is a privilege. Anxiety, sickness, suffering or danger, now and then, with a foregoing of the common conveniences and charities of this life, may make us pause, and cause the spirit to waver, and the soul to sink; but let this only be for a moment.
>
> I go to open the door to Central Africa. It is probable I may die there; but, brethren, I pray you, see to it that the door is never closed again.[8]

We have also a record of the significant missionary prayer:

> Give success to our endeavours to introduce civilization and Christianity into this benighted country. Thou has promised, *Ethiopia shall soon stretch out her hands unto God:* make us, we pray Thee, instruments in fulfilling this Thy promise.[9]

The problem of rehabilitating the ex-slaves was also a great factor in bringing missions into Africa. In at least one case there was a definite invitation—'For Christ's sake, come quick. Let nothing but sickness prevent you. . . . Do, do, for God's sake, start at this moment; do not neglect me and all this burden; it is more than I can bear!' This was in a letter to Thomas Dove from one of the ex-slaves who had gone back to his homeland, Abeokuta.[10]

The means by which African converts were made may be outlined as follows:

(*a*) *The early missionary was a committed Christian in the service of his Lord.* This was the sole key-note of his life, which was therefore a testimony to the Gospel he preached. He identified himself wholeheartedly with the people among whom he laboured. People saw in him the Lord Whom he commended to them and believed. This was an effective factor, more so than any amount of preaching, in the work of evangelism.

[8] Maxwell, n.d., p. 34.
[9] Deaville Walker, 1931, p. 20.
[10] Deaville Walker, 1942, p. 14.

(*b*) Side by side with European missionaries worked African leaders, trained or untrained, but all ardent converts to the faith. De Graft Johnson of the Gold Coast, who worked selflessly both in his own country and in Nigeria, Bishop Crowther, who was a pioneer in many areas of the Church's life in Nigeria and the father of the Niger Mission of Nigeria, and Bishop James Johnson, who worked in Sierra Leone and in Nigeria and who foresaw that the true life of the Church in Africa could be realized only through its indigenization and worked zealously towards that end, are examples. These African workers were used everywhere by God for the foundation of the Church in ways which only they, and no foreigner, could have been used.

(*c*) *Christianity came as a religion of demonstrated salvation.* On 1 June 1840 the Prince Consort presiding over a meeting in the Exeter Hall, London, spoke as follows: 'I sincerely trust that this great country will not relax its efforts until it has, finally and for ever, put an end to a state of things so repugnant to the principles of Christianity. . . . I do trust that Providence will prosper our exertions in so holy a cause. . . .' The object of the meeting was the abolition of slave-trade, and 'to stop the supply of slaves at its source'.[11]

We of today cannot really know the amount of suffering brought upon Africa, and inflicted especially upon those who were enslaved. Horrors and atrocities may describe the situation; but what these meant to them is beyond our imagination. We can, however, appreciate the relief and consequent gratitude to the deliverers which the liberated slaves felt. They knew or were told that they were rescued in consequence of Christianity and in the name of the Saviour of mankind. This was something new and, inevitably, there was a ground prepared for the seed of the Gospel. It was not only that the slaves were liberated. They were rehabilitated and taught, besides the truths of Christianity, to read and write. To them there was something 'magical' in this. And it meant deliverance from ignorance. The rehabilitation of the ex-slaves involved finding them gainful occupations, the improvement in their conditions and ways of living and therefore deliver-

[11] Deaville Walker, 1931, p. 14 f.

ance from material want. This three-fold deliverance—physical, spiritual and mental, and material—constituted another effective factor in the promotion of Christianity in Africa. Wherever the ex-slaves spoke of Christianity, they were speaking from first-hand and genuine experience of the salvation which they had proved and which had been demonstrated in their lives. And in many parts of Africa people were quick to see this and sought to embrace the religion, either from genuine desire to be 'saved' or from the personal motives of the material benefits which they could get from Christianity.

(*d*) *The European backing of Christianity*. Africa had known the Europeans as people with immense power, wisdom, and wealth. Europeans had demonstrated their power either as tormentors of Africans before whom the latter were entirely powerless; or as their deliverers whose benefactions appeared to be inexhaustible. In commercial wares brought by Europeans, in their bearing and comportment, there was every sign of wealth, and of this wealth Africans were already having a taste in the gifts brought to them by explorers. The general impression was great and arresting. One result of this was that in many areas Africans readily developed immense admiration for the Europeans. In Edoland in Nigeria, for example, the original cults of the arch-divinity of Yorubaland and that of the goddess of the sea have become hybridized into the cult of Poseidon or Neptune. The image of this divinity, Olokun, in Uronigbe (the headquarters of the cult) is fully dressed in what is a combination of the regalia of an ancient Portuguese Roman Catholic priest and that of a Portuguese general. The images of his courtiers are either those of Portuguese priests or soldiers. The regalia of the king of Benin as well as that of the Benin chief is also based on that of an old Portuguese or Spanish priest.

History is emphatic on the fact that Christianity was sponsored by the Governments of the countries of origin of each mission and by the imperial power of each local mission field. When the C.M.S. missionary arrived at the court of Mutesa I of Buganda, he presented two letters of commendation, one from the Church Missionary Society, and another from the Foreign Office. It was the Colonial Governor, Maclean, who welcomed Thomas Birch Freeman to the Gold Coast. And when Thomas Birch Freeman visited King Osai Tutu Kwamina at Kumasi, it was with the commendation and backing of the European Governor of the Gold Coast. The C.M.S. in Sierra Leone actually received an annual subsidy of £500 from the Government for over a period, and this is a common feature of missionary work all over Africa. About 1904, we are told that the white missionaries in East Africa were supported by the authority of the Colonial Government and that they enjoyed an almost limitless freedom to make and carry out their own schemes. Missionaries were also used in certain areas as liaison officers between the Colonial Government and the people. Some of them became part-time civil servants. And some even fought in a war of supremacy between tribes.

Christianity conferred a status upon its converts: they were in a class by themselves. Even today in Abeokuta Christians are called 'the bookish ones' or 'the people with books'. It is a religion with a prestige value. Christians were in the forefront of a new enlightenment throughout the continent and they and their children set the fashion which the impressionable Africans followed. Christianity also enabled people to earn their livelihood in 'clean' jobs, a situation which was greatly exploited by the Church. Chiefs became friends of missionaries and either professed Christianity themselves or surrendered their children for education and baptism, undoubtedly because of expected political or material benefits; but the Church found this acceptable and rejoiced at it.

Thus, the European backing of Christianity was a true asset. Pax Britannica and other European influences came to the Church's aid in her fight against what she considered to be unwholesome or evil in her surroundings. Observances of, and respect for, her institutions were imposed upon the whole continent by the colonial rulers—Sunday, Christmas, and Easter were foremost among the Christian Feasts which were made occasions of public holidays for all civil servants, employees of the mercantile houses, school children, and teachers, irrespective of the religious affiliations of individuals.

Westernism and Christianity became mixed up. Converts to Christianity despised their own cultures, preferring European customs. In certain areas the imitation or aping of European ways of life went so far that today the people no longer remember their native traditions. One may quote as an example the Portuguese evangelization of the Congo, where the King of Congo was asked to throw away all that might remind him of the old ways. Before long, a Portuguese veneer had spread over Congolese Society: Portuguese dress was adopted, Portuguese names were given at baptism, the king's capital city was renamed San Salvador, and the feudal system was introduced into the Court.[12]

(*e*) *Education.* Church schools became the recruiting grounds for Christians. The Church was the pioneer in the work of education in many parts of Africa. As people became more and more hungry for education, more and more schools were built. The work has now expanded to such an extent that it appears to be putting even the work of evangelism to which the Church is called in the second place. But the real motive has been Christian education. To this end, ministers and teachers had persuaded immature children to embrace Christianity; the bait often used was that if they were baptized and could show their certificates of baptism, they would be able to secure jobs in the civil service or in the mercantile houses. One old Anglican priest told me, 'I became a Christian in order to learn to read and write and secure a good job afterwards.' He happened to be one of those who in the process became truly converted.

SUPPRESSION OF INDIGENOUS BELIEFS AND PRACTICES

The European missionary came to Africa with the preconceived notion that there was either no religion at all in Africa or that it was entirely of the Devil. Leo Frobenius, the German explorer, says that before ever he visited Africa, 'a great light of the Church' had declared that 'the "niggers" have no souls, but are burnt-out husks of men'. He read in a Berlin Journal that

[12] From the contribution by Mrs. Ruth Reardon to the discussion on this paper.

Africa was a place governed entirely by 'insensible fetish'.[13] The early Lutheran Missionaries who came to East Africa in the service of the C.M.S. saw the African as the unrelieved model of the 'fallen man'.[14] Missionaries therefore considered it their duty not only to convert Africans to Christianity but also to make them give up and forget their past entirely and live up to their new dignity. The result was that the Church did not take account of the traditional beliefs of the people; little effort was made to understand them and to know their basic hopes and fears and traditional yearnings for God, and in what way God had met this yearning. The Church in Africa came into being with prefabricated theology, liturgies, and traditions. In the matter of Christian ethics, the converts found themselves in the position of those early converts before the Council of Jerusalem (Acts 15): 'Unless you are circumcised after the custom of Moses, you cannot be saved'; and that is virtually the position today.

THE PHENOMENA OF CHANGE

The world in which we live is changing, and Africa with it. As far back as 1926, Edwin Smith had written of 'The New Africa'.[15] But that newness is nothing compared with that of the present-day Africa through which Mr. Harold Macmillan, one-time British Prime Minister, clearly saw that the 'Wind of Change' is blowing. There have been phenomenal developments and achievements throughout the continent. Africa is no longer exposed helplessly (some had thought hopelessly) to economic and social exploitation, to rape and sacrilege, to the violation of her personality by the technologically superior races of the world. She is awake and has been making the fact known in unmistakable ways. She is showing that she is fully alive by asserting that she is created to be an autonomous being and claiming the inalienable rights of a corporate personality to self-expression and the guidance of her own destiny.

Africa has been passing through the birth-throes of her new life. But she is entering into that life fully conscious of an urgent sense of responsibility, which though often ill or vaguely defined,

[13] 1913, vol. I, pp. xiii ff. [14] Oliver, 1952, p. 9. [15] 1926, pp. 1 ff.

has its joy and pain, often resulting in chaos or bewilderment, but which nevertheless she will not now surrender to any other.

THE CHURCH IN A CHANGING WORLD

The world of Africa into which the Church came in the first instance was ready for her because of her circumstances. By and large, the material upon which the Church worked was receptive and docile. There were complete conversions of many who did not pause to ask any questions but were ready always to trust and obey.

This receptive attitude gradually changed, however, as the first brand of missionaries and Christian workers and the first generation of Christian Africans were passing away, and there came a change in the structure of Church administration; there were also growing up generations of Christians who did not share the first-hand, arresting experiences of the first Christian Africans. Also, education, however well geared to a particular purpose, has a way of exceeding its set limits and making the mind free to an extent not foreseen. This actually happened rather early in the Church. Some of her children began to ask awkward questions and even to turn into recalcitrants or rebels. Thus, changes within the Church and the external world around her have brought about the present predicament which may be analysed as follows:

(a) *African Nationalism*

The Church has every right to claim that she is the pioneer, or even the author of African nationalism. Her evangelism inculcated that every person is created free and a child of God; her system of Christian education directly or indirectly liberated people's minds; through her, Africans were exposed to the ways and wisdom of the European world through literature and education in European institutions; all these laid the foundation for African nationalism, gave it its initial impetus and even today maintain it indirectly in consequence of the children of the Church—'loyal' and 'disloyal'—whom she has 'reared and brought up'. Henry Venn of the C.M.S., for example, has been described as the father of African nationalism because of his faith in the potential of Africans and his consequent fruitful efforts in their training and his advocacy of ecclesiastical 'home rule' for them. But the Church did not set out to produce African nationalists. And nationalism in Africa does not recognize her as its author or promoter. Wherever nations in the continent are free, or are striving to be free from foreign domination, therefore, the extreme nationalist tends to see the Church as one of those instruments of bondage from which Africa should break free.

(b) *Incidental Means of Conversion*

With developments all over Africa, and the gradual recognition of her corporate personality, the Church is being denuded of what had appeared to be its prestige and economic values. Unrestricted areas of education and the coming into the new political power of adherents of all religions without discrimination have created equal opportunity for all. It is no longer a thing desirable or even useful for a person to be a Christian in order to secure a good job or to get to the topmost post in the government of any particular country. For example, the Prime Minister of Nigeria today is a Muslim.

It is now being realized that it was something of a misfortune that Christianity as a religion was sought after for its interim incidental advantages. A good number of those who became adherents for these reasons have now either reverted to their old beliefs or become indifferent, and often antagonistic, to it.

(c) *School Education*

Hitherto, the Church has concentrated much of her resources on school education in Africa. In fact she was not only the pioneer in many areas if not in most, but also had the monopoly of it. Now that changes are taking place, the governments of Africa are gradually taking over the organization of school education from the Church. In some countries, it has already become law that no child should be compelled to attend Christian instruction classes or to join in school worship. In almost every one of the Government Advanced Teacher Training Colleges in

Nigeria, for example, Religious Knowledge is not in the curriculum. Where governments pay the full salaries of teachers and pay for school equipment, it means virtually the cessation of the control which the Church used to have over the teachers with regard to the ethics of their work, the tone of the school, and their own personal morality. This is an area where the Church is being hard hit, for it means that her educational influence through the schools upon African young people generally is being removed.

(d) *The European Connexions of the Church*

These have now become rather a handicap to the Church. This predicament was not unforeseen: Mackay of Uganda once said, 'I believe we shall gain a great point when Christianity ceases to be called the white man's religion.' This fact of the European connexions of the Church is now affecting her adversely in several ways:

(i) We have observed that to the extreme nationalist, the Church is only an agent of imperialism. And we can see now that it was an error of judgement for the Church to identify herself closely with the ruling colonial powers on the Continent. There is no doubt but that there are illustrative justifications for the cry of the nationalists against the Church. For example, it takes an exuberance of the grace of God for the harrassed and oppressed South African who is being treated as sub-human with the approval of a section of the Church (which to him is 'The Church') to remain a Christian or to believe that the Church is here for any other purpose than the rape of Africa.

There is the fact also that Africans believed for a long time (and there is a great multitude who still do) that all Europeans were Christians. The effect of this is that Africans are thoroughly confused when they find Europeans behaving in ways which contradict the Gospel which 'they' preach. Either they conclude then that the Europeans do not believe what 'they' preach or that they think that 'since the whitemen are doing it, why can't we?' About 1913, Bishop James Johnson in Sierra Leone spoke of 'European civilization and the deteriorating tendencies of some form of it, and the unChristian and ungodly lives of many a

European among us, a people whom it has been natural for us to look to for example on account of the superior advantages they had been blessed with, and the claim and bid they make for respect for this. . .'.

(ii) Within the Church in Africa there has been a sign that all has not been well from quite early times. While there were missionaries of very sound spiritual and moral calibre, there have always been those who may be described as the black sheep of the family, whose main attraction to the field appears to have been the excitement of the game. There was indeed a time, especially during the period of the scramble for Africa and since, when the mission field in Africa became swamped with missionaries to whom the imperial flags meant more than the Cross of Christ, who had more regard for their white skins, European dignity, and 'superior status' than they had for the brothers and sisters for whom Christ died, whose relationship even with the African ministers and other Church workers was not one of colleagueship but strictly official, always or, too often, that of master and servant; at best their attitude to the whole congregation was one of paternalism. Naturally, the attitude of these unconverted persons had the effect of creating doubts in people's minds with regard to the validity of the Church's teaching of the Fatherhood of God and the brotherhood of all believers.

The paternalistic or domineering attitude of European missionaries led early to a smouldering resentment within the Church and broke out eventually in open rupture. By 1821, the first African independent Church had come into being in Sierra Leone. It took the name of 'African Methodist Church'. By 1835, six more had been formed. The African Church (incorporated) of Nigeria came into being for the same reason. There are examples of all these splinter churches throughout Africa.

Earlier, we have remarked on the vital significance of African workers in the foundation of the Church. But they were not allowed to continue this significant role as they were guided by the Spirit. Some of the new brand of missionaries who came in with the scramble for Africa took it into their heads to criticize and discredit the earlier faithful African workers; and as a result of the changed attitude of Europeans towards them, these African workers were considered no longer good enough for certain key situations. Bishop Crowther, for example, had much heart-rending trouble in this way. It was these Europeans who opposed very vigorously, and to a great extent successfully, the Native Pastorate scheme advocated for West Africa by Henry Venn and to which Bishop James Johnson devoted so much of his life. As these Africans in key-posts died or were transferred, they were invariably replaced with Europeans. This process gained ground as progress in tropical medicine made it possible for Europeans to live in any part of Africa. Thus, African leadership in the Church became relegated to the background. The result of that deliberate sin is now one of the Church's main embarrassments in Africa. Today, African leadership is inadequate both qualitatively and quantitatively. This makes it difficult for the Church to answer adequately the questions that educated Africans are asking, to be able to cope with their spiritual problems which are more often than not beyond the capacity of the European; and, of course, the process of indigenization has been retarded with a menacing consequence.

With the above goes the important matter of stewardship. The Church in Africa has been allowed to remain for too long a Church which is dependent upon foreign aid. On the whole, there has been disastrously insufficient training in stewardship. Too much foreign aid has had a crippling effect on the Church. That is why at the present time almost all the European-related churches in Africa are either not fully self-maintaining or are finding it impossible to fulfil certain urgent, vital obligations for lack of funds. They are all beggars, therefore. There are places where the little they have is being spent on the non-essentials while the essentials are being neglected.

(e) *Conflict of Religions*

During the period when the Church enjoyed unrivalled privileges under the colonial governments, she had been lulled into a sense of false security. Islam, however, has never accepted a defeat from Christianity and has been finding a way of establishing itself as the 'universal' religion in Africa. As far back as 1910, there was a debate in Sierra Leone on the subject, 'Which is more beneficial to Society, Christianity or Islam?' And the Muslims in the 'Protectorate' had predicted then that Christianity would pass away with the progress of civilization! In many parts of Africa Christianity-within-colonialism had an apparent supremacy over Islam. Today, the situation is different. Islam has become aggressively missionary and is promoting school education and charitable institutions in the same way as Christianity has been doing; the voice of Islam is heard in daily radio programmes and its hand seen in the daily papers. It is engaged in a kind of *jihad*, openly or secretly, against Christianity. The Sudan of today is our best example. The Church has been forced to recognize the 'menace of Islam' and to begin a painful rethinking of her position with regard to it.

There has been a disturbing sign suggesting that probably the old traditional religion has only stooped to conquer. It is certain that the religion in its old conservative form is passing away. But with the aid of nationalism and the injection of a new life which it receives indirectly through the two world religions of Christianity and Islam, it is now taking a new form. Everywhere we are beginning to see a resurgence or recrudescence of the old cults in 'reformed' garbs. The slogan of these new movements is based upon the notion that Christianity is the religion of the white man and Islam that of the Arabs. Africans must, therefore, revive their own God-given religion. We may quote here the Reformed Ogboni Fraternity, the National Church, and the Aruosa Church, all of Nigeria.[16] The interesting thing about these illustrations is that they are erected with scaffoldings borrowed from the Christian Church.

There is a third element, and this may be described as 'humanistic secularism'. With the return from Europe of Africans educated in all branches of learning, the coming of African Universities which attract all types of professors and lecturers with many different, or no, moral and spiritual standards, and

[16] For 'Reformed Ogboni fraternity', see Idowu, 1962, pp. 24, 28, 212; and for 'The National Church' and 'The Aruosa Church', see Idowu, 1965, p. 9.

with all kinds of literature flooding the continent, Africa is being assailed by a medley of ideologies; there are militant political ideas which are set against anything that savours of European domination or of the European's superior attitude. The result of these is either to confuse Africans or to make a good many of the intelligentsia become indifferent to, or to repudiate, all European-introduced spiritual values, or in fact, any spiritual values at all. Recently, in a conference, one African physician who was trained in Europe described God as preached by Christians as *mumbo-jumbo*—an idea which is certainly unAfrican. It is no wonder that this kind of attitude is resulting in neurotic traits or unmistakable signs of lack of sense of direction all over Africa.

(f) *Result of Prefabricated Theology and Traditions*[17]

It was a serious mistake that the Church took no account of the indigenous beliefs and customs of Africa when she began her work of evangelization. It is now obvious that by a misguided purpose, a completely new God who had had nothing to do with the past of Africa was introduced to her peoples. Thus, there was no proper foundation laid for the Gospel message in the hearts of the people and no bridge built between the old and the new; the Church has in consequence been speaking to Africans in strange tongues because there was no adequate communication. In consequence, the Church has on her hands communities of believers who, by and large, live ambivalent spiritual lives. Christianity to them is a fashionable religion which has the habit of beginning and ending within the walls of a church building; it does not reach those vital areas of the personal needs of Africans. Thus, it is possible for an African to sing lustily in Church, 'Other refuge have I none', while still carrying an amulet somewhere on his person, or being able to go out of Church straight to his diviner, without feeling that he is betraying any principle.

Here also is the reason why the Church authorities and African Christians do not see eye-to-eye on certain matters of Christian ethics. Polygamy is a popular example.[18] The Church has been asking Africans to produce the fruit of Christianity

[17] See Idowu, 1965.

[18] See Webster, 1965.

without adequate theological basis, at least one that they can grasp intelligently. The basis of African beliefs and practices is the covenant. It is the heart of all cults in Africa. Africans count it a serious sin to break covenant. The various tabu with which his life is surrounded stem largely from his covenant relationships and they are binding for that very reason. The African's covenant-relationship with his fellow man is a consequence often of his covenant-relationship first with an object of worship common to him and the fellow man. This in sum-total determines his behaviour. The Church took the wrong step when she retreated to the position before the first Council of Jerusalem by demanding 'of its converts some cultural equivalent of circumcision'.[19] If the effort had been directed at making Christians, showing clearly to Africans that they are entering into personal, covenant-relationship with the Living God and a personal Saviour, we should not have been facing our present embarrassment.

Added to the above is the fact which has now become obvious that the prefabricated liturgies which have been imported from Europe and imposed upon this continent have proved inadequate. There are certain emotional depths which are not being reached in Africans by these liturgies and the whole system is making for spiritual sterility as far as they are concerned. Hymns are European verses sung to European tunes, the phraseology of the liturgies are either archaic, barely intelligible, or often irrelevant in Africa.

The sum-total effect is partly, as we have seen, a resurgence or recrudescence of the old cults. But in the main, we see it in the rise of the 'Independent Churches',[20] described variously as 'prophetism', 'pentecostalism', etc. The real meaning of these is that they are a reaction against the European complexion of the European-related Church in Africa and a rebuke to the aridity of her spiritual and liturgical life. Here we see Africans seeking a way of Christian self-expression, groping for the selfhood of the Church, and asking to be allowed to worship as Christian Africans and not to be turned into Europeans before they can worship. The most significant elements in these movements are

[19] Taylor, pp. 109–11. [20] Welbourn, 1961; Baëta, 1962.

that they seek to fulfil that which is lacking in the European-led churches, that is, to give Africans a form of worship which will 'satisfy' both spiritually and emotionally, and to make Christianity cover every area of human life and fulfil all human needs. Thus, for example, the 'prophetic' element in them is to the Africans a satisfactory substitute for the old system of divination. An urgent indigenization of the Church is what they indicate. Whether they are succeeding in their purpose or not is another question into which we have no time and space to go here. The main point is that in a bewildering way, they have forced the attention of the European-related Church upon themselves and although her attitude to them is as yet uncertain, it is nevertheless currently moving away from that of definite antagonism.

CONCLUSION

The Church is facing a real predicament in African today. Although she has achieved great things in and for Africa in the work of evangelization, education, healing, general enlightenment and liberation from the shackles of wickedness, ignorance, fear, and superstition, and although she has been the pioneer and leader in the spirit of freedom which is culminating in the political independence of the nations of Africa, she is now being faced with certain situations which place her on severe trial. Her position is being made the more painful because it appears that the enterprise she launched has grown beyond her control. It is clear that she has not developed enough resources, in men and material, for the maintenance of her life. The training of her workers has not kept pace either qualitatively or numerically with her expansion and relatively to the changing needs and challenges of modern Africa.

Pastoral care and instructions in the fundamentals of Christianity are inadequate and this situation is affecting her membership adversely with reference to steadfastness and Christian practice. She has been trying to maintain her workers on inadequate stipends which inevitably expose them to the temptations and allurements which the new Africa affords in abundance. She herself is a house divided against herself, which is a real menace to her life in an Africa in search of a corporate personality. The problem of the indigenization of the Church presses upon her urgently—it is a razor-edge course which nevertheless she cannot evade if she is to have real life in Africa.[21]

The opportunity for evangelism has never been greater than it is now in Africa; but it will take a Church which is alive and vigorous with the power which only God can supply to be equal to the task.

REFERENCES

Works Cited in the Text

Baëta, C. G.
(1962) *Prophetism in Ghana*. S.C.M.

Deaville Walker, F.
(1931) *The Romance of the Black River*. C.M.S.
(1942) *A Hundred Years in Nigeria*. Cargate.

Frobenius, Leo
(1913) *The Voice of Africa*. Oxford.

Idowu, E. Bolaji
(1962) *Olodumare: God in Yoruba Belief*. Longmans.
(1965) *Towards an Indigenous Church*. Oxford University Press.

Maxwell, J. L.
(n.d.) *Half a Century of Grace*. S.U.M.

Oliver, R.
(1952) *The Missionary Factor in East Africa*. Longmans.

Smith, Edwin
(1926) *The Christian Mission in Africa*. I.M.C.

Taylor, John V.
(1963) *Primal Vision*. S.C.M.

Webster, J. B.
(1965) *The African Churches among the Yoruba*. Oxford University Press.

Welbourn, F. B.
(1961) *East African Rebels*. S.C.M.

Further References

Ajayi, J. F. A.
(1965) Christian Missions in Nigeria. Longmans.

Ayandele, E. A.
(n.d.) 'The Political and Social Implications of Missionary Enterprise in the Evolution of Modern Nigeria.' (Ph.D. Thesis, Senate House, London; Library, University of Ibadan.)

Bane, M. J.
(1956) *Catholic Pioneers in West Africa*. Clonmore and Reynolds.

Duffy, James
(1962) *Portugal in Africa*. Penguin Books.

[21] See Idowu, 1965.

Gale, H. P.
(1959) *Uganda and the Mill Hill Fathers.* Macmillan.
Miller, Walter R.
(1947) *Have we Failed in Nigeria?* Lutterworth Press.
(1917) Sierra Leone Native Church, Jubilee Volume.
Southon, Arthur E.
(1934) *Gold Coast Methodism.* C.M.S., Lagos.
Sundkler, B.
(1962) *The Christian Ministry in Africa.* S.C.M.
Taylor, John V.
(1958) *The Growth of the Church in Buganda.* S.C.M.
Taylor, J. V. and Lehmann, D. A.
(1961) *Christians of the Copperbelt.* S.C.M.
Thorpe, C.
(1951) *Limpopo to Zambesi.* Cargate.
Vicedom, C. F.
(1961) *Church and People in New Guinea.* U.S.C.L.

Résumé

LA SITUATION DE L'ÉGLISE EN AFRIQUE

La date exacte de l'arrivée du Christianisme en Afrique reste inconnue mais il est certain qu'il y fut introduit dès les premiers temps de son histoire. Le Christianisme dans les temps modernes est entré en Afrique à un moment où, à cause de plusieurs raisons dûes à certaines circonstances, le continent était prêt à le recevoir.

L'Évangile a été prêché afin que tous ceux qui l'entendraient puissent recevoir son message et s'abriter au sein de l'Église. L'histoire montre néanmoins que dans la plupart des régions ce furent les esclaves libérés qui formèrent les premiers centres chrétiens. La réadaptation des anciens esclaves constitua l'un des pôles d'attraction des missions en Afrique.

Les raisons des activités missionnaires en Afrique font depuis longtemps l'objet de discussions, discussions qui ont pris un nouvel essor de nos jours. Des opinions diverses ont été exprimées. Les missions étaient-elles simplement un outil de la politique coloniale, un moyen permettant 'd'adoucir' les Africains et de les rendre ainsi plus faciles à gouverner? Il semble qu'il soit juste de dire que, même si les raisons ne furent que rarement absolument désintéressées, il est certain cependant qu'à l'origine elles étaient fondées sur une foi chrétienne et des sentiments humanitaires réels.

Les moyens par lesquels des conversions furent obtenues étaient les suivants:

(*a*) les premiers missionnaires, chrétiens véritables, ardents et zélés, qui voulaient apporter la 'Bonne Nouvelle' du Salut aux Africains;

(*b*) les catéchistes africains qui à l'origine travaillaient main dans la main avec les missionnaires;

(*c*) le fait que le Christianisme fut présenté comme une religion de salut réel: libération des atrocités et horreurs de l'esclavage, libération de l'obscurantisme spirituel, de l'ignorance et des carences matérielles;

(*d*) l'appui de l'Europe au Christianisme: admiration des Européens à cause de leur puissance et de leur richesse; prestige et valeur économiques du Christianisme, et finalement:

(*e*) l'éducation—les écoles fournissant de jeunes recrues au Christianisme.

Le fait que les missions ne tînrent absolument pas compte des croyances religieuses indigènes des populations africaines dans leurs efforts d'évangélisation revêt une importance essentielle. Cette attitude provenait de ce que les missions estimaient que tout ce qui existait en Afrique avant la venue de l'Église 'venait du diable'. C'est ainsi que l'Église en Afrique s'est construite sur une théologie préfabriquée, des liturgies préfabriquées et des traditions préfabriquées.

Il était inévitable que des changements se produisent en Afrique et c'est à ce phénomène que l'on peut imputer la situation actuelle de l'Église en Afrique.

(*a*) Le nationalisme africain dans son aile extrémiste refuse de trouver quoi que ce soit de bon au travail de l'Église et la considère comme un instrument de servitude impérialiste qu'on devrait abolir et rejeter.

(*b*) Toutes les raisons secondaires de conversion qui s'étaient avérées utiles à l'Église ont disparu. L'Église a perdu sa valeur de prestige et son attrait économique n'existe plus. On n'a plus besoin d'être chrétien pour obtenir un poste très élevé dans la fonction publique ou le gouvernement du pays.

(*c*) L'instruction a été reprise par les gouvernements africains et là l'Église a été très atteinte car l'enseignement direct de la religion risque de cesser dans les écoles.

(*d*) Les rapports de l'Église avec l'Europe sont devenus une sorte de handicap en Afrique. Beaucoup d'Africains considèrent encore le christianisme comme la religion de l'homme blanc ce qui est très dangereux. Le fait qu'il existe des Européens en Afrique dont l'attitude est en violente contradiction avec l'Évangile de l'Amour—en Afrique du Sud, par exemple—permet difficilement à certains Africains de prendre le Christianisme au sérieux car malheureusement ils croient encore que tous les Européens sont chrétiens et font front commun avec les missionnaires. L'attitude de certains groupes de missionnaires et la position d'opposition généralement adoptée à l'égard des groupes religieux établis par les Africains ont créé un grand mécontentement qui est allé parfois jusqu'à une rupture complète avec l'Église.

(*e*) Le conflit entre les diverses religions a eu un mauvais effet pour l'Église. L'Islam de nos jours a un caractère missionnaire agressif et se présente à l'Afrique comme la religion universelle. On peut observer partout une recrudescence on une résurgence des cultes traditionnels ceci dans le but très net de répudier le Christianisme, religion de l'homme blanc, pour adopter une religion propre à l'Afrique.

Le sécularisme humaniste s'est introduit en Afrique avec l'enseignement universitaire européen, la littérature européenne et l'avènement des universités africaines et leurs professeurs d'obédiences spirituelles et morales diverses. Tout ceci a rendu la situation plus complexe encore surtout parmi les intellectuels africains.

(*f*) On voit maintenant apparaître les résultats fort gênants de l'erreur commise par les premiers missionnaires qui ne voulaient tenir aucun compte des coutumes et de la sagesse traditionnelles de l'Afrique. On voit maintenant que la théologie, les liturgies et les traditions 'préfabriquées' sont extrêmement inadéquates. Cette erreur a apporté une grande confusion dans la vie spirituelle des Africains chrétiens, car elle a doté les Africains, hommes et femmes, d'une sorte de vie spirituelle ambivalente ne leur permettant que très difficilement de comprendre ce que l'on entend par morale chrétienne.

La chemin du Salut a été abandonné au détriment de la vie spirituelle et morale de nombreux croyants. C'est en partie à cela qu'est dûe la résurgence ou la recrudescence des anciens cultes.

La conséquence la plus importante de tout cela est le développement des 'Églises indépendantes' qui indique que l'indigénisation de l'Église d'Afrique est non seulement très souhaitable mais encore urgente et impérative.

L'Église à l'heure actuelle se trouve dans une situation très difficile quoiqu'elle ait tant ouvré pour le continent. Néanmoins, la possibilité d'évangéliser reste toujours bien vivante, à condition bien sûr que l'Église elle-même soit vigoureuse et animée de la puissance divine que Dieu seul peut lui insuffler.

INDEX